N

DATE DUE

ALL THE
PEOPLE AND PLACES
OF THE BIBLE

ALL THE PEOPLE AND PLACES OF THE BIBLE

Edited by

JAMES I. PARKER, A.M., D.PHIL.
Regent College

MERRILL C. TENNEY, A.M., Ph.D.
Wheaton Graduate School

WILLIAM WHITE, JR., Th.M., Ph.D.

THOMAS NELSON PUBLISHERS
NASHVILLE • CAMDEN • NEW YORK

Published in Nashville, Tennessee, by Thomas Nelson, Inc., Publishers and distributed in Canada by Lawson Falle, Ltd., Cambridge, Ontario.

Printed in the United States of America.

Library of Congress Cataloging in Publication Data
Main entry under title:

All the people and places of the Bible.

   1. Bible—Dictionaries.   I. Packer, J. I.
(James Innell)   II. Tenney, Merrill Chapin, 1904–
III. White, William, 1934–
BS440.A46   1982   220'.3'21   82-12564
ISBN 0-8407-5819-7

INTRODUCTION

This volume identifies all of the people and places of the Bible, excluding the Apocrypha. Names are arranged alphabetically by their spellings in the King James Version. When a person and a place share the same name, separate entries are made for each with the person listed first.

A typical entry lists the name, followed by any variant spellings enclosed within brackets. Parentheses surround the phonetic spelling of the word and the English meaning of the name in its original language. A short description of the person or place follows plus selected biblical references where it may be found.

The meanings of biblical names are far from certain. Many have such obscure origins that they can present only interesting possibilities at best. The fact that reference books vary in defining these meanings attests to this uncertainty.

Biblical names also present other challenges. Because countless generations continuously inhabited a certain area, throughout its history it might be known by different names. Thus, Accho and Ptolemais refer to the same city, but each in a different period of history. Because these changes often confuse Bible students, in this volume names are grouped under the most familiar biblical word and are cross-referenced to others.

Names of people are challenging for other reasons. Frequently, more than one person bears the same name. For instance, no less than eleven men are called Joseph. When this is the case, each person is listed in the entry in correct biblical order. A bracketed number designates each individual.

Some biblical characters are called by more than one name. Often this is due to nothing more than foreign speakers refering to someone in their own languages. Thus, Saul (Hebrew) of Tarsus is also called Paul (Greek). However, many differences are not explained as easily. For example, why is the same person called both Reuel and Deuel? Or why is Jemuel also called Nemuel? In some cases, scribes could have made errors in transcribing Scripture and their errors were passed from generation to generation without correction. Whatever the reason, this volume harmonizes many of these differences. Note that the Deuel entry includes a reference to Reuel.

Many of these difficulties arise because biblical names originated in ancient and foreign settings. The variant spellings of people and places could be contractions that posed little difficulty for readers in ancient times. Also, some names were altered or omitted from genealogies for reasons that were clear then but are unclear to us. Therefore, even genealogies do not always help us to distinguish one person from an ancestor with the same name. The user of this volume will be spared some frustration if the differences between the ancient and modern situations are kept in mind.

In a few cases, English versions of the Bible use the same word to transliterate several similar, but different, Hebrew names. In these instances, a separate entry for each Hebrew name is recorded (*See for instance,* Iddo).

LIST OF MAPS

A

Aaron (ār'un; "enlightened, rich, mountaineer"). The brother of Moses. He became the first high priest of Israel (Exod. 4:14, 30; 7:2, 19; 17:9-12; 29; Num. 12; 17).

Abagtha (a-bag'tha; "happy, prosperous"). One of the seven chamberlains of King Ahasuerus (Esther 1:10).

Abana (a-ba'na; "stony"). A river that runs through Damascus, purported to have healing qualities (2 Kings 5:12). A more accurate rendering of the name would be Amana.

Abarim (ab'a-rim; "mountain beyond"). A large mountain range in Moab near Heshbon, which includes Mount Nebo (Num. 27:12; 33:47-48; Deut. 32:49).

Abda (ab'da; "servant worshiper"). [1] Father of Solomon's tribute officer, Adoniram (1 Kings 4:6). [2] A chief Levite after the Exile (Neh. 11:17). He is called Obadiah in First Chronicles 9:16.

Abdeel (ab'dē-el; "servant of God"). The father of Shelemiah, who was commanded to arrest Baruch and Jeremiah (Jer. 36:26).

Abdi (ab'di; "servant of Jehovah"). [1] One whom David set over the song service (1 Chron. 6:44). [2] One who took a foreign wife during the Exile (Ezra 10:26). [3] A Levite contemporary with Hezekiah (2 Chron. 29:12).

Abdiel (ab'di-el; "servant of Jehovah"). Ancestor of a clan of Gad (1 Chron. 5:15).

Abdon (ab'don; "service, servile"). [1] A judge of Israel for eight years (Judg. 12:13, 15). See Bedan. [2] A descendant of Benjamin who dwelt in Jerusalem (1 Chron. 8:23). [3] Firstborn son of Jehiel, mentioned in Chronicles (1 Chron. 8:30; 9:36). [4] One sent to Huldah to inquire of the meaning of the Law (2 Chron. 34:20). He is called Achbor in Second Kings 22:12. Possibly he is identical with [2].

Abdon (ab'don; "service"). A city belonging to the tribe of Asher, located at the present site of Khirbet Abdeh (Josh. 21:30; 1 Chron. 6:71). It was once called Hebron; see Hebron [2].

Abed-nego (a-bed'ne-gō; "servant of Nego; servant of Ishtar"). Name given to Azariah, one of the three friends of Daniel who were carried captive to Babylon. He was thrown into a fiery furnace (Dan. 1:7; 2:49; 3:12-30).

Abel (ā'bel; "a breath, vapor; shepherd"). Second son of Adam and Eve, slain by his brother Cain (Gen. 4:1-10; Heb. 11:4; 12:24).

1

Abel (ā'bel; "meadow," "brook," "stream"). A prefix attached to several towns. [1] In Second Samuel 20:14-18, a city specifically related to Abel-beth-maacah is mentioned. Some suppose that Abel and Beth-maacah were towns so close together that they were thought of as being one. However, others believe only one town is referred to in this passage. [2] The KJV reading in First Samuel 6:18, "the great stone of Abel," is not very likely. It is a combination of the Hebrew, "the great meadow [*abel*]," and the Septuagint, "the great stone." A city is not referred to here. See Abel-beth-maacah.

Abel-beth-maacah (ā'bel-beth-mā'a-ka; "meadow [brook] of the house of Maacah"). A town of the tribe of Naphtali, located in northern Palestine (2 Sam. 20:14-15). Verse 14 probably refers to one city, not two. In verse 18 the city is simply called Abel. See also Abel [1], Abel-maim.

Abel-maim (ā'bel-mā'im; "meadow [brook] of waters"). Probably another name for Abel-beth-maacah (2 Chron. 16:4).

Abel-meholah (ā'bel-me-hō'lah; "meadow [brook] of dancing"). The birthplace of Elisha, located on the western side of the Jordan Valley (Judg. 7:22; 1 Kings 4:12).

Abel-mizraim (ā'bel-miz'rā-im; "meadow of Egypt"). See Atad.

Abel-shittim (ā'bel-shit'im; "meadow [brook] of Acacias"). Largest campsite of the wandering Israelites, located on the plains of Moab (Num. 33:49).

Abez (ā'bez; "lofty"). A town in northern Palestine apportioned to the tribe of Issachar (Josh. 19:20).

Abi (a'bi; "my father"). The mother of King Hezekiah (2 Kings 18:2). *Abi* is a contraction of *Abijah* ("Jehovah is father"), which she is called in Second Chronicles 29:1. See Abi-albon; Abi-ezer.

Abia [Abiah, Abijah] (a-bī'a [a-bī'a, a-bī'ja]; "Jehovah is father"). [1] A son of Samuel and wicked judge of Israel (1 Sam. 8:2; 1 Chron. 6:28). [2] The wife of Hezron (1 Chron. 2:24). [3] Son of Rehoboam and successor to the throne of Judah, an ancestor of Christ (1 Chron. 3:10; 2 Chron. 11:20-14:1; Matt. 1:7). He was also known as Abijam. [4] The seventh son of Becher the son of Benjamin (1 Chron. 7:8). [5] A descendant of Aaron appointed by David in connection with the priestly courses (1 Chron. 24:10; cf. Luke 1:5). [6] A son of Jeroboam I of Israel (1 Kings 14:1-8). [7] A priest of Nehemiah's time who sealed the covenant (Neh. 10:7). Possibly the same as the priest mentioned in Nehemiah 12:1, 4, 17. [8] See Abi.

Abi-Albon (a'bī-al'bon; "father of strength"). One of David's "valiant men" (2 Sam. 23:31). Also called Abiel (1 Chron. 11:32).

Abiasaph [Ebiasaph] (a-bī'a-saf [e-bī'a-saf]; "my father has gathered"). A Levite whose descendants were doorkeepers of the Tabernacle (Exod. 6:24; 1 Chron. 6:23; 9:19).

Abiathar (a-bī'a-thar; "father of super-excellence or pre-eminence"). The only priest to escape Saul's massacre at Nob, he was a high priest in David's time. He was deposed by Solomon (1 Sam. 22:20-23; 1 Kings 2:27; 1 Chron. 15:11-12). First Samuel 21 says that Ahimelech [1] was the high priest when David ate the showbread, yet Mark 2:26 states this occurred in the days of Abiathar, the high priest. There are several possible ways to resolve this problem: (a) An old rabbinic tradition says that the son of a high priest could also be designated a high priest; however, we cannot be sure how old this tradition is. (b) Abiathar may have been assisting his father as high priest and thus could be so designated. (c) Abiathar was more prominent in history than was his father Ahimelech, so he is mentioned here instead of Ahimelech. If this is so (and it seems to be), then Abiathar is called the "high priest" before he actually assumed that office. Notice that Mark does *not* say that Abiathar was present when David ate the showbread; there is no need to suppose an error in this passage.

Abida [Abidah] (a-bī'da [a-bī'da]; "father of knowledge"). A son of Midian listed in Genesis and Chronicles (Gen. 25:4; 1 Chron. 1:33).

Abidan (a-bī'dan; "father is judge"; "my father"). A prince of Benjamin (Num. 1:11; 2:22; 7:60, 65; 10:24).

Abiel (ā'bi-el; "God is father"). *See* Abi-albon, Ner.

Abi-ezer [Abiezer] (ā'bi-ē'zer [a'bi-ē'zer]; "father of help"). [1] A descendant of Manasseh (Josh. 17:2; 1 Chron. 7:18). *See* Jeezer. [2] One of David's mighty men (2 Sam. 23:27; 1 Chron. 11:28; 27:12).

Abigail (ab'i-gāl; "father [i.e., cause] of delight"). [1] A wife of Nabal and afterwards of David (1 Sam. 25:3, 14-44). [2] Mother of Amasa, whom Absalom made captain (2 Sam. 17:25; 1 Chron. 2:16-17).

Abihail (ab'i-hāl; "father of might"). [1] A chief man of the descendants of Merari (Num. 3:35). [2] The wife of Abishur (1 Chron. 2:29). [3] Head of a family of Gad (1 Chron. 5:14). [4] A wife of Rehoboam (2 Chron. 11:18). [5] Father of Esther (Esther 2:15; 9:29).

Abihu (a-bī'hū; "he is my father"). A son of Aaron, destroyed with his brother for offering strange fire to God (Exod. 6:23; Lev. 10:1).

Abihud (a-bī'hud; "father of honor"). A son of Bela listed in Chronicles (1 Chron. 8:3).

Abijah (a-bī'ja; "the Lord is my father"). *See* Abia.

Abijam (a-bī'jam; "father of the sea [or west]"). *See* Abia [3].

Abilene (ab-i-lē'ne; "stream," "brook"). A Syrian tetrarchy located 29 to 32 km. (18 to 20 mi.) northwest of Damascus (Luke 3:1).

Abimael (a'bim'a-el; "my father is God"). A son of Joktan listed in Genesis and Chronicles (Gen. 10:26-28; 1 Chron. 1:20-22). The name may denote an Arabian tribe. Some scholars suggest a locality in Arabia is intended.

Abimelech (a-bim'e-lek; "father of the king"). [1] Many scholars believe the King(s) Abimelech(s) of Gerar in Genesis 20, 21, and 26 are not proper names but a royal title borne by the Philistine kings.

The Psalm 34 title mentions Abimelech where Achish should occur. Since the story of Achish was well known, it seems improbable to regard this as a mistake, but rather a royal title of Achish, king of Gath. *See* Phichol. **[2]** A son of Gideon who tried to become king of Israel, and did reign for three years (Judg. 8:30–10:1). **[3]** *See* Ahimelech [2].

Abinadab (a-bin′a-dab; "father or source of liberality or willingness"). **[1]** A man of Judah in whose house the ark was placed (1 Sam. 7:1; 2 Sam. 6:3-4; 1 Chron. 13:7). **[2]** A brother of David (1 Sam. 16:8; 17:13; 1 Chron. 2:13). **[3]** Son of Saul slain by the Philistines (1 Sam. 31:2; 1 Chron. 8:33; 9:39; 10:2). **[4]** Father of one of Solomon's officers (1 Kings 4:11).

Abiner (ab′i-ner). *See* Abner.

Abinoam (a-bin′ō-am; "father of pleasantness"). Father of Barak the general (Judg. 4:6, 12; 5:1, 12).

Abiram (a-bī′ram; "father of elevation"). **[1]** One who conspired against Moses and was destroyed (Num. 16:27; Psa. 106:17). **[2]** Firstborn son of Hiel who died when his father began to rebuild Jericho (1 Kings 16:34; cf. Josh. 6:26).

Abishag (ab′i-shag; "my father was a wanderer"). A beautiful woman chosen to nurse the aged David (1 Kings 1:3, 15; 2:17, 21-22). This woman may also be the heroine of the Song of Solomon, where she is simply called "the Shulamite."

Abishai (a-bish′a-ī; "my father is Jesse; source of wealth"). A son of David's sister, Zeruiah. He was one of David's mighty men (1 Sam. 26:6-9; 2 Sam. 2:18; 10:10; 23:18).

Abishalom [Absalom] (a-bish′a-lom; "father of peace"). Father of Maachah, the wife of Rehoboam (1 Kings 15:2, 10). He is called Absalom, another form of the name, in Second Chronicles 11:20-21, and Uriel in Second Chronicles 13:2. *See* Absalom.

Abishua (a-bish′ū-a; "father of safety"). **[1]** A son of Phinehas, descendant of Aaron mentioned in Chronicles and Ezra (1 Chron. 6:4-5, 50; Ezra 7:5). **[2]** A descendant of Benjamin listed in Chronicles (1 Chron. 8:4).

Abishur (ab′i-shur; "father of oxen"). A son of Shammai listed in Chronicles (1 Chron. 2:28-29).

Abital (ab′i-tal; "source of dew"). A wife of David (2 Sam. 3:4; 1 Chron. 3:3).

Abitub (ab′i-tub; "source of good"). A descendant of Benjamin listed in Chronicles (1 Chron. 8:11).

Abiud (a-bī′ud; "my father is majesty; father of honor"). A son of Zerubbabel and ancestor of Christ (Matt. 1:13).

Abner [Abiner] (ab′ner [ab′i-ner]; "my father of light"). A shortened form of *Abiner;* the captain of the host under Saul and Ishbosheth (1 Sam. 14:50-51; 26:5, 7; 2 Sam. 2; 3).

Abraham [Abram] (ā′bra-ham [ā′bram]). The founder of the Jewish nation and an ancestor of Christ. His name was changed from Abram ("the father is exalted") to Abraham ("father of multitudes") (Gen. 11–26; Matt. 1:1-2).

Absalom (ab'sa-lom; "father of peace"). A son of David who tried to usurp the throne from his father (2 Sam. 3:3; 13–19). *See* Abishalom.

Accad [Akkad] (ak'ac [ak'ad]; "fortress"). A city built by Nimrod on the Plain of Shinar (Sumer), north of Babylonia (Gen. 10:10).

Accho (ac'kō; "compressed"). A town on the coast of Palestine about 40 km. (25 mi.) scuth of Tyre, apportioned to the tribe of Asher (Judg. 1:31); also called Ptolemais in Acts 21:7.

Aceldama [Potter's Field] (a-sel'da-ma; "field of blood"). A field purchased by the priests of Jerusalem with the 30 pieces of silver that bought the betrayal of Jesus (Acts 1:19); also called Potter's Field (Matt. 27:7).

Achaia (a-kā'ya; "trouble"). An ancient district of the Peloponnesus in Greece ruled by the Romans (Acts 18:12; Rom. 15:26).

Achaicus (a-kā' i-kus; "belonging to Achaia"). A Corinthian Christian who visited Paul at Philippi (1 Cor. 16:17).

Achan [Achar] (ā'kan [ā'kar]; "trouble"). One who stole part of the spoil of Jericho and brought "trouble" on his people. He was killed for this (Josh. 7:1-24). In First Chronicles 2:7, he is called *Achar*.

Achaz (a'kaz; "he holds"). Greek form of Ahaz (q.v.).

Achbor (ak'bor; "a mouse"). [1] Father of a king of Edom (Gen. 36:38-39; 1 Chron. 1:49). [2] The father of the one sent to bring Urijah from Egypt (Jer. 26:22; 36:12). [3] *See* Abdon [4].

Achim (ā'kim; "woes"). Ancestor of Christ (Matt. 1:14).

Achish (ā'kish; "serpent-charmer"). [1] A king of Gath to whom David fled for safety (1 Sam. 21; 27-29). [2] Another king of Gath who bore the same name but reigned during Solomon's time (1 Kings 2:39-40). However, many believe the kings to be identical.

Achmetha [Ecbatana] (ak'me-tha [ek-ba-ta'na]; "a place of horses"). A provincial city of the Medes that was the summer residence of Persian kings (Ezra 6:2); also called Ecbatana. The city stood near present-day Hamadan.

Achor (ā'kōr; "trouble"). A valley south of Jericho, in which Achan was stoned (Josh. 7:24); and which formed the northern boundary of Judah (Josh. 15:7).

Achsa [Achsah] (ak'sa [ak'sah]; "serpent-charmer"). A daughter of Caleb who married her uncle Othniel (Josh. 15: 16-17; Judg. 1:12-13; 1 Chron. 2:49).

Achshaph (ak'shaf; "sorcery"). A city of Canaan captured by Joshua (Josh. 12:20), and a landmark on the boundary of the land apportioned to the tribe of Asher (Josh. 19:25).

Achzib [Chezib] (ak'zib [ke'zib]; "false"). [1] A Canaanite city in the lowlands of Judah, captured by Joshua (Gen. 38:5; Josh. 15:44). [2] A seashore town on the northern side of Galilee near the Lebanon border (Josh. 19:29; Judg. 1:31).

Adadah (ad'a-dah; "holiday"). A town in the southern district of Judah (Josh. 15:22).

Adah (ā'da; "pleasure; beauty"). [1] One of the two wives of Lamech (Gen. 4:19-20, 23). [2] One of the wives of Esau (Gen. 36:2, 4, 10, 12, 16). See Esau's Wives.

Adaiah (ad-ā'ya; "pleasing to Jehovah; Jehovah has adorned"). [1] A son of Shimhi found in First Chronicles 8:12-21. [2] A Levite ancestor of Asaph (1 Chron. 6:41). Also called Iddo (1 Chron. 6:21). [3] Father of a captain who aided Jehoiada (2 Chron. 23:1). [4] Father of Jedidah, the mother of King Josiah (2 Kings 22:1). [5] One whose descendants resided in Jerusalem (Neh. 11:5). [6] One who married a foreign wife (Ezra 10:29). [7] Another who did the same (Ezra 10:39). [8] A Levite descendant from Aaron (1 Chron. 9:12; Neh. 11:12).

Adalia (a-dā'li-a; "honor of Ized"). One of the sons of Haman slain by the Jews (Esther 9:8).

Adam (ad'am; "of the ground; firm"). The first man. His sin caused a curse to fall upon all the race (Gen. 2–3; 1 Cor. 15:22, 45). He is listed in the genealogy of Christ (Luke 3:38).

Adam (ad'am; "red; of the earth"). A city on the east bank of the Jordan River that was given to the tribe of Reuben (Josh. 3:16).

Adamah (ad'a-ma; "earth"). A fortified city in northern Palestine apportioned to the tribe of Naphtali (Josh. 19:36); its exact location is not known.

Adami [Adami-Nekeb] (ad'a-mī [ad'a-mī-ne'keb]; "fortified"). A border town assigned to the tribe of Naphtali (Josh. 19:33); perhaps located on the site of modern Khirbet ed-Damiyeh, 8 km. (5 mi.) southwest of Tiberias. Some consider this to be the same as Nekeb and hence join the words to form one: Adami-Nekeb. Others deny this—either view is possible. Adami also might be identical with Adamah (q.v.).

Adar [Hazar-Addar] (ā'dar [hā'zar-ad'ar]; "height"). A fortress town located on the southwestern border of Judah between Kadesh-barnea and Karka (Josh. 15:3). This place is called Hazar-Addar in Numbers 34:4.

Adbeel (ad'bi-el; "languishing for God"). A son of Ishmael listed in Genesis and Chronicles (Gen. 25:13; 1 Chron. 1:29).

Addan (ad'dan). See Addon.

Addan [Addon] (ad'dan [ad'don]; "stony"). A place in Babylon that served as a staging area for exiles returning to Israel (Ezra 2:59; Neh. 7:61).

Addar (ad'dar; "height; honor"). A son of Bela listed in Chronicles (1 Chron. 8:3). See Ard [2].

Addi (ad'dī; "my witness"). An ancestor of Christ (Luke 3:28).

Addon [Addan] (ad'don [ad'dan]; "strong"). A man who was unable to prove his Jewish ancestry when he returned from Exile (Neh. 7:61; Ezra 2:59).

Ader (ā'der; "a flock"). A son of Beriah listed in Chronicles (1 Chron. 8:15).

Adiel (ā'di-el; "ornament of God"). [1] A descendant of Simeon listed in Chronicles (1 Chron. 4:36). [2] A descendant of Aaron (1 Chron. 9:12). [3] Father of David's treasurer, Asmaveth (1 Chron. 27:25).

Adin (ā'din; "ornament"). [1] Ancestor of returned capt ves (Ezra 2:15; Neh. 7:20). [2] One whose descendant returned with Ezra (Ezra 8:6). [3] A family who sealed the covenant (Neh. 10:14-16).

Adina (ad'i-na; "ornament"). A captain of David's (1 Chron. 11:42).

Adino (ad'i-nō; "orrament"). A chief of David's mighty men (2 Sam. 23:8). Some identify him with Jashobeam [1]; others deny this.

Adithaim (ad-i-tha'im; "double crossing"). A town in the lowlands of Judah (Josh. 15:36).

Adlai (ad'lā-i; "lax; weary"). Father of an overseer of David's herds (1 Chron. 27:29).

Admah (ad'mah; "redness"). One of the Cities of the Plain that God destroyed with Sodom and Gomorrah (Gen. 19:25-29); its location may now be submerged by the southern end of the Dead Sea.

Admatha (ad'ma-tha; "God-given"). One of the seven princes of Persia (Esther 1:14).

Adna (ad'na; "pleasure"). [1] One who took a foreign wife (Ezra 10:30). [2] A priest listed in Nehemiah (Neh. 12:12-15). *See also* Adnah.

Adnah (ad'nah; "pleasure"). [1] A captain who joined David at Ziklag (1 Chron. 12:20). [2] A chief captain of Jehoshaphat (2 Chron. 17:14). *See also* Adna.

Adoni-bezek (a-dō'ni-bē'zek; "lord of lightning [Bezek]"). A king of Bezek who was captured by Israel (Judg. 1:5-7).

Adonijah (a-dō-nī'jah; "Jehovah is my lord"). [1] A son of David, executed by Solomon for trying to usurp the throne (2 Sam. 3:4; 1 Kings 1:2). [2] One sent by Jehoshaphat to teach the law (2 Chron. 17:8). [3] One who sealed the new covenant with God after the Exile (Neh. 10:14-16). [4] *See* Tob-adonijah.

Adonikam (a-don-ī'kam; "my lord has risen"). Ancestor of returned captives (Ezra 2:13; 8:13; Neh. 7:18).

Adoniram (a-do-nī'ram; "lord of height"). *See* Hadoram [3].

Adoni-zedek (a-do'ni-ze'dek; "lord of justice or righteousness"). A king of Jerusalem defeated by Joshua (Josh. 10:1-27).

Adoraim (ad-ō-rā'im; "two mounds"). A city in Judah built by Rehoboam (2 Chron. 11 9).

Adoram (a-dō'ram). *See* Adoniram; Hadoram [3].

Adrammelech (a-dram'mel-ek; "honor of the king; Adar is king"). A son of the Assyrian king Sennacherib who, with his brother, killed his father (2 Kings 19:37; Isa. 37:38).

Adramyttium (a-dra-mit'ti-um; "from Adramys, brother of Craesus"). A port city of Mysia in the northwestern part of the Roman province of Asia (Acts 27:2; cf. 16:7).

Adria (ā'dri-a; "from [the city] Adria of Italy"). Originally a name referring to the sea east of Italy. In later times, the term included the Mediterranean between Greece and Sicily (Acts 27:27).

Adriel (ā'dri-el; "honor of God; my help is God"). The man whom Merab married although she had been promised to David (1 Sam. 18:19; 2 Sam. 21:8).

Adullam (a-dul'lam; "refuge"). A town of Judah near Succoth. David made the headquarters of his rebellion against Saul in a cave near this town (Josh. 12:7-15; 1 Sam. 22; 2 Sam. 23:13).

Adummim (a-dum'im; "bloody things"). A pass from the Jordan Valley to the hill country of Judah. It is the shortest route from Jericho to Jerusalem, and may have been the setting for Jesus' parable of the good Samaritan (Josh. 15:7; cf. Luke 10:30-37).

Aeneas (e nē'as; "praise"). The paralytic of Lydda who was healed by Peter (Acts 9:33-34).

Aenon (ē'non; "fountains"). A place noted for its abundant supply of water, where John baptized his converts. Most likely this site was at the head of the Valley of Shechem (John 3:23).

Agabus (ag'a-bus; "locust"). A prophet of Jerusalem who foretold suffering for Paul if he went to Jerusalem (Acts 11:28; 21:10).

Agag (ā'gag; "high; warlike"). A name or title of the kings of Amalek; it is probably not a proper name. However, if it is a proper name, it is used to refer to two persons: [1] A king mentioned by Balaam (Num. 24:7). [2] A king that Saul spared, but who was later executed by Samuel (1 Sam. 15).

Agar (ā'gar; "wandering"). The Greek form of Hagar (q.v.).

Agee (ag'ē; "fugitive"). Father of one of David's mighty men (2 Sam. 23:11).

Agrippa (a-grip'a). See Herod.

Agur (ā'gur; "gathered"). A sage who wrote Proverbs 30.

Ahab (ā'hab; "father's brother [uncle]"). [1] The seventh king of Israel. He was wicked and idolatrous and married a woman of the same character—Jezebel (1 Kings 16:28–22:40). [2] A false prophet killed by Nebuchadnezzar (Jer. 29:21-22).

Aharah (a-har'ah; "brother's follower"). See Ahiram.

Aharhel (a-har'hel; "after might; brother of Rachel"). A descendant of Judah (1 Chron. 4:8).

Ahasai (a-hā'sī; "my holder; protector"). A priest of the family of Immer (Neh. 11:13). See Jahzerah.

Ahasbai (a-has'bī; "blooming; shining"). Father of one of David's mighty men (2 Sam. 23:34).

Ahasuerus (a-haz-u-ē'rus; "prince") [1] The king of Persia whom Esther married. He is known as Xerxes to historians (Esther 1:1; 2:16;

10:3) [2] The father of Darius the Mede (Dan. 9:1). [3] Another name for Cambyses, king of Persia (Ezra 4:6).

Ahava (a-hā'va; "water"). A site about 14 km. (9 mi.) north of Babylon; a staging area for Jews preparing to return to Palestine (Ezra 8:15, 31).

Ahaz [Achaz] (ā'haz a'kaz]; "he holds"). [1] The eleventh king of Judah and an ancestor of Christ (1 Kings 15:38–16:20; Matt. 1:9). [2] A descendant of Benjamin (1 Chron. 8:35-36; 9:41-42).

Ahaziah [Azariah] (ē-ha-zi'a [a-za-rī'a]; "Jehovah holds or sustains"). [1] The eighth king of Israel. He was weak and idolatrous (1 Kings 22:51–2 Kings 1:18). [2] The sixth king of Judah; he reigned only one year (2 Kings 8:24-29; 9:16ff.). He was also known as Jehoahaz (2 Chron. 21: 7; 25:23). His being called Azariah in Second Chronicles 22:6 is an error; over fifteen Hebrew manuscripts and all recent versions read Ahaziah. See Jehoahaz.

Ahban (a'ban; "brother of intelligence"). The son of Abishur of Judah (1 Chron. 2:29).

Aher (ā'her; "one that is behind"). A descendant of Benjamin (1 Chron. 7:12). See also Ahiram.

Ahi (ā'hī; "my brother"). [1] Head of a family of Gad (1 Chron. 5:15). [2] A man of the tribe of Asher (1 Chron. 7:34).

Ahiah (a-hī'a; "Jehovah is brother"). [1] A grandson of Phinehas (1 Sam. 14:3, 18). Some identify him with Ahimelech [2]. [2] One of Solomon's scribes (1 Kings 4:3). [3] A descendant of Benjamin (1 Chron. 8:7). See also Ahijah.

Ahiam (a-hī'am; "a mother's brother"). One of David's mighty men (2 Sam. 23:33; 1 Chron. 11:35).

Ahian (a-hī'an; "brother of day"). A descendant of Manasseh (1 Chron. 7:19).

Ahiezer (a-hī-ē'zer; "helping brother"). [1] A prince of Dan who helped Moses take a census (Num. 1:12; 2:25; 7:66). [2] One who joined David at Ziklag (1 Chron. 12:3).

Ahihud (a-hī'hūd; "brother of honor"). [1] A prince of Asher (Num. 34:27). [2] A member of the family of Ehud, descended from Benjamin (1 Chron. 8:7).

Ahijah (a-hī'jāh; "Jehovah is brother; my brother is Jehovah"). [1] A prophet who prophesied the splitting away of the ten tribes (1 Kings 11:29-30; 14:2, 4-5). [2] Father of Baasha who conspired against Nadab (1 Kings 15:27, 33; 21:22). [3] A son of Jerahmeel (1 Chron. 2:25). [4] One of David's mighty men (1 Chron. 11:36). [5] One who sealed the new covenant with God after the Exile (Neh. 10:26). [6] One set over the temple treasures (1 Chron. 26:20). See also Ahiah; Ahimelech.

Ahikam (a-hī'kam; "my brother has risen"). A member of the group sent to consult Huldah the prophetess (2 Kings 22:12, 14; 25:22; Jer. 26:24; 39:14).

Ahilud (a-hī'lud; "a brother born; child's brother"). Father of a

recorder appointed by David (2 Sam. 8:16; 20:24; 1 Kings 4:3, 12).
Ahimaaz (a-him′a-az; "powerful brother"). [1] Father of Ahinoam, wife of Saul (1 Sam. 14:50). [2] One of Solomon's officers (1 Kings 4:15). [3] Son of Zadok who remained loyal to David (2 Sam. 15:27, 36; 17:17, 20; 18:19-29).

Ahiman (a-hī′man; "brother of man or fortune"). [1] A son of Anak who dwelt in Hebron (Num. 13:22; Josh. 15:14; Judg. 1:10). [2] A porter in the temple (1 Chron. 9:17).

Ahimelech (a-him′e-lek; "brother of the king; my brother is king"). [1] A Hittite friend of David (1 Sam. 26:6). [2] A priest, son of Abiathar and grandson of [3] (2 Sam. 8:17; 1 Chron. 24:6). Some think the readings in these passages have been transposed (i.e., they speak of Ahimelech the son of Abiathar instead of Abiathar the son of Ahimelech). But this seems unlikely, especially in First Chronicles 24. He is called Abimelech in First Chronicles 18:16. The Septuagint has Ahimelech here also. [3] One of the priests of Nob slain for helping David (1 Sam. 21:1-8; 22:9-20). See also Abimelech; Ahiah.

Ahimoth (a-hī′moth; "brother of death"). A descendant of Kohath (1 Chron. 6:25).

Ahinadab (a-hin′a-dab; "brother of liberality or willingness"). One of Solomon's royal merchants (1 Kings 4:14).

Ahinoam (a-hin′ō-am; "pleasant brother"). [1] Wife of King Saul (1 Sam. 14:50). [2] A woman of Jezreel who married David (1 Sam. 25:43; 27:3; 1 Chron. 3:1).

Ahio (a-hi′ō; "his brother"). [1] Son of Abinadab, in whose house the ark stayed for 20 years (2 Sam. 6:3-4; 1 Chron. 13:7). [2] A descendant of Benjamin (1 Chron. 8:14). [3] A descendant of Saul (1 Chron. 8:31; 9:37).

Ahira (a-hī′ra; "brother of evil"). A chief of the tribe of Naphtali (Num. 1:15; 2:29; 7:78).

Ahiram (a-hī′ram; "exalted brother; my brother is exalted"). A descendant of Benjamin (Num. 26:38). He is called Ehi, possibly a contraction of Ahiram, in Genesis 46:21 and Aharah in First Chronicles 8:1. He is possibly the same as Aher (q.v.).

Ahisamach (a-his′a-mach; "supporting brother"). One who helped build the tent of meeting (Exod. 31:6; 35:34; 38:23).

Ahishahar (a-hish′a-har; "brother of the dawn"). One of the sons of Bilhan (1 Chron. 7:10).

Ahishar (a-hī′shar; "brother of song; my brother has sung"). An officer of Solomon (1 Kings 4:6).

Ahithophel (a-hith′o-fel; "brother of foolishness"). The real leader of Absalom's rebellion against David. When he saw that victory was impossible, he committed suicide (2 Sam. 15–17).

Ahitub (a-hī′tub; "a good brother; my brother is goodness"). [1] A son of Phinehas (1 Sam. 14:3; 22:9, 11-12, 20). [2] Father of Zadok the high priest (2 Sam. 8:17; 15:27; 1 Chron. 6:7-8). [3] A high priest of the same family who served during Nehemiah's time (1 Chron. 6:11; 9:11; Neh. 11:11).

Ahlab (ah'lab; "ferti e"). A town assigned to Asher, but never captured from the Canaanites (Judg. 1:31); its probable location is about 6 km. (4 mi.) northeast of Tyre.

Ahlai (a'lī; "Jehovah s staying"). [1] A daughter of Sheshan listed in First Chronicles 2:3. [2] Father of one of David's mighty men (1 Chron. 11:41).

Ahoah (a-hō'ah; "a brother's reed; brotherly"). A son of Bela (1 Chron. 8:4).

Aholiab (a-hō'li-ab; "a father's tent"). One of the workers who erected the tabernacle (Exod. 31:6; 35:34; 36:1-2).

Aholibamah (a-hōl-i-bē'mah; "tent of the high place"). [1] A wife of Esau (Gen. 36:2, 5, 14, 18). [2] A duke of Edom (Gen. 36:41). *See also* Esau's Wives.

Ahumai (a-hū'mī; "heated by Jehovah"). A descendant of Judah (1 Chron. 4:2).

Ahuzam (a-hū'zam; "possession"). A son of Ashur, a descendant of Judah through Caleb (1 Chron. 4:16).

Ahuzzath (a-huz'zath; 'holding fast"). A friend of Abimelech, king of Philistia (Gen. 26:26).

Ai [Aiath; Aija] (ā'ī [ā-ī'ath; ā-ī'ja]; "heap of ruins"). [1] One of the strongest Canaanite cities, located east of Bethel (Josh. 7:2; Neh. 11:31). In Isaiah 10:28 the Hebrew feminine form of the name (Aiath) occurs. [2] A city of the Ammonites, probably located near Heshbon (Jer. 49:3).

Aiah [Ajah] (ā-ī'ah [ā'ja]; "a vulture"). [1] A son of Zibeon (Gen. 36:24; 1 Chron. 1:40). [2] Father of Saul's concubine, Rizpah (2 Sam. 3:7; 21:8, 10-11).

Aijalon [Ajalon] (ā'ja-lon [aj'a-lon]; "place of harts"). [1] A town located 22.5 km. (14 mi.) northwest of Jerusalem, designated as a Levitical city (Josh. 19:42 21:24; 2 Chron. 28:18). [2] A site belonging to the tribe of Zebulun west of the Sea of Galilee, where the judge Elon was buried (Judg. 12:12). Its exact location is unknown.

Ain (a'ēn; "eye"). [1] A town of Judah near Rimmon, assigned to the Levites serving the tribe of Simeon (Josh. 15:32; 19:7 21:16; 1 Chron. 4:32). [2] A site on the boundary line of the Promised Land, west of Riblah (Num. 34:11). Its exact location is unknown.

Ajalon (aj'a-lon). *See* Aijalon.

Akan (ā'kan). *See* Jaakan.

Akkub (ak'kub; "lain in wait; pursuer"). [1] One descendant from David mentioned in Chronicles (1 Chron. 3:24). [2] A porter in the temple (1 Chron. 9:17; Neh. 11:19; 12:25). [3] Ancestor of a family of porters (Ezra 2:42; Neh. 7:45). [4] Ancestor of Nethinim who returned from the Exile (Ezra 2:45). [5] A priest who helped the people understand the Law (Neh. 8:7).

Akrabbim (a'krab'bim). *See* Maaleh-acrabbim.

Alameth (al'a-meth; "hidden"). A son of Becher (1 Chron. 7:8).

Alammelech (a-lam'me-lek; "king's oak"). A village assigned to the tribe of Asher (Josh. 19:26).

Alemeth (al'e-meth; "hiding place"). A descendant of Jonathan (1 Chron. 8:36; 9:42).

Alemeth [Almon] (al'e-meth [al'mōn]; "hidden"). A city given to the priests of the tribe of Benjamin (1 Chron. 6:60; Josh. 21:18).

Alexander (al-ex-an'der; "helper of man"). [1] A son of the Simon who bore Christ's cross (Mark 15:21). [2] A kinsman of Annas and a leading man in Jerusalem (Acts 4:6). [3] A Christian with Paul when the Ephesians had a riot (Acts 19:33). Perhaps the same as [1]. [4] A convert who apostatized (1 Tim. 1:20). [5] A person who did much harm to Paul (2 Tim. 4:14). Perhaps the same as [4].

Alexandria (al-ex-an'dri-a; "city of Alexander the Great"). A city on the Mediterranean coast of Egypt, which served as Egypt's capital city for many years (Acts 27:6; 28:11-13).

Aliah [Alvah] (a-lī'ah [al'va]; "sublimity"). A duke of Edom (1 Chron. 1:51). He is called Alvah in Genesis (Gen. 36:40).

Alian [Alvan] (a-lī'an [al'van]; "sublime"). A descendant of Seir (1 Chron. 1:40). He is called Alvan in Genesis 36:23.

Allon (al'lon; "an oak"). A chief of Simeon (1 Chron. 4:37).

Allon (al'lon; "an oak"). A town in south Naphtali (Josh. 19:33).

Almodad (al-mō'dad; "the agitator"). A son of Joktan (Gen. 10:26; 1 Chron. 1:20). Perhaps the name refers to an Arabian people that settled in South Arabia.

Almon (al'mōn). *See* Alemeth.

Almon-diblathaim (al'mon-dib-la-tha'im; "hiding place of two fig sacks"). A site between the Arnon River and Shittim where the Israelites camped during their wandering in the wilderness (Num. 33:46).

Aloth (ā'loth; "ascents; steeps"). A district from which King Solomon drew provisions (1 Kings 4:16).

Alphaeus (al-fē'us; "leader; chief"). [1] The father of Levi (Matthew) (Mark 2:14). [2] The father of the apostle James (Matt. 10:3; Mark 3:18; Acts 1:13). Some identify him with Cleophas. *See* Cleophas.

Alush (ā'lush; "crowd"). A site where the Israelites camped on their journey from Egypt to Mount Sinai (Num. 33:14).

Alvah (al'va). *See* Aliah.

Alvan (al'van). *See* Alian.

Amad (a'mad; "enduring"). A frontier town of the tribe of Asher (Josh. 19:26).

Amal (a'mal; "laboring"). A descendant of Asher (1 Chron. 7:35).

Amalek (am'a-lek; "warlike; dweller in the vale"). A son of Eliphaz and progenitor of the Amalekites (Gen. 36:12, 16; 1 Chron. 1:36; cf. Exod. 17:8-9).

Amam (a'mam; "gathering place"). A village located on the Wadi-es-Sini in southern Judah (Josh. 15:26).

Amana (a-ma'na; "forth"). A range of mountains in Lebanon, probably south of the Amana [Abana] River (Song of Sol. 4:8).

Amariah (am-a-rī'a; "Jehovah has said"). [1] Grandfather of Zadok the high priest (1 Chron. 6:7, 52; Ezra 7:3). [2] Son of Azariah, a high priest in Solomon's time (1 Chron. 6:11). [3] A descendant of Kohath (1 Chron. 23:19; 24:23). [4] A chief priest in the reign of Jehoshaphat (2 Chron. 19:11). [5] The one appointed to distribute the tithes (2 Chron. 31:15). [6] One who took a foreign wife during the Exile (Ezra 10:42). [7] One who sealed the new covenant with God after the Exile (Neh. 10:3; 12:2, 13). [8] One whose descendants dwelled in Jerusalem after the Exile (Neh. 11:4). [9] Ancestor of Zephaniah the prophet (Zeph. 1:1).

Amasa (am'a-sa; "burden-bearer; people of Jesse"). [1] A nephew of David who became the commander of Absalom's army (2 Sam. 17:25; 19:13; 20:4-12). [2] One who opposed making slaves of captured Jews (2 Chron. 28:12).

Amasai (a-mas'ā-ī; "burden-bearer"). [1] A man in the genealogy of Kohath (1 Chron. 6:25, 35; 2 Chron. 29:12). [2] A captain who joined David at Ziklag (1 Chron. 12:18). [3] A priest who assisted in bringing up the ark of the covenant to Obed-edom (1 Chron. 15:24).

Amashai (a-mash'ā-ī; "carrying spoil"). A priest of the family of Immer (Neh. 11:13).

Amasiah (am-a-sī'a; "Jehovah bears; Jehovah has strength"). A chief captain of Jehoshaphat (2 Chron. 17:16).

Amaziah (am-a-zī'a; "Jehovah has strength"). [1] Son and successor of Joash to the throne of Judah. He was murdered at Lachish (2 Kings 12:21–14:20). [2] A man of the tribe of Simeon (1 Chron. 4:34). [3] A Levite descendant from Merari (1 Chron. 6:45). [4] An idolatrous priest of Bethel (Amos 7:10, 12, 14).

Ami [Amon] (ā'mī [ā'mon]; "faithful"). A servant of Solomon whose descendants returned from captivity (Ezra 2:57). In Nehemiah 7:59, he is called Amon.

Aminadab (a-min'a-dab; "people of liberality"). Greek form of Amminadab (q.v.).

Amittai (a-mit'ī; "truthful"). Father of the prophet Jonah (2 Kings 14:25; Jon. 1:1).

Ammah (am'ma; "head"). A hill in the wilderness of the Jordan Valley near Gibeon; Joab and Abner fought here (2 Sam. 2:24).

Ammiel (am'i-el; "my people are strong; my kinsman is God"). [1] One of those who spied out the Promised Land (Num. 13:12). [2] Father of Machir, David's friend (2 Sam. 9:4-5; 17:27). [3] See Eliam [1]. [4] A porter of the tabernacle in the time of David (1 Chron. 26:5).

Ammihud (am-mi'hud; "my people are honorable or glorious"). [1] Father of Elishama, the chief of Ephraim (Num. 1:10; 2:18; 7:48) [2] A Simeonite whose son helped to divide the Promised Land (Num.

34:20). **[3]** A Naphthalite whose son helped divide the Promised Land (Num. 34:28). **[4]** Father of Talmai, king of Geshur (2 Sam. 13:37). **[5]** A descendant of Pharez (1 Chron. 9:4).

Amminadab [Aminadab] (am-min′a-dab [a-min′a-dab]; "my people are willing or noble"). **[1]** Aaron's father-in-law (Exod. 6:23). **[2]** A prince of Judah and ancestor of Christ (Num. 1:7; 2:3; Ruth 4:19-20; Matt. 1:4). **[3]** A son of Kohath (1 Chron. 6:22). **[4]** One who helped to bring the ark of the covenant from the house of Obed-edom (1 Chron. 15:10-11).

Ammishaddai (am-mi-shad′dā-ī; "the Almighty is my kinsman; my people are mighty"). Father of Ahiezer, a captain of Dan during the wilderness journey (Num. 1:12; 2:25).

Ammizabad (am-miz′a-bad; "my people are endowed; my kinsman has a present"). One of David's captains (1 Chron. 27:6).

Ammon (am′mon). *See* Ben-ammi.

Amnon (am′non; "upbringing; faithful"). **[1]** Eldest son of David, by Ahinoam, slain by Absalom (2 Sam. 3:2; 13:1-39). **[2]** A son of Shimon of the family of Caleb (1 Chron. 4:20).

Amok (a′mok; "deep"). A priest who returned to Jerusalem with Zerubbabel (Neh. 12:7, 20).

Amon (ā′mon; "workman" or "trustworthy"). **[1]** Governor of Samaria in Ahab's time (1 Kings 22:26; 2 Chron. 18:25). **[2]** Son and successor of Manasseh to the throne of Judah; an ancestor of Christ (2 Kings 21:19-25; Jer. 1:2; Zeph. 1:1; Matt. 1:10). **[3]** *See* Ami.

Amos (ā′mos; "burden-bearer; burdensome"). **[1]** A prophet during the reigns of Uzziah and Jeroboam (Amos 1:1; 7:10-12, 14). **[2]** An ancestor of Christ (Luke 3:25).

Amoz (ā′moz; "strong"). Father of the prophet Isaiah (2 Kings 19:2, 20; Isa. 1:1; 2:1; 13:1).

Amphipolis (am-fip′o-lis; "surrounded city"). The chief city of Macedonia, located in the region of Thrace (Acts 17:1).

Amplias (am′pli-as; "large"). A Roman Christian to whom Paul sent greetings (Rom. 16:8).

Amram (am′ram; "people exalted; red"). **[1]** A descendant of Levi and father or ancestor of Aaron, Moses, and Miriam (Exod. 6:18, 20; Num. 3:19; 26:58-59). **[2]** One who had taken a foreign wife (Ezra 10:34). **[3]** *See* Hemdan.

Amraphel (am′ra-fel; "powerful people"). A king of Shinar who warred against Sodom (Gen. 14:1, 9).

Amzi (am′zi; "my strength"). **[1]** A Levite of the family of Merari (1 Chron. 6:46). **[2]** An ancestor of returned exiles (Neh. 11:12).

Anab (ā′nab; "grape"). A town in the mountains of Judah (Josh. 11:21; 15:50).

Anah (ā′nah; "answering"). **[1]** The mother (father?) of one of Esau's wives (Gen. 36:2, 14, 18, 25). If the father, he is the same as Beeri the Hittite (Gen. 26:34). *See* Esau's Wives. **[2]** A son of Seir and a chief of Edom (Gen. 36:20, 29; 1 Chron. 1:38). [3] A son of Zibeon (Gen. 36:24; 1 Chron. 1:40-41).

Anaharath (a-ña'ha-rath; "gorge"). A frontier town of the tribe of Issachar (Josh. 19:19).

Anaiah (a-nī'a; "Jehovah has covered; Jehovah answers"). [1] One who stood with Ezra at the reading of the Law (Neh. 8:4). [2] One who sealed the new covenant with God after the Exile (Neh. 10:22).

Anak (ā'nak; "giant; long necked"). Ancestor of the giant Anakim (Num. 13:22, 28, 33; Josh. 15:14).

Anamim (an'a-mim). A descendant of Mizraim (Gen. 10:13; 1 Chron. 1:11). Possibly an unknown Egyptian tribe.

Anan (ā'nan; "he beclouds; cloud"). One who sealed the new covenant with God after the Exile (Neh. 10:26).

Anani (a-nā'nī; "my cloud"). A descendant of David who lived after the Babylonian Captivity (1 Chron. 3:24).

Ananiah (an-a-nī'a; "Jehovah is a cloud [i.e., protector]"). Ancestor of a returned exile (Neh. 3:23).

Ananiah (an-a-nī'a; "Jehovah has covered"). A town inhabited by the tribe of Benjamin after the Exile (Neh. 11:32).

Ananias (an-a-nī'as; "Jehovah is gracious"). [1] A disciple struck dead for trying to deceive the apostles (Acts 5:1, 3, 5). [2] A disciple of Damascus who helped Paul after receiving a vision (Acts 9:10-17; 22:12). [3] A high priest in Jerusalem who opposed Paul (Acts 23:2; 24:1).

Anath (ā'nath; "answer"). Father of the judge Shamgar (Judg. 3:31; 5:6).

Anathoth (an'a-thoth; "answers"). [1] A son of Becher (1 Chron. 7:8). [2] One who sealed the new covenant with God after the Exile (Neh. 10:19).

Anathoth (an'a-thoth; 'answer"). A town of the tribe of Benjamin, located about 4 km. (2.5 mi.) northeast of Jerusalem (Josh. 21:18; Ezra 2:23); the birthplace of the prophet Jeremiah (Jer. 1:1; 11:21).

Andrew (an'drew; "manly; conqueror"). The brother of Peter and one of the twelve apostles (Matt. 4:18; 10:2; John 1:40, 44; 6:8).

Andronicus (an-dro-nī kus; "conqueror"). A kinsman of Paul at Rome, to whom Paul sent greetings (Rom. 16:7).

Anem (ā'nem; "two fountains"). A city of the tribe of Issachar, assigned to the Levites (1 Chron. 6:73). It is identical with En-gannim [2].

Aner (ā'ner; "sprout; waterfall"). An Amorite chief (Gen. 14:13, 24).

Aner (ā'ner; "sprout; waterfall"). A city of the tribe of Manasseh located west of the Jordan; it was assigned to the Levites (1 Chron. 6:70).

Aniam (a-nī'am; "lamentation of the people"). A descendant of Manasseh (1 Chron. 7:19).

Antioch. The modern city of Antakya stands on the site of Antioch, where the early church launched Paul's first missionary campaign (Acts 13:1-3). This photo is taken from the ruins of the Seleucid fortress above Antioch, which was still standing in Paul's day.

Anim (a'nim; "fountains"). A town in the hills of Judah (Josh. 15:50).

Anna (an'a; "grace"). A prophetess of the tribe of Asher in Christ's time (Luke 2:36).

Annas (an'as; "grace of Jehovah"). High priest of the Jews who first tried Christ (Luke 3:2; John 18:13, 24; Acts 4:6).

Antioch (an'ti-ok; "speedy as a chariot"). [1] A Syrian city on the south side of the Orontes River, where the followers of Jesus were first called Christians (Acts 11:19-26). [2] A city of Phrygia near the border of Pisidia, visited by Paul and Barnabas on their missionary journey (Acts 13:14).

Antipas (an'ti-pas). A Christian martyr of Pergamos (Rev. 2:13).

Antipatris (an-tip'a-tris; "for his father"). A city built on the Plain of Sharon by Herod the Great (Acts 23:31).

Anto-thijah (an-to-thī'jah; "answers of Jehovah; belonging to Ana-thoth"). A son of Shashak (1 Chron. 8:24).

Anub (ā'nub; "strong; high"). A descendant of Judah through Caleb (1 Chron. 4:8).

Apelles (a-pel'ēz). A Roman Christian to whom Paul sent greetings (Rom. 16:10).

Aphek [Aphik] (ā'fek [ā'fik]; "strength"). [1] A city north of Sidon (Josh. 13:4). [2] A town assigned to the tribe of Asher but never captured from the Canaanites; located just southeast of Accho (Josh. 19:30; Judg. 1:31). [3] A town on the Plain of Sharon northeast of Joppa, whose king was killed by Joshua (Josh. 12:18). [4] A town between Shunem and Jezreel, whose soldiers fought in the war between Saul and the Philistines (1 Sam. 28:4; 29:1, 11; 31:1). This may have been the town where Ben-hadad fought Ahab (1 Kings 20:26-30), and where "Jehoash" of Israel would defeat the Syrians (2 Kings 13:14-19). However, these two passages may refer to Aphek in Golan, about 5 km. (3 mi.) east of the Sea of Galilee.

Aphekah (a-fē'kah; "fortress"). A city of Judah (Josh. 15:53).

Aphiah (a-fī'a; "striving"). An ancestor of Saul (1 Sam. 9:1).

Aphrah (aph'rah; "house of dust"). A city of Philistia (Mic. 1:10).

Aphses (aph'ses; "the dispersed"). Chief of the eighteenth temple chorus (1 Chron. 24:15).

Apollonia (ap-o-lō'ni-a; "city of Apollo"). A Macedonian town visited by Paul on his way to Thessalonica (Acts 17:1).

Apollos (a-pol'los; "a destroyer"). A Jewish Christian, mighty in the scripture, who came to Ephesus and was instructed by Acuila and Priscilla (Acts 18:24; 19:1; 1 Cor. 1:12; 3:4-6; Titus 3:13).

Appaim (ap'pa-yim; "face; presence; nostrils"). A son of Nadab (1 Chron. 2:30).

Apphia (af'i-a). A female Christian Paul mentioned when writing Philemon (Philem. 2).

Appii Forum (ap-i-ī fō'rum; "marketplace of Appius"). A town in Italy about 64 km. (40 mi.) from Rome. Roman Christians met Paul here when he was brought to plead his case before Caesar (Acts 28:15).

Aquila (ak'wi-la; "eagle"). A pious Jewish Christian, husband of Priscilla and friend of Paul (Acts 18:2, 18, 26; Rom. 16:3; 1 Cor. 16:19).

Ar (ar; "city"). The chief city of Moab, located on the northern boundary of Moabite territory (Num. 21:15; Isa. 15:1).

Ara (a'ra; "strong"). A son of Jether (1 Chron. 7:38).

Arab (a'rab; "ambush"). A town in the hills of Judah east of Dumah (Josh. 15:52).

Arabah (ar'a-bah; "steppe"). The depression of land holding the Sea of Galilee and the Dead Sea (Josh. 18:18). The "valley" of Joshua 11:2 probably refers to the Arabah.

Arabia (a-rā'bia; "desert"). A large peninsula bounded on the east by the Persian Gulf and the Gulf of Oman, on the west by the Red Sea, and on the south by the Indian Ocean. It was the home of many nomadic tribes, and was sometimes called the "East Country" (2 Chron. 21:16; Isa. 13:20).

Arad (a'rad; "fugitive"). One of the chief men of Aijalon (1 Chron. 8:15).

Arad (a'rad; "wild ass"). A Canaanite city in the wilderness of Judea (Josh. 12:14).

Arah (a'rah; "wayfarer"). **[1]** A son of Ulla; member of the tribe of Asher (1 Chron. 7:39). **[2]** Ancestor of a family returned from the Exile (Ezra 2:5; Neh. 7:10). **[3]** Grandfather of the wife of Tobiah, who opposed Nehemiah in rebuilding the temple (Neh. 6:18).

Aram (a'ram; "high; exalted"). **[1]** A son of Shem (Gen. 10:22-23; 1 Chron. 1:17). The Aramean people possibly are referred to. **[2]** A son of Abraham's nephew, Kemuel (Gen. 22:21). **[3]** A descendant from Asher (1 Chron. 7:34). **[4]** The Greek form of Ram (q.v.).

Aram (a'ram; "high"). The plain extending eastward from the Lebanon Mountains beyond the Euphrates River, occupied by the Aramaeans, mistakenly termed "Syrians" by the KJV (Num. 23:7; 1 Kings 20:1).

Aran (ar'an; "firmness"). A son of Seir (Gen. 36:28; 1 Chron. 1:42).

Ararat (ar'a-rat; "high land"). A mountainous, hilly land in western Asia (Jer. 51:27) later known as Armenia (Isa. 37:38; 2 Kings 19:37). Noah's ark rested on mountains in this area (Gen. 8:4).

Araunah (a-ra'na; "Jehovah is firm"). *See also* Ornan.

Arba (ar'ba; "four; strength of Baal"). An ancestor of the Anakim (Josh. 14:15; 15:13; 21:11).

Archelaus (ar-ke-lā'us; "people's chief"). The son of Herod the Great who succeeded his father as the ruler of Idumea, Judea, and Samaria (Matt. 2:22).

Archippus (ar-kip'us; "chief groom"). A "fellow-soldier" whom Paul addresses (Col. 4:17; Philem. 2).

Ard (ard; "sprout; descent"). **[1]** A son of Benjamin (Gen. 46:21). **[2]** A son of Bela listed in Numbers 26:40. Possibly identical with the Adar of First Chronicles 18:3.

Ardon (ar'don; "descendant"). A son of Caleb of Judah mentioned in Chronicles (1 Chron. 2:18).

Areli (a-rē'li; "valiant; heroic; God's hearth"). One of the sons of Gad (Gen. 46:16; Num. 26:17).

Areopagus (ar-e-op'a-gus; "hill of Ares [Mars]"). A hill west of the acropolis in Athens, where Paul addressed several Greek philosophers; also known as Mars Hill (Acts 17:19-34).

Aretas (ar'e-tas; "pleasing; virtuous"). Aretas IV, Philopatris, King of the Nabataeans whose deputy tried to seize Paul (2 Cor. 11:32).

Argob (ar'gob; "mound"). An officer of Pekahiah slain by Pekah (2 Kings 15:25).

Argob (ar'gob; "region of clods"). A district of Bashan that was taken by King Solomon (Deut. 3:4; Josh. 13:30; 1 Kings 4:13).

Aridai (a-rid'ā-ī; "delight of Hari"). A son of Haman slain by the Jews (Esther 9:9).

Aridatha (a-rīd'a-tha; "given by Hari"). A son of Haman, hanged with his father (Esther 9:8).

Arieh (ar-yā; "lion of Jehovah"). A man of Israel killed by Pekah (2 Kings 15:25).

Ariel (ar'i-el; "lion of God"). One sent by Ezra to secure the temple ministers (Ezra 8:16).

Arimathaea (a-ri-ma the'a; "heights"). The home of a businessman named Joseph, who gained permission to bury the body of Jesus (Matt. 27:57; Luke 23:51). Its exact location is not known, but is generally believed to have been about 16 km. (10 mi.) northeast of Lydda on the western edge of the hill country of Ephraim. *See also* Ramah.

Arioch (ar'i-ok; "lion-like"). [1] A king of Ellasar in Assyria who took part in the expedition against Sodom and Gomorrah (Gen. 14:1, 9). [2] A captain of Nebuchadnezzar's guard commanded to slay the "wise men" (Dan. 2:14-15, 24-25).

Arisai (a-ris'ī). A son of Haman slain by the Jews (Esther 9:9).

Aristarchus (a-ris-tar'kus; "the best ruler"). A faithful companion who accompanied Paul on his third missionary journey (Acts 19:29; 20:4; Col. 4:10).

Aristobulus (a-ris-to-bū'lus; "best counselor"). A person in Rome whose household Paul saluted (Rom. 16:10).

Armageddon (ar-ma-ged'on; Hebrew, *Har Megiddo*—"hill of Megiddo"). The site of the final battle between Christ and Satan (Rev. 16:16). *See also* Megiddo.

Armenia (ar-mē'ni-a). *See* Ararat.

Armoni (ar-mō'ni; "of the palace"). A son of Saul by Rizpah (2 Sam. 21:8).

Arnan (ar'nan; "joyous; strong"). A descendant of David and founder of a family (1 Chron. 3:21).

Arnon (ar'non; "rushing water"). A river that pours into the Dead Sea (Num. 21:13; Josh. 13:16).

Arod (ā'rod; "descent; posterity"). A son of Gad, progenitor of the tribe of Arodi (Num. 26:17; cf. Gen. 46:16).

Aroer (ar'ō-er; "naked"). [1] A town on the northern bank of the Arnon River (Deut. 2:36; Josh. 12:2). [2] A city of Gilead east of Rabbath-Ammon (Josh. 13:25). [3] A village of Judah about 19 km. (12 mi.) southeast of Beer-sheba (1 Sam. 30:28).

Arpad [Arphad] (ar'pad [ar'fad]; "strong"). A Syrian city 20 km. (13 mi.) north of Aleppo (Isa. 36:19; Jer. 42:23).

Arphaxad (ar-fax'ad). A son of Shem and an ancestor of Christ (Gen. 10:22, 24; 1 Chron. 1:17-18; Luke 3:36). Possibly the reference is to a tribe or people. Formerly identified with the mountainous land north of Nineveh.

Artaxerxes (ar-ta-zerk'sēz; "fervent to spoil"). [1] A king of Persia, Artaxerxes I Longimanus, at whose court Ezra and Nehemiah were officials (Ezra 7:1, 7, 11-12; Neh. 2:1; 5:14). [2] Some suppose that Ezra 4:7 uses "Artaxerxes" to refer to the pseudo-Smerdis king of Persia, but the reference is probably to [1].

Artemas (ar'te-mas; "whole; sound"). A friend of Paul's at Nicopolis (Titus 3:12).

Aruboth (ar'u-bōth; "windows"). A district belonging to King Solomon (1 Kings 4:10).

Arumah (a-rū'ma; "heights"). A town near Shechem once occupied by Abimelech (Judg. 9:41).

Arvad (ar'vad; "wandering"). The northernmost Phoenician city, noted for its mariners (Ezek. 27:8). The modern city of Ruwad is located on this site.

Arza (ar'za; "firm"). A steward of King Elah of Israel (1 Kings 16:9).

Arzob (ar'zob). See Bashan.

Asa (ā'sa; "physician; healer"). [1] The third king of Judah and an ancestor of Christ (1 Kings 15:8-16:29; Matt. 1:7-8). [2] Head of a Levite family (1 Chron. 9:16).

Asahel (ās'a-hel; "God is doer; God has made"). [1] A son of David's sister, Zeruiah. He was slain by Abner (2 Sam. 2:18-32; 3:27, 30). [2] A Levite sent to teach the Law (2 Chron. 17:8). [3] A Levite employed as an officer of the offerings and tithes (2 Chron. 31:13). [4] Father of Jonathan, appointed to take a census of foreign wives (Ezra 10:15).

Asahiah [Asaiah] (ā-sa-hī'a [ā-sa-ī'a]; "Jehovah is doer; Jehovah has made"). One sent to inquire of the Lord concerning the Book of the Law (2 Kings 22:12, 14; 2 Chron. 34:20).

Asaiah (ā-sa-ī'a; "Jehovah is doer; Jehovah has made"). [1] A prince of Simeon who helped defeat the people of Gedor (1 Chron. 4:36). [2] A descendant of Merari who helped bring up the ark (1 Chron. 6:30; 15:6, 11). [3] A resident of Jerusalem (1 Chron. 9:5). [4] See also Asahiah.

Asaph (ā'saf; "collector; gatherer"). [1] One of David's three chief musicians (1 Chron. 6:39; 15:17, 19). Author of Psalms 50, 73–83. [2] Father of Joah the recorder to Hezekiah (2 Kings 18:18, 37; 2 Chron. 29:13). [3] A Levite whose descendants lived in Jerusalem (1 Chron. 9:15). [4] One whose descendants were porters in David's time (1 Chron. 26:1). The text should possibly read Abiasaph (q.v.). [5] A keeper of the royal forests in Judah (Neh. 2:8).

Asareel (a-sar'e-el; "God is joined or ruler"). A descendant of Judah through Caleb (1 Chron. 4:16).

Asarelah (as-a-re'la; "Jehovah is joined; whom God has bound"). One appointed to the temple service by David (1 Chron. 25:2). He is called Jesharelah ("of Jesharel") in verse 14. This may be another name for Azarael [2].

Asenath (as'e-nath; "dedicated to [the deity] Neit"). The Egyptian wife of Joseph (Gen. 41:45, 50; 46:20).

Aser (ā'ser). Greek form of Asher (q.v.).

Ashan (ā'shan; "smoke"). A lowland town assigned to the tribe of

Judah, then to Simeon (Josh. 15:42; 19:7; 1 Chron. 4:32); probably located just northwest of Beer-sheba. It is possibly identical with Chor-ashan (q.v.).

Ashbea (ash'be-a; "man of Baal"). A family of linen workers that sprang from Shelah, son of Judah (1 Chron. 4:21).

Ashbea (ash'be-a; "idolatry"). A place where linen workers lived (1 Chron. 4:21); its exact location is unknown.

Ashbel (ash'bel; "man of Baal"). Son of Benjamin (Gen. 46:21; Num. 26:38; 1 Chron. 8 1).

Ashchenaz [Ashkenaz] (ash'ken-az [ash'ken-az]; "a fire that spreads"). A son of Gomer (Gen. 10:3; 1 Chron. 1:6). Possibly a race or tribe who dwelt near Ararat and Minni in eastern Armenia.

Ashdod (ash'dod; "stronghold"). One of the five chief Canaanite cities; the seat of the worship of the fish god Dagon; located halfway between present-day Jaffa and Gaza (Josh. 11:22; 1 Sam. 5:1). In the N.T. the city is called Azotus (Acts 8:40).

Asher [Aser] (ash'er [ā'ser]; "happy"). The eighth son of Jacob and an ancestor of one of the twelve tribes of Israel (Gen. 30:13; 35:26; 46:17; 49:20; 1 Chron. 2 2).

Asher (ash'er; "happy "). A town on the southern border of Manasseh (Josh. 17:7).

Ashkelon [Askelon] (ash'ke-lon [as'ke-lon]; "wandering"). One of the five chief Canaanite cities, the seat of the worship of the goddess Derceto; located about 19 km. (12 mi.) north of the present-day city of Gaza (Josh. 13:3; Jer. 47:5).

Ashkenaz (ash'ke-naz) See Ashchenaz.

Ashnah (ash'na; "hard firm"). [1] A village in the lowlands of Judah near Zorah (Josh. 15:33) [2] Another village of Judah, farther south (Josh. 15:43).

Ashpenaz (ash'pe-naz) Prince of Nebuchadnezzar's eunuchs who had charge of the captives from Judah (Dan. 1:3).

Ashriel (ash'ri-el). See Asriel.

Ashtaroth (ash'ta-roth). See Ashteroth-karnaim.

Ashteroth-karnaim (ash'te-roth-kar-na'im; "[the goddess] Ashtaroth of the two horns"). A town of Bashan, the seat of the worship of the goddess Ashtaroth (Gen. 14:5). The city is possibly to be identified with Astaroth (Ashtaroth) (Deut. 1:4; Josh. 9:10), though this is not certain.

Ashur (ash'ur; "free man; man of Horus"). A son of Hezron and head of the inhabitants of Tekoa (1 Chron. 2:24; 4:5).

Ashvath (ash'vath; "made; wrought"). A son of Japhlet; a descendant of Asher (1 Chron. 7:33).

Asia (ā'sha; "eastern") The term used by the Bible to refer to Asia Minor (1 Cor. 16:19; Acts 2:9).

Asiel (ā'si-el; "God is doer or maker"). A descendant of Simeon and grandfather of Jehu (1 Chron. 4:35).

Askelon (as'ke-lon). *See* Ashkelon.

Asnah (as'na; "thornbush"). One whose descendants returned from Exile (Ezra 2:50).

Asnapper (as'nap-er; alternative form of Osnapper). One who brought men from Susa and Elam to Samaria (Ezra 4:9). Formerly believed to be Esarhaddon, he is now believed to have been Ashurbanipal, king of Assyria and Esarhaddon's son.

Aspatha (as-pā'tha; "horse-given"). Son of Haman, slain by the Jews (Esther 9:7).

Asriel [Ashriel] (as'ri-el [ash'ri-el]; "God is joined; vow of God"). A son of Manasseh (Num. 26:31; 1 Chron. 7:14).

Asshur [Assur] (ash'ur [as'ur]; "level plain"). [1] A son of Shem (Gen. 10:22; 1 Chron. 1:17). Possibly the people of Assyria are intended. [2] Genesis 10:11, if denoting a person, refers to a son of Ham or to [1]. However, many scholars translate: "From that land he (Nimrod) went into Assyria (Asshur)."

Asshur [Assur] (ash'ur [as'ur]; "level plain"). A city in Assyria which was sometimes the capital, or the nation itself may be referred to (Num. 24:22, 24).

Assir (as'sir; "prisoner"). [1] A son of Korah (Exod. 6:24; 1 Chron. 6:22). [2] A son of Ebiasaph (1 Chron. 6:23, 37). [3] A son of Jeconiah (Jehoiachin), king of Judah (1 Chron. 3:17).

Assos (as'os; "approaching"). A seaport of Mysia, near Troas (Acts 20:13).

Assur (as'ur). *See* Asshur.

Assyria (a-sir'i-a; "country of Assur"). A Semitic nation on the Tigris River, whose capital was Nineveh (Gen. 2:14; 2 Kings 15:10, 20).

Asuppim (a-sup'im). A word which should be translated "storehouse" as in Nehemiah 12:25. First Chronicles 26:15 should read: "The lot for the South Gate (southward) fell to Obed-edom, and the lot for the storehouse fell to his sons."

Asyncritus (a-sing'kri-tus; "incomparable"). One at Rome whom Paul salutes (Rom. 16:14).

Atad (ā'tad; "a thorn"). The campsite near Hebron used by Joseph and his brothers as they prepared to take Jacob's body back to Canaan (Gen. 50:11). The new name given the site was a pun: The Canaanites saw the mourning [Hebrew, *ēbhel*] of the Egyptians and called the place *Abel* [Hebrew, *ābhel*]—"meadow"; *mizraim*—"of the Egyptians."

Atarah (at'a-ra; "crown; ornament"). A wife of Jerahmeel (1 Chron. 2:26).

Ataroth (at'a-roth; "crowns"). [1] A town east of the Jordan River rebuilt by the tribe of Gad (Num. 32:3, 34). [2] A town on the edge of the Jordan Valley at the border of Ephraim (Josh. 16:7). [3] The house of Joab mentioned in the genealogy of Judah (1 Chron. 2:54). The site is unknown. Some take the "House of Joab" to be part of the town's title; in Hebrew this would be Atroth-bethjoab. [4] *See also* Ataroth-addar.

Ataroth-addar [**Ataroth-adar**] (at'a-roth-ad'dar [at-a-roth-a'dar]; "crown of Addar"). A village on the southern frontier of Ephraim (Josh. 16:5; 18:13). The town is probably to be identified with Ataroth (Josh. 16:2).

Ater (ā'ter; "bound; lame"). [1] One who sealed the new covenant with God after the Exile (Neh. 10:17). [2] Ancestor of a family of gatekeepers (Ezra 2:42; Neh. 7:45). [3] Ancestor of a family that returned from the Exile (Ezra 2:16; Neh. 7:21).

Athach (ā'thak; "stopping place"). A town in southern Judah, to which David sent some of the spoil of Ziklag (1 Sam. 30:30).

Athaiah (ath-a'ya; "Jehovah is helper"). A descendant of Judah dwelling in Jerusalem (Neh. 11:4).

Athaliah (a-tha-lī'ah; "whom Jehovah has afflicted; Jehovah is strong"). [1] The daughter of Jezebel, wife of King Jehoram, and afterwards ruler of Israel for six years (2 Kings 8:26; 11:1-20; 2 Chron. 22:2-23:21). [2] A son of Jeroham (1 Chron. 8:26). [3] Father of a returned exile (Ezra 8:7).

Athens (ath'enz; "city of Athena"). The greatest city of classical Greece, capital of the Greek city-state of Attica, where Paul founded a Christian church (Acts 17:15-18).

The Areopagus. Sixteen steps lead to the top of rocky Mars Hill in Athens, called the *Areopagus*. This rocky bluff served as a meeting place of the city court and council of elders. Here Paul preached his famous sermon to the Athenians (Acts 17:21-34). A stronghold of the Athenian aristocracy during the sixth and fifth centuries B.C., the council of the Areopagus gradually lost power in subsequent years.

Athlai (ath'lī; "Jehovah is strong"). One who married a foreign wife (Ezra 10:28).

Atroth (at'roth; "crowns"). A city of the tribe of Gad (Num. 32:35). Some believe Atroth and Shophan are one city and render the name Atroth-shophan. *See also* Shophan.

Attai (ā'tā-ī; "seasonable; timely"). **[1]** One who joined David at Ziklag (1 Chron. 12:11). **[2]** A son of king Rehoboam (2 Chron. 11:20). **[3]** Descendant of Pharez (1 Chron. 2:35-36).

Attalia (at-a-li'a). A seaport of Pamphylia near Perga through which Paul and Barnabas passed after their first missionary journey (Acts 14:25).

Augustus (a-gus'tus; "consecrated" or "holy"). Acts 25:21, 25; 27:1 use the Greek rendering of the title "reverend" in this fashion, since Augustus had been dead many years.

Augustus Caesar (a-gus'tus sē'zer). The imperial name of Octavian, a nephew of Julius Caesar who became emperor of Rome. During his reign, Christ was born (Luke 2:1).

Ava (āv'a; "legion"). An Assyrian city that sent settlers to colonize Samaria (2 Kings 17:24).

Aven (ā'ven; "nothingness"). **[1]** Another name for the Egyptian city of On, called Heliopolis by the Greeks (Ezek. 30:17). **[2]** A valley town in the kingdom of Damascus; probably Awaniyek (Amos 1:5).

Avim (av'im). A city of the tribe of Benjamin, probably near Bethel (Josh. 18:23). Some translate "Bethel and (the village of) the Arvim," thus indicating a group of people.

Avith (ā'vith; "ruins"). A city of Edom, home of King Hadad (Gen. 36:35; 1 Chron. 1:46).

Azal (ā'zal; "noble; slope"). A place near Jerusalem (Zech. 14:5).

Azaliah (az-a-lī'a; "Jehovah is noble"). Father of Shaphan the scribe (2 Kings 22:3; 2 Chron. 34:8).

Azaniah (az-a-nī'a; "Jehovah is hearer"). Father of one who signed the new covenant with God after the Exile (Neh. 10:9).

Azarael [Azareel] (a-zā'rē'el [a-zā'rē'el]; "God is helper"). **[1]** One who joined David at Ziklag (1 Chron. 12:6). **[2]** One who ministered in the song service of the temple (1 Chron. 25:18). **[3]** A prince of Dan (1 Chron. 27:22). **[4]** One who took a foreign wife (Ezra 10:41). **[5]** A priest of the family of Immer (Neh. 11:13). **[6]** One who played the trumpet at the dedication of the new temple (Neh. 12:36).

Azariah (az-a-rī'a; "Jehovah has helped"). **[1]** *See* Uzziah. **[2]** A ruler of Solomon's officers (1 Kings 4:5). **[3]** A descendant of David's high priest (1 Kings 4:2). **[4]** A descendant of Judah (1 Chron. 2:8). **[5]** A descendant of Jerahmeel (1 Chron. 2:38-39). **[6]** A son of Ahimaaz (1 Chron. 6:9). **[7]** A high priest and grandson of **[6]** (1 Chron. 6:10-11). **[8]** A son of Hilkiah the high priest under Josiah (1 Chron. 6:13-14; 9:11; Ezra 7:1). **[9]** An ancestor of Samuel the prophet

(1 Chron. 6:36). **[10]** A prophet who went to Asa (2 Chron. 15:1). **[11]**, **[12]** Two sons of King Jehoshaphat (2 Chron. 21:2). **[13]** *See* Ahaziah **[2]**. **[14]** A captain who helped to place Joash on the throne (2 Chron. 23:1). **[15]** Another man who helped Joash (2 Chron. 23:1). **[16]** A high priest who opposed Uzziah (2 Chron. 26:17, 20). **[17]** A chief of Ephraim (2 Chron. 28:12). **[18]** A descendant of Kohath and father of Joel (2 Chron. 29:12). **[19]** One who helped cleanse the temple (2 Chron. 29:12). **[20]** A chief of the family of Zadok, priest in Hezekiah's time (2 Chron. 31:10, 13). **[21]** Ancestor of Zadok and Ezra (Ezra 7:3). **[22]** One who repaired the wall of Jerusalem (Neh. 3:23-24). **[23]** One who came up to Jerusalem with Zerubbabel (Neh. 7:7). Perhaps this is another name of Seraiah (Ezra 2:2); if not, his name is omitted in this passage. **[24]** A priest who explained the Law (Neh. 8:7). **[25]** *See* Ezra [1]. **[26]** A prince of Judah (Neh. 12:33). **[27]** One who charged Jeremiah with false prophecy (Jer. 43:2). **[28]** A captive carried to Babylon with Daniel (Dan. 1:6-7, 11, 19; 2:17). *See* Abed-nego.

Azaz (ā'zaz; "strong; powerful"). A descendant of Reuben (1 Chron. 5:8).

Azaziah (ă-za-zī'a; "Jehovah is strong"). **[1]** A Levite who took part in the musical service when the ark was brought to the temple (1 Chron. 15:21). **[2]** Father of a prince of Ephraim in David's time (1 Chron. 27:20). **[3]** A Levite who had the oversight of the dedicated things of the temple under Hezekiah (2 Chron. 31:13).

Azbuk (az'buk; "pardon"). The father of a man named Nehemiah (Neh. 3:16).

Azekah (a-zē'ka; "dug up place"). A city in the lowlands of Socoh, less than 32 km. (20 mi.) southwest of Jerusalem; the kings besieging Gibeon were driven here (Josh. 10:10; 1 Sam. 17:1).

Azel (ā'zel; "noble"). A descendant of King Saul (1 Chron. 8:37-38; 9:43-44).

Azem (ā'zem). *See* Ezem.

Azgad (az'gad; "worship; supplication; Gad is strong"). **[1]** One whose descendants returned from the Exile with Zerubbabel (Ezra 2:12; Neh. 7:17). **[2]** One who came back to Jerusalem with Ezra (Ezra 8:12). **[3]** One who sealed the new covenant with God after the Exile (Neh. 10:15).

Aziel (ā'zi-el; "God is might"). *See* Jaaziel.

Aziza (a-zī-za; "strong"). One who married a foreign wife (Ezra 10:27).

Azmaveth (az-ma'veth; "counsel or strength of death"). **[1]** One of David's mighty men (2 Sam. 23:31; 1 Chron. 11:33). **[2]** A descendant of Saul (1 Chron. 8:36; 9:42). **[3]** Father of two men who joined David at Ziklag (1 Chron. 12:3). **[4]** A treasury officer of David's (1 Chron. 27:25).

Azmaveth (az-ma'veth). *See* Beth-Azmaveth.

Azmon (az'mon; "strong"). A place on the western boundary of Canaan (Num. 34:4).

Aznoth-Tabor (az'noth-tā'bor; "peaks [ears] of Tabor"). An incline near Mount Tabor, west of Kadesh-Barnea (Josh. 19:34).

Azor (ā'zōr; "helper"). An ancestor of Christ (Matt. 1:13-14).

Azotus (a-zo'tus). *See* Ashdod.

Azriel (az'ri-el; "God is helper"). **[1]** A chief of the tribe of Manasseh (1 Chron. 5:24). **[2]** Father of a ruler of Naphtali in David's time (1 Chron. 27:19). **[3]** Father of an officer sent to capture Baruch (Jer. 36:26).

Azrikam (az'ri-kam; "my help has risen"). **[1]** One of the family of David (1 Chron. 3:23). **[2]** A son of Azel of the family of Saul (1 Chron. 8:38; 9:44). **[3]** A descendant of Merari (1 Chron. 9:14; Neh. 11:15). **[4]** The governor of Ahaz's house (2 Chron. 28:7).

Azubah (a-zu'bah; "forsaken"). **[1]** The mother of King Jehoshaphat (1 Kings 22:42; 2 Chron. 20:31). **[2]** Wife of Caleb, the son of Hezron (1 Chron. 2:18-19).

Azur (ā'zur; "helper; helpful"). **[1]** Father of a prince that Ezekiel saw in a vision (Ezek. 11:1). **[2]** Father of the false prophet Hananiah (Jer. 28:1). *See also* Azzur.

Azzah (az'zah). *See* Gaza.

Azzan (az'zan; "sharp; thorn"). Father of a chief of Issachar (Num. 34:26).

Azzur (az'zur; "helper; helpful"). One who sealed the covenant (Neh. 10:17). *See also* Azur.

B

Baal (bā'al; "master; lord"). **[1]** A descendant of Reuben (1 Chron. 5:5). **[2]** The fourth of ten sons of Jehiel (1 Chron. 8:29-30; 9:36).

Baal (bā'al; "master"). A city of Simeon, identical with Baalath-beer (1 Chron. 4:33).

Baalah (bā'a-la; "mistress"). **[1]** A Simeonite town in southern Judah (Josh. 15:29). The city is also called Bilhah (1 Chron. 4:29) and Balah in Joshua 19:3. **[2]** A hill in Judah between Ekron and Jabneel (Josh. 15:11). **[3]** *See* Kirjath-jearim.

Baalath (bā'a-lath; "mistress"). A town of the tribe of Dan, located near Gezer (Josh. 19:44; 1 Kings 9:18; 2 Chron. 8:6).

Baalath-beer (bā'a-lath-bē'er; "mistress of a well"). A border town of the tribe of Simeon, sometimes called "Ramoth (or Ramath) of the south" (Josh. 19:8). It is identical with Baal (q.v.).

Baale-judah (bā'a-lē-jū'da). *See* Kirjath-jearim.

Baal-gad (bā'al-gad; "the lord of fortune; Gad is lord"). A town at the foot of Mount Hermon that marked the northern limit of Joshua's conquest (Josh. 11:17; 12:7).

Baal-hamon (bā'al-hā'mon; "lord of a multitude"). A place where King Solomon had a vineyard (Song of Sol. 8:11); its exact location is unknown.

Baal-hanan (bā'al-hā'nan; "the lord is gracious"). [1] The seventh of the kings of Edom (Gen. 36:38-39; 1 Chron. 1:49-50). [2] A tender of olive and sycamore trees in David's time (1 Chron. 27:28).

Baal-hazor (bā'al-hā'zcr; "lord of Hazor [enclosure]"). The place near Ephraim where Absalom killed Ammon (2 Sam. 13:23); the probable site is about 7 km. (4.5 mi.) northeast of Bethel.

Baal-hermon (bā'al-her'mon; "lord of Hermon"). The site of Canaanite rituals on the eastern slope of Mount Hermon, which marked the northwest boundary of the half-tribe of Manasseh (Judg. 3:3; 1 Chron. 5:23).

Baalis (bā'a-lis; "lord of joy"). The king of the Ammonites after Jerusalem was taken (Jer. 40:14).

Baal-meon (bā'al-me-ōn'; "lord of the house"). An Amorite city on the north border of Moab (Num. 32:38; Ezek. 25:9). The city is called Beon in Numbers 32:3, Beth-baal-meon in Joshua 13:17 and Beth-meon in Jeremiah 48:23.

Baal-perazim (bā'al-pe-rā'zim; "lord of breaches"). A place near the Valley of Rephaim, where King David won a battle with the Philistines (2 Sam. 5:20). It is called simply Perazim in Isaiah 28:21.

Baal-shalisha (bā'al-shal'i-sha; "lord of a third part"). A village that presented food to the prophet Elisha; probably located about 22 km. (13.5 mi.) northwest of Gilgal (2 Kings 4:42).

Baal-tamar (bā'al-tā'mar; "lord of palms"). A place near Gibeah and Bethel in the territory of Benjamin, where the Israelites repelled the army of Gibeah (Judg. 20:33).

Baal-zephon (bā'al-se'fon; "lord of the North"). The site that the Israelites faced when they encamped between Migdol and the Red Sea on their Exodus from Egypt (Exod. 14:2; Num. 33:7).

Baana [Baanah] (bā'a-na [bā'a-na]; "son of grief; patient"). [1] One of Solomon's royal merchants (1 Kings 4:12). [2] Another merchant of Solomon, responsible for Asher (1 Kings 4:16). [3] Father of Zadok, the builder of the temple (Neh. 3:4). [4] Father of one of David's mighty men (2 Sam. 23:29; 1 Chron. 11:30). [5] A captain in Ishbosheth's army (2 Sam. 4:2, 5-6, 9). [6] One who returned from the Exile with Zerubbabel (Ezra 2:2; Neh. 7:7; 10:27).

Baara (bā'a-ra; "a wood; the burning one"). A wife of Shaharaim (1 Chron. 8:8).

Baaseiah (bā'a-sē'ya; "Jehovah is bold"). An ancestor of Asaph (1 Chron. 6:40).

Baasha (bā'a-sha; "boldness"). The third king of Israel; war and wickedness characterized his reign (1 Kings 15:16–16:13).

Babel (ba'bel; "gate of God"). A city built by Nimrod on the Plain of Shinar (Gen. 10:10).

Babylon (bab'i-lon; meaning unknown). [1] The capital city of the Babylonian Empire, famous for its hanging gardens; a focal point of the Jewish captivity beginning in 586 B.C. (2 Kings 17:24-25; Isa. 39:3, 6-7). [2] Most scholars believe the references in First Peter 5:13 and Revelation 14:8; 18:2, 10-21 are to Rome. However, some believe Peter refers to [1].

Babylonia (bab-i-lō'ni-a; meaning unknown). The eastern portion of the Fertile Crescent having Babylon (2 Kings 17:24-25) for its capital. It is also called Shinar (Gen. 10:10) and the land of the Chaldeans (Jer. 24:5; Ezek. 12:13) in the Old Testament.

Baca (bā'ka; "weeping; balsam tree"). A valley of Palestine; possibly the Valley of Rephaim, where many balsam trees are found (Psa. 84:6).

Bahurim (ba-hū'rim; "low ground"). A village near the Mount of Olives on the road from Jerusalem to the Jordan River (2 Sam. 3:16; 16:5; 17:18; 19:16).

Bakbakkar (bak-bak'er; "diligent; searcher"). A Levite who returned from the Babylonian Captivity (1 Chron. 9:15). See Bakbukiah [1].

Bakbuk (bak'būk; "waste; hollow"). One whose descendant returned from the Exile (Ezra 2:51; Neh. 7:53).

Bakbukiah (bak-bū-kī'a; "wasted by Jehovah"). [1] A Levite who lived in Jerusalem (Neh. 11:17). Perhaps identical with Bakbakkar (q.v.). [2] A Levite who returned with Zerubbabel (Neh. 12:9). [3] A Levite and guard of the temple storehouse (Neh. 12:25).

Bajith (bā'jith; "house"). A Moabite city or temple (Isa. 15:2).

Balaam (bā-lam; "a pilgrim; lord [Baal] of the people"). A prophet that the king of Moab induced to curse Israel. Instead, God put words of blessing in his mouth (Num. 22–24; 31:8).

Balac (bā'lak). Greek form of Balak (q.v.).

Baladan (bal'a-dan; "having power"). Father of the king of Babylon in Hezekiah's time (2 Kings 20:12; Isa. 39:1).

Balah (bā'la). See Baalah [1].

Balak [Balac] (bā'lak [ba'lak]; "void; empty"). The king of Moab that hired Balaam to curse Israel (Num. 22–24; Josh. 24:9).

Bamah (bā'ma; "high place"). The reference in Ezekiel 20:29 is possibly to a prominent high place of idolatrous worship like the one at Gibeon (1 Kings 3:4).

Bamoth (bā'moth; "high places"). An Israelite encampment north of the Arnon River (Num. 21:19). The city is probably the Baal of Numbers 22:41.

Bamoth-baal (bā'moth-bā'al; "high places of Baal"). See Bamoth.

Bani (bā'nī; "posterity"). [1] One of David's mighty men (2 Sam.

Babylonian record of conquest. This clay tablet from Babylonia tells about the first 11 years of Nebuchadnezzar's reign and mentions his conquest of Jerusalem in 586 B.C. Bible scholars are able to use secular records like this to confirm the dates of biblical events.

23:36). **[2]** A descendant of Merari (1 Chron. 6:46). **[3]** A descendant of Pharez (1 Chron. 9:4). **[4]** Father of a family that returned from the Babylonian Captivity (Ezra 2:10; 10:29). In Nehemiah 7:15, he is called Binnui. **[5]** One whose descendants had taken foreign wives during the Exile (Ezra 10:34). **[6]** A descendant of [5] who took a foreign wife during the Exile (Ezra 10:38). **[7]** A Levite who helped to repair the wall of Jerusalem (Neh. 3:17; 8:7). **[8]** A Levite who assisted in the devotions of the people (Neh. 9:4; 10:13). **[9]** One who sealed the new covenant with God after the Exile (Neh. 10:14). **[10]** A Levite whose son was an overseer of the Levites after the Exile. Perhaps the same as [7] or [8] (Neh. 11:22). **[11]**, **[12]**, **[13]** Three Levites who participated in the temple worship (Neh. 9:4-5).

Bar (bar; Aramaic for the Hebrew "bēn," "son.") "Bar" and "ben" are frequently prefixed to names to indicate direct relationship. Thus Peter is called Bar-jonah (son of Jonah) because his father was named Jonah (Matt. 16:17) and perhaps Nathanael was called Bartholomew (son of Tolmai) because his father was named Tolmai. It can also designate characteristics or conditions. For example, Joses was called Barnabas ("son of consolation") because of the aid he rendered the apostles (Acts 4:36).

Barabbas (bar-ab′as; "father's son"). A murderer whom the people demanded that Pontius Pilate should release instead of Christ (Matt. 27:17, 20-21, 26; Mark 15 7). *See* Bar.

Barachel (bar'a-kel; "blessed of God"). Father of Elihu, a figure in Job (Job 32:2, 6).

Barachias (bar-a-kī'as; Greek form of Barachiah). The father of a prophet whom the Jews killed (Matt. 23:35). It is quite possible the reference is to the author of the Book of Zechariah. Zechariah [11], or else an unknown prophet. See Berechiah.

Barak (bar'ak; "lightning"). The general of the judge Deborah; he helped to defeat Sisera (Judg. 4:6–5:15).

Bariah (ba-rī'ah; "fugitive"). A descendant of David (1 Chron. 3:22).

Bar-jesus (bar-jē'sus). See Elymas; Bar.

Bar-jonah (bar-jō'nah). See Peter; Bar.

Barkos (bar-kos; "partly colored"). An ancestor of captives returning from the Exile (Ezra 2:53; Neh. 7:55).

Barnabas (bar'na-bas; "son of consolation"). A Jewish Christian who traveled widely with Paul (Acts 4:36; 9:27; 11:22-30; Gal. 2:1). His original name was Joses, but he was named Barnabas by the apostles (Acts 4:36); obviously they considered him to be *their* consoler. See Bar.

Barsabas (bar'sa-bas; "son of Saba"). See Bar; Joseph [11]; Juda [12].

Bartholomew (bar-thol'ō-mū; "son of Tolmai"). One of Jesus' twelve apostles (Matt. 10:3; Mark 3:18; Acts 1:13). He is probably the same as Nathanael (q.v.). See Bar.

Bartimaeus (bar-ti-mē'us; Aramaic *bar,* "son" and Greek *timaios,* "honorable"). A blind beggar healed by Christ (Mark 10:46-52). See Bar.

Baruch (ba'ruk; "blessed"). [1] Jeremiah's friend and scribe (Jer. 32:12-13, 16; 36). [2] One who helped to rebuild the wall of Jerusalem (Neh. 3:20; 10:6). [3] A descendant of Perez who returned from the Exile (Neh. 11:5).

Barzillai (bar-zil'ā-i; "strong"). [1] One who befriended David when he fled from Absalom (2 Sam. 17:27; 19:31-39). [2] Husband of Merab, Saul's eldest daughter, and father of Adriel (2 Sam. 21:8). [3] A priest whose genealogy was lost during the Exile (Ezra 2:61; Neh. 7:63).

Bashan (ba'shan; "fertile plain"). A district stretching from the Upper Jordan Valley to the Arabian Desert, containing "the whole region of Arzob" (Deut. 3:4-5, 10, 13; 1 Kings 4:13; Psa. 22:12; Ezek. 27:6; 39:18).

Bashan-havoth-jair (ba'shan-hā'voth-jā'ir). See also Havoth-jair.

Bashemath [Basmath] (bash'e-math [bas'math]; "fragrant"). [1] A daughter of Solomon (1 Kings 4:15). [2] A wife of Esau (Gen. 26:34). See also Esau. [3] Another wife of Esau, whom he married to appease his father (Gen. 36:3-4, 10, 13). See also Esau's Wives.

Basmath (bas'math). See Bashemath.

Bath-rabbim (bath-rab'im; "daughter of multitudes"). A gate of Heshbon (Song of Sol. 7:4).

Bath-sheba (bath-shē'ba; "the seventh daughter; daughter of the oath"). The beautiful wife of Uriah the Hittite, and afterward the wife of David (2 Sam. 11:3; 12:24; 1 Kings 1:11–2:19). She was the mother of Solomon and an ancestor of Christ (Matt. 1:6). She is called Bathshua in First Chronicles 3:5.

Bath-shua (bath-shū'a; "daughter of prosperity"). [1] Another name of Bath-sheba (q.v.). [2] The wife of Judah. In Genesis 38:2 and First Chronicles 2:3, the KJV incorrectly renders her name as "daughter of Shua"; Bath-shua is really a proper name.

Bavai (bav'a-i; "wisher"). One who helped to rebuild the wall of Jerusalem (Neh. 3:18).

Bazlith [Bazluth] (baz' ith [baz'luth]; "asking"). One whose descendants returned from the Exile (Ezra 2:52; Neh. 7:54).

Bealiah (be-a-li'a; "Jehovah is lord"). A man who joined David at Ziklag (1 Chron. 12:5).

Bealoth (bē'a-loth; "mistresses; possessors"). A village in southern Judah (Josh. 15:24).

Beautiful Gate. A portion of the east gate of Jerusalem where Peter and John healed a lame man (Acts 3:2).

Bebai (bē'bā-ī; "fatherly"). [1] An ancestor of captives returning from the Exile (Ezra 2 11; Neh. 7:16). [2] An ancestor of some returning from the Exile with Ezra (Ezra 8:11; 10:28); perhaps the same as [1]. [3] One who sealed the new covenant with God after the Exile (Neh. 10:15).

Becher (bē'ker; "youth; firstborn"). [1] A son of Benjamin (Gen. 46:21). [2] A son of Ephraim (Num. 26:35); perhaps the same as Bered in First Chronicles 7:20.

Bechorath (be-kō'rath; "first birth"). An ancestor of Saul (1 Sam. 9:1).

Bedad (bē'dad; "alone"). Father of Hadad, fourth king of Edom (Gen. 36:35; 1 Chron. 1:46).

Bedan (bē'dan; "son of judgment"). [1] A leader of Israel mentioned as a deliverer of the nation (1 Sam. 12:11). The Septuagint, Syriac, and Arabic read *Barak* instead; however, many think this is a reference to Abdon. [2] A descendant of Manasseh (1 Chron. 7:17).

Bedeiah (be-dē'ya; "servant of Jehovah"). One who had married a foreign wife during the Exile (Ezra 10:35).

Beeliada (bē'e-li'a-da; "the lord knows"). A son of David (1 Chron. 14:7) also known as Eliada (2 Sam. 5:16; 1 Chron. 3:8).

Beer (bē'er; "a well"). [1] A temporary encampment of the Israelites in the wilderness (Num. 21:16-18); possibly the same as Beerelim. [2] A place where Jotham sought refuge from his brother Abimelech (Judg. 9:21); possibly the same as Beeroth.

Beera [Beerah] (be-ē'ra [be-ē'ra]; "expounder"). [1] A descendant of Asher (1 Chron. 7:37). [2] A prince of Reuben who was carried captive to Assyria (1 Chron. 5:7).

Beer-elim (bē′er-ē′lim; "well of Elim"). A village in southern Moab (Isa. 15:8).

Beeri (be-ē′ri; "man of the springs" or "expounder"). [1] Father of Judith, a wife of Esau (Gen. 26:34). See also Esau's Wives. [2] Father of the prophet Hosea (Hos. 1:1).

Beer-lahai-roi [**Lahai-roi**] (bē′er-la-hī′roi [la-hī′roi]; "well of the living one who sees me"). The well of Hagar, located between Kadesh and Bered on the road to Shur, about 80 km. (50 mi.) southwest of Beer-sheba (Gen. 16:14). It is shortened to Lahai-roi in Genesis 24:62.

Beeroth (bē-ē′roth; "wells"). [1] A place on the border of Edom where the wandering Israelites camped; also called Beeroth, Bene-Jaakan or Bene-jaakan (Deut. 10:6; Num. 33:31). [2] A city of Gibeon assigned to the tribe of Benjamin (Josh. 9:17; 18:25).

Beer-sheba (bē′er-shē′ba; "well of oaths"). A city in southern Judah, site of Abraham's covenant with Abimelech; it is located about 45 km. (28 mi.) southwest of Hebron (Gen. 21:14, 22-31; Josh. 15:28).

Beeshterah (bē′esh-tē′ra; "temple of Ashterah"). See Ashtaroth-Karnaim.

Bela [**Belah**] (bē′la [be′la]; "consumption"). [1] A king of Edom, the first mentioned in Scripture (Gen. 36:32-33; 1 Chron. 1:43-44). [2] A son of Benjamin and one of the left-handed heroes (Gen. 46:21; 1 Chron. 7:6-7). [3] Descendant of Reuben (1 Chron. 5:8).

Bela [**Belah**] (bē′la [be′la]; "destroying"). One of the Cities of the Plain, probably Zoar (Gen. 14:2).

Belshazzar (bel-shaz′er; Hebrew form of the Babylonian name Bel-shar-usur—"[the god] Bel has protected the king [ship]"). The son of Nabonidus and co-regent in Babylon. He witnessed strange handwriting on the wall of his palace before his kingdom was overthrown by Persia (Dan. 5; 7:1; 8:1).

Belteshazzar (bel-te-shaz′er; Hebrew form of the Babylonian name, Balat-usu-usur—"Protect his life!"). The name given to Daniel in Babylon (Dan. 1:7). See Daniel.

Ben (ben; "son"). An assistant in the temple musical service at the time of David (1 Chron. 15:18).

Benaiah (be-nā′ya; "Jehovah has built"). [1] The third leader of David's army, counselor to the kings, and loyal friend of both David and Solomon (2 Sam. 8:18; 20:23; 1 Kings 1:8–2:46). [2] One of David's mighty men (2 Sam. 23:30; 1 Chron. 11:31). [3] Head of a family of the tribe of Simeon (1 Chron. 4:36). [4] One of David's priests (1 Chron. 15:18, 20, 24; 16:5-6). [5] Father of one of David's counselors (1 Chron. 27:34). [6] The grandfather of Jahaziel (2 Chron. 20:14). [7] An overseer of the temple during Hezekiah's reign (2 Chron. 31:13). [8], [9], [10], [11] Four men who married foreign wives during the Exile (Ezra 10:25, 30, 35, 43). [12] Father of Pelatiah, a prince of Judah (Ezek. 11:1, 13).

Ben-ammi (ben-am′i; "son of my people"). The ancestor of the Ammonites (Gen. 19:38), born to Lot and his daughter.

Bene-berak (ben'e-bē'rak; "sons of lightning"). A town of the tribe of Dan, about 6 km. (‹ mi.) east of modern Jaffa (Josh. 19:45).

Bene-jaakan (ben'ē-jā'a-kan; "sons of Jaakan"). *See* Beeroth [1].

Ben-hadad (ben-hā'dad; "sons of [the god] Hadad"). [1] Ben-hadad I, the king of Syria who made a league with Asa of Judah and invaded Israel (1 Kings 15:18, 20; 2 Chron. 10:2, 4). [2] Ben-hadad II, another king of Syria defeated by Ahab; he eventually laid siege to Samaria itself (1 Kings 20; 2 Kings 6:24; 8:7, 9. [3] The son of Hazael who reigned over Syria as the empire disintegrated (2 Kings 13:3, 24-25; Amos 1:4). [4] Possibly a general title of the Syrian kings (Jer. 49:27).

Ben-hail (ben-hā'il; ' strong; son of strength"). A prince of Judah under Jehoshaphat (2 Chron. 17:7).

Ben-hanan (ben-hā'nan; "son of grace"). A son of Shimon of the tribe of Judah (1 Chron. 4:20).

Beninu (be-ni'nū; "our son"). One who sealed the new covenant with God after the Exile (Neh. 10:13).

Benjamin (ben'ja-mir; "son of the right hand"). [1] The youngest son of Jacob; his descendants became one of the twelve tribes of Israel (Gen. 35:18, 24; 42:4, 36; 43–45. [2] A descendant of Benjamin (1 Chron. 7:10). [3] A descendant of Harim (Ezra 10:32). [4] One who helped to repair the wall of Jerusalem (Neh. 3:23). [5] One who helped to dedicate the wall of Jerusalem (Neh. 12:34).

Beno (bē'nō; "his son"). A descendant of Merari (1 Chron. 24:26-27).

Benoni (ben-ō'ni; "son of my sorrow"). Name given to Rachel's child as she died bearing him; Jacob changed his name to Benjamin (q.v.).

Ben-zoheth (ben-zō'heth; "son of Zoheth; corpulent; strong"). A descendant of Judah through Caleb (1 Chron. 4:20).

Beon (be-ōn'; "house of On"). *See* Baal-meon.

Beor [Bosor] (bē'ōr [bō'sor]; "shepherd"). [1] Father of Bela, the king of Edom (Gen. 36:32; 1 Chron. 1:43). [2] Father of the prophet Balaam (Num. 22:5; 24:3, 15; 31:8).

Bera (bē'ra; "gift"). A king of Sodom in the time of Abram (Gen. 14:2).

Berachah (ber'a-ka; "blessing"). One who joined David at Ziklag (1 Chron. 12:3).

Berachah (ber'a-ka; "blessing"). A valley in Judah near Tekoa, named by Jehoshaphat (2 Chron. 20:26).

Berachiah (ber-a-kī'a). *See* Berechiah [2].

Beraiah (ber-a-ī'a; "unfortunate"). A chief of Benjamin (1 Chron. 8:21).

Berea (be-rē'a; "watered"). A city in Macedonia about 80 km. (50 mi.) west of Thessalonica (Acts 17:10); now called Verria, or Salonica.

Berechiah [Berachiah] (ber-a-kī'a [ber-a-kī'a]; "Jehovah is blessing"). [1] A descendant of Jehoiakim (1 Chron. 3:20). [2] Father of Asaph, the chief singer (1 Chron. 6:39; 15:17). [3] A Levite who lived near Jerusalem (1 Chron. 9:16). [4] One of the tabernacle doorkeepers (1 Chron. 15:23). [5] A descendant of Ephraim in the time of Pekah (2 Chron. 28:12). [6] Father of one who repaired the wall of Jerusalem (Neh. 3:4, 30; 6:18). [7] The father of the prophet Zechariah (Zech. 1:1, 7). *See* Barachias.

Bered (bē'red; "seed place"). A descendant of Ephraim (1 Chron. 7:20); perhaps the same as Becher (Num. 26:35).

Bered (bē'red; "hail"). A place in the wilderness of Shur in southern Palestine, not far from Kadesh (Gen. 16:14).

Beri (bē'ri; "expounder"). A descendant of Asher (1 Chron. 7:36).

Beriah (be-rī'a; "unfortunate"). [1] A descendant of Asher (Gen. 46:17; Num. 26:44-45; 1 Chron. 7:30-31). [2] A descendant of Ephraim (1 Chron. 7:23). [3] A descendant of Benjamin (1 Chron. 8:13, 16). [4] A descendant of Levi (1 Chron. 23:10-11).

Bernice (ber-nī'sē; "victorious"). The immoral daughter of Herod Agrippa I. She and her brother Agrippa (with whom she was living in incest) sat in judgment on Paul (Acts 25:13, 23; 26:30).

Berodach-baladan (be-rō'dak-bal'a-dan). A copyist's mistake or another form of Merodach-baladan (q.v.).

Berothah [Berothai; Chun] (be-rō'tha [be-rō'thī; kun]; "of a well"). A town in northern Palestine between Hamath and Damascus, captured by David; also called Chun (2 Sam. 8:8; 1 Chron. 18:8; Ezek. 47:16).

Besai (bē'sī; "treading down"). One who returned to Jerusalem with Zerubbabel (Ezra 2:49; Neh. 7:52).

Besodeiah (bes-o-dē'ya; "given to trust in Jehovah"). One of the repairers of the old gate of Jerusalem (Neh. 3:6).

Besor (bē'sōr; "cold"). A brook south of Ziklag (1 Sam. 30:9-10, 21).

Betah (bē'ta; "confidence"). A city of Amam-Zobah (2 Sam. 8:8). It is identical with Tibhath (q.v.).

Beten (bē'ten; "valley"). A village of the tribe of Asher (Josh. 19:25); Eusebius noted that it was about 12 km. (7.5 mi.) east of Accho.

Beth-abara (beth-ab'a-ra; "house at the ford"). A place on the eastern side of the Jordan River where John the Baptist baptized his converts (John 1:28). The majority of Greek manuscripts read Bethany here instead; however, this city was not identical with Bethany proper.

Beth-anath [Beth-anoth] (beth-ā'nath [beth-ā'noth]; "house of reply"). [1] A fortress town of the tribe of Naphtali (Josh. 19:38; Judg. 1:33). [2] A town in the mountains of Judah, about 6 km. (4 mi.) from Hebron (Josh. 15:59).

Bethany (beth'a-ni; "house of affliction; place of unripe figs"). [1] A settlement on the hill leading to the Mount of Olives, about 2.6 km. (1.6 mi.) from Jerusalem (Mark 11:1; Luke 19:29).

Beth-arabah (beth-ar'a-ba; "house of the desert"). A village in the Judean wilderness on the boundary between the territories of Judah and Benjamin (Josh. 15:6, 61; 18:22).

Beth-aram [Beth-haran] (beth-a'ram [beth-a'ran]; "house of the heights"). A town of the tribe of Gad, located in the Jordan Valley and noted for its hot springs (Num. 32:36; Josh. 13:27).

Beth-arbel (beth-ar'bel; "house of ambush"). A town destroyed by Shalman (Hos. 10:14). Now known as Irbid, it is located about 6 km. (4 mi.) west-northwest of Tiberias.

Beth-aven (beth-ā'ven; "house of idols"). A town of the tribe of Benjamin, located in the wilderness near Ai (Josh. 7:2; 18.12; 1 Sam. 13:5).

Beth-azmaveth (beth-az-mā'veth; "house of Azmaveth"). A town near Jerusalem, halfway between Geba and Anathoth; perhaps the same as Hizmeh (Neh. 7:28). It is also called simply Azmaveth (Ezra 2:24; Neh. 12:29).

Beth-baal-meon (beth-bā'al-mē'on; "Baal's dwelling place"). *See also* Baal-meon.

Beth-barah (beth-ba'ra). A place in the vicinity of the Jordan Valley,

Ben-hadad's capital.
When Ben-hadad II united the Arameans (who lived in the territory northwest of Israel) he strengthened Damascus as the capital of his domain Ben-hadad's armies defeated the combined forces of Israel and Judah in a battle at Ramoth-gilead, in which King Ahab was killed (1 Kings 22:1-35). Modern Damascus shows the strong influence of Muslim culture.

possibly a ford or crossing near the confluence of the Jordan and the Wadi Farah (Judg. 7:24).

Beth-birei [Beth-biri] (beth-bir'e-ī [beth-bir'ī]; "house of my creation"). A town of the tribe of Simeon (1 Chron. 4:31); perhaps the same as Beth-lebaoth (q.v.).

Beth-car (beth-kar'; "house of the lamb"). A Philistine stronghold in Judah, site of a battle between the Israelites and the Philistines (1 Sam. 7:11).

Beth-dagon (beth-dā'gon; "house of Dagon"). [1] A town located on the border between Asher and Zebulun (Josh. 19:27); probably modern Jelamet el-Atika at the foot of Mount Carmel. [2] A town in the Judean lowlands (Josh. 15:33, 41); possibly modern Khirbet Dajun.

Beth-diblathaim (beth-dib-la-thā'im; "house of fig cakes"). A town in Moab (Jer. 48:21-22); possibly the same as Almon-diblathaim (q.v.).

Beth-el [Bethel] (beth'-el; "house of God"). [1] A town located about 18 km. (11 mi.) north of Jerusalem; an important site throughout the history of Israel (cf. Gen. 13:3; 28:18-19; Josh. 16:2; Judg. 21:19). It was formerly called Luz. The modern town of Bertin is located near the ruins. [2] *See also* Bethuel.

Beth-emek (beth-ē'mek; "house of the valley"). A town near the border of Asher; it is bounded on the north side by the ravine of Jipthah-el (Josh. 19:27). The modern name of this site is Amkah.

Bether (bē'ther). Many scholars believe the text of The Song of Solomon 2:17 should read "rugged mountains" instead of Bether. Others suggest the reference is to "the hills where the spice [cinnamon?] grows."

Bethesda (be-thez'da; "house of outpouring or overflowing water"). A pool near the Sheep Gate of Jerusalem reputed to have healing qualities (John 5:2-3).

Beth-ezel (beth-ē'zel; "a place near"). A town of southern Judah (Micah 1:11); present-day Deil el-'Asal.

Beth-gader (beth-gā'der; "house of walls"). A town of Judah founded by Hareph (1 Chron. 2:51).

Beth-gamul (beth-gā'mul; "camel house"). A city of Moab about 10 km. (6 mi.) east of Dibon (Jer. 48:23).

Beth-haccerem (beth-hak-sē'rem; "house of vines"). A town of Judah that maintained a beacon station (Neh. 3:14; Jer. 6:1); probably present-day Ain Karim, 7 km. (4 mi.) west of Jerusalem.

Beth-haran (beth-ha'ran). See Beth-aram.

Beth-hogla [Beth-hoglah] (beth-hog'la [beth-hog'lah]; "partridge house"). A Benjamite village about 6 km. (4 mi.) southeast of Jericho (Josh. 15:6; 18:19).

Beth-horon (beth-hō'ron; "cave house"). Twin towns located on the boundary between the territories of Ephraim and Benjamin. Upper Beth-horon was situated on a mountain pass between Jerusalem and the plain to the west. Lower Beth-horon was about 2 km. (1.5 mi.)

farther northwest (Josh. 16:3; 18:13; 2 Chron. 8:5; 1 Kings 9:17). The modern names for these towns are Beit 'Ur et Tahta (Lower) and Beit 'Ur el Foka (Upper).

Beth-jeshimoth [Beth-jesimoth] (beth-jesh'i-moth [beth-jes'i-moth]; "house of deserts"). A town in Moab near the Dead Sea (Num. 33:49; Josh. 12:3).

Beth-lebaoth (beth-le-bā'oth; "house of lionesses"). A town of southern Judah assigned to the tribe of Simeon (Josh. 19:6). The city is also known as Lebaoth (Josh. 15:32). It is perhaps identical with Beth-birei (q.v.).

Bethlehem (beth'-le-hem; "house of bread"). [1] A town about 10 km. (6 mi.) south of Jerusalem; birthplace of Jesus Christ (Matt. 2:5) and Ephrath (Gen. 35:16, 19; Ruth 4:11; cf. Mic. 5:2). Only in later times was it known as Bethlehem. It was originally called Ephratah (Ephrath) (Gen. 35:16: Ruth 4:11). [2] A city of the tribe of Zebulun located about 11 km. (7 mi.) northwest of Nazareth (Josh. 19:15).

Beth-maachah (beth-mā'a-ka). See also Abel-beth-maachah.

Beth-marcaboth (beth-mar'ka-both; "house of chariots"). A city in the Negeb near Ziklag (Josh. 19:5).

Beth-meon (beth-mē'on; "dwelling place"). See also Baal-meon.

Beth-nimrah (beth-nim'ra; "house of the leopardess"). A fortified city built by the tribe of Gad east of the Jordan River (Num. 32:36); also called Nimrah (Num. 32:3).

Beth-palet [Beth-phelet] (beth-pā'let [beth-fē'let]; "house of escape"). A town in the southernmost part of Judah (Josh. 15:27; Neh. 11:26); probably modern el-Meshash.

Beth-pazzez (beth-paz'ez; "house of dispersion"). A town of the tribe of Issachar (Josh. 19:21); its modern name is Kerm el-Haddatheh.

Beth-peor (beth-pē'or; "house of Peor"). A site near Pisgah where the Israelites placed their main camp while warring against Og (Deut. 3:29; 4:46).

Bethphage (beth'fa-jē; "house of unripe figs"). A settlement near Bethany on the road from Jerusalem to Jericho, probably at the descent from the Mount of Olives (Matt. 21:1; Mark 11:1).

Beth-rapha (beth-ra'fa; "place of fear"). A descendant of Judah or a city Eshton built (1 Chron. 4:12).

Beth-rehob (beth-rē'hob; "place of a street" [or market]). A town of the Upper Jordan Valley (Judg. 18:28; 2 Sam. 10:6). The city is called Rehob (Num. 13:21).

Bethsaida (beth-sā'i-da; "fish house"). A fishing town on the Sea of Galilee; birthplace of Philip, Andrew, and Simon (Matt. 11:21; Luke 9:10; Mark 6:45).

Beth-shean [Beth-shan] (beth-shē'an [beth-shan]; "house of rest"). The southern border town of the region of Galilee; largest of the ten cities of the Decapolis (Josh. 17:11; 1 Chron. 7:29).

Beth-shemesh (beth-shē'mesh; "house of the sun"). [1] A town on the road from Ashkelon and Ashdod to Jerusalem; it is located about 38 km. (24 mi.) west of Jerusalem (Josh. 15:10). **[2]** A Canaanite city in the territory of Naphtali (Josh. 19:38; Judg. 1:33). **[3]** A city of the tribe of Issachar, probably on the Jordan River near the Sea of Galilee (Josh. 19:22). **[4]** Another name for the Egyptian city of Heliopolis (Jer. 43:13).

Beth-shittah (beth-shit′a; "house of acacia"). A town of the Jordan Valley between Jezreel and Zerarah, noted for its acacia trees (Judg. 7:22).

Beth-tappuah (beth-tap′u-a; "house of apricots"). A settlement in the hills of Judah about 8 km. (5 mi.) west of Hebron (Josh. 15:53).

Bethuel (be-thū′el; "dweller in God"). A son of Nahor, Abraham's brother (Gen. 22:22-23; 28:5).

Bethuel [Bethul] (be-thū′el [bē′thul]; "dweller of God"). A town apportioned to the tribe of Simeon (Josh. 19:4; 1 Chron. 4:30). The town was also called Bethel (1 Sam. 30:27).

Beth-zur (beth-zur′; "house of rock"). A city in the hill country of Judah, fortified during the era of Rehoboam (Josh. 15:58; 2 Chron. 11:7).

Betonim (bet′o-nim; "bellies"). A town assigned to the tribe of Gad (Josh. 13:26).

Beulah (bū′la; "married"). Isaiah's name for the Promised Land after the Babylonian Captivity (Isa. 62:4).

Bezai (bē′za-ī; "shining; high"). **[1]** An ancestor of 323 captives returning from the Exile (Ezra 2:17; Neh. 7:23). **[2]** One who sealed the new covenant with God after the Exile (Neh. 10:18).

Bezaleel (be-zal′e-el; "God is protection"). **[1]** A chief worker and designer of the tabernacle (Exod. 31:2; 35:30; 36:1-2). **[2]** One who had married a foreign wife (Ezra 10:30).

Bezek (bē′zek; "lightning"). **[1]** A town near Jerusalem (Judg. 1:4-5). **[2]** The place where Saul assembled his army (1 Sam. 11:8).

Bezer (bē′zer; "strong"). One of the heads of Asher (1 Chron. 7:37).

Bezer (bē′zer; "fortress"). A fortified city within the territory of Reuben (Deut. 4:43; Josh. 20:8); probably present-day Unim el-Ammad, about 9 km. (5.5 mi.) east of Heshbon.

Bichri (bik′ri; "youth; firstborn"). An ancestor of Sheba, who rebelled against David (2 Sam. 20:1).

Bidkar (bid′kar; "servant of Ker [Kar]"). A captain in the service of Jehu who executed the sentence on Ahab's son (2 Kings 9:25).

Bigtha (big′tha; "given by fortune"). A chamberlain of Ahasuerus (Esther 1:10).

Bigthan [Bigthana] (big′than [big-thā′na]; "given by fortune"). A chamberlain who conspired against Ahasuerus (Esther 2:21; 6:2).

Bigvai (big′va-ī; "happy; of the people"). **[1]** Head of one of the families who returned with Zerubbabel (Ezra 2:2, 14; 8:14; Neh. 7:7, 19). **[2]** One who sealed the covenant with Nehemiah (Neh. 10:16).

Bildad (bil'dad; "lord Adad; son of contention"). One of Job's three "friends" (Job 2:11; 8:1; 18:1; 25:1; 42:9).

Bileam (bil'e-am; "foreigners"). A settlement on the western side of the Jordan River assigned to the tribe of Manasseh (1 Chron. 6:70).

Bilgah (bil'ga; "bursting forth; firstborn"). [1] A priest in the tabernacle service (1 Chron. 24:14). [2] A priest who came up to Jerusalem with Zerubbabel (Neh. 12:5, 18).

Bilgai (bil'ga-i; "bursting forth"). One who sealed the new covenant with God after the Exile (Neh. 10:8); perhaps the same as Bilgah [2].

Bilhah (bil'ha; "tender"). The handmaid of Rachel and mother of Dan and Naphtali (Gen. 29:29; 30:3-5, 7).

Bilhah (bil'ha). See Baalah [1].

Bilhan (bil'han; "tender"). [1] A descendant of Seir (Gen. 36:27; 1 Chron. 1:42). [2] A descendant of Benjamin (1 Chron. 7:10).

Bilshan (bil'shan; "searcher"). A prince who returned from the Exile (Ezra 2:2; Neh. 7:7).

Bimhal (bim'hal; "circumcised"). A descendant of Asher (1 Chron. 7:33).

Binea (bin'e-a; "wanderer"). A descendant of Saul (1 Chron. 8:37; 9:43).

Binnui (bin'nū-i; "being a family"). [1] A Levite appointed by Ezra to weigh gold and silver (Ezra 8:33). [2],[3] Two men who married foreign wives during the Exile (Ezra 10:30, 38). [4] One who repaired the wall of Jerusalem (Neh. 3:24; 10:9). [5] A Levite who came up with Zerubbabel (Neh. 12:8). [6] See Bani [4].

Birsha (bir'sha; "thick; strong"). A king of Gomorrah in the days of Abraham (Gen. 14:2).

Birzavith (bir'za-vith; "olive well"). Descendant of Asher (1 Chron. 7:31).

Bishlam (bish'lam; "peaceful"). A foreign colonist who wrote a letter of complaint against the Jews (Ezra 4:7).

Bithiah (bi-thī'a; "daughter of Jehovah"). A daughter of the pharaoh and wife of Mered (1 Chron. 4:18); her name implies her conversion.

Bithron (bith'ron; "ravine"). A gorge in the Aravah east of the Jordan River (2 Sam. 2:29).

Bithynia (bi-thin'i-a; "violent rainfall"). A country of northwestern Asia Minor, bounded on the north by the Black Sea (Acts 16:7; 1 Pet. 1:1).

Bizjothjah (biz-joth'ja; meaning uncertain). A town in the southernmost portion of Judah (Josh. 15:28).

Biztha (biz'tha; "eunuch"). One of Ahasuerus' eunuchs (Esther 1:10).

Blastus (blas'tus; "a bud"). The chamberlain of Herod Agrippa I (Acts 12:20).

Boanerges (bo-a-nur'jez). The surname bestowed upon James and John, the sons of Zebedee. It means "sons of thunder" (Mark 3:17).

Boaz [Booz] (bō'az [bō'oz]; "fleetness; strength"). A Bethlehemite of Judah who became the husband of Ruth and an ancestor of Christ (Ruth 2–4; Matt. 1:5; Luke 3:32).

Bocheru (bō'ke-roo; "youth"). A descendant of King Saul (1 Chron. 8:38; 9:44).

Bochim (bō'kim; "weepers"). A site near Gilgal where the Israelites repented of their sins (Judg. 2:1-5).

Bohan (bō'han; "stumpy"). A descendant of Reuben for whom a boundary stone between Judah and Benjamin was named (Josh. 15:6; 18:17).

Bohan (bō'han; "thumb; stumpy"). The "stone of Bohan" was a boundary mark separating the northeast frontier of Judah from Benjamin. The site is uncertain (Josh. 18:17).

Booz (bō'oz). Greek form of Boaz (q.v.).

Boscath (bos'kath). See Bozkath.

Bosor (bō'sor). Greek form of Beor (q.v.).

Bozez (bōz'es; "shining"). The name of two crags near Geba; the northernmost crag faces Michmash (1 Sam. 14:4).

Bozkath [Boscath] (boz'kath [bos'kath]; "craggy"). A town near Lachish in southern Judah (Josh. 15:39; 2 Kings 22:1).

Bozrah (boz'ra; "stronghold"). [1] The capital of Edom (Gen. 36:33; 1 Chron. 1:44). [2] A city of Moab; probably Bezer (Jer. 48:24).

Brook of the Willows. See Willows, Brook of the.

Bukki (buk'ī; "proved of Jehovah; mouth of Jehovah"). [1] An ancestor of Ezra and descendant of Aaron (1 Chron. 6:5, 51; Ezra 7:4). [2] A prince of the tribe of Dan (Num. 34:22).

Bukkiah (bu-kī'a; "proved of Jehovah; mouth of Jehovah"). A son of Heman and musician in the temple (1 Chron. 25:4, 13).

Bunah (boo'na; "understanding"). A son of Jerahmeel (1 Chron. 2:25).

Bunni (bun'ī; "my understanding"). [1] An ancestor of Shemaiah the Levite (Neh. 11:15). [2] A Levite who helped Ezra in teaching the Law (Neh. 9:4). [3] One who sealed the new covenant with God after the Exile (Neh. 10:15).

Buz (booz; "contempt"). [1] The second son of Nahor, the brother of Abraham (Gen. 22:21). [2] A descendant of Gad (1 Chron. 5:14).

Buzi (booz'i; "despised by Jehovah"). A descendant of Aaron and father of Ezekiel (Ezek. 1:3).

C

Cabbon (kab'on; "understanding"). A town of lowland Judah (Josh. 15:40).

Cabul (kā'bul; "displeasing; obscurity"). [1] A town of the tribe of Asher noted for its dry climate (Josh. 19:27). [2] A district of Galilee; the northern part of the territory of Naphtali (1 Kings 19:13).

Caesar (sē'zer). The name of a branch of the aristocratic family of the Julii, which gained control of the Roman government; afterward it became a formal title of the Roman emperors. *See* Augustus Caesar; Tiberius Caesar; Claudius Caesar.

Caesarea [Caesarea Maritima] (ses-a-rē'a [ses-a-rē'a ma-ri-tē'ma]; "city of Caesar"). Coastal city of Palestine that served as capital of the Roman province (Acts 8:40). Built by Herod the Great, it is located 37 km. (23 mi.) from the foot of Mount Carmel; also called Caesarea Maritima.

Caesarea Philippi (ses-a-rē'a fi-lip'ī; "Caesar's city of Philippi"). A town located at the foot of Mount Hermon; the northernmost extent of Jesus' ministry (Matt. 16:13-20).

Caiaphas (kā'ya-fas; "depression"). The high priest who took a leading role in the trial of Jesus (Matt. 26:3, 57-68; John 11:49).

Cain (kān; "acquired; spear"). The eldest son of Adam who killed his brother Abel (Gen. 4:1-25). *See also* Tubal-cain.

Cain (kān; "acquired; spear"). A town in the hill country of Judah (Josh. 15:57).

Cainan [Kenan] (ka-ī'nan [kē'nan]; "acquired"). [1] A son of Enosh and ancestor of Christ (Gen. 5:9; Luke 3:37). The KJV inconsistently spells the same name *Kenan* in First Chronicles 1:2. [2] A son of Arphaxad and an ancestor of Christ (Luke 3:36). It should be noted that this name occurs in the Septuagint text and not in the Hebrew of Genesis 10:24; 11:12. The presence of this name shows that the early lists in Genesis were not meant to be complete.

Calah (kā'la; "old age"). A city built by Nimrod that later became the capital of the Assyrian Empire; located about 29 km. (18 mi.) south of Nineveh (Gen. 10:11).

Calcol (kal'kol; "sustaining" or "nourishment"). A descendant of Judah (1 Chron. 2:6). *See also* Chalcol.

Caleb [Chelubai] (kā'leb [ke-lū'bī]; "impetuous; raging with madness"). [1] One of the spies sent out by Moses to see the Promised Land (Num. 13:6; Josh. 14–15). [2] A son of Hezron and grandfather of [1] (1 Chron. 2:18-19, 42).

Caleb-ephratah (kā'leb-ef'ra-tha). The place where Hezron died (1 Chron. 2:24). Many scholars translate the verse: "after the death of Hezron, Caleb went into Ephrathah, the wife of Hezron his father, and she bore him Ashhur, the father of Tekoa" (RSV) following the LXX. *See also* Ephratah.

Calneh (kal'ne; "fortress"). [1] A Babylonian city belonging to Nimrod (Gen. 10:10). [2] A city located about 10 km. (6 mi.) from Arpad (Amos 6:2); probably the present-day Kullani.

Calno (kal'nō; "futility"). A city conquered by the Assyrians (Isa. 10:9); probably the same as Calneh [2].

Calvary (kal'var-ē). *See* Golgotha.

Camon (kā'mon; "standing place"). The place Jair was buried (Judg. 10:5).

Cana (kā'na; "reeds"). A village of Galilee where Jesus performed the miracle of changing water into wine. It is located 16 km. (10 mi.) northeast of Nazareth (John 2:1, 11; 4:46).

Canaan (kā'nan; "low"). A son of Ham and grandson of Noah (Gen. 10:6-19; 1 Chron. 1:8, 13). Possibly a reference to the inhabitants of Canaan.

Canaan (kā'nan; "purple"). The native name of Palestine, the land given to Abraham and his descendants (Gen. 11:31; Exod. 6:4).

Candace (kan'da-sē; "contrite one"). A dynastic title of Ethiopian queens (Acts 8:27).

Canneh (kā'neh; "distinguished"). A town on the southern coast of Arabia (Ezek. 27:23); present-day Canne.

Capernaum (ka-per'na-um; "village of Nahum"). A town on the northwest shore of the Sea of Galilee; an important center of Jesus' ministry (Matt. 4:13; Luke 4:31).

Caphtor (kaf'tor; "isle"). The island or seacoast region from which the Philistines originally came (Jer. 47:4; Amos 9:7); probably Crete and other nearby islands.

Caphtorim [Caphthorim] (kaf-tor-im' [kaf-thor-im']. A son of Mizraim (Gen. 10:14; 1 Chron. 1:12). Possibly a reference to the people from Caphtor.

Cappadocia (kap-a-dō'shi-a; "five horses"). A Roman district in eastern Asia Minor (Acts 2:9; 1 Pet. 1:1).

Carcas (kar'kas; "severe"). A chamberlain of Ahasuerus (Esther 1:10).

Carchemish [Charchemish] (kar'ke-mish [kar'kem-ish]; "city [fortress] of Chemosh"). A city west of the Euphrates River; the eastern capital of the Hittites (2 Chron. 35:20; Isa. 10:9; Jer. 46:2).

Careah (ka-rē'a). *See* Kareah.

Carmel (kar'mel; "orchard"). [1] A string of mountains that run about 24 km. (15 mi.) through central Palestine and jut into the Mediterranean Sea (Jer. 46:18). [2] A town in the mountains of Judah about 14 km. (9 mi.) south-southeast of Hebron (Josh. 15:55; 1 Sam. 25:5); modern Kermel. [3] *See* Rachal.

Carmi (kar'mī; "fruitful; noble"). [1] A son of Reuben who went to Egypt with him (Gen. 46:9; Exod. 6:14; 1 Chron. 5:3). [2] A descendant of Judah (Josh. 7:1; 1 Chron. 2:7). [3] Another son of Judah (1 Chron. 4:1); some identify him with [2].

Carpus (kar'pus; "fruit; wrist"). A friend with whom Paul left his cloak (2 Tim. 4:13).

Carshena (kar-shē'na; "distinguished; lean"). One of the seven princes of Persia and Media during Ahasuerus' reign (Esther 1:14).

Casiphia (ka-sif'i-a). An unidentified place in Babylon to which Ezra sent for ministers of the house of God (Ezra 8:17).

Casluhim (kas'lū-him; "fortified"). A son of Mizraim (Gen. 10:14;

1 Chron. 1:12). Possibly a people related to the Egyptians. They were the ancestors of the Phi istines.

Cedron (ke'dron). *See* Kidron.

Cenchrea (sen'kre-a; "millet"). A harbor about 11 km. (7 mi.) east of Corinth, visited by Paul (Acts 18:18).

Cephas (se'fas). *See* Peter.

Chalcol (kal'kol; "sustaining"). A wise man with whom Solomon was compared (1 Kings 4:31).

Chaldea (kal-de'a; "demons"). The southern region of the Babylonian Empire (Jer. 50:10; Ezek. 11:24).

Champaign (sham-pān'). A word derived from the Latin campus, a field. The Hebrew text reads Arabah (Deut. 11:30).

Charashim [Charran] (kar'a-shim [kar'an]; "ravine of craftsmen"). A valley that ran along the back of the Plain of Sharon, east of modern Jaffa (1 Chron. 4:14). Compare Nehemiah 11:35, where the valley is called Charran.

Charran (kar'an). Greek form of Haran (q.v.). *See* Charashim.

Chebar (ke'bar; "strength"). A river of Chaldea; the Jewish exiles, including Ezekiel, lived along its banks (Ezek. 1:3).

Chedorlaomer (ked-or-la-ō'mer; Elamite, Kutir-Lakamar— "servant of [the goddess] Lakamar"). A king of Elam who came up against Sodom and Gomorrah (Gen. 14:1-24).

Chelal (ke'lal; "completeness"). A man who took a foreign wife during the Exile (Ezra 10:30).

Chelluh (kel'a; "robust"). A man who married a foreign wife during the Exile (Ezra 10:35).

Chelub (ke'lub; "boldness"). [1] A descendant of Judah (1 Chron. 4:11). [2] Father of Ezri (1 Chron. 27:26).

Chelubai (ke-lū'bī). *See* Caleb [2].

Chenaanah (ke-nā'a-na; "flat; low"). [1] A son of Bilhan (1 Chron. 7:10). [2] Father of the false prophet Zedekiah (1 Kings 22:11, 24).

Chenani (ken'a-nī; "Jehovah, creator"). A Levite in the time of Ezra (Neh. 9:4).

Chenaniah (ken-a-ni'a; "established by Jehovah"). [1] A head Levite when David brought the ark of the covenant to the temple (1 Chron. 15:22, 27). [2] An officer of David (1 Chron. 26:29). *See also* Conaniah.

Chephar-haammonai (ke'far-ha-am'o-ni; "village of the Ammonites"). A town assigned to the tribe of Benjamin (Josh. 18:24); probably modern Khirbet Kafr 'Ana, east of Jifna.

Chephirah (ke-fī'ra; "town"). A city of Gibeon given to the tribe of Benjamin (Josh. 9:17); modern Kefireh, located 13 km. (8 mi.) west-northwest of Jerusalem.

Cheran (ke'ran; "lyre; lamb; union"). A son of Dishon (Gen. 36:26).

Cherith (ke'rith; "gorge"). A small stream east of the Jordan River, where birds fed the prophet Elijah (1 Kings 17:3-5).

Cherub (kē'rub). A place in Babylonia (Ezra 2:59; Neh. 7:61).

Chesalon (kes'a-lon; "hopes"). A town on Mount Jearim of Judah, about 16 km. (10 mi.) west of Jerusalem (Josh. 15:10).

Chesed (ke'sed; "gain"). Son of Nahor and Milcah and nephew of Abraham (Gen. 22:22).

Chesil (ke'sil; "fool"). A village in the southernmost portion of Judah (Josh. 15:3); perhaps the same as Bethuel (q.v.).

Chesulloth (ke-sul'oth; "loins"). A town 6 km. (4 mi.) southeast of Nazareth in the territory of Issachar (Josh. 19:18).

Chezib (ke'zib; "deceitful"). See Achzib.

Chidon [Nachon] (kī'don [nā'kon]; "javelin"). The place where Uzzah was struck dead for touching the ark of the covenant (1 Chron. 13:9); in Second Samuel 6:6 the place is called Nachon. Its exact location is unknown.

Chileab (kil'e-ab; "restraint of father"). A son of David (2 Sam. 3:3); probably also called Daniel (1 Chron. 3:1).

Chilion (kil'i-un; "pining"). Son of Naomi and husband of Orpah (Ruth 1:2, 5).

Chilmad (kil'mad; "closed"). A nation on the Euphrates River that traded with Tyre (Ezek. 27:23).

Chimham (kim'ham; "pining"). A friend and political supporter of David (2 Sam. 19:37-38, 40; Jer. 41:17).

Chinnereth [Chinneroth; Cinneroth] (kin'e-reth [kin'e-roth; sin'e-reth]; "harps"). [1] Another name for the Sea of Galilee (Num. 34:11; Josh. 12:3). [2] A city on the north shore of the Sea of Galilee (Deut. 3:17). [3] The region surrounding the city of Chinnereth (1 Kings 15:20).

Chios (kī'os; "open"). An island of the Greek chain at the entrance to the Gulf of Smyrna (Acts 20:15).

Chislon (kis'lon; "strength"). A prince of the tribe of Benjamin (Num. 34:21).

Chisloth-tabor (kis'loth-ta'bor; "loins of tabor"). A city of Zebulun at the foot of Mount Tabor (Josh. 19:12). It is perhaps identical with Tabor [2].

Chittim (kit'im). The island of Cyprus (Isa. 23:1, 12). The term referred in a more general way to the coastlands of the Mediterranean (Jer. 2:10). The ships of Chittim in Daniel 11:30 probably refer to Rome. See also Kittim.

Chloe (klō'e; "a tender sprout"). A Corinthian woman or an Ephesian woman who knew of the problems at Corinth (1 Cor. 1:11).

Chor-ashan (kōr'a-shan; "smoking furnace"). A town in Judah given to Simeon (1 Sam. 30:30). It is possibly identical with Ashan (q.v.).

Chorazin (ko-rā'zin; "secret"). A coastal city of the Sea of Galilee where Jesus Christ performed many miracles (Matt. 11:21; Luke 10:13).

Chozeba (ko-zē'ba; "untruthful"). A village of Judah inhabited by the descendants of Shelah (1 Chron. 4:22); probably the same as Achzib [1].

Christ (krīst). See Jesus.

Chub (kub). Many scholars believe this is a textual error and should be read as in the LXX, "Lub," i.e., Libya (q.v.) (Ezek. 30:5).

Chun (kun; "founding"). See Berothah.

Chushan-rishathaim (kū'shan-rish-a-thā'im; "man of Cush; he of the twofold crime"). A king of Mesopotamia that God chose to punish Israel (Judg. 3:8, 10).

Chuza (koo'za; "seer"). Steward of Herod Antipas whose wife ministered to Christ and the apostles (Luke 8:3).

Cilicia (si-lish'i-a; "rolling"). A district of southeast Asia Minor. Paul was born in Tarsus, the principal city of this district (Acts 21:39).

Cis (sis). Greek form of Kish (q.v.).

Cities of Refuge. Six Levitical cities set aside as sanctuaries for certain criminals: Bezer, Ramoth-gilead, Golan, Kedesh, Shechem, and Kirjath-arbu (Deut. 4:41-43; Josh. 20:7-9).

Cities of the Plain. Five cities located on the Plain of Jordan: Sodom, Gomorrah, Admah, Zeboim, and Zoar (Gen. 10:19; 13:10).

City of David. [1] Jebusite city of Zion captured by David's men. David made it his royal city and renamed it Jerusalem (2 Sam. 5:6-9; 1 Chron. 11:5, 7). [2] See Bethlehem.

City of Salt. A city in the wilderness of Judah near En-gedi (Josh. 15:62).

Clauda (klo'da; "lamentable"). An island southwest of Crete passed by Paul during his journey to Rome (Acts 27:16).

Claudia (klo'di-a; "lame"). A Roman Christian who sent greetings to Timothy (2 Tim. 4:21).

Claudius Caesar (klo'di-us sē'zer; "lame ruler"). Roman emperor who banished the Jews from Rome (Acts 18:2).

Claudius Lysias (klo'di-us lis'i-as; "lame dissolution"). A Roman officer, chief captain in Jerusalem (Acts 23:26).

Clement (klem'ent; "mild"). A co-worker with Paul at Philippi (Phil. 4:3).

Cleopas (klē'o-pas; "renowned father"). One of the disciples whom Jesus met on the way to Emmaus (Luke 24:18). See also Cleophas.

Cleophas (klē'o-fas; "renowned"). The husband of one of the Marys who followed Jesus (John 19:25); possibly the same as Alphaeus (q.v.). See also Alphaeus; Cleopas.

Cnidus (nī'dus; "age"). A city on the southwestern coast of Asia Minor near the Isle of Cos passed by Paul on his journey to Rome (Acts 27:7).

Col-hozeh (kol-hō'zeh; "wholly a seer"). [1] Father of Shallum, who helped to rebuild the wall of Jerusalem (Neh. 3:15). [2] A man of Judah (Neh. 11:5); possibly the same as [1].

Colosse [Colossae] (ko-los′e [ko-los′e]; "punishment"). A city in the district of Phrygia in Asia Minor (Col. 1:2).

Conaniah [Cononiah]. (kon-a-nī′a [kon-on-ī′a]; "Jehovah has founded"). [1] A Levite appointed to be overseer of the tithes and offerings at the temple (2 Chron. 31:12-13). [2] A chief of the Levites (2 Chron. 35:9). *See also* Chenaniah.

Coniah (cō-nī′a). *See* Jehoiachin.

Cononiah (kon-on-ī′a). *See* Conaniah.

Coos (kō′os). An island between Rhodes and Miletus (Acts 21:1).

Core (kō′re). Greek form of Korah (q.v.).

Corinth (kor′inth; "ornament"). A Greek city located on the isthmus between the Peloponnesus and mainland Greece, about 64 km. (40 mi.) west of Athens (Acts 18:1; 1 Cor. 1:2).

Cornelius (kor-nē′li-us; "of a horn"). A Roman centurion who was converted to Christianity (Acts 10:1-31).

Corner Gate. A gate near the northwest corner of the wall of Jerusalem (2 Kings 14:13).

Co-sam (kō′sam; "diviner"). An ancestor of Christ (Luke 3:28).

Coz (koz; "thorn; nimble"). A descendant of Judah through Caleb (1 Chron. 4:8).

Cozbi (koz′bi; "deceitful"). A Midianite woman slain by Phinehas at Shittim (Num. 25:6-18).

Crescens (kres′enz; "increasing"). An assistant with Paul at Rome (2 Tim. 4:10).

Crete (krēt; "carnal"). A large island southeast of Greece (Titus 1:5).

Crispus (kris′pus; "curled"). A ruler of the Jewish synagogue at Corinth who was converted to Christ (Acts 18:7-8; 1 Cor. 1:14).

Cush (kūsh; "black"). [1] Eldest son of Ham (Gen. 10:6-8; 1 Chron. 1:8-10). [2] A descendant of Benjamin and enemy of David (Psa. 7, title).

Cush (kūsh; "black"). The area of the Upper Nile south of Egypt; traditional homeland of the descendants of Ham (Gen. 10:6-8).

Cushan (kū′shan). The name of a place or people, possibly Midian (Hab. 3:7).

Cushi (kū′shi; "black"). [1] Father of Zephaniah (Zeph. 1:1). [2] Great-grandfather of Jehudi (Jer. 36:14). [3] The messenger that told David of the defeat of Absalom (2 Sam. 18:21-32).

Cuth (kūth; "burning"). A Babylonian city (2 Kings 17:30); present-day Tell Ibrahim, northeast of Babylon.

Cyprus (sī′prus; "fairness"). An island in the northeastern Mediterranean Sea about 96 km. (60 mi.) east of Syria (Acts 13:4; 15:39).

Cyrene (sī-rē′nē; "wall"). A city of Libya in Northern Africa (Matt. 27:32); probably modern Shahhat.

Corinth at the Crossroads

Corinth rose from ashes to occupy a position of prominence at the trading crossroads of the ancient world. The original city was destroyed in 146 B.C. in a Greek revolt against the Roman Empire. Rebuilt in the time of Julius Caesar (*ca.* 46 B.C.), Corinth soon regained its former position as a center of commerce. Within twenty-one years, this rapidly growing metropolis became the capital of the province of Achaia in Greece.

Corinth was one of the wealthiest and most influential cities of its time. Located on a narrow strip of land between mainland Greece and the Peloponnesus (the peninsula of southern Greece), Corinth had two main harbors, which gave the city access to the Aegean and Ionian seas. This strategic location allowed Corinth to control the traffic of the eastern and western seas, along a principal trade route of the Roman Empire. Corinth was the fourth largest city of the empire (after Rome, Alexandria, and Antioch), and had a population of nearly half a million.

Corinth was also situated at a cultural crossroads. Residents migrated to this rapidly developing area from every corner of the Mediterranean world. Egyptians, Syrians, Orientals, and Jews who settled there brought a wide variety of cultural influences.

One might well call ancient Corinth a "sin city." While rather low moral values were held by the general Roman public, Corinth had a reputation for embracing the lowest of the low. Even prior to the time of the apostle Paul, "to live like a Corinthian" was a slang phrase denoting loose, immoral conduct.

Oddly, religion contributed to this atmosphere of moral corruption. Many of the fertility cults that existed in the city included acts of magic and sexual perversion as part of their "worship." Corinth's temple of Aphrodite, the goddess of love, at one time had one thousand priestess-prostitutes within its confines.

To this complex city came the apostle Paul. Arriving around A.D. 52, Paul remained there for about a year and a half, ministering to one of the greatest churches of Jesus Christ. A city at the crossroads, both physically and spiritually, Corinth heard the gospel of Christ through Paul's ministry.

Corinth was rebuilt after earthquakes in 1858 and 1928. The Doric columns of one old temple of Apollo are one of the few reminders of Corinth's early days left. Corinth today has a population of about 20,000. It is still an important sea town, with exports of olive oil, silk, and currants, which take their name from the city.

Cyrenius [Quirinius] (sī-rē′ni-us [kwī-rin′i-us]; "of Cyrene"). The governor of Syria (Luke 2:2).

Cyrus (sī′rus). Founder of the Persian Empire; he returned the Jews to their land (Ezra 1:1-4, 7; 3:7; Isa. 44:28; 45:1-4; Dan. 6:28).

D

Dabbasheth (dab′e-sheth; "camel hump"). A border town of the tribe of Zebulun (Josh. 19:11).

Daberath [Dabareh] (dab′e-rath [dab′a-reh]; "pasture"). A city of the tribe of Issachar, assigned to the Levites (Josh. 19:12; 1 Chron. 6:72); probably modern Daburiyeh at the western base of Mount Tabor. The KJV renders the same Hebrew word as Dabareh in Joshua 21:28.

Dalaiah (da-lī′a; "Jehovah is deliverer" or "Jehovah has raised"). A descendant of Judah (1 Chron. 3:24). *See also* Delaiah.

Dale, the King's. *See* Shaveh.

Dalmanutha (dal-ma-nū′tha; "bucket"). A fishing village on the western coast of the Sea of Galilee (Mark 8:10).

Dalmatia (dal-mā′shē-a; "deceitful"). A province of Illyricum on the eastern shore of the Adriatic Sea; noted for its wild inhabitants (Rom. 15:19; 2 Tim. 4:10). Dalmatia later became the official name of the province.

Dalphon (dal′fon; "swift"). A son of Haman slain by the Jews (Esther 9:6-7, 10).

Damaris (dam′a-ris; "heifer"). An Athenian woman converted by Paul (Acts 17:34).

Damascus (da-mas′kus; "sackful of blood"). An important Syrian trade center; Paul was converted on the road from Jerusalem to this city (Gen. 14:15; Acts 9:2).

Dan (dan; "judge"). The fifth son of Jacob and ancestor of one of the twelve tribes of Israel (Gen. 30:6; 49:16-17).

Dan (dan; "judge"). A town of the tribe of Dan in the northwest portion of Palestine (Josh. 19:47; Judg. 20:1).

Daniel (dan′yel; "God is my judge"). [1] A prophet at the time of Nebuchadnezzar and Cyrus. His wisdom and faith earned him a

David. David is portrayed here as a boy with his sling. This young shepherd killed Goliath (1 Sam. 17:4-50) and became a hero to the Israelites.

position of esteem under Nebuchadnezzar and Darius (Dan. 1:1-6; 2; 6:1-2. **[2]** One of the sons of David (1 Chron. 3:1). *See* Chileab. **[3]** A Levite of the line of Ithamar (Ezra 8:2; Neh. 10:6).

Dan-jaan (dan-jā'an; "judgment"). A place or city between Gilead and Sidon: possibly Dan (2 Sam. 24:6).

Dannah (dan'na; "judging"). A small village in the hill country of Judah (Josh. 15:49); modern Deir esh Shenish or Simya.

Dara (da'ra; "bearer [pearl] of wisdom"). A son of Zerah (1 Chron. 2:6). Possibly the same as Darda (q.v.).

Darda (dar'da; "bearer [pearl] of wisdom"). A wise man with whom Solomon was compared (1 Kings 4:31). *See also* Dara.

Darius (da-rī'us; "he that informs himself"). **[1]** The sub-king of Cyrus who received the kingdom of Belshazzar (Dan. 5:30–6:28); also known as Darius the Mede. **[2]** The fourth king of Persia (Ezra 4:5; Hag. 1:1; Zech. 1:1); also called Hystaspis. **[3]** Darius II (Nothus) who ruled Persia and Babylon (Neh. 12:22).

Darkon (dar'kon; "carrier"). A servant of Solomon whose descendants returned to Palestine after the Exile (Ezra 2:56; Neh. 7:58).

Dathan (dā'than; "front"). A chief of the tribe of Reuben who tried to overthrow Moses and Aaron (Num. 16; 26:9; Deut. 11:6).

David (dā'vid; "beloved"). The great statesman, general, and king of Israel. He united the divided tribes of Israel and made many preparations for the temple, which his son Solomon would complete (1 Sam. 16–1 Kings 2:11). He was an ancestor of Christ (Matt. 1:6).

Dead Sea. *See* Salt Sea.

Debir (dē'bir; "oracle"). A king of Eglon defeated by Joshua (Josh. 10:3).

Debir (dē'bir; "oracle"). **[1]** A town in the hill country of Judah assigned to the Levites (Josh. 15:15). The city is also called Kirjath-sannah (Josh. 15:49) and Kirjath-sepher (Judg. 1:11-13). **[2]** A town near the Valley of Achor, probably on the road between Jerusalem and Jericho (Josh. 15:7). **[3]** A border town of the tribe of Gad, located east of the Jordan River near Mahanaim (Josh. 13:26).

Deborah (deb'ō-ra; "bee"). **[1]** The nurse of Rebekah (Gen. 24:59; 35:8). **[2]** Prophetess and judge of Israel who helped to deliver her people from Jabin and Sisera (Judg. 4:4-14; 5).

Decapolis (de-kap'ō-lis; "ten cities"). A league of ten cities forming a Roman district on the Plain of Esdraelon and the Upper Jordan Valley (Matt. 4:25).

Dedan (dē'dan). **[1]** A descendant of Cush (Gen. 10:7). Possibly a people of Arabia in the neighborhood of Edom. **[2]** A son of Jokshan and grandson of Abraham (Gen. 25:3).

Dedan (dē'dan; "low"). A district near Edom between Sela and the Dead Sea (Jer. 25:23; Ezek. 25:13). Isaiah 21:13 mentions the "caravans of the Dedanim" in the wilds of Arabia.

Dekar (dē'kar; "lancer"). Father of one of Solomon's commissaries (1 Kings 4:9).

Delaiah (de-lī'a; "Jehovah has raised; Jehovah is deliverer"). [1] One of David's priests (1 Chron. 24:18). [2] A prince who urged Jehoiakim not to destroy the roll containing Jeremiah's prophecies (Jer. 36:12, 25). [3] Ancestor of a postexilic family that had lost its genealogy (Ezra 2:60; Neh. 7:62). [4] The father of Shemaiah (Neh. 6:10). See also Dalaiah.

Delilah (de-lī'la; "longing; dainty one"). A woman whom the Philistines paid to find Samson's source of strength (Judg. 16).

Demas (dē'mas; "popular"). A friend of Paul at Rome who later forsook him (Col. 4:14; 2 Tim. 4:10; Philem. 24).

Demetrius (de-mē'tri-us; "belonging to Demeter"). [1] A Christian praised by John (3 John 12). [2] A silversmith who led the opposition against Paul at Ephesus (Acts 19:24-41).

Derbe (der'bē; "sting"). A city of southeastern Asia Minor, where Paul sought refuge after being stoned at Lystra (Acts 14:6-20).

Deuel (dū'el; "knowledge of God"). Father of Eliasaph (Num. 1:14). He is called Reuel in Numbers 2:14; we do not know which name is original.

Diblaim (dib'lā-im; "two cakes; double embrace"). Father-in-law of Hosea (Hos. 1:3).

Diblath (dib'lath; "round cake"). A place or city in Palestine (Ezek. 6:14); its exact location is unknown, but it was probably Riblah [1].

Dibon [Dimon; Dimonah] (dī'bon [dī'mon; di-mō'na]; "wasting"). [1] A city of the tribe of Gad located north of the Arnon River (Num. 21:30; 32:3; Isa. 15:9); the famous Moabite Stone was found here in 1868. [2] A village of Judah, also known as Dimonah (Neh. 11:25; Josh. 15:22).

Dibon-gad (dī'bon-gad; "wasting of Gad"). A halting place of the Israelites leaving Egypt (Num. 33:45-46). It is probably the same as Dibon [1].

Dibri (dib'ri; "eloquent" or "on the pasture born"). A descendant of Dan whose daughter married an Egyptian; her son was stoned for blasphemy (Lev. 24:11).

Didymus (did'i-mus). See Thomas.

Diklah (dik'la; "place of palms"). A son of Joktan (Gen. 10:27; 1 Chron. 1:21). Possibly a people who dwelt in Arabia is intended.

Dilean (dil'e-an; "cucumber"). A city in the lowlands of Judah (Josh. 15:38).

Dimnah (dim'na; "dung"). See Rimmon [3].

Dimon (dī'mon). See Dibon.

Dimonah (dī'mō'na). See Dibon [2].

Dinah (dī'na; "justice"). The daughter of Jacob and Leah who was violated by Hamor; this resulted in a tribal war (Gen. 34).

Dinhabah (din'ha-ba; "give judgment"). A city belonging to the king of Edom (Gen. 36:32); its exact location is unknown.

Dionysius (di-o-nish'i-us; "Bacchus"). A member of the supreme court at Athens converted by Paul (Acts 17:34).

Diotrephes (dī-ot're-fēz; "nourished by Jupiter"). A person who opposed John's authority (3 John 9-10).

Diphath (dif'ath). *See* Riphath.

Dishan (dī'shan; "antelope" or "leaping"). A son of Seir (Gen. 36:21, 28, 30; 1 Chron. 1:38, 42). *See also* Dishon.

Dishon (dī'shon; "antelope" or "leaping"). [1] A son of Seir (Gen. 36:21, 30; 1 Chron. 1:38). [2] A grandson of Seir (Gen. 36:25; 1 Chron. 1:41). *See also* Dishan.

Dizahab (dīz'a-hab; "have gold"). A place near where Moses gave his farewell speech to the nation of Israel (Deut. 1:1); its exact location is unknown, but it may be Edh-Dheilbeh, east of Heshbon.

Dodai (dō'dī). *See* Dodo.

Dodanim [Rodanim] (dōd'a-nim [rod'a-nim]). The son of Javan (Gen. 10:4). First Chronicles 1:7 states his name as Rodanim; many scholars consider Rodanim to be original. Possibly a reference to the inhabitants of Rhodes and the neighboring islands.

Dodavah (dōd'a-va; "loved of Jehovah"). Father of Eliezer (2 Chron. 20:37).

Dodo [Dodai] (dō'do [dō'dī]; "beloved"). [1] The grandfather of Tola, a judge (Judg. 10:1). [2] A commander of one of the divisions of David's army and father of Eleazar [3] (2 Sam. 23:9; 1 Chron. 11:12; 27:4). [3] Father of Elhanan [2] (2 Sam. 23:24; 1 Chron. 11:26).

Doeg (dō'eg; "anxious; cared for"). A servant of King Saul who executed the priests of Nob on Saul's orders (1 Sam. 21:7; 22:9-19).

Dophkah (dof'ka; "drover"). A place in the wilderness of Sinai between the Red Sea and Rephidim (Num. 33:12-13).

Dor (dōr; "dwelling"). A Canaanite town on the Mediterranean coast about 13 km. (8 mi.) north of Caesarea (Josh. 11:2; 12:23).

Dorcas (dor'kas). *See* Tabitha.

Dothan (do'than; "two wells"). A city of the tribe of Manasseh west of the Jordan River and northeast of Samaria, near Mount Gilboa; here Joseph was sold into slavery (Gen. 37:17; 2 Kings 6:13).

Dragon Well [Jackal's Well]. A well located between the Dung Gate and the Valley Gate of Jerusalem (Neh. 2:13).

Drusilla (drū-sil'a; "watered by dew"). A Jewess, the daughter of Herod Agrippa I and wife of Felix; she and Felix heard a powerful message of Paul's (Acts 24:24-25).

Dumah (dū'ma; "silence"). A descendant of Ishmael (Gen. 25:14; 1 Chron. 1:30).

Dumah (dū'ma; "silence"). [1] A town in Judah (Josh. 15:52). [2] A symbolic name of Edom or a place in Arabia (Isa. 21:11).

Dung Gate. A gate in the southwest wall of Jerusalem (Neh. 2:13; 12:31).

Dura (dū'ra; "fortress"). The Babylonian plain where King Nebuchadnezzar set up a golden idol (Dan. 3:1).

E

East Land [East Country; Dawn Land]. A general reference to all of the lands east of Palestine; sometimes used to refer specifically to the Arabian and Syrian Deserts (Zech. 8:7).

East Sea. *See* Salt Sea.

Ebal [Obal] (ē'bal [ō'bal]; "bare" or "naked"). **[1]** A son of Shobal the Horite (Gen. 36:23; 1 Chron. 1:40). **[2]** A son of Joktan, descendant of Shem (1 Chron. 1:22). He is called Obal in Genesis 10:28. Possibly an Arabian people is meant.

Ebal (ē'bal; "stone"). A mountain beside Mount Gerizim (Deut. 27:12-13); modern Jebel Eslamiyeh.

Ebed (ē'bed; "servant"). **[1]** A companion of Ezra on his return to Jerusalem (Ezra 8:6). **[2]** Father of Gaal who rebelled against Abimelech (Judg. 9:26-35).

Ebed-Melech (ē'bed-mē'lek; "the king's servant"). An Ethiopian eunuch who rescued Jeremiah (Jer. 38:7-12; 39:16).

Eben-ezer (eb'en-ē'zer; "stone of help"). **[1]** The site of the defeat of Israel by the Philistines (1 Sam. 4:1-22). It was in the north of Sharon near Aphek. **[2]** Name of a stone Samuel erected to commemorate his victory over the Philistines (1 Sam. 7:12). The stone was possibly named after [1] to give the idea that Israel's defeat there had been reversed.

Eber (ē'ber; "the other side; across"). **[1]** A descendant of Shem and an ancestor of Christ (Gen. 10:21, 24-25; 11:14-17; Luke 3:35). His name occurs as Heber in Luke 3:35. Possibly the Hebrews and certain Aramean people are intended. **[2]** A descendant of Benjamin (1 Chron. 8:12). **[3]** Head of a priestly family (Neh. 12:20). *See* Heber.

Ebez (ē'bez). *See* Abez.

Ebiasaph (e-bī'a-saf). *See* Abiasaph.

Ebronah (eb-rō'na; "passage; opposite"). A stopping place for the Israelites in the wilderness just north of Ezion-Geber on the Gulf of Aqabah (Num. 33:34-35).

Eden (ē'den; "delight"). **[1]** A descendant of Gershom (2 Chron. 29:12). **[2]** A Levite in the time of Hezekiah (2 Chron. 31:15).

Eden (ē'den; "pleasure"). **[1]** The garden that God created as the first residence of man (Gen. 2:15); its exact location is unknown. It may have been between the Tigris and Euphrates Rivers near the head of the Persian Gulf. **[2]** A region in Mesopotamia (2 Kings 19:12; Isa. 37:12).

Eder (ē'der; "flock"). A grandson of Merari, son of Levi (1 Chron. 23:23; 24:30).

Eder [Edar] (ē'der [ē'dar]; "flock"). [1] A tower of possibly a town between Bethlehem and Hebon; Jacob once camped near here (Gen. 35:21). [2] A town of southern Judah about 7 km. (4.5 mi.) south of Gaza (Josh. 15:21); modern el-Adar.

Edom (ē'dom; "red"). Name given to Esau, the elder son of Isaac, because of his red skin (Gen. 25:30). *See* Esau; Obed-edom.

Edom (ē'dom; "red"). A mountainous region south of Moab, which stretches from the Dead Sea to the Gulf of Aqabah. It was settled by the descendants of Esau, the Edomites (Gen. 32:3; Exod. 15:15).

Edrei (ed're-ī; "fortress"). [1] The capital of Bashan; site of Israel's battle with Og (Deut. 3:10; Josh. 12:4). [2] A city of Naphtali between Kedesh and En-hazor (Josh. 19:37).

Eglah (eg'la; "calf"). One of David's wives (2 Sam. 3:5. 1 Chron. 3:3).

Eglaim (eg'la-im; "pond"). A town of Moab (Isa. 15:8).

Eglon (eg'lon; "circle"). A king of Moab who oppressed Israel in the days of the judges (Judg. 3:12-17).

Eglon (eg'lon; "of a calf"). A town in the lowlands of Judah (Josh. 15:39); its exact location is unknown.

Egypt (ē'jipt; "land of the soul of Ptah"). Northeast corner of Africa where the Israelites were held in bondage until Moses led them to the Promised Land (Gen. 45:9; 47:6).

Ehi (ē'hi). *See* Ahiram.

Ehud (ē'hud; "strong"). [1] A judge who delivered Israel from the oppression of Eglon of Moab (Judg. 3:15-30). [2] Great-grandson of Benjamin (1 Chron. 7:10; 8:6); perhaps the same as [1].

Eker (ē'ker; "root"). A descendant of Judah (1 Chron. 2:27).

Ekron (ek'ron; "migration"). The northernmost of the five chief cities of Palestine, apportioned to the tribe of Judah (Josh. 13:3); present-day 'Akir, located 10 km. (6 mi.) west of Gezer.

Eladah (el'a-da; "God is ornament"). A descendant of Ephraim (1 Chron. 7:20).

Elah (ē'la; "oak"). [1] A chieftain of Edom (Gen. 36:41; 1 Chron. 1:52). [2] Father of a commissary officer under Solomon (1 Kings 4:18). [3] The son and successor of Baasha, king of Israel. He was murdered by Zimri (1 Kings 16:6-14). [4] The father of Hoshea, last king of Israel (2 Kings 15:30; 17:1). [5] A son of Caleb, son of Jephunneh (1 Chron. 4:15). [6] A descendant of Benjamin (1 Chron. 9:8).

Elah (ē'la; "oak" or "terebinth"). A valley mentioned in First Samuel 17:2. Quite possibly the Wadi Es-Sant ("valley of the terebinth") or part of it is intended. Es-Sant is 11 mi. southwest of Jerusalem.

Elam (ē'lam; "high land"). [1] A son of Shem (Gen. 10:22; 1 Chron. 1:17). Many scholars consider the people of Elam, a region beyond the Tigris east of the Babylonia, to be intended. It was bounded on the north by Assyria and Media, on the south by the Persian Gulf, and on the east and southeast by Persia. [2] A descendant of Benjamin (1 Chron. 8:22). [3] A descendant of Korah (1 Chron. 16:3). [4] A leader of the people who sealed the new covenant with God after the Exile (Neh. 10:14). [5] A priest of Nehemiah's time who helped to cleanse Jerusalem (Neh. 12:42). [6] One whose descendants returned from the Exile (Ezra 2:7). [7] Another whose descendants returned from the Exile (Ezra 2:31). [8] Yet another whose descendants returned from the Exile (Ezra 8:7). [9] Ancestor of some who married foreign wives during the Exile (Ezra 10:2).

Elasah (el'a-sa; "God is doer"). [1] One who married a foreign wife (Ezra 10:22). [2] Ambassador of Zedekiah (Jer. 29:3). [3] *See* Eleasah.

Elath [Eloth] (e'lath [ē'loth]; "terebinth tree"). A major port city of the Gulf of Elath or Aqabah on the Red Sea (Deut. 2:8).

El-beth-el (el-beth'el; "God of Bethel"). Name Jacob gave the scene of his vision at Luz (Bethel) (Gen. 35:7).

Eldaah (el'da; "whom God calls"). A son of Midian (Gen. 25:4; 1 Chron. 1:33).

Eldad (el'dad; "God is a friend"). One of two elders who received the prophetic powers of Moses (Num. 11:26-27).

Elead (el'e-ad; "God is witness"). A descendant of Ephraim slain by invaders (1 Chron. 7:21).

Elealeh (e-le-a'le; "ascent of God"). A town of the tribe of Reuben about 3 km. (2 mi.) north-northeast of Heshbon (Num. 32:3); modern el-Al.

Eleasah (el-ē'a-sa; "God is doer"). [1] A descendant of Judah (1 Chron. 2:39-40). [2] A descendant of King Saul (1 Chron. 8:37; 9:43). *See* Elasah.

Eleazar (el-e-ā'zer; "God is helper"). [1] Third son of Aaron and successor to the high priest's office (Exod. 6:23; Num. 3:32; 20:28). [2] One sanctified to keep the ark of the covenant (1 Sam. 7:1). [3] One of David's mighty men (2 Sam. 23:9; 1 Chron. 11:12). [4] A descendant of Merari who had no sons (1 Chron. 23:21-22; 24:28). [5] A priest who accompanied Ezra when he returned to Jerusalem (Ezra 8:33). [6] A priest who assisted at the dedication of the walls of Jerusalem (Neh. 12:42); possibly the same as [5]. [7] An ancestor of Jesus (Matt. 1:15).

Eleph (e'lef; "ox"). A city of the tribe of Benjamin, near Jerusalem (Josh. 18:28).

Elhanan (el-hā'nan; "whom God gave; God is gracious"). [1] The warrior who killed Lahmi, the brother of Goliath (1 Chron. 20:5; 2 Sam. 21:19). [2] One of David's mighty men (2 Sam. 23:24; 1 Chron. 11:26).

Eli (ē'lī; "Jehovah is high"). High priest at Shiloh and judge of Israel. He is remembered for his lack of firmness (1 Sam. 1-4). *See also* Heli.

Eliab (e-lī'ab; "God is father"). [1] A prince of Zebulun (Num. 1:9;

2:7; 7:24, 29; 10:16). [2] Father of the wicked pair, Dathan and Abiram (Num. 16:1, 12; 26:8). [3] Son of Jesse and brother of David (1 Sam. 16:6); he is called Elihu in First Chronicles 27:18. [4] Ancestor of Samuel (1 Chron. 6:27); he is called Eliel in First Chronicles 6:34 and Elihu in First Samuel 1:1. [5] A warrior of David (1 Chron. 12:8-9, 14). [6] A Levite musician in the time of David (1 Chron. 15:18, 20; 16:5). [7] See Eliel.

Eliada [Eliadah] (e-lī a-da [e-lī′a-da]; "God is knowing"). [1] A mighty man of Jehoshaphat (2 Chron. 17:17). [2] Father of Rezon (1 Kings 11:23). [3] See Beeliada.

Eliah (e-lī′a). See Elijah.

Eliahba (e-lī′a-ba; "God hides"). One of David's 30-man guard (2 Sam. 23:32; 1 Chron. 11:33).

Eliakim (e-lī′a-kim; "God is setting up"). [1] Successor of Shebna as master of Hezekiah's household (2 Kings 18:18, 26; Isa. 22:20). [2] Original name of King Jehoiakim (q.v.). [3] A priest in Nehemiah's time (Neh. 12:41). [4] An ancestor of Christ (Matt. 1:13).

Eliam (ē′li-am; "my God is a kinsman; God is founder of the people"). [1] Father of Bathsheba (2 Sam. 11:3). By transposition of the two parts of the name he is called Ammiel (1 Chron. 3:5). [2] One of David's mighty men (2 Sam. 23:34).

Elias (e-lī′as). Greek form of Elijah (q.v.).

Eliasaph (e-lī′a-saf; "God is gatherer"). [1] Head of the tribe of Gad (Num. 1:14; 2:14; 7:42, 47). [2] A prince of Gershon (Num. 3:24).

Eliashib (e-lī′a-shib; "God is requiter"). [1] A priest in the time of David (1 Chron. 24:12). [2] A descendant of David (1 Chron. 3:24). [3] The high priest in Nehemiah's time (Neh. 3:1, 20-21). [4], [5], [6] Three men who married foreign wives during the Exile (Ezra 10:24, 27, 36). [7] One who assisted Ezra in resolving the matter of the foreign wives (Ezra 10:6; Neh. 12:10); possibly the same as [3].

Eliathah (e-li′a-tha; "God is come"). One appointed for the song service in the temple (1 Chron. 25:4, 27).

Elidad (e-lī′dad; "God is a friend"). A chief of the tribe of Benjamin (Num.34:21).

Eliel (ē′li-el; "God, my God"). [1] Head of a family of the tribe of Manasseh (1 Chron. 5:24). [2] A descendant of Benjamin (1 Chron. 8:20). [3] Another descendant of Benjamin in Chronicles (1 Chron. 8:22). [4] A captain of David's army (1 Chron. 11:46). [5] One of David's mighty men (1 Chron. 11:47). [6] One who joined David at Ziklag (1 Chron. 12:11); perhaps the same as [4] or [5]. [7] A chief of Judah (1 Chron. 15:9); perhaps [4]. [8] A chief Levite whom David commissioned to bring the ark of the covenant to the temple (1 Chron. 15:11). [9] The Levite overseer of the dedicated things of the temple under Hezekiah (2 Chron. 31:13). [10] See Eliab [4].

Elienai (el-i-ē′nī; "unto God are my eyes"). A chief of Benjamin (1 Chron. 8:20).

Eliezer (el-i-ē'zer; "God is help"). **[1]** Abraham's chief servant (Gen. 15:2). **[2]** The second son of Moses and Zipporah (Exod. 18:4; 1 Chron. 23:15, 17). **[3]** A descendant of Benjamin (1 Chron. 7:8). **[4]** A priest who assisted with bringing the ark of the covenant to the temple (1 Chron. 15:24). **[5]** A prince of Reuben in the time of David (1 Chron. 27:16). **[6]** A prophet who rebuked Jehoshaphat (2 Chron. 20:37). **[7]** A leader who induced others to return to Jerusalem (Ezra 8:16). **[8]**, **[9]**, **[10]** Three men who took foreign wives during the Exile (Ezra 10:18, 23, 31). **[11]** An ancestor of Christ (Luke 3:29).

Elihoenai (el-i-ho-ē'nī; "to Jehovah are my eyes"). Ancestor of some returned exiles (Ezra 8:4). *See also* Elioenai.

Elihoreph (el-i-hō'ref; "God of harvest grain"). A scribe of Solomon (1 Kings 4:3).

Elihu (e-lī'hū; "God himself"). **[1]** One who joined David at Ziklag (1 Chron. 12:20). **[2]** A porter at the tabernacle at the time of David (1 Chron. 26:7). **[3]** The youngest "friend" of Job (Job 32:2, 4-6). **[4]** *See* Eliab [3]. **[5]** *See* Eliab [4].

Elijah [Eliah; Elias] (e-lī'ja [e-lī'a; e-lī'as]; "Jehovah is my God"). **[1]** A great prophet of God; he strenuously opposed idolatry and was caught up in a chariot of fire at death (1 Kings 17:1—2 Kings 2:11; Matt. 17:3). **[2]** A chief of the tribe of Benjamin (1 Chron. 8:27). **[3]** One who married a foreign wife during the Exile (Ezra 10:26). **[4]** Another who took a foreign wife during the Exile (Ezra 10:21).

Elika (e-lī'ka; "God is rejector"). One of David's warriors (2 Sam. 23:25).

Elim (ē'lim; "oaks"). The second resting place of the Israelites after they crossed the Red Sea (Exod. 15:27; 16:1); probably the modern oasis of Wadi Gharandel, located 101 km. (63 mi.) from Suez.

Elimelech (e-lim'e-lek; "my God is King"). The husband of Naomi and father-in-law of Ruth. He died in Moab (Ruth 1:2-3; 2:1, 3; 4:3, 9).

Elioenai (e-li-o-ē'nī; "to Jehovah are my eyes"). **[1]** A descendant of David (1 Chron. 3:23-24). **[2]** A chief of the tribe of Simeon (1 Chron. 4:36). **[3]** A chief of Benjamin (1 Chron. 7:8). **[4]**, **[5]** Two men who had married foreign wives during the Exile (Ezra 10:22, 27). **[6]** A priest in the days of Nehemiah (Neh. 12:41); possibly the same as [4]. **[7]** A doorkeeper of the temple (1 Chron. 26:3). **[8]** *See* Elihoenai.

Eliphal (e-lī'fal; "God is judge"). One of David's mighty men (1 Chron. 11:35).

Eliphalet [Eliphelet; Elpalet] (e-lif'a-let [e-lif'e-let; el-pā'let]; "God is escape"). **[1]** The last of David's thirteen sons (2 Sam. 5:16; 1 Chron. 3:8; 14:7). **[2]** Another of David's sons (1 Chron. 3:6); called Elpalet in First Chronicles 14:5. **[3]** One of David's mighty men (2 Sam. 23:34). **[4]** A descendant of Benjamin and Saul (1 Chron. 8:39). **[5]** One who came back to Jerusalem with Ezra (Ezra 8:13). **[6]** One who took a foreign wife during the Exile (Ezra 10:33).

Eliphaz (el'i-faz; "God is dispenser"). [1] The leader of Job's three "friends" who confronted him (Job 2:11; 4:1; 15:1). [2] A son of Esau (Gen. 36:4, 10-12; 1 Chron. 1:35-36).

Elipheleh (e-lif'e-le; "Jehovah is distinction"). A Levite set over the choral service of the temple when the ark of the covenant was returned (1 Chron. 15:18, 21).

Eliphelet (e-lif'e-let). *See* Eliphalet.

Elisabeth (e-liz'a-beth; "God is swearer; oath of God"). The wife of Zacharias and mother of John the Baptist (Luke 1:5-57).

Eliseus (el-i-sē'us). Greek form of Elisha (q.v.).

Elisha [**Elishah; Eliseus**] (e-lī'sha [e-lī'sha; el-i-sē'us]; "God is Savior"). [1] The disciple and successor of Elijah: he held the prophetic office for 55 years (1 Kings 19:16-17, 19; 2 Kings 2-6; Luke 4:27). [2] Eldest son of Javan and grandson of Noah (Gen. 10:4). Possibly the people of Cyprus or the inhabitants of Alasiya, a country near Cilicia. Others suggest it includes the Italians and Peloponnesians.

Elishama (e-lish'a-ma; "God is hearer"). [1] Grandfather of Joshua (Num. 1:10; 2:18; 1 Chron. 7:26). [2] A son of King David (2 Sam. 5:16; 1 Chron. 3:8). [3] Another son of David (1 Chron. 3:6); also called Elishua in Second Samuel 5:15 and First Chronicles 14:5. [4] A descendant of Judah (1 Chron. 2:41). [5] One of the "royal seed" and grandfather of Gedaliah (2 Kings 25:25; Jer. 41:1). [6] A scribe or secretary of Jehoiakim (Jer. 36:12, 20-21). [7] A priest sent by Jehoshaphat to teach the Law (2 Chron. 17:8).

Elishaphat (e-lish'a-fat; "God is judge"). One of the captains of hundreds commissioned by Jehoiada (2 Chron. 23:1).

Elisheba (e-lish'e-ba; "God is swearer; God is an oath"). The wife of Aaron and mother of Nadab, Abihu, Eleazar, and Ithamar (Exod. 6:23).

Elishua (e-līsh-u-a; "God is rich"). *See* Elishama [3].

Eliud (e-lī'ud; "God my praise"). An ancestor of Jesus (Matt. 1:14-15).

Elizaphan [**Elzaphan**] (e-liz'a-fan [el'za-fan]; "God is protector"). [1] A chief of the family of Kohath (Num. 3:30; 1 Chron. 15:3); he is also called Elzaphan (Exod. 6:22; Lev. 10:4). [2] A prince of the tribe of Zebulun (Num. 34:25).

Elizur (e-lī'zur; "God is a rock"). A chief of the tribe of Reuben who assisted Moses in taking the census (Num. 1:5; 2:10; 7:30, 35).

Elkanah [**Elkonah**] (el-kā'na [el-kō'na]; "God is possessing"). [1] Grandson of Korah (Exod. 6:24; 1 Chron. 6:23). [2] Father of the prophet Samuel and a descendant of [1] (1 Sam. 1:1-23; 2:11, 20). [3] A descendant of Levi (1 Chron. 6:25, 36). [4] A descendant of Levi (1 Chron. 6:26, 35); perhaps the same as [3]. [5] A Levite ancestor of Berechiah (1 Chron. 9:16). [6] One who joined David at Ziklag

(1 Chron. 12:6). **[7]** A doorkeeper of the ark of the covenant (1 Chron. 15:23); perhaps the same as [6]. **[8]** An officer of King Ahaz (2 Chron. 28:7).

Elkosh (el'kosh; meaning unknown). The birthplace of Nathan the prophet (Nah. 1:1).

Ellasar (el-lā'sar; "oak"). A city of lower Babylonia, formerly known as Larsa (Gen. 14:1, 9); present-day Senkereh.

Elmodam (el-mō'dam; "measure"). An ancestor of Christ (Luke 3:28).

Elnaam (el-nā'am; "God is pleasant"). The father of two of David's warriors (1 Chron. 11:46).

Elnathan (el-nā'than; "God is giving"). **[1]** Father of Nehushta, Jehoiakim's queen (2 Kings 24:8; Jer. 26:22). **[2], [3], [4]** Three Levites in the time of Ezra (Ezra 8:16).

Elon (ē'lon; "oak; strong"). **[1]** Father of a wife of Esau (Gen. 26:34; 36:2). **[2]** A son of Zebulun (Gen. 46:14; Num. 26:26). **[3]** A judge of Israel for ten years (Judg. 12:11-12).

Elon (ē'lon; "oak; terebinth tree"). A city assigned to the tribe of Dan (Josh. 19:43); its exact location is unknown.

Elon-Beth-Hanan (ē'lon-beth-hā'nan; "oak of the house of grace"). One of three towns of the tribe of Dan that formed a district of King Solomon (1 Kings 4:9).

Eloth (ē'loth). *See* Elath.

Elpaal (el-pā'al; "God is working"). A descendant of Benjamin (1 Chron. 8:11-12).

Elpalet (el-pā'let). *See* Eliphalet [2].

El-Paran (el-pā'ran; "oak of Paran"). *See* Paran.

Eltekeh (el'te-keh; "grace"). A town of the tribe of Dan assigned to the Levites (Josh. 19:40, 44; 21:20, 23); probably modern Khirbet el-Mukanna, located about 10 km. (6 mi.) south-southeast of Akir (Ekron).

Eltekon (el'te-kon; meaning uncertain). A village in the hill country of Judah (Josh. 15:59); probably modern Khirbet el-Deir, located about 6 km. (4 mi.) west of Beer-sheba.

Eltolad (el-tō'lad; "kindred of God"). A town about 21 km. (13 mi.) southeast of Beer-sheba in southern Judah; appointed to the tribe of Simeon (Josh. 19:4) in First Chronicles 4:29 the city is simply called Tolad.

Eluzai (e-lū'zā-ī; "God is strong"). One who joined David at Ziklag (1 Chron. 12:5).

Elymas (el'i-mas "a sorcerer"). A false prophet who opposed Saul and Barnabas at Paphos (Acts 13:8); he was also called Bar-jesus (v. 6).

Elzabad (el'za-bad; "God is endowing"). **[1]** One who joined David at Ziklag (1 Chron. 12:12). **[2]** A descendant of Levi (1 Chron. 26:7).

Elzaphan (el'za-fan). *See* Elizaphan.

Emmaus (e-mā'us; "despised people"). A settlement about 16 km. (10 mi.) west of Jerusalem (Luke 24:13); its exact location is unknown.

Emmor (em'mor). Greek form of Hamor (q.v.).

Enam (ē'nam; "double fountains"). A village of lowland Judah near Jarmuth (Josh. 15:20, 34).

Enan (ē'nan; "eyes; fountain"). Father of a prince of Naphtali (Num. 1:15; 2:29).

En-dor (en'dor; "fountain of habitation"). A town of the tribe of Manasseh where Saul consulted a witch about his future (Josh. 17:11); probably modern Indur on the northeastern shoulder of the Little Hermon Mountain, 10 km. (6 mi.) southeast of Nazareth.

En-eglaim (en-eg'la-im "fountain of two calves"). A place on the northwestern coast of the Dead Sea (Ezek. 47:10).

En-gannim (en-gan'im; "fountain of gardens"). [1] A town of lowland Judah (Josh. 15:20, 34). [2] A border town of the tribe of Issachar, about 11 km. (7 mi.) southwest of Mount Gilboa (Josh. 19:21); sometimes called Anem (1 Chron. 6:73). Its modern name is Jenin.

En-gedi (en-gē'dī; "fountain of the goat"). A town on the western shore of the Dead Sea assigned to the tribe of Judah; originally called Hazazon-tamar (Josh. 15:62; 2 Chron. 20:2).

En-haddah (en-had'a; "flowing strongly"). A village of the tribe of Issachar, located about 10 km. (6 mi.) east of Mount Tabor (Josh. 19:21).

En-hakkore (en-hak'o-re; "well of the one who called"). A spring at

En-gedi. This spring of fresh water is En-gedi, where David hid from Saul (1 Sam. 23:29). Located in the northeast corner of the Negev Desert, the fountain creates an oasis rich with semi-tropical vegetation and celebrated for its palms, vineyards, and balsam (Song of Sol. 1:14).

Lehi, which God brought forth as an answer to Samson's prayer (Judg. 15:18-19).

En-hazor (en-hā'zor; "fountain of the village"). A fortified city of the tribe of Naphtali (Josh. 19:37). It has been identified with modern Khirbet Hasireh, near the ruins of Hazyter.

En-mishpat (en-mish'pat; "fountain of judgment"). *See also* Kadesh-barnea.

Enoch [Henoch] (ē'nuk [hē'nuk]; "teacher"). [1] The eldest son of Cain (Gen. 4:17-18). [2] A son of Jared and an ancestor of Christ (Gen. 5:18-19, 21; 1 Chron. 1:3; Luke 3:37; Heb. 11:5).

Enoch (ē'nuk; "initiated"). A city built by Cain (Gen. 4:17).

Enos [Enosh] (ē'nos [ē'nosh] "mortal"). Son of Seth and ancestor of Christ (Gen. 4:26; 5:6-11; 1 Chron. 1:1; Luke 3:38).

Enosh (ē'nosh). *See* Enos.

En-rimmon (en'rim'on). *See* Rimmon [1].

En-rogel (en-rō'gel; "fuller's fountain"). A spring outside the city of Jerusalem near the Hinnom Valley (2 Sam. 17:17).

En-shemesh (en-she'mesh; "eye of the sun"). A well and town east of Bethany on the road between Jerusalem and Jericho (Josh. 15:1, 7).

En-tappuah (en-tap'u-a; "apple spring"). A town on the border of Ephraim (Josh. 17:7-8).

Epaenetus (e-pē'ne-tus "praised"). A Christian at Rome to whom Paul sent greetings (Rom. 16:5).

Epaphras (ep'a-fras; shortened form of *Epaphroditus*—"lovely"). A Christian worker with Paul who served as missionary to Colossae (Col. 1:7; 4:12; Philem. 23).

Epaphroditus (e-paf-ro-dī'tus; "lovely"). A Philippian Christian who worked so strenuously that he lost his health (Phil. 2:25; 4:18).

Ephah (ē'fa; "obscurity"). [1] A concubine of Caleb (1 Chron. 2:46). [2] A descendant of Judah (1 Chron. 2:47). [3] A grandson of Abraham (Gen. 25:4; 1 Chron. 1:33).

Ephai (ē'fa; "obscuring"). One whose children were left in Judah after the Exile (Jer. 40:8).

Epher (ē'fer; "calf; young deer"). [1] A grandson of Abraham and son of Midian (Gen. 25:4; 1 Chron. 1:33). [2] One of the descendants of Judah (1 Chron. 4:17). [3] A chief of the tribe of Manasseh east of the Jordan River (1 Chron. 5:24).

Ephes-dammim [Pas-dammim] (ē'fes-dam'im [pas'dam'im]; "boundary of blood"). A Philistine settlement near Socoh, apportioned to the tribe of Judah (1 Sam. 17:1). It is called Pas-dammim ("portion of blood") in First Chronicles 11:13.

Ephesus (ef'e-sus; "desirable"). A town on the western coast of Asia Minor between Miletus and Smyrna; an important trading center (Acts 19:1).

Ephlal (ef'lal; "judging"). A descendant of Pharez through Jerahmeel (1 Chron. 2:37).

Ephod (ē-fod; "oracular"). Father of a prince of the tribe of Manasseh (Num. 34:23).

Ephraim (e'fra-im; "doubly fruitful"). The second son of Joseph by Asenath. Although Ephraim was the younger of the two sons of Joseph, he received the firstborn's blessing. He was an ancestor of one of the twelve tribes of Israel (Gen. 41:52; 46:20; 48; 50 23).

Ephraim (e'fra-im; "fruitful"). [1] The territory allotted to the tribe of Ephraim in the Promised Land (Num. 1:33). [2] A city near Baalhazor, probably the same as "Ephraim near the Wilderness" (2 Sam. 13:23; John 11:54). It is identified with modern et-Taiyibeh, about 6 km. (4 mi.) northeast of Bethel. [3] A gate on the north wall of old Jerusalem (2 Kings 14:13; 2 Chron. 25:23). [4] A rough area (not forest) where Absalom was slain (2 Sam. 18:6). [5] A mountain allotted to the tribe of Ephraim (1 Sam. 1:1).

Ephrain (e'fra-in; "fruitful"). A city that Abijah took from Jeroboam (2 Chron. 13:19); probably another name for Ephraim [2].

Ephratah [Ephrath] (ef'ra-ta [ef'rath]; "fertility"). The second wife of Caleb (1 Chron. 2:19, 50; 4:4).

Ephratah (ef'ra-ta). See Bethlehem [1].

Ephrath (ef'rath). See Bethlehem [1].

Ephron (ē'fron; "strong"). A Hittite from whom Abraham bought a field with a cave, which became Sarah's burial place (Gen. 23:8, 10, 13-14; 49:30).

Ephron (ē'fron; "dust"). A ridge of mountains between Nephtoah and Kirjath-jearim on the boundary between Judah and Benjamin (Josh. 15:1, 9).

Er (ur; "watcher"). [1] Eldest son of Judah, slain by God (Gen. 38:3, 6-7; 1 Chron. 2:3). [2] A son of Shelah (1 Chron. 4:21). [3] An ancestor of Jesus (Luke 3:28).

Eran (ē'ran; "watcher; watchful"). The son of Ephraim's oldest son (Num. 26:36).

Erastus (e-ras'tus; "beloved"). [1] Christian sent with Timothy into Macedonia while Paul stayed in Asia (Acts 19:22). [2] An important person in Corinth sending greetings to Rome (Rom. 16:23). [3] One who remained at Corinth (2 Tim. 4:20). Perhaps some or all of the above are identical.

Erech (ē'rek; "length"). A city built by Nimrod on the Plain of Shinar, south of Babylon (Gen. 10:10).

Eri (ē'rī; "watcher"). A son of Gad (Gen. 46:16; Num. 26:16).

Esaias (e-zā'yas). Greek form of Isaiah (q.v.).

Esarhaddon (e-sar-had'on; "Ashur has given a brother"). The son of Sennacherib and a powerful king of Assyria (2 Kings 19:37; Ezra 4:2; Isa. 37:38).

Esau (ē'so; "hairy"). Eldest son of Isaac and twin brother of Jacob. He is the progenitor of the tribe of Edom (Gen. 25:25). He sold his birthright to Jacob (Gen. 25:26-34; 27; 36).

Esau's Wives: There are two lists of Esau's wives—Genesis 26:34; 28:9 list them in this fashion: [1] Judith, the daughter of Beeri the Hittite. [2] Bashemath, daughter of Elon the Hittite and [3] Mahalath, the daughter of Ishmael, Abraham's son. The other list in Genesis 36:2-3 runs thus: [1] Aholibamah, the daughter of Anah the daughter of Zibeon. [2] Adah, the daughter of Elon the Hittite and [3] Bashemath, the daughter of Ishmael. Some scholars suppose we are dealing with six women, but this seems unlikely. In the ancient world, many women received new names at marriage and this fact would account for the different names. Thus, [1] Judith is Aholibamah, [2] Bashemath is Adah, and [3] Mahalath is Bashemath. As far as Judith is concerned, Beeri might be her father and Anah her mother; or perhaps Anah is another name of Beeri. Some even think Beeri ("man of the springs") is a nickname rather than a proper name.

Esek (ē'sek; "strife"). A well dug by Isaac in the Valley of Gerar; claimed by the Philistines (Gen. 26:20).

Eshan (ē'shan; "support"). A mountain village near Dumah, about 16 km. (10 mi.) from Hebron; apportioned to the tribe of Judah (Josh. 15:52).

Esh-baal (esh'ba-al; "man or servant of Baal"). Altered to a curse. *See* Ish-bosheth.

Eshban (esh'ban; "man of understanding"). Son of Dishon (Gen. 36:26; 1 Chron. 1:41).

Eshcol (esh'kol; "a cluster of grapes"). The brother of Mamre and Aner who helped Abraham defeat Chedorlaomer (Gen. 14:13-24).

Eshcol (esh'kol; "cluster of grapes"). A valley north of Hebron, famous for its grapes (Num. 13:24).

Eshean (esh'e-an). *See* Eshan.

Eshek (ē'shek; "oppressor"). A descendant of King Saul (1 Chron. 8:39).

Eshtaol (esh'ta-ol; "way"). A settlement in the hills of Judah about 21 km. (13 mi.) west of Jerusalem; burial place of Samson (Josh. 15:33; Judg. 13:25).

Eshtemoa (esh-te-mō'a; "bosom of women"). A Maacathite, a son of Ishbah (1 Chron. 4:17, 19).

Eshtemoa [Eshtemoh] (esh-te-mō'a [esh-te-mō]; "bosom of women"). A village in the hill country of Judah about 14 km. (9 mi.) south of Hebron, famed for its prophetic oracle (Josh. 15:20, 50).

Eshton (esh'ton; "rest"). A descendant of Judah through Caleb (1 Chron. 4:11-12).

Esli (es'lī; "reserved"). An ancestor of Christ (Luke 3:25).

Esrom (ez'rom). Greek form of Hezron (q.v.).

Esther (es'ter; "star; [the goddess Ishtar]"). The Persian name of Hadassah, who was chosen by Ahasuerus to be his queen. The Book of Esther tells her story.

Etam (ē'tam; "wild beast's lair"). A name occurring in Judah's genealogy list (1 Chron. 4:3). It may be a place name.

Etam (ē'tam; "lair"). **[1]** A town of the tribe of Simeon (1 Chron. 4:32); identified with modern 'Aitun, about 18 km. (11 mi.) west-southwest of Hebron. **[2]** A cleft of rock near Zorah (Judg. 15:8, 11). **[3]** A resort town near Jerusalem, used by King Solomon (2 Chron. 11:6); Josephus wrote that it was located about 11 km. (7 mi.) from Jerusalem.

Etham (ē'tham; "sea-bound"). A place where the Israelites camped before they entered the wilderness of Sinai (Exod. 13:20; Num. 33:6); apparently it was located north of Timsah Lake.

Ethan (ē'than; "ancient"). **[1]** A wise man in the days of Solomon (1 Kings 4:31; Psa. 89 title). **[2]** A descendant of Judah (1 Chron. 2:6, 8). He is possibly identical with [1]. **[3]** See Jeduthun. **[4]** A descendant of Levi (1 Chron. 6:42).

Ethbaal (eth'ba-al; "Baal's man; with Baal"). King of Sidon and father of Ahab's wife Jezebel (1 Kings 16:31).

Ether (ē'ther; "plenty"). **[1]** A village of the tribe of Judah located within 3 km. (2 mi.) of modern Beit-Jibrin (Josh. 15:42). **[2]** A village of the tribe of Simeon (Josh. 19:7), sometimes called Tochen (1 Chron. 4:32). This is probably modern Khirbet 'Attic, 25 km. (15.5 mi.) northeast of Beer-sheba.

Ethiopia [Cush?] (e-thi-ō'pi-a [Kush]; "burnt face"). A nation located in the upper region of the Nile River (Psa. 68:31; Isa. 18:1). It is not the same as modern Ethiopia. See also Cush.

Ethnan (eth'nan; "gift"). Grandson of Ashur through Caleb, son of Hur (1 Chron. 4:7).

Ethni (eth'ni; "my gift"). One whom David set over the song service of the temple (1 Chron. 6:41).

Eubulus (u-bū'lus; "of good counsel"). One of the Roman Christians that remained loyal to Paul (2 Tim. 4:21).

Eunice (u-nī'se; "conquering well"). The pious mother of Timothy (2 Tim. 1:5; cf. Acts 16:1).

Euodias (u-ō'di-as; "fragrant"). A Christian woman at Philippi (Phil. 4:2). The KJV is mistaken at this point, giving a man's name for a woman's. The name should read *Euodia*.

Euphrates (u-frā'tēz; meaning unknown). A major river of western Asia, which begins in Armenia and joins the Tigris River before flowing into the Persian Gulf. It formed the western boundary of Mesopotamia (Gen. 2:14; 15:18).

Eutychus (u'ti-kus; "fortunate"). A young man at Troas whom Paul restored to life (Acts 20:6-12).

Eve (ēv; "life; life-giving"). The first woman, Adam's wife (Gen. 3:20; 4:1; 2 Chron. 11:3).

Evi (ē'vī; "desire"). One of the five kings of Midian slain by Israel (Num. 31:8; Josh. 13:21).

Evil-merodach (ē'vil-me-rō'dak; Babylonian, Arvil-Marduk—"the man of [the god] Marduk"). The king of Babylon who released Jehoiachin from imprisonment. He succeeded his father, Nebuchadnezzar (2 Kings 25:27-30; Jer. 52:31).

Ezar (ē'zar). *See* Ezer [6].

Ezbai (ez'bā-ī; "shining; beautiful"). The father of one of David's mighty men (1 Chron. 11:37).

Ezbon (ez'bon; "bright"). [1] A son of Gad (Gen. 46:16), called Ozni ("Jehovah hears") in Numbers 26:16. [2] A descendant of Benjamin (1 Chron. 7:7).

Ezekias (ez-e-kī'as). Greek form of Hezekiah (q.v.).

Ezekiel (e-zēk'yel; "God strengthens"). A prophet of a priestly family carried captive to Babylon. He prophesied to the exiles in Mesopotamia by the river Chevar, and is the author of the book bearing his name (Ezek. 1:3; 24:24).

Ezel (ē'zel; "division; separation"). A craggy hiding place of David during his rebellion against Saul (1 Sam. 20:19).

Ezem [Azem] (ē'zem [ā'zem]; "bone"). A village about 5 km. (3 mi.) south of Beer-sheba, near the border of Edom (Josh. 15:29).

Ezer (ē'zer; "help"). [1] A son of Ephraim slain by the inhabitants of Gath (1 Chron. 7:21). [2] A priest in Nehemiah's time (Neh. 12:42). [3] A descendant of Judah through Caleb (1 Chron. 4:4); perhaps the same as Ezra [2]. [4] A valiant man who joined David at Ziklag (1 Chron. 12:9). [5] A Levite who assisted in repairing the wall of Jerusalem (Neh. 3:19). [6] ("union"), a son of Seir (Gen. 36:21, 27, 30;

Where Felix and Festus held court. Scattered columns, broken walls, and a large open well are the only remains of Caesarea Maritima, the lavish Roman port where Felix and Festus heard Paul's testimony (Acts 24-26). Paul remained imprisoned in this city for about two years before facing the emperor in Rome.

1 Chron. 1:42); he is also called Ezar (1 Chron. 1:38). *See* Abi-ezer; Romamti-ezer.

Ezion-geber [**Ezion-gaber**] (ē'zi-on-gē'ber [ē'zi-on-gā'ber]; "giant's backbone"). A village west of the port of Elath on the Gulf of Aqaba (Num. 33:35).

Ezra (ez'ra; "help"). [1] Head of one of the courses of priests that returned from the Exile (Neh. 12:1). The full form of his name, *Azariah*, occurs in Nehemiah 10:2. [2] A descendant of Judah through Caleb (1 Chron. 4:17). *See* Ezer [3]. [3] A prominent scribe and priest descended from Hilkiah the high priest (Ezra 7:1-12; 10:1; Neh. 8:1-13). *See* Azariah.

Ezri (ez'rī; "my help"). One of David's superintendents of farm workers (1 Chron. 27:26).

F

Fair Havens. An anchorage on the southern coast of the island of Crete, near Lasea (Acts 27:8).

Felix (fē'lix; "happy"). Roman governor of Judea that presided over the trial of Paul at Caesarea (Acts 23:23-27; 24:22-27).

Festus (fes'tus; "swine-like"). Successor of Felix to the governorship of Judea. He continued the trial of Paul begun under Felix (Acts 25; 26).

Fortunatus (for-tu-na'tus "fortunate"). A Corinthian Christian who cheered and comforted Paul at Ephesus (1 Cor. 16:17-18).

G

Gaal (gā'al; "rejection"). A son of Ebed. He tried to lead a rebellion against Abimelech (Judg. 9:26-41).

Gaash (gā'ash; "earthquake"). A hill in the territory of Ephraim, just south of Timnath-serah; the burial place of Joshua (Josh. 24:30).

Gaba (gā'ba). *See* Geba.

Gabbai (gab'a-ī; "collector"). A chief of the tribe of Benjamin after the return from the Exile (Neh. 11:8).

Gabbatha (gab'a-tha; "pavement"). An open space at the front of Herod's temple in Jerusalem, where Pontius Pilate sat to judge Jesus Christ (John 19:13).

Gad (gad; "fortune"). [1] The seventh son of Jacob and an ancestor of one of the twelve tribes (Gen. 30:11; 49:19). [2] David's seer who frequently advised him (1 Sam. 22:5; 1 Chron. 21:9-19).

Gad (gad; "lot; fortune"). The territory settled by the tribe of Gad, east of the Jordan River (1 Sam. 13:7; Josh. 13:24).

Gadara (gad'a-ra; "walls"). A town located east of the Jordan River, 11 km. (7 mi.) south of the Sea of Galilee (Mark 5:1; Luke 8:26). It was one of the Decapolis cities (q.v.). *See also* Gergesa.

Gaddi (gad'ī; "my fortune"). One of those sent to spy out Canaan (Num. 13:11).

Gaddiel (gad'i-el; "fortune of God"). One of the spies (Num. 13:10).

Gadi (gā'dī; "fortunate"). Father of King Menahem of Israel (2 Kings 15:14, 17).

Gaham (gā'ham; "blackness"). A son of Nahor (Gen. 22:24).

Gahar (gā'har; "prostration; concealment"). One whose family returned from captivity (Ezra 2:47; Neh. 7:49).

Gai (gā'ī). *See* Gath.

Gaius (gā'yus; "lord"). [1] One to whom John's third epistle is addressed (3 John 1). [2] A native of Macedonia and a companion of Paul (Acts 19:29). [3] A man of Derbe who accompanied Paul as far as Asia (Acts 20:4). [4] The host to Paul when he wrote to the Romans (Rom. 16:23). [5] A convert whom Paul baptized at Corinth (1 Cor. 1:14); some think he is identical with [4].

Galal (ga'lal; "great; rolling"). [1] A returned exile (1 Chron. 9:15). [2] A Levite who returned from the Exile (1 Chron. 9:16; Neh. 11:17).

Galatia (ga-lā'shi-a; "land of Galli"). A district of central Asia Minor (Acts 16:6).

Galeed (gal'e-ed). *See* Jegar-sahadutha.

Galilee (gal'i-lē; "circle"). One of the largest Roman districts of Palestine; the primary region of Jesus' ministry (Luke 3:1; 23:6).

Galilee, Sea of. A large lake in northern Palestine, fed by the Jordan River; several of Jesus' disciples worked as fishermen on this lake (John 6:1). The lake was also known as the Sea of Chinnereth (q.v.), the Sea of Tiberias, and the Sea of Gennesaret (q.v.). *See also* Chinnereth [1] and Gennesaret [2].

Gallim (gal'im; "heaps"). A village near Gibeah of Saul (Isa. 10:29-30; 1 Sam. 25:44); probably modern Kirbet Ka'Kūl.

Gallio (gal'i-ō; meaning unknown). Roman proconsul of Achaia before whom Paul was tried in Corinth (Acts 18:12-17).

Gamaliel (ga-mā'li-el; "reward or recompense of God"). [1] A prince of the tribe of Manasseh (Num. 1:10; 2:20). [2] A great Jewish teacher of the Law. He persuaded his fellow Jews to let the apostles go free (Acts 5:33-40; 22:3).

Gamul (gā'mul; "weaned"). A chief priest (1 Chron. 24:17).

Gareb (ga'reb; "reviler; despiser"). One of David's mighty men (2 Sam. 23:38; 1 Chron. 11:40).

Gareb (ga'reb; "scab"). A hill in the vicinity of Jerusalem (Jer. 31:39).

Gashmu (gash'mu). *See* Geshem.

Gatam (gā'tam; "burnt valley"). An Edomite chief, grandson of Esau (Gen. 36:11, 16; 1 Chron. 1:36).

Sea of Galilee. This freshwater lake, fed by the Jordan River, is enclosed by hills except where the Jordan enters and leaves. Called a "sea" because of its considerable size, the lake is below sea level and has a semi-tropical climate. Violent storms can suddenly sweep down onto the lake from nearby Mount Hermon.

Gath (gath; "wine press"). One of the five chief Philistine cities; home of the giant Goliath (1 Sam. 17:4; 2 Kings 12:17; 2 Chron. 26:6). Its exact location is not known.

Gath-hepher [Gittah-hepher] (gath-hē'fer [git-a-hē'fer]; "wine press of digging"). A city of the tribe of Zebulun, located about 5 km. (3 mi.) northeast of Nazareth; home of the prophet Jonah (Josh. 19:13; 2 Kings 14:25).

Gath-rimmon (gath-rim'on; "pomegranate press"). [1] A city of the tribe of Dan assigned to the Levites; it probably was located on the Plain of Joppa (Josh. 19:45; 1 Chron. 6:69). [2] A town of the tribe of Manasseh, assigned to the Levites (Josh. 21:25); probably the same as Bileam.

Gaza [Azzah] (gā'za [az'zah]; "strong"). [1] The southernmost of the five chief Philistine cities, located 72 km. (44.5 mi.) south of modern Jaffa and 4 km. (2.4 mi.) from the Mediterranean Sea. It was the scene of Samson's exploits (Josh. 11:22; Judg. 16:1-3; 2 Kings 18:8; Jer. 25:20). [2] A town of the tribe of Ephraim located on a small plain near Shiloh (1 Chron. 7:28).

Gazer (gā'zer). *See* Gezer.

Gazez (gā'zez; "shearer"). [1] A son of Caleb (1 Chron. 2:46). [2] A grandson of Caleb (1 Chron. 2:46).

Gazzam (gāz'am; "devourer; swaggerer"). One whose descendants returned (Ezra 2:48; Neh. 7:51).

Geba [Gaba] (gē'ba [gā'ba]; "hill"). A Benjamite city in the extreme northern portion of Judah, about 10 km. (6 mi.) north-northeast of Jerusalem (Josh. 18:24); modern Jeba'.

Gebal (gē'bal; "mountain"). **[1]** A Phoenician seaport 68 km. (42 mi.) north of Sidon; also called Byblos (Ezek. 27:9). **[2]** The northern portion of the mountains of Edom (Psa. 83:7).

Geber (gē'ber; "man; strong one"). **[1]** The father of one of Solomon's officers (1 Kings 4:13). **[2]** One of Solomon's commissaries (1 Kings 4:19).

Gebim (gē'bim; "ditches"). A settlement just north of Jerusalem near Michmash (Isa. 10:31).

Gedaliah (ged-a-lī'a; "Jehovah is great"). **[1]** Governor of Jerusalem after the Exile (2 Kings 25:22; Jer. 40:5-6). **[2]** A Levite musician (1 Chron. 25:3, 9). **[3]** A priest who had married a foreign wife during the Exile (Ezra 10:18). **[4]** A chief of Jerusalem that imprisoned Jeremiah (Jer. 20:1-6). **[5]** Grandfather of the prophet Zephaniah (Zeph. 1:1).

Gedeon (ged'e-on). Greek form of Gideon (q.v.).

Ruins of Gebal. King Solomon hired stone masons from the Phoenician coastal city of Gebal (later called Byblos) to help build the temple in Jerusalem (1 Kings 5:18, RSV). Their skill is evidenced by these stone monuments at Gebal, 40 km. (25 mi.) north of Beirut. The craftsmen of Gebal also had a reputation for shipbuilding (Ezek. 27:9).

Geder (gē′der; "wall"). A town in the extreme southern portion of Judah, captured by Joshua (Josh. 12:13); perhaps the same as modern Beth-gador or Gedor.

Gederah (ge-de′ra; "sheepfold"). A town in the lowlands of Judah, 6 km. (4 mi.) northwest of Zorah (Josh. 15:36); modern Jedireh.

Gederoth (ged′e-roth; "sheepfolds"). A town in the lowlands of Judah, about 6 km. (4 mi.) southwest of Ekron (Josh. 15:41); modern Katrah.

Gederothaim (ged′e-ro-thā′im; "two sheepfolds"). A town of Judah (Josh. 15:36), perhaps the same as Gederoth.

Gedor (gē′dor; "wall"). [1] An ancestor of Saul (1 Chron. 8:31). [2] A descendant of Judah (1 Chron. 4:4). [3] A descendant of Judah (1 Chron. 4:18).

Gedor (gē′dor; "wall"). [1] A town in the hills of Judah about 11 km. (7 mi.) northwest of Hebron (Josh. 15:58). [2] A town of the tribe of Simeon, near the southwestern limits of Palestine (1 Chron. 4:39). [3] A village in the territory of Benjamin (1 Chron. 12:7); modern Khirbet el-Judeira.

Geharashim (gi-har′a-shim). See Charashim.

Gehazi (ge-hā′zī; "valley of vision; diminisher"). The dishonest servant of Elisha (2 Kings 4:12-37; 5:20-27; 8:4).

Geliloth (gel′i-lōth; "circles"). A landmark on the southern boundary of Benjamin (Josh. 18:17). See also Gilgal [4].

Gemalli (ge-mal′i; "camel owner"). Father of Ammiel (Num. 13:12).

Gemariah (gem-a-rī′a; "Jehovah has accomplished"). [1] One who sought to stop Jehoiakim from burning Jeremiah's prophecies (Jer. 36:10-12, 25). [2] One of Zedekiah's ambassadors to Babylon (Jer. 29:3).

Gennesaret (ge-nes′a-ret; "garden of the prince"). [1] The region on the northwest shore of the Sea of Galilee (Matt. 14:34). [2] Another name for the Sea of Galilee (Luke 5:1).

Genubath (ge-nū′bath; "theft"). A son of Hadad the Edomite (1 Kings 11:20).

Gera (gē′ra; "enmity" or "grain"). [1] A son of Benjamin (Gen. 46:21). [2] A son of Bela (1 Chron. 8:3, 5, 7). [3] Father of Ehud (Judg. 3:15). [4] Father or ancestor of Shimei (2 Sam. 16:5; 19:16, 18; 1 Kings 2:8). [Note: All of these may be identical.]

Gerar (gē′rar; "halting place"). A Philistine city on the southern edge of Palestine, near Gaza (Gen. 26:1; 2 Chron. 14:13); its exact location is unknown.

Gergesa (gur′ge-sa; "pilgrims"). A town or district which would have been located on the eastern side of the Lake of Galilee. Its location is not certain, but some have suggested modern-day Kersa (Matt. 8:28). Some scholars have questioned the reliability of the Gospel accounts of the healing of the demoniac, for Matthew says that it occurred in Gergesa while Mark 5:1 and Luke 8:26 say that it

Mount Gerizim and Mount Ebal. As the Israelites prepared to enter the Promised Land, Joshua gathered them in front of Gerizim (1) and Ebal (2) to hear him read the Law of Moses (Josh. 8:30-35). The two mountains form a natural amphitheater, where thousands of people could have listened to Joshua's voice.

occurred in Gadara. However, this really is no problem for Gadara was a strong city and probably had economic and political influence over the entire area.

Gerizim (ger'i-zīm; "cutters; wasteland"). A steep mountain in central Palestine facing Mount Ebal (Deut. 11:29); its peak is 872 m. (2,840 ft.) above sea level.

Gershom (gur-shom; "exile"). [1] Firstborn son of Moses and Zipporah (Exod. 2:22; 18:3). [2] *See* Gershon. [3] A descendant of Phinehas (Ezra 8:2). [4] Father of Jonathan, a Levite during the time of the judges (Judg. 18:30).

Gershon [Gershom] (gur'shun [gur'shom]; "exile"). An important priest, the eldest son of Levi (Gen. 46:11; Exod. 6:16; 1 Chron. 6:1). He is also called Gershom (1 Chron. 6:16-17, 20; 15:7).

Gesham (ge'sham; "firm"). A descendant of Caleb (1 Chron. 2:47).

Geshem [Gashmu] (ge'shem [gash'mu]; "rainstorm" or "corporealness"). An Arabian opponent of Nehemiah (Neh. 2:19; 6:1-2).

Geshur (ge'shur; "bridge"). An Aramean kingdom just east of Maacah, between Mount Hermon and the district of Bashan. Absalom sought refuge here after he killed his half-brother Amnon (2 Sam. 3:3; 13:37).

Gether (ge'ther) [1] A descendant of Shem (1 Chron. 1:17). Possibly an unknown family of Arameans is meant. [2] The third of Aram's sons (Gen. 10:23).

Gethsemane (geth-sem'a-nē; "oil press"). A garden east of Jerusalem, beyond the brook Kidron at the foot of Mount Olivet; the site of Christ's betrayal (Matt. 26:36-56).

Geuel (ge-ū'el; "salvation of God"). The spy sent out from Gad to bring back word about Canaan (Num. 13:15).

Gezer [Gazer] (gez'er [gā'zer]; "dividing"). A Canaanite town beside the Mediterranean Sea near Lachish and Lower Beth-horon; a battleground in King David's wars (2 Sam. 5:25; 1 Chron. 14:16).

Giah (gī'ah; "waterfall"). A settlement between Gibeon and a ford across the Jordan River (2 Sam. 2:24).

Gibbar (gib'ar; "high; mighty"). One who returned to Jerusalem with Zerubbabel (Ezra 2:20).

Gibbethon (gib'e-thon; "high house"). A village of the tribe of Dan where Nadab was assassinated (Josh. 19:44; 1 Kings 15:27); probably modern Tell el-Milat, directly east of Ekron.

Gibea (gib'e-a; "highlander"). A descendant of Caleb (1 Chron. 2:49).

Gibeah (gib'e-a; "hill"). [1] A Judean town about 16 km. (10 mi.) northwest of Hebron (Josh. 15:57). [2] A town midway between Jerusalem and Ramah; home and capital of King Saul (1 Sam. 10:26; 15:34). The town is called Gibeath in Joshua 18:28. [3] A town or hill in the territory of Ephraim (Josh. 24:33); probably near Timnah [1]. [4] A hill in Kiriath-jearim on which was located the house of Abinadad (2 Sam. 6:3-4).

Gibeon (gib'e-on; "hill height"). The chief city of the Hivites, assigned to the tribe of Benjamin; located 9 km. (5.5 mi.) north-northwest of Jerusalem (Josh. 11:19; 2 Sam. 20:1-9). Its modern name is El-Jib.

Giddalti (gi-dal'tī; "I have magnified"). A son of Heman in charge of one of the courses at the temple (1 Chron. 25:4).

Giddel (gid'el; "very great"). [1] One whose descendants returned

Gibeon (?) Archaeologists believe that this site, known as el-Jib, is the biblical Gibeon. God instructed Joshua to destroy all of the people of Canaan when the Israelites took the land, but the people of Gibeon tricked him into making a treaty with them. Neighboring Amorite kings attacked Gibeon for defecting to the Israelites, and Joshua came to their aid. God granted a hailstorm and an extension of the daylight hours to help Joshua defeat the Amorites (Josh. 9-10; 11:19). The treaty remained in force during the time of Saul and David. When the Gibeonites demanded justice for murders that Saul had committed there, David gave them seven of Saul's sons to be executed (2 Sam. 21:1-11).

to Jerusalem with Zerubbabel (Ezra 2:47; Neh. 7:49). **[2]** Head of a family of Solomon's servants (Ezra 2:56; Neh. 7:58).

Gideon [Gedeon] (gid'e-on [ged'e-on]; "feller [i.e., great warrior]"). The great judge of Israel who delivered his people from Midian (Judg. 6–8); he was given the name Jerubbaal (q.v.).

Gideoni (gid-e-ō'ni; "feller"). A descendant of Benjamin (Num. 1:11; 2:22).

Gidom (gī'dom; "desolation"). A village of the tribe of Benjamin, located between Gibeah [1] and Rimmon [2] (Judg. 20:45).

Gihon (gī'hon; "stream; bursting forth"). **[1]** One of the four rivers of Eden [1] (Gen. 2:13). **[2]** An intermittent spring outside the walls of Jerusalem, south of the temple area (1 Kings 1:38-45; 2 Chron. 32:30).

Gilalai (gil'a-lī; "rolling; weighty"). One of a party of priests who played on David's instruments at the consecration of the Jerusalem walls under Ezra (Neh. 12:36).

Gilboa (gil-bō'a; "hill country"). A mountain overlooking the Plain of Jezreel; site of King Saul's death (1 Sam. 28:4; 31:1); modern Jebel Fuku'a.

Gilead (gil'e-ad; "strong; rocky"). **[1]** A son of Machir (Num. 26:29-30). **[2]** Father of Jephthah the judge (Judg. 11:1-2). **[3]** A descendant of Gad (1 Chron. 5:14).

Gilead (gil'e-ad; "strong; rocky; rough"). A region east of the Jordan River, stretching from Moab to the Yarmuk River (Deut. 3:16-17). **[2]** A mountain jutting onto the Plain of Jezreel (Judg. 7:3). **[3]** A city in the region of Gilead (Hos. 6:8).

Gilgal (gil'gal; "rolling"). **[1]** The first campsite of the Israelites after they crossed the Jordan River into Canaan, probably near Jericho (Josh. 4:19-24). **[2]** A village 11 km. (7 mi.) northeast of Bethel, from which Elijah and Elisha began their journey (2 Kings 2:1-4; 4:38); present-day Jiljilia. **[3]** A town on the edge of the Plain of Sharon, about 8 km. (5 mi.) north-northeast of Antipatris (Josh. 10:6-9, 15). **[4]** A place on the northern boundary of Judah, near Debir (Josh. 15:7); perhaps the same as Geliloth.

Giloh (gī'lo; "he that overturns"). A town in the hill country of Judah, 8 km. (5 mi.) north-northwest of Hebron (Josh. 15:51).

Gimzo (gim'zo; "sycamore"). A town of northern Judah, about 5 km. (3 mi.) southeast of Lydda (2 Chron. 28:18); modern Jimzu.

Ginath (gī'nath; "protection"). Father of Tibni (1 Kings 16:21-22).

Ginnetho [Ginnethon] (gin'e-tho [gin'e-thon]; "great protection"). A prince or priest who sealed the new covenant with God after the Exile (Neh. 10:6; 12:4, 16).

Ginnethon (gin'e-thon). *See* Ginnetho.

Gispa (gis'pa; "listening; attentive"). An overseer of the Nethinim (Neh. 11:21).

Gittah-hepher (git'a-hē'fer) *See* Gath-hepher.

Gittaim (git'a-im "two winepresses"). A Benjamite town of refuge near Beeroth (Neh. 11:33); probably the site of modern el-Ramleh.

Goath (gō'ath; "constancy"). A site near Jerusalem (Jer. 31:39); its exact location is unknown.

Gob (gob; "cistern"). A site of several battles during Israel's wars with the Philistines (2 Sam. 21:18); its exact location is unknown, but may be the same as Gezer or Gath.

Gog (gog; "high; mountain"). [1] A descendant of Reuben (1 Chron. 5:4). [2] A prince of Rosh, Meshech, and Tubal (Ezek. 38:2; 39:1, 11). In Revelation 20:7 Gog appears to have become a nation as is Magog, thus indicating the name is to be understood symbolically. *See also* Magog.

Golan (gō'lan; "passage"). A city of Bashan east of the Jordan River, assigned to the Levites as a city of refuge (Deut. 4:43; Josh. 21:27). It is probably the site of modern Sam el-Jaulan, 27 km. (17 mi.) east of the Sea of Galilee.

Golgotha [Calvary] (gol'go-tha; "skull"). A hill just outside the walls of ancient Jerusalem; the site of Jesus' crucifixion (Matt. 27:33; John 19:17). Its exact location is unknown, but it was probably inside the walls of what is now called the "old city."

Goliath (go-lī'ath; "an exile or soothsayer"). [1] The Philistine giant who was slain by David (1 Sam. 17:4-54). [2] Another giant, possibly the son of [1] (2 Sam. 21:19).

Gomer (gō'mer). [1] Eldest son of Japheth (Gen. 10:2-3; 1 Chron. 1:5-6). Possibly a people inhabiting the north, probably including or identical with the Cimmerians of classical history. [2] The immoral wife of Hosea (Hos. 1:3; 3:1-4).

Gomorrah (go-mor'ra; "submersion"). One of the five Cities of the Plain destroyed along with Sodom (Gen. 18:20; 19:24, 28). Many scholars believe it was submerged by the southeastern tip of the Dead Sea.

Goshen (gō'shen; "drawing near"). [1] A cattle-raising district of the Nile delta assigned to the Israelites before they were placed in bondage (Gen. 46:28). [2] A town in the hill country of Judah (Josh. 15:51); probably modern Dahariyeh, about 21 km. (13 mi.) southwest of Hebron. [3] A region of Judah that probably derived its name from the town of Goshen (Josh. 10:41; 11:16).

Gozan (gō'zan; "food"). A district and town of Mesopotamia, located on the Habor River (2 Kings 17:6; 18:11). The KJV refers to it as a river, but this does not seem likely.

Greece [Grecia] (grēs [grē'shi-a]; meaning uncertain). A country of Southern Europe between Italy and Asia Minor; one of the most powerful nations of the ancient world (Dan. 8:21; Zech. 9:13; Acts 16:1).

Gudgodah (gud-gō'da; "incision"). A place where the Israelites camped in the wilderness, near En-gedi (Deut. 10:7); perhaps the same as Hor-hagidgad (q.v.).

Guni (gū'nī; "protected"). [1] Son of Naphtali found in three lists (Gen. 46:24; Num. 26:48; 1 Chron. 7:13). [2] Father of Abdiel (1 Chron. 5:15).

Gur (gur; "whelp"). A hill near Ibleam where Jehu killed Ahaziah (2 Kings 9:27).

Gur-baal (gur-bā'al; "dwelling place of Baal"). A desert district south of Beer-sheba between Canaan and the Arabian peninsula (2 Chron. 26:7).

H

Haahashtari (hā-a-hash'ta-ri; "the courier"). A son of Ashur listed in the descendants of Judah (1 Chron. 4:6).

Habaiah (ha-ba'ya; "Jehovah is protection"). Ancestor of a priestly family (Ezra 2:61; Neh. 7:63).

Habakkuk (ha-bak'uk; "love's embrace"). A prophet during the reigns of Jehoiakim and Josiah (Hab. 1:1; 3:1).

Habaziniah (hab-a-zi-nī'a; "Jehovah's light"). The grandfather of Jaazaniah, the founder of a Jewish sect (Jer. 35:3).

Habor (hā'bor; "fertile"). A tributary of the Euphrates River (2 Kings 17:6; 18:11); probably the Khabur River.

Hachaliah (hak-a-lī'a; "Jehovah is hidden"). The father of Nehemiah the governor of Israel (Neh. 1:1).

Hachilah (ha-kī'la; "gloomy"). A hill in the wilderness southeast of Hebron, near Maon (1 Sam. 26:1-3).

Hachmoni (hak'mo-nī; "the wise"). Father of Jehiel, the royal tutor (1 Chron. 27:32).

Hadad (hā'dad; "thunderer"). [1] One of the twelve sons of Ishmael and grandson of Abraham (1 Chron. 1:30). He is called Hadar, due to a copyist's mistake or a dialectal variant in Genesis 25:15. [2] A king of Edom who fought Midian (Gen. 36:35-36; 1 Chron. 1:46). [3] The last of Edom's early kings (1 Chron. 1:50-51). Due to a copyist's mistake or dialectal variant he is called Hadar in Genesis 36:39. [4] A member of the royal family of Edom who opposed Israel's rule of Edom (1 Kings 11:14-22, 25).

Hadadezer [Hadarezer] (ha-dad-ē'zer [ha-da-rē'zer]; "[the god] Hadad is my help"). The king of Zobah in Syria that warred against David and Joab (2 Sam. 8:3-12). His name is also written Hadarezer; perhaps this is a dialectal variant (2 Sam. 10:16; 1 Chron. 18:3-10).

Hadadrimmon (ha-dad-rim'on; compound of two divine names: Hadad and Rimmon). The KJV takes this as a reference to a place in the Valley of Jezreel, near Megiddo (Zech. 12:11). Many believe, however, the reference is to the lamentation for a divinity analogous to the weeping for Tammuz (Ezek. 8:14).

Hadar (hā'dar). *See* Hadad [1], [3].

Hadarezer (ha-da-rē'zer). *See* Hadadezer.

Hadashah (had'-a-sha; "new"). A village in the lowlands of Judah about 5 km. (3 mi.) from Beth-horon (Josh. 15:37); perhaps modern Khirbet el-Judeideh.

Hadassah (ha-das'sa; "myrtle"). The Hebrew name of Esther (q.v.).

Hadattah (ha-dat'a; "new"). A town in southern Judah (Josh. 15:25), probably near Hazor [2].

Hades (hād'ēz). *See* Hell.

Hadid (hā-did; "point"). A Benjamite town located 5 km. (3 mi.) east-northeast of Lydda (Ezra 2:33; Neh. 11:34).

Hadlai (had'lī; "resting"). The father of Amasa, a chief man of the tribe of Ephraim (2 Chron. 28:12).

Hadoram (ha-dō'ram; "Hadad is high"). [1] The son of Joktan, a descendant of Noah (Gen. 10:27; 1 Chron. 1:21). Possibly the name denotes an Arabian tribe. [2] The son of the king of Hamath; he bore presents to David (1 Chron. 18:10). He is called Joram, in Second Samuel 8:9-10, perhaps as a token to honor David's God (i.e., Joram means "Jehovah is high"). [3] The superintendent of forced labor under David, Solomon, and Rehoboam. He is variously called Adoniram ("my lord is exalted"), and Adoram, a contraction of the former (2 Sam. 20:24; 1 Kings 4:6; 12:18; 2 Chron. 10:18). *See also* Jehoram.

Hadrach (hā-drak; "dwelling"). A Syrian country associated with Hamath and Damascus, encompassing an area along the Orontes River south of Hamath (Zech. 9:1).

Hagab (hā'gab; "locust"). An ancestor of captives returning with Zerubbabel (Ezra 2:46). *See* Hagaba.

Hagaba [Hagabah] (hag'a-ba [hag'a-ba]; "locust"). An ancestor of some of the captives returning with Zerubbabel (Ezra 2:45; Neh. 7:48). *See* Hagab.

Hagabah (hag'a-ba). *See* Hagaba.

Hagar [Agar] (hā'gar [ā'gar]; "wandering"). An Egyptian servant of Sarah; she became the mother of Ishmael by Abraham (Gen. 16:1-16; 21:14-17).

Haggai (hag'gā-ī; "festive"). The first of the prophets who prophesied after the Babylonian Captivity (Ezra 5:1; Hag. 1:1, 3, 12).

Haggeri (hag'ge-ri; "wanderer"). The father of one of David's mighty men (1 Chron. 11:38).

Haggi (hag'i; "festive"). The second son of Gad (Gen. 46:16; Num. 26:15).

Haggiah (hag-gī'a; "feast of Jehovah"). A descendant of Levi (1 Chron. 6:30).

Haggith (hag'gith; "festal"). The fifth wife of David and mother of Adonijah (2 Sam. 3:4; 1 Kings 1:5, 11).

Hakkatan (hak'a-tan; "the little one"). The father of Johanan, who returned with Ezra (Ezra 8:12).

Hakkoz (hak'oz; "the nimble"). A priest and chief of the seventh course of service in the sanctuary (1 Chron. 24:10). *See* Koz [1].

Hakupha (ha-kū'fa; "incitement"). Ancestor of a family returning from captivity (Ezra 2:51; Neh. 7:53).

Halah (hā'la; "moist table"). A portion of the Assyrian kingdom, encompassing the basin of the Habor and Saorkas Rivers (2 Kings 17:6; 1 Chron. 5:26).

Halak (hā'lak; "smooth"). A mountain in southern Palestine (Josh. 11:17; 12:7); possibly present-day Jebel Halog, just north-northeast of Abdeh.

Halhul (hal'hul; "tremble"). A Judean village located about 6 km. (4 mi.) north of Hebron (Josh. 15:58); said to be the burial place of Jonah.

Hali (hā'lī; "sickness"). A town of Judah, located near the border of Asher (Josh. 19:25).

Hallohesh [Halohesh] (ha-lō'hesh [ha-lō'hesh]; "the whisperer; the slanderer"). [1] The father of one who repaired the wall (Neh. 3:12). [2] A man or family that sealed the new covenant with God after the Exile (Neh. 10:24); some identify him with [1].

Halohesh (ha-lō'hesh). *See* Hallohesh.

Hamath. The modern Syrian city of Hama stands on the site of biblical Hamath. The city marked the northern boundary that God assigned to the people of Israel (Num. 34:8; Josh. 13:5). In King David's time, the Aramean people of Hamath were friendly toward Israel (2 Sam. 8:9-10). The Orontes River flows through the city.

Ham (ham; "hot"). The youngest son of Noah. Because of his wickedness, his son Canaan was cursed (Gen. 5:32; 9:22-27).

Ham (ham; "hot"). [1] A name for Egypt used only in poetry (Psa. 78:51). [2] A place between Ashteroth-Karnaim in Bashan and the Moabite country (Gen. 14:5). Possibly modern Ham about 5 mi. south of Irbid in the 'Ajlūn district.

Haman (hā'man; "celebrated Human [Humban]"). The prime minister of Ahasuerus who plotted against the Jews (Esther 3-9).

Hamath (hā'math). See Hemath.

Hamath [Hemath] (hā'math [hē'math]; "anger"). [1] A Hittite city on the Orontes River about 200 km. (125 mi.) north of Damascus; a supply base for Solomon's armies (2 Chron. 8:4). [2] The ideal northern boundary of Israel (Num. 13:21; 34:8).

Hamath-zobah (hā'moth-zō'ba). A city captured by Solomon (2 Chron. 8:3).

Hammath [Hemath] ([hē'math] hām'ath; "hot springs"). A city on Naphtali allotted to the Levites (Josh. 19:35). It is probably identical with Hammon (1 Chron. 6:76) and Hammoth-dor (Josh. 21:32).

Hammedatha (ham-e-dā'tha; "given by the moon"). The father of Haman (Esther 3:1).

Hammelech (ham'e-lek). This is not a proper name. It is a general title that means "the king" (Jer. 36:26; 38:6).

Hammoleketh (ha-mol'e-keth; "the queen"). An ancestor of Gideon. It may be a proper name or title (1 Chron. 7:18).

Hammon (ham'on; "hot waters"). [1] A frontier village of the tribe of Asher, assigned to the Levites, located about 16 km. (10 mi.) south of Tyre (Josh. 19:28). [2] See Hammath.

Hammoth-dor (ham'moth-dōr). See Hammath.

Hamonah (ham'o-na; "multitude"). Symbolic name of the city where Gog is to be defeated (Ezek. 39:16).

Hamon-gog (hā'mon-gog; "multitude of Gog"). The valley where Gog and his armies will be defeated in their final struggle against God's people (Ezek. 39:11-15).

Hamor [Emmor] (hā'mor [em'mor]; "ass"). The prince of Shechem whose son Shechem brought destruction on himself and his family (Gen. 33:19; 34:2-26).

Hamran (ham'ran). See Hemdan.

Hamuel (ha-mū'el; "wrath of God"). A descendant of Simeon (1 Chron. 4:26).

Hamul (hā-mul; "pity"). The younger son of Pharez (Gen. 46:12; 1 Chron. 2:5).

Hamutal (ha-mū'tal; "kinsman of the dew"). One of King Josiah's wives (2 Kings 23:31; 24:18; Jer. 52:1).

Hanameel (ha-nam'e-el; "gift of grace of God"). A cousin of Jeremiah's who sold him a field (Jer. 32:6-9).

Hanan (hā'nan; "merciful"). [1] A descendant of Benjamin

(1 Chron. 8:23). **[2]** A descendant of Benjamin through Saul (1 Chron. 8:38; 9:44). **[3]** One of David's heroes (1 Chron. 11:43). **[4]** A returned captive (Ezra 2:46; Neh. 7:49). **[5]** A Levite who assisted Ezra when reading the Law (Neh. 8:7). **[6]** A Levite who sealed the covenant with Nehemiah (Neh. 10:10; 13:13). Perhaps identical with [5]. **[7]** A chief or family who sealed the covenant with Nehemiah (Neh. 10:22). **[8]** A chief or family who also sealed the covenant (Neh. 10:26). **[9]** A temple officer whose sons had a chamber in the temple (Jer. 35:4). [Note: This name should not be confused with Baal-hanan.]

Hananeel (ha-nan'e-el; "given of God"). A tower of Jerusalem, located near the Sheep's Gate (Jer. 31:38; Zech. 14:10).

Hanani (ha-nā'nī; "gracious"). **[1]** A musician and head of one of the courses of the temple services (1 Chron. 25:4, 25). **[2]** The father of the prophet Jehu; cast into prison by Asa (1 Kings 16:1, 7; 2 Chron. 16:7-10). **[3]** A priest who married a foreign wife (Ezra 10:20). **[4]** A brother of Nehemiah and a governor of Jerusalem under him (Neh. 1:2; 7:2). **[5]** A priest and musician who helped to purify the walls of Jerusalem (Neh. 12:36).

Hananiah (han-a-nī'a; "Jehovah is gracious"). **[1]** A descendant of Benjamin (1 Chron. 8:24). **[2]** An officer of Uzziah (2 Chron. 26:11). **[3]** The father of a prince under Jehoiakim (Jer. 36:12). **[4]** The leader of the sixteenth division of David's musicians (1 Chron. 25:4, 23). **[5]** The grandfather of Irijah (Jer. 37:13). **[6]** A false prophet who opposed Jeremiah (Jer. 28). **[7]** One of Daniel's friends at Babylon (Dan. 1:7, 11, 19). *See also* Shadrach. **[8]** A son of Zerubbabel (1 Chron. 3:19, 21). **[9]** A Levite who married a foreign wife during the Exile (Ezra 10:28). **[10]** A druggist and priest who helped to rebuild the wall of Jerusalem (Neh. 3:8). **[11]** One who helped to rebuild the gate of Jerusalem (Neh. 3:30); perhaps the same as [10]. **[12]** A faithful Israelite placed in charge of Jerusalem (Neh. 7:2). **[13]** One who sealed the new covenant with God after the Exile (Neh. 10:23). **[14]** A priest present at the dedication of the walls of Jerusalem (Neh. 12:12, 41).

Hanes (ha'nez; "Mercury"). An Egyptian town about 80 km. (50 mi.) south of Memphis (Isa. 30:4).

Haniel [Hanniel] (han'i-el; "God is gracious"). **[1]** A prince of the tribe of Manasseh (Num. 34:23). **[2]** A hero of Asher (1 Chron. 7:39).

Hannah (han'a; "grace"). A prophetess, the mother of Samuel (1 Sam. 1).

Hannathon (han'a-thon; "dedicated to grace"). A town of the tribe of Zebulun located on a road between Megiddo and Accho (Josh. 19:14).

Hanniel (han'i-el). *See* Haniel.

Hanoch [Henoch] (hā'nok [hē'nuk]; "dedicated"). **[1]** A grandson of Abraham (Gen. 25:4), called Henoch in First Chronicles 1:33. **[2]** The eldest son of Reuben, and founder of the Hanochite clan (Gen. 46:9; 1 Chron. 5:3). **[3]** Enoch, the son of Jared (1 Chron. 1:3).

Hanun (hā'nun; "gracious"). [1] A king of Ammon who involved the Amonites in a disastrous war with David (2 Sam. 10:1-6). [2] One who repaired the wall (Neh. 3:30). [3] One who repaired the valley gate of Jerusalem (Neh. 3:13).

Haphraim (haf-ra'yim; "two pits"). A frontier town assigned to the tribe of Issachar (Josh. 19:19). It may be modern Khirbet el-Farriyeh, about 10 km. (6 mi.) northwest of Megiddo; or it may be modern et Faryibeh, northwest of Bethshean.

Hara (ha'ra; "hill"). A place in Assyria to which the Israelite captives were taken (1 Chron. 5:26); it may be the proper name of a settlement or the Hebrew term for "mountains of the Medes."

Haradah (har'a-da; "fear"). A place where the Israelites camped during their wilderness wanderings (Num. 33:24); its exact location is unknown.

Haran (ha'ran; "strong; enlightened"). [1] A brother of Abraham who died before his father (Gen. 11:26-31). [2] A descendant of Levi (1 Chron. 23:9). [3] A son of Caleb (1 Chron. 2:46).

Haran [Charran] (ha'ran [ká ran]; "mountains"). A Mesopotamian city located 386 km. (240 mi.) northwest of Nineveh and 450 km. (280 mi.) north-northeast of Damascus (Gen. 11:31; 12:4-5).

Harbona [Harbonah] (har-bō'na; "ass-driver"). A chamberlain under Ahasuerus (Esther 1:10; 7:9).

' **Hareph** (ha'ref; "early born"). A son of Caleb (1 Chron. 2:51), not to be confused with Hariph (q.v.).

Hareth (ha'reth; "thicket"). A forest of Judah in which David hid (1 Sam. 22:5).

Harhaiah (har-hā'ya; "Jehovah is protecting"). Father of Uzziel, a builder of the wall of Jerusalem (Neh. 3:8).

Harhas [Hasrah] (har'has [has'ra]; "glitter"). Grandfather of Shallum, the husband of the prophetess Huldah (2 Kings 22:14). Another form of the name is Hasrah (2 Chron. 34:22).

Harhur (har'hur; "nobility; distinction"). Ancestor of returned captives (Neh. 7:53; Ezra 2:51).

Harim (hā'rim; "snub-nosed"). [1] A priest in charge of the third division of temple duties (1 Chron. 24:8; Ezra 2:39; 10:21; Neh. 3:11). [2] An ancestor of some returning from captivity (Ezra 2:32; Neh. 7:35). [3] One whose descendants took foreign wives during the Exile (Ezra 10:31). [4] One who sealed the new covenant with God after the Exile (Neh. 10:5). [5] A family that sealed the new covenant with God after the Exile (Neh. 10:27). [6] An ancestor of a family, perhaps [4] (Neh. 12:15). [Note: Many of those named Harim may be identical; there are many uncertainties.]

Hariph (hā'rif; "early born"). [1] An ancestor of returning captives (Neh. 7:24). [2] Head of a family who sealed the new covenant with God after the Exile (Neh. 10:19). He is called Jorah in Ezra 2:18.

Harmon (har'mon; KJV reads "the palace"). A place to which the people of Samaria were exiled, perhaps in the area of Rimmon (Amos 4:3).

Harnepher (har-nē'fer; "panting"). A descendant of Asher (1 Chron. 7:36).

Harod (hā'rod; "trembling"). A spring (Judg. 7:1); commonly thought to be modern 'Ain Jalud on the northwest side of Mount Gilboa, about 1.5 km. (1 mi.) southeast of Jezreel.

Haroeh (har'o'e; "the seer"). A descendant of Judah (1 Chron. 2:52); perhaps Reaiah (1 Chron. 4:2).

Harosheth (ha-rō'sheth; "carving"). A small village on the northern bank of the Kishon River 26 km. (16 mi.) north-northwest of Megiddo (Judg. 4:2, 13).

Harsha (har'sha; "artificer"). An ancestor of returning captives (Ezra 2:52; Neh. 7:54).

Harum (hā'rum; "elevated"). A descendant of Judah (1 Chron. 4:8).

Harumaph (ha-rū'maf; "slit-nosed"). Father of Jedaiah the wall-builder (Neh. 3:10).

Haruz (hā'ruz; "industrious"). Mother of King Amon (2 Kings 21:19).

Hasadiah (has-a-dī'a; "Jehovah is kind"). A descendant of Jehoiakim (1 Chron. 3:20).

Hasenuah (has-e-nū'a; "the violated"). A descendant of Benjamin (1 Chron. 9:7). The original name was probably Senuah, to which the Hebrew definite article (Ha-) is prefixed. *See also* Senuah.

Hashabiah (hash-a-bī'a; "Jehovah is associated"). [1] A descendant of Levi (1 Chron. 6:45). [2] Another descendant of Levi (1 Chron. 9:14). [3] A son of Jeduthun (1 Chron. 25:3). [4] A descendant of Kohath (1 Chron. 26:30). [5] A son of Kemuel who was a prince of the Levites (1 Chron. 27:17). [6] A chief of a Levite clan (2 Chron. 35:9). [7] A Levite who returned with Ezra from Babylon (Ezra 8:19). [8] A chief of the family of Kohath (Ezra 8:24). [9] One who repaired the wall of Jerusalem (Neh. 3:17). [10] One who sealed the covenant with Nehemiah (Neh. 10:11). [11] A Levite in charge of certain temple functions (Neh. 11:15). [12] An attendant of the temple (Neh. 11:22). [13] A priest in the days of Jeshua (Neh. 12:21). [14] A chief Levite (Neh. 12:24). [Note: It is quite possible that [9], [12], and [14] refer to the same person.]

Hashabnah (ha-shab'na; "Jehovah is a friend"). One who sealed the new covenant with God after the Exile (Neh. 10:25).

Hashabniah (ha-shab-nī'a; "Jehovah is a friend"). [1] Father of Hattush who helped to rebuild the wall of Jerusalem (Neh. 3:10). [2] A Levite who officiated at the fast under Ezra and Nehemiah when the covenant was sealed (Neh. 9:5).

Hashbadana (hash-bad'a-na; "judge"). An assistant to Ezra at the reading of the Law (Neh. 8:4).

Hashem (hā-shem; "shining"). Father of several of David's guards (1 Chron. 11:34).

Hashmonah (hash-mō'na; "fruitfulness"). A place where the Israelites camped in the wilderness (Num. 33:29-30); possibly modern Wadi el-Hashim.

Hashub [Hasshub] (Fā'shub [has 'shub]; "associate"). [1] A Levite chief (1 Chron. 9:14; Neh. 11:15). [2] A builder of the wall of Jerusalem (Neh. 3:11). [3] One of the signers of the new covenant with God after the Exile (Neh. 10:23). [4] One who repaired the wall of Jerusalem (Neh. 3:23).

Hashubah (ha-shū'ba; "association"). A descendant of Jehoiakim (1 Chron. 3:20).

Hashum (hā'shum; "shining"). [1] One whose descendants returned from the Babylonian Captivity (Ezra 2:19; 10:33; Neh. 7:22). [2] One who sealed the covenant (Neh. 8:4; 10:18).

Hashupha [Hasupha] (ha-shoo'fa]; "stripped"). An ancestor of returning captives (Ezra 2:43; Neh. 7:46).

Hasrah (has'ra). See Harhas.

Hassenaah (has-en-ā'a; "the thorn hedge"). An ancestor of those who rebuilt the Fish Gate at Jerusalem (Neh. 3:3). The name is probably identical with the Senaah of Ezra 2:35 and Nehemiah 7:38, which most English translators have understood to have the Hebrew definite article (Ha-) prefixed.

Hasshub (has'shub). See Hashub.

Hasupha (ha-soo'fa). See Hashupha.

Hatach (ha'tach). A chamberlain of Ahasuerus (Esther 4:5-10).

Hathath (hā'thath; "terror"). Son of Othniel (1 Chron. 4:13).

Hatipha (ha-tī'fa; "taken; captive"). An ancestor of returning captives (Ezra 2:54; Neh. 7:56).

Hatita (hat'i-ta; "exploration"). A temple gatekeeper or porter whose descendants returned from the Babylonian Captivity (Ezra 2:42; Neh. 7:45).

Hattil (hat'il; "decaying"). An ancestor of some who returned from the Babylonian Captivity (Ezra 2:57; Neh. 7:59).

Hattush (hat'ush; "contender"). [1] Descendant of the kings of Judah, perhaps of Shechaniah (1 Chron. 3:22). [2] A descendant of David who returned from the Exile with Ezra (Ezra 8:2). [3] A priest who returned from the Exile with Zerubbabel (Neh. 12:2). [4] One who helped to rebuild the wall of Jerusalem (Neh. 3:10). [5] A priest who signed the covenant (Neh. 10:1, 4). [Note: entries [1], [2], [3], and [5] may refer to the same person.]

Hauran (ha-oo-ran'; "black land"). A district bordering the region of Gilead south of Damascus, noted for the fertility of its soil (Ezek. 47:16, 18).

Havilah (hav'i-la; perhaps "sandy"). [1] Son of Cush (Gen. 10:7; 1 Chron. 1:9). Possibly an unknown tribe is intended. [2] A descendant of Shem in two genealogies (Gen. 10:29; 1 Chron. 1:23). Possibly a tribe of Arabians who inhabited central or south Arabia is meant.

Havilah (hav'i-la; "circle"). A region of central Arabia populated by

Hazor. Joshua defeated King Jabin of Hazor during the conquest of Canaan (Josh. 11:1-13; 12:19). King Solomon later fortified the city, but the Assyrians destroyed it in the eighth century B.C. and carried away its people (1 Kings 9:15; 2 Kings 15:29). From 1955 to 1958, Israeli archaeologists led by Yigael Yadin excavated the ruins of Hazor, just northwest of the Sea of Galilee.

the descendants of Cush (Gen. 10:7; 1 Sam. 15:7; cf. Gen. 25:18). This term may have referred to the territory of the Arabian Desert for several hundred miles north of modern Al-Yamanah.

Havoth-jair (hā'voth-jā'ir; "tent villages of Jair"). An area in the northwest part of Bashan, containing several unwalled cities (Num. 32:41). The area is called Bashan-havoth-jair in Deuteronomy 3:14.

Hazael (haz'a-el; "God sees"). The murderer of Ben-hadad II who usurped the throne of Syria (1 Kings 19:15, 17; 2 Kings 8:8-29).

Hazaiah (ha-zā'ya "Jehovah is seeing"). A descendant of Judah (Neh. 11:5).

Hazar-Addar (hā'zar-ad'ar). *See* Adar.

Hazar-enan (hā'zar-ē'nan; "village of fountains"). A small village on the northern border of Palestine (Num. 34:9; Ezek. 48:1); probably modern Kiryatein.

Hazar-gaddah (hā'zar-gad'a; "town of Gadah"). A village on the southern border of Judah southwest of Ras Zuiveira (Josh. 15:27); possibly modern Khirbet Ghazza.

Hazar-hatticon (hā'zar-hat'i-kon; "enclosure"). A village on the border of Havran (Ezek. 47:16).

Hazar-maveth (hā'zar-mā'veth; "court of death"). The third son of Joktan (Gen. 10:26; 1 Chron. 1:20). Possibly the name refers to a people who dwelt in the peninsula of Arabia.

Hazar-maveth (hā'zar-mā'veth; "enclosure"). A very small district of Arabia in the southern portion of the Arabian Peninsula (Gen. 10:26).

Hazar-shual (hā'zar-shū'al; "fox village"). A town in southern Judah apportioned to the tribe of Simeon (Josh. 15:28; 19:3). Perhaps it is modern el-Watan, located between Beer-sheba and Tell es-Saba.

Hazar-susah [Hazar-susim] (hā′zar-soo′za [hā′zar-soo′zim]; "captive mare[s]"). A small village in the extreme south of the territory of Simeon (Josh. 19:5; 1 Chron. 4:31); it may be modern Susiyeh, located 3 km. (2 mi.) east of Eshtemoa.

Hazazon-tamar [Hazezon-tamar] (haz′a-zon-tā′mar [haz′e-zon-tā′◯ mar]; "sandy surface of the palm tree"). Said to be another name for En-gedi (Gen. 14:7; 2 Chron. 20:2); this name may in fact refer to modern Tamar, about 32 km. (20 mi.) south-southeast of the Dead Sea on the road to Elath.

Hazelelponi (haz-e-lel-pō′nī; "protection of the face of"). A daughter of Etam in the genealogy of Judah (1 Chron. 4:3).

Hazeroth (ha-zē′roth; "enclosures"). A place where the Israelites camped in the wilderness (Num. 11:35); possibly modern Ain Hudra, about 58 km. (36 mi.) north-northeast of Mount Sinai.

Haziel (hā′zi-el; "God is seeing"). A descendant of Levi in the time of David (1 Chron. 23:9).

Hazo (hā′zō; "vision; seer"). A son of Nahor and nephew of Abraham (Gen. 22:22).

Hazor (hā′zor; "enclosure"). [1] The capital of the Canaanite kingdom, later included in the territory of Naphtali in northern Palestine (Josh. 11:1, 10, 13); site of a major archaeological excavation. [2] A place in extreme southern Judah (Josh. 15:23); possibly modern el-Jebariyeh. [3] Another city in southern Judah (Josh. 15:25). Hezron was a district or region of the city or another name for the city itself (v. 25). [4] A village of the tribe of Benjamin, to which the Jewish exiles returned (Neh. 11:33); modern Khirbet Hazzur, 6 km. (4 mi.) north-northwest of Jerusalem. [5] A region of the Arabian Desert east of Palestine (Jer. 49:28, 30, 33).

Heber (hē′ber; properly Eber—"the other side; across"). [1] Head of a family of Gad (1 Chron. 5:13). [2] A descendant of Benjamin (1 Chron. 8:22). See Eber.

Heber (hē′ber; "companion"). [1] A descendant of Asher (Gen. 46:17; 1 Chron. 7:31-32). [2] The husband of Jael, who killed Sisera (Judg. 4:11, 17, 21; 5:24). [3] Head of a clan of Judah (1 Chron. 4:18). [4] A descendant of Benjamin (1 Chron. 8:17). [5] Used in Luke 3:35 to refer to Eber [1].

Hebron (hē′brun; "ford; company"). [1] A son of Kohath (Exod. 6:18; Num. 3:19; 1 Chron. 6:2, 18). [2] A descendant of Caleb (1 Chron. 2:42-43).

Hebron (hē′brun; "friendship"). [1] A city in the hills of Judah, 32 km. (20 mi.) south of Jerusalem (Gen. 13:18; Num. 13:22). [2] A town of the tribe of Asher, more frequently called Abdon (Josh. 19:28).

Hegai [Hege] (heg′a-ī [hē′ge]). A chamberlain of Ahasuerus (Esther 2:3, 8, 15).

Helah (hē′lah; "tenderness"). A wife of Asher (1 Chron. 4:5, 7).

Helam (hē′lam). A place east of the Jordan, where David defeated

Hebron and History

The city of Hebron is first mentioned in the Bible when Abram separated his camp from Lot's and settled at Hebron (Gen. 13:18). Years later, Abraham bought the cave at Machpelah in Hebron to bury Sarah. The burial place later served for Abraham, Isaac and Rebecca, and Jacob and Leah (Gen. 49:29-33).

When the Hebrews returned from Egyptian bondage to inhabit the Promised Land, they feared the size of the inhabitants; so they only gradually captured Canaan from the clans of Anak, or made alliances with them (Num. 13:14). After Hebron's king joined with other kings to attack a Hebrew ally, Gibeon, the Hebrews attacked and captured Hebron and other cities (Josh. 10). The Bible gives credit for the capture of Hebron to three people or groups of people: Caleb (Josh. 15:13-15), the tribes of Judah (Judg. 1:8-10), and Joshua (Josh. 10:36-37). After the capture, Hebron was turned over to Caleb, as God had promised earlier (Num. 14).

Generations later, the inhabitants of Hebron assisted David and his army as he pursued the Philistines. Victorious, David shared "the spoil of the enemies of the Lord (1 Sam. 30-31) with the people of Hebron and other cities. As David grew in power, the men of Judah gathered at Hebron and anointed him their king. David ruled the southern kingdom from Hebron.

After David united the two kingdoms (with the seat of government at Jerusalem), Hebron is mentioned only briefly in the Bible. David's son Absalom launched an unsuccessful revolt against him from Hebron (2 Sam. 15:7-10). Later Rehoboam strengthened the city's fortifications so that Hebron could protect Jerusalem, which lay about nineteen miles to the north (2 Chron. 11:5, 10).

Hebron was designated a city of the Levites. The descendants of Levi (i.e., the priests) were given these cities and surrounding pastures as places to live (cf. Josh. 21:1-12). Hebron was also named a city of refuge. If a person unintentionally killed someone, he could flee to one of the six cities of refuge, where he would be protected until he stood trial (Num. 35:9-15).

Modern Hebron has a population of about 40,000 and is located on an important road junction in the highland area of western Jordan. The stone-built town has small, winding streets, and active marketplaces, which sell the wares of local craftsmen, such as glassblowers. Dr. Philip C. Hammond of the University of Utah, who has excavated many artifacts at Hebron, considers the city the oldest continuously occupied unwalled city in the world.

---

the king of Syria (2 Sam. 10:16-19). Possibly 'Almā or 'Ilmā, 10 mi. southwest of Busr el-Harīrī.

Helbah (hel'ba; "fertile"). A town of the tribe of Asher on the Phoenician plain northeast of Tyre (Judg. 1:31); probably the same as Ahlah.

Helbon (hel'bon; "fat"). A village of Syria near Damascus, known for its wines (Ezek. 27:18); probably modern Khalbun, 21 km. (13 mi.) north-northwest of Damascus.

Heldai (hel'dī; "enduring"). [1] A captain of the temple service (1 Chron. 27:15). [2] An Israelite who returned from the Babylonian Captivity and was given special honors (Zech. 6:10); he is called Helem in verse 14.

Heleb [Heled] (hē'leb [hē'led]; "fat"). One of David's mighty men (2 Sam. 23:29; 1 Chron. 11:30).

Heled (hē'led). See Heleb.

Helek (hē′lek; "port on"). A descendant of Manasseh (Num. 26:30; Josh. 17:2).

Helem (hē′lem; "strength"). [1] A descendant of Asher (1 Chron. 7:35). [2] Another name for Heldai [2] (q.v.).

Heleph (hē′lef; "passing over"). A town marking the boundary of the tribe of Naphtali, just northeast of Mount Tabor (Josh. 19:33).

Helez (hē′lez; "vigor"). [1] One of David's mighty men (2 Sam. 23:26; 1 Chron. 11:27; 27:10). [2] A descendant of Judah (1 Chron. 2:39).

Heli (hē′lī; "high," perhaps a contracted form of "God is high." Heli is the Greek form of Eli.). The father of Joseph in Luke's genealogy (Luke 3:23).

Helkai (hel′ka-ī; "Jehovah is my portion"). The head of a priestly family (Neh. 12:15).

Helkath (hel′kath; "part"). A town marking the boundary of the tribe of Asher (Josh. 19:25); probably modern Tell el-Harboj.

Helkath-hazzurim (hel′kath-haz′u-rim; "field of rock"). An area of smooth ground near the pool of Gibeon (2 Sam. 2:16).

Hell (hel; "conceal"). The place of woe for the departed. "Hades" is the New Testament name for "Sheol," which was conceived as a place where the souls of all dead resided (Psa. 16:10; Matt. 11:23; Acts 2:27). The KJV also has *hell* as its translation of *Gehenna*, a valley outside Jerusalem that Jesus used as a symbol of woe for lost souls. For believers, He said that Hades would be a paradise (Luke 23:43); for the godless, it would be "Gehenna" (cf. Luke 16:22-23).

Helon (hē′lon; "valorous"). The father of Eliab, the prince of Zebulun (Num. 1:9; 2:7; 7:24; 10:16).

Hemam (hē′mam). See Homam.

Heman (hē′man "faithful"). [1] A musician and seer appointed by David as a leader in the temple's vocal and instrumental music (1 Chron. 6:33; 15:17; 2 Chron. 5:12; 35:15). [2] A wise man with whom Solomon was compared (1 Kings 4:31; 1 Chron. 2:6). He composed a meditative Psalm (Psa. 88, title).

Hemath (hē′math; "warmth"). Father of the house of Rechab (1 Chron. 2:55); also called Hamath (Amos 6:14). See also Hammath.

Hemdan (hem′dan; "pleasant"). A descendant of Seir (Gen. 36:26). The KJV wrongly rendered his name *Amram* in First Chronicles 1:41—the reading there is Hamran, possibly a copyist's mistake.

Hen (hen; "favor"). A son of Zephaniah (Zech. 6:14); he is probably the same as *Josiah* in verse 10.

Hena (hē′na; "troubling"). A city about 32 km. (20 mi.) from Babylon (2 Kings 19:13; Isa. 37:13); probably the same as modern Anah on the Euphrates River.

Henadad (hen′a-dad; "Hadad is gracious"). A head of a Levite family that helped to rebuild the temple (Ezra 3:9; Neh. 3:18, 24; 10:9).

Henoch (hē′nuk). See Hanoch [1] and Enoch [2].

Hepher (hē'fer; "a digging; a well"). **[1]** The youngest son of Gilead and founder of the Hepherites (Num. 26:32; Josh. 17:2). **[2]** A man of Judah (1 Chron. 4:6). **[3]** One of David's heroes (1 Chron. 11:36).

Hepher (hē'fer; "pit"). A town west of the Jordan River (Josh. 12:17); probably modern Tell Ibshar on the Plain of Sharon.

Hephzi-bah (hef'zi-ba; "my delight is in her"). The mother of King Manasseh (2 Kings 21:1).

Heres (hē'rez; "sun"). **[1]** A mountain in the district of Aijalon (Judg. 1:35). **[2]** An Egyptian city that the KJV calls "the city of destruction" (Isa. 19:18).

Heresh (he'resh; "work; silence"). Head of a Levite family (1 Chron. 9:15).

Hermas (hur'mas; "Mercury; interpreter"). A Christian to whom Paul sent greetings (Rom. 16:14).

Hermes (hur'mēz; "Mercury [the god]; interpreter"). A Greek Christian in Rome to whom Paul sent greetings (Rom. 16:14).

Hermogenes (hur-moj'e-nēz; "born of Hermes"). A Christian who deserted Paul at Rome or Ephesus (2 Tim. 1:15).

Hermon (hur'mun; "devoted to destruction"). The highest mountain of the Anti-Lebanon range, marking the northeast boundary of Palestine (Deut. 3:8; Josh. 11:17; 1 Chron. 5:23).

Herod (her'ud; "heroic"). **[1]** Herod the Great, the sly king of Judea when Christ was born. In order to maintain power, he murdered the children of Bethlehem, thinking that he would be killing the Messiah (Matt. 2:1-22; Luke 1:5). **[2]** Herod Antipas, son of the former, was tetrarch of Galilee and Perea. He was the murderer of John the Baptist (Matt. 14:1-10; Luke 13:31-32; Luke 23:7-12). **[3]** Herod Philip, son of Herod the Great, was tetrarch of Iturea and Trachonitis (Luke 3:1). **[4]** Herod Philip, another son of Herod the Great, is the Philip whose wife Herod Antipas lured away (Matt. 14:3). **[5]** Herod Agrippa I, tetrarch of Galilee and eventual ruler of his grandfather's (i.e., Herod the Great's) old realm. He bitterly persecuted Christians (Acts 12:1-23). **[6]** Herod Agrippa II, son of Agrippa I and king of various domains, witnessed the preaching of Paul (Acts 25:13-26; 26:1-32).

Herodias (he-rō'di-as; "heroic"). Granddaughter of Herod the Great, wife of Antipas, and ultimate cause of John the Baptist's death (Matt. 14:3-9; Luke 3:19).

Herodion (he-rō'di-on; "heroic"). A Jewish Christian to whom Paul sent greetings (Rom. 16:11).

Hesed (hē'sed; "kindness"; [God has kept] "faithfulness"). Father of one of Solomon's officers (1 Kings 4:10); not to be confused with Jushab-hesed (q.v.).

Heshbon (hesh'bon; "stronghold"). The Amorite capital on the boundary between Reuben and Gad, standing between the Arnon and Jabbok Rivers (Num. 21:26; Josh. 13:17).

Heshmon (hesh'mon; "rich soil"). A place in the far southern region of Judah (Josh. 15:27); possibly same as Azmon.

Heth (heth). A son of Canaan (Gen. 10:15; 1 Chron. 1:13). Possibly a reference to the Hittite people.

Hethlon (heth'lon; "fearful dwelling"). A mountain pass at the northern border of Palestine, connecting the Mediterranean coast with the Plain of Hamath (Ezek. 47:15; 48:1).

Hezeki (hez'e-kī; "Jehovah is strength"). A descendant of Benjamin (1 Chron. 8:17).

Hezekiah [Ezekias; Hizkijah] (hez-e-kī'a [ez-e-kī'as; hiz-kī'a]; "Jehovah is strength"). **[1]** One who returned from Babylon (Ezra 2:16; Neh. 7:21). He, or his representative, is called Hizkijah (a form of Hezekiah) in Nehemiah 10:17. **[2]** The twelfth king of Judah; an ancestor of Christ. He instituted religious reform and improved the overall safety and prosperity of the nation (2 Kings 18–20; 2 Chron. 29–32; Matt. 1:9-10). **[3]** A son of Neariah, a descendant of the royal family of Judah (1 Chron. 3:23).

Hezion (hē'zi-on; "vision"). The grandfather of Ben-hadad, king of Syria (1 Kings 15:18). Many scholars identify him with Rezon (q.v.).

Hezir (hē'zir; "returning home"). **[1]** A Levite in the time of David (1 Chron. 24:15). **[2]** A chief of the people that sealed the new covenant with God after the Exile (Neh. 10:20).

Hezrai [Hezro] (hez'rī [hez'rō]; "blooming; beautiful"). One of David's warriors (2 Sam. 23:35). He is also called Hezro (1 Chron. 11:37).

Hezro (hez'rō). *See* Hezrai.

Hezron [Esrom] (hez'ron [ez'rom]; "blooming"). **[1]** A son of Perez and an ancestor of Christ (Gen. 46:12; 1 Chron. 2:5, 9, 18, 21, 24-25; Matt. 1:3; Luke 3:33). **[2]** A son of Reuben (Gen. 46:9; Exod. 6:14).

Hezron (hez'ron; "blooming"). **[1]** *See* Hazor [5]. **[2]** A place on the southern border of Judah, not far from Kadesh-barnea (Josh. 15:3).

Hiddai [Hurai] (hid'a-ī [hū'ra-ī]; "mighty; chief"). One of David's mighty men (2 Sam. 23:30). He is called Hurai ("free; noble") in First Chronicles 11:32.

Hiddekel (hid'e-kel; "sound"). An archaic name for the Tigris River (Gen. 2:14; Dan. 10:4). It is narrower than the Euphrates, but carries more water. It joins the Euphrates 100 miles from the Persian Gulf at Al Qurna.

Hiel (hī'el; "God is living"). A man who rebuilt Jericho (1 Kings 16:34) and sacrificed his sons, in fulfillment of Joshua's curse (Josh. 6:26).

Hierapolis (he-er-ap'o-lis; "holy city"). A city of the province of Phrygia in Asia Minor, at the confluence of the Lycas and Meander Rivers (Col. 4:13).

Hilen [Holon] (hī'len [hō'lon]; "grief"). A city of the tribe of Judah, allotted to the Levites (Josh. 15:51; 1 Chron. 6:58).

Hilkiah (hil-kī'a; "Jehovah is protection" or "my portion"). **[1]** One who stood with Ezra at the reading of the Law (Neh. 8:4). **[2]** A Levite who kept the children of the temple officials (1 Chron. 6:45). **[3]** A gatekeeper of the tabernacle (1 Chron. 26:11). **[4]** Master of the household of King Hezekiah (2 Kings 18:18, 26; Isa. 22:20; 36:3). **[5]** A priest of Anathoth and father of Jeremiah (Jer. 1:1). **[6]** High priest and the discoverer of the Book of the Law in the days of Josiah (2 Kings 22:4, 8; 23:4). **[7]** The father of Gemariah (Jer. 29:3). **[8]** A chief of priests who returned from captivity (Neh. 12:7) and his later descendants (Neh. 12:12, 21).

Hillel (hil'lel; "praised greatly"). The father of Abdon, one of the judges (Judg. 12:13, 15).

Hinnom (hin'om). An unknown person who had a son(s) after whom a valley near Jerusalem was named. Human sacrifices took place there in Jeremiah's day, and garbage was later incinerated in this defiled place (Josh. 15:8; 18:16; Neh. 11:30; Jer. 7:31-32).

Hinnom (hin'om; "their riches"). A narrow valley southwest of Jerusalem (Josh. 15:8; 18:16; 2 Chron. 28:3).

Hirah (hī'ra; "distinction"). A friend of Judah (Gen. 38:1, 12).

Hiram [Huram] (hī'ram [hū'ram]; abbreviated form of Ahiram, "My brother is the exalted"). **[1]** A king of Tyre who befriended David and Solomon (2 Sam. 5:11; 1 Kings 5; 9:11; 10:11). **[2]** The skillful worker in brass whom Solomon secured from King Hiram (1 Kings 7:13, 40, 45; 2 Chron. 4:11, 16). **[3]** A descendant of Benjamin (1 Chron. 8:5).

Hizkiah [Hizkijah] (hiz-kī'a [hiz-ki'ja]; "Jehovah is strength"). **[1]** An ancestor of the prophet Zephaniah (Zeph. 1:1). *See* Hezekiah [1].

Hobab (hō'bab; "beloved"). The father-in-law or brother-in-law of Moses (Num. 10:29; Judg. 4:11). The phrase "father-in-law" in Judges 4:11 may possibly mean nothing more than "in-law," or perhaps Jethro was also named Hobab; but the identity is uncertain. *See also* Jethro.

Hobah (hō'ba; "love"). The town north of Damascus that was the farthest point to which Abraham pursued the defeated eastern kings (Gen. 14:15).

Hod (hod; "majesty"). One of the sons of Zophah (1 Chron. 7:37).

Hodaiah (hō-dā'ya; "honorer of Jehovah"). A descendant of the royal line of Judah (1 Chron. 3:24); possibly an alternate spelling of Hodaviah (q.v.).

Hodaviah (hō-da-vī'a; "honorer of Jehovah"). **[1]** A chief of the tribe of Manasseh (1 Chron. 5:24). **[2]** A descendant of Benjamin (1 Chron. 9:7).**[3]** An ancestor of returning captives (Ezra 2:40). He is also called Hodevah ("Jehovah is honor") in Nehemiah 7:43. *See also* Hodaiah.

Hodesh (hō'desh; "new moon"). A wife of Shaharaim (1 Chron. 8:9).

Hodevah (ho-dē'va). *See* Hodaviah.

Hodiah [Hodijah] (ho-dī'a [ho-dī'ja]; "splendor [or honor] of Jehovah"). **[1]** A brother-in-law of Naham (1 Chron. 4:19). The KJV incorrectly identifies him as the "wife" of Naham. **[2]** One of the

Mount Hor. The burial place of Aaron (Deut. 32:50), Mount Hor is traditionally identified with the modern-day peak of Jebel Nebi Harun. Over 1,500 m. (4,800 ft.) high, the mountain stands to the west of Edom.

Levites who explained the Law (Neh. 8:7; 10:10, 13). **[3]** One who sealed the new covenant with God after the Exile (Neh. 10:18).

Hodijah (ho-dī'ja). *See* Hodiah.

Hoglah (hog'la; "partridge"). A daughter of Zelophehad (Num. 26:33; 27:1; Josh. 17:3).

Hoham (hō'ham; "whom Jehovah impels; Jehovah protects the multitude"). An Amorite king slain by Joshua (Josh. 10:1-27).

Holon (hō'lon; "grief"). **[1]** A Moabite town (Jer. 48:21); possibly modern Horon. **[2]** *See* Hilen.

Homam [Hemam] (hō'mam [hē'mam]; "raging"). A Horite descendant of Esau (1 Chron. 1:39). He is called Hemam in Genesis 36:22 (probably a copyist's error).

Hophni (hof'nī; "strong"). The unholy son of Eli slain at the battle of Aphek (1 Sam. 1:3; 2:22-24, 34).

Hor (hōr; "hill"). **[1]** A mountain on the boundary of Edom (Num. 20:22; 33:37); tradition identifies it as modern Jebel Harun, but Jebel Madeirch is more likely the location. **[2]** A mountain between the Mediterranean Sea and the entrance of Hamath [2], possibly in the Lebanon range (Num. 34:7-8).

Horam (hō'ram; "height"). A king of Gezer defeated by Joshua (Josh. 10:33).

Horeb (hō'reb; "desert"). A range of mountains on the Sinai Peninsula, of which Mount Sinai is the highest (Exod. 17:6); now called the Serbal range.

Horem (hō'rem; "dedicated to God"). A fortress of the tribe of Naphtali (Josh. 19:38); modern Hurah at the southern end of the Wadi el-Ain.

Hor-Hagidgad (hōr'-ha-gid'gad; "cleft mountain"). A place where the wandering Israelites camped (Num. 33:32); probably located on what is now called the Wadi Ghadaghed. It is perhaps identical with Gudgodah (q.v.).

Hori (hō'rī; "free; noble"). [1] A descendant of Esau (Gen. 36:22; 1 Chron. 1:39). [2] The father of one of the men sent to spy out the Promised Land (Num. 13:5).

Hormah (hor'ma; "dedicated to God"). A Canaanite city located near Ziklag; originally called Zephath (1 Sam. 30:30); perhaps the same as modern Tell el-Milk, east-southeast of Beersheba.

Horonaim (hor'o-nā'im; "double caves"). A sanctuary town of Moab, near Zoar (Isa. 15:5; Jer. 48:3).

Hosah (hō'sa; "refuge"). One of the first doorkeepers of the ark of the covenant (1 Chron. 16:38; 26:10-11, 16).

Hosah (hō'sa; "refuge"). A landmark city of the tribe of Asher on the boundary near Tyre (Josh. 19:29).

Hosea [Osee] (ho-zē'a [ō'zē]; "help; i.e., Jehovah is help"). A prophet of Israel; he denounced the idolatries of Israel and Samaria (Hos. 1:1-2).

Hoshaiah (ho-shā'ya; "whom Jehovah helps"). [1] The father of Jezaniah or Azariah (Jer. 42:1; 43:2). [2] A man who led half of the princes of Judah in procession at the dedication of the walls (Neh. 12:32).

Hoshama (ho-shā'ma; "whom Jehovah heareth"). A son or descendant of Jeconiah or Jehoiakim (1 Chron. 3:18).

Hoshea [Hosea] (ho-shē'a [hō-sā'a]; "Jehovah is help or salvation"). [1] A chief of the tribe of Ephraim in the days of David (1 Chron. 27:20). [2] The last king of Israel; he was imprisoned by Sargon of Assyria (2 Kings 15:30; 17:1, 4, 6; 18:1). [3] One who sealed the covenant with Nehemiah (Neh. 10:23). [3] The original name of Joshua (q.v.).

Hotham [Hothan] (hō'tham [hō'than]; "determination"). [1] A descendant of Asher (1 Chron. 7:32). [2] Father of two of David's best men (1 Chron. 11:44).

Hothan (hō'than). *See* Hotham.

Hothir (hō'thir; "abundance"). Son of Heman in charge of the twenty-first course of the tabernacle service (1 Chron. 25:4, 28).

Hukkok (huk'ok; "hewn"). A place on the border of Naphtali (Josh. 19:34); probably modern Yakuk.

Hukok (huk'ok; "ditch"). A city marking the boundary of Asher (1 Chron. 6:75). It is identical with Helkath (q.v.).

Hul (hul; "circle"). Grandson of Shem (Gen. 10:23; 1 Chron. 1:17). Possibly an Aramean tribe is referred to; some have suggested the people of Hūlīa near Mount Masius.

Huldah (hul'da; "weasel"). A prophetess in the days of King Josiah (2 Kings 22:14; 2 Chron. 34:22).

Humtah (hum'tah; "place of lizards"). A city in the mountains of Judah near Hebron (Josh. 15:54).

Hupham (hū'fam; "coast-inhabitant; protected"). The head of a family descendant from Benjamin (Num. 26:39). In Genesis 46:21 and First Chronicles 7:12, his name is listed as Huppim ("coast-people" or "protection").

Huppah (hup'a; "protection"). A priest in the time of David who had charge of one of the courses of service in the sanctuary (1 Chron. 24:13).

Huppim (hup'ēm). See Hupham.

Hur (hur; "free; noble"). [1] One of the men who held up Moses' arms during the battle with Amalek (Exod. 17:10, 12; 24:14). [2] A son of Caleb (Exod. 31:2; 35:30; 38:22; 1 Chron. 2:19, 50; 4:1, 4). [3] A Midianite king slain by Israel (Num. 31:8; Josh. 13:21). [4] An officer of Solomon on Mount Ephraim (1 Kings 4:8). [5] The ruler of half of Jerusalem under Nehemiah (Neh. 3:9).

Hurai (hū'ra-ī; "free; noble"). See Hiddai.

Huram (hū'ram). See Hiram.

Huri (hū'rī; "linen weaver"). A descendant of Gad (1 Chron. 5:14).

Hushah (hū'sha; "haste"). A descendant of Judah (1 Chron. 4:4).

Hushai (hu'sha-ī; "quick"). A friend and counselor of David (2 Sam. 15:32, 37; 16:16-18; 17:5-15).

Husham (hū'sham; "hasting; alert"). A descendant of Esau who became king of Edom (Gen. 36:34-35; 1 Chron. 1:45-46).

Hushim (hū'shim; "hasting; hasters"). [1] A son of Dan (Gen. 46:23); in Numbers 26:42, his name is Shuham. [2] A descendant of Benjamin (1 Chron. 7:12). [3] One of the two wives of Shaharaim (1 Chron. 8:8, 11).

Huz (huz). See Uz.

Hymenaeus (hi-men-ē'us; "nuptial"). An early Christian who fell into apostasy and error (1 Tim. 1:20; 2 Tim. 2:17).

I

Ibhar (ib'har; "chooser; Jehovah chooses"). One of David's sons born at Jerusalem (2 Sam. 5:15; 1 Chron. 3:6).

Ibleam (ib'le-am; "ancient people"). A city of the tribe of Manasseh (Josh. 17:11; Judg. 1:27) generally believed to be another name for Bileam (q.v.).

Ibneiah [Ibnijah] (ib-nē'ya [ib-nī'ja]; "Jehovah builds up"). [1] A descendant of Benjamin (1 Chron. 9:8). [2] A man of Benjamin whose descendants lived in Jerusalem (1 Chron. 9:8).

Ibnijah (ib-nī'ja). See Ibneiah.

Ibri (ib'rē; "one who passes over; a Hebrew"). A descendant of Merari in the time of David (1 Chron. 24:27).

Ibzan (ib'zan; "famous; splendid"). A Bethlehemite who judged Israel for seven years (Judg. 12:8-10).

Ichabod (ik′a-bod; "inglorious"). Son of Phinehas, born after his father's death and after the ark was taken (1 Sam. 4:19-22).

Iconium (ī-kō′ni-um; "coming"). Capital of the province of Lycaonia in Asia Minor (Acts 13:51; 14:1).

Idalah (id′a-la; "land of slander"). A city of the tribe of Zebulun (Josh. 19:15); modern Khirbet el-Huvara.

Idbash (id′bash; "honey-sweet"). One of the sons of Abi-etam (1 Chron. 4:3).

Iddo (id′ō; "honorable; happy"). The official of Casiphia who provided Levites for Ezra (Ezra 8:17).

Iddo (id′ō; "beloved"). [1] Captain of the tribe of Manasseh in Gilead (1 Chron. 27:21). [2] A descendant of Gershon (1 Chron. 6:21); called Adaiah in First Chronicles 6:41.

Iddo (id′ō; "timely"). [1] Father of Abinadab (1 Kings 4:14). [2] Grandfather of the prophet Zechariah (Ezra 5:1; Zech. 1:7).

Iddo (id′ō; "adorned"). [1] A prophet who wrote about the kings of Israel (2 Chron. 9:29; 12:15). [2] A priest who returned to Jerusalem with Zerubbabel (Neh. 12:4); perhaps the same as [1].

Idumea (id-u-mē′a; "red"). An area in southwestern Palestine. After the fall of Jerusalem in 586 B.C. many Edomites migrated into this area thus giving it the name Idumea (the Greek form of the Hebrew Edom) (Mark 3:8).

Igal [Igeal] (ī′gal [i′ge-al]; "Jehovah redeems"). [1] One of the twelve spies sent to search out Canaan (Num. 13:7). [2] One of David's heroes (2 Sam. 23:36). [3] A descendant of the royal house of Judah (1 Chron. 3:22).

Igdaliah (ig-da-lī′a; "Jehovah is great"). Ancestor of persons who had a "chamber" in the temple (Jer. 35:4).

Igeal (i′ge′al). *See* Igal.

Iim (ī′im; "heaps"). [1] A town in extreme southern Judah (Josh. 15:29); modern Deir el-Ghawi. [2] A town east of the Jordan River, perhaps the Moabite fortress of Mahaiy (Num. 33:45); probably the same as Ije-abarim.

Ije-abarim (ī′je-ab′a-rim; "ruins of Abraham"). A place where the Israelites camped in the territory of Moab (Num. 33:45). *See also* Iim [2].

Ijon (ī′jon; "heap; ruin"). A city of northern Palestine belonging to the tribe of Naphtali (1 Kings 15:20); modern Merj 'Ayun, a few kilometers northwest of Dan.

Ikkesh (ik′kesh; "subtle" or "crooked"). Father of Ira, one of David's mighty men (2 Sam. 23:26; 1 Chron. 11:28; 27:9).

Ilai (ī′la-ī; "exalted"). *See* Zalmon.

Illyricum (i-lir′i-kum; "joy"). A Roman province on the east coast of the Adriatic Sea, stretching from Italy on the north to Macedonia on the south (Rom. 15:19). It was later renamed Dalmatia (q.v.).

Imla [Imlah] (im′la; "fullness"). Father of Micaiah (2 Chron. 18:7-8).

Imlah (im'la). *See* Imla.

Immer (im'er; "loquacious; prominent"). [1] A priest in the time of David (1 Chron. 24:14). [2] A priest of Jeremiah's time (Jer. 20:1). [3] The father of Zodak (Neh. 3:29). [4] A family of priests who gave their name to the sixteenth course of the temple service (1 Chron. 9:12; Ezra 2:37; Neh. 7:40).

Immer (im'er; "lamb"). A person or place in Babylonia (Ezra 2:59; Neh. 7:61); its exact location is unknown.

Imna [Jimna; Jimnah, Imnah] (im'na [jim'na; im'na]; "lugging"). [1] A descendant of Asher (Gen. 46:17; 1 Chron. 7:35). [2] A son of Asher (Num. 26:44; 1 Chron. 7:30). [3] Father of Kore in Hezekiah's reign (2 Chron. 31:14).

Imnah (im'na). *See* Imna.

Imrah (im'ra; "height of Jehovah" or "stubborn"). A descendant of Asher (1 Chron. 7:36).

Imri (im'rī; "talkative; projecting"). [1] A descendant of Judah (1 Chron. 9:4). [2] Father of Zaccur, one of Nehemiah's assistants (Neh. 3:2).

India (in-dē'ah; meaning unknown). A land on the eastern limit of the Persian Empire, surrounding the Indus River (Esther 1:1; 8:9).

Iphedeiah (if-e-dē'ya; "Jehovah redeems"). A descendant of Benjamin (1 Chron. 8:25).

Ir (ir; "watcher" or "city"). A descendant of Benjamin (1 Chron. 7:12); possibly the same as Iri (v. 7). Not to be confused with Irnahash.

Ira (ī'ra; "watchful"). [1] A priest to David (2 Sam. 20:26). [2] One of David's thirty mighty men (1 Chron. 11:28; 2 Sam. 23:38) and a captain of the temple guard (1 Chron. 27:9). [3]Another of David's thirty (1 Chron. 11:40; 2 Sam. 23:26).

Irad (ī'rad; "fleet"). A descendant of Enoch (Gen. 4:18).

Iram (ī'ram; "citizen"). A duke of Edom (Gen. 36:43).

Iri (ī'ri; "watchful"). A descendant of Benjamin (1 Chron. 7:7); possibly the same as Ir (v. 12).

Irijah (i'rī'ja; "seen of Jehovah"). A captain of the gate who arrested Jeremiah (Jer. 37:13-14).

Ir-nahash (ir-nā'hash; "serpent city"). A descendant of Judah (1 Chron. 4:12).

Ir-nahash (ir-nā'hash; "serpent city"). A town of Judah (1 Chron. 4:12); its exact location is unknown, but it is probably the same as modern Deir Nahhas, near Beit Jibrin.

Iron (ī'ron; "pious; place of terror"). A city of the tribe of Naphtali (Josh. 19:38); probably modern Yarun, 16 km. (10 mi.) west of Hula Lake.

Irpeel (ir'pe-el; "God heals"). A city of the tribe of Benjamin (Josh. 18:27); perhaps the same as modern Rafat, 10 km. (6 mi.) northwest of Jerusalem.

Ir-shemesh (ir-she'mesh; "city of the sun"). A city of the tribe of

Dan (Josh. 19:41); probably another name for Beth-shemesh (q.v.).

Iru (ī'rū; "watch"). A son of Caleb (1 Chron. 4:15).

Isaac (ī'zak; "laughter"). The son of Abraham and Sarah, born to them in their old age. He was the father of Jacob and Esau and an ancestor of Christ (Gen. 21–25; Matt. 1:2).

Isaiah [Esaias] (ī-zā'ya [e-zā'yas]; "salvation of Jehovah"). Called the "prince of prophets"; his career lasted over sixty years. He foretold the coming of Christ (Isa. 1:1; 7:14; 9:6; 52:12-53).

Iscah (is'ka; "Jehovah is looking" or "who looks"). Daughter of Haran, sister of Milcah, and niece of Abraham (Gen. 11:29).

Iscariot (is-kar'i-ot). *See* Juda(s) [8].

Ishbah (ish'ba; "praising; appeaser"). A descendant of Judah (1 Chron. 4:17).

Ishbak (ish'bak; "leaning; free"). Son of Abraham and father of a northern Arabian tribe (Gen. 25:2; 1 Chron. 1:32).

Ishbi-benob (ish'bī-bē'nob; "dweller at Nob"). One of the sons of Rapha the Philistine; he attacked David but was killed by Abishai (2 Sam. 21:15-22).

Ish-bosheth (ish-bō'sheth; "man of shame"). Son and successor of King Saul. He reigned two years before being defeated by David (2 Sam. 2:8-15; 3:8, 14-15; 4:5-12). He also was known as Esh-baal (1 Chron. 8:33; 9:39).

Ishi (ish'ī; "my husband" or "salutary"). [1] A descendant of Pharez, son of Judah (1 Chron. 2:31). [2] A descendant of Judah (1 Chron. 4:20). [3] A descendant of Simeon (1 Chron. 4:42). [4] A chief of the tribe of Manasseh (1 Chron. 5:24).

Ishiah (ī-shī'a). *See* Isshiah.

Ishijah (ish-ī'ja). *See* Isshiah.

Ishma (ish'ma; "high" or "desolate"). A brother of Jezreel and Idbash, all descendants of Caleb (1 Chron. 4:3).

Ishmael (ish'ma-el; "God hears"). [1] Son of Abraham and Hagar; his descendants are the Arabian nomads (Gen. 16:11-16; 17:18-26; 25:9-17; 28:9; 36:3). [2] The cunning son of Nethaniah and traitor of Israel (Jer. 40:8–41:18). [3] A descendant of Benjamin (1 Chron. 8:38). [4] Father of Zebadiah (2 Chron. 19:11). [5] A captain in the time of Jehoiada and Joash (2 Chron. 23:1). [6] A Levite who married a foreign wife during the Exile (Ezra 10:22).

Ishmaiah [Ismaiah] (ish-ma'ya [is-ma'ya]; "Jehovah hears"). [1] A chief of Zebulun in David's time (1 Chron. 27:19). [2] A chief of Gibeon who joined David at Ziklag (1 Chron. 12:4).

Ishmerai (ish'me-rī; "Jehovah is keeper" or "to guard"). A descendant of Benjamin (1 Chron. 8:18).

Ishod (ī'shod; "man of majesty"). A man of Manasseh (1 Chron. 7:18).

Ish-pan (ish'pan; "he will hide"). A chief man of Benjamin (1 Chron. 8:22).

Ishuah [Isuah] (ish'u-a; [is'u-a]; "he will level" or "even"). Second son of Asher (Gen. 46:17; 1 Chron. 7:30).

Ishui [Ishuai; Isui; Jesui] (ish'u-ī [ish'u-ī; is'u-ī; jes'u-ī]; "equal"). [1] Third son of Asher (Gen. 46:17; Num. 26:44; 1 Chron. 7:30). [2] A son of King Saul by Ahinoam (1 Sam. 14:49). Some believe he is identical with Ish-bosheth.

Ismachiah (is-ma-kī'a; "Jehovah will sustain"). An overseer under King Hezekiah (2 Chron. 31:13).

Ismaiah (is-mā'ya). See Ishmaiah.

Ispah (is'pa; "firm"). A descendant of Benjamin (1 Chron. 8:16).

Israel (iz'ra-el). See Jacob.

Israel (iz'ra-el; "who prevails with God"). The northern kingdom of the Hebrews in Palestine, inhabited by the ten tribes that followed Ish-bosheth and Jeroboam. The cities of Jericho and Gezer marked its southern boundary (2 Chron. 35:18; cf. Gen. 32:32). See also Jacob.

Issachar (is'a-kar; "reward"). [1] Ninth son of Jacob and ancestor of one of the twelve tribes of Israel (Gen. 30:17-18; 49:14-15). [2] A tabernacle porter (1 Chron. 26:5).

Isshiah [Ishiah; Ishijah] (is-shī'a [ī-shī'a; ish-ī'ja]; "Jehovah exists"). [1] One of David's chiefs (1 Chron. 7:3). [2] See Jesiah [2]. [3] A man who took a foreign wife during the Exile (Ezra 10:31). [4] A descendant of Moses (1 Chron. 24:21). See Isaiah.

Ish-tob (ish'tob; "good man"). A small state of Aram (2 Sam. 10:6, 8).

Isuah (is'u-a). See Ishuah.

Isui (is'u-ī). See Ishui.

Italy (it'a-li; "abounding with calves"). The peninsula jutting from the Alps into the Mediterranean Sea, bounded on the south by the straits of Messina (Acts 18:2; 27:1).

Ithai (ith'a-ī; "being"). One of David's thirty mighty men (1 Chron. 11:31). He is called Ittai in Second Samuel 23:29.

Ithamar (ith'a-mar; "land; island of palms"). A son of Aaron (Exod. 6:23; 28:1); Eli was high priest of his line (1 Chron. 24:6).

Ithiel (ith'i-el; "God is"). A man of the tribe of Benjamin (Neh. 11:7).

Ithiel and Ucal (ith'i-el; ū'kal; "signs of God"; or verb meaning "to be weary"). The names of two wise men to whom Agur spoke his words. Some scholars believe these are not proper names, but two verbs. If so, the last part of verse 1 would read: "The man said, I have wearied myself, O God, I have wearied myself, O God, and am consumed" (Prov. 30:1).

Ithmah (ith'ma; "purity"). A Moabite, one of David's guards (1 Chron. 11:46).

Ithnan (ith'nan; "given"). A town in extreme southern Judah (Josh. 15:23).

Ithra (ith'ra; "abundance"). The father of Amasa, Absalom's captain (2 Sam. 17:25). He was also known as Jether (1 Kings 2:5, 32).

Ithran (ith'ran; "excellent"). [1] A descendant of Seir (Gen. 36:26). [2] A son of Zophah of Asher (1 Chron 7:37).

Ithream (ith're-am; "residue of the people"). A son of David probably by Eglah (2 Sam. 3:5).

Ittah-kazin (it'a-kā'zin; "gather"). A landmark on the boundary of Zebulun near modern Sepphoris (Josh. 19:13).

Ittai (it'a-ī; "timely"). [1] A Philistine friend and general of David (2 Sam. 15:11-22; 18:2, 4, 12). [2] *See* Ithai.

Ituraea (it-u-rē'a; "mountains"). A small province on the northwest boundary of Palestine at the base of Mount Hermon (Luke 3:1). It probably derived its name from Jetur, a son of Ishmael.

Ivah (ī'va; "hamlet"). A city located on the Euphrates River (2 Kings 18:34; 19:13); perhaps the same as Ava.

Izehar [Izhar] (īz'e-har [īz'har]; "shining"). A Levite, the father of Korah (Exod. 6:18-21; Num. 3:19).

Izrahiah (iz-ra-hī'a; "Jehovah shines"). A descendant of Issachar (1 Chron. 7:3).

Izri (iz'rī; "creator"). Leader of the fourth musical course (1 Chron. 25:11); perhaps the same as Zeri (v. 3).

J

Jaakan [Jakan] (jā'a-kan [jā'kan]; "intelligent"). A son of Ezer, son of Seir (Deut. 10:6; 1 Chron. 1:42). In Genesis 36:27, he is called Akan. Many scholars believe the reference in the Deuteronomy passage is to a city. *See* Beeroth.

Jaakobah (ja-a-kō'ba; "to Jacob"). A descendant of Simeon (1 Chron. 4:36).

Jaalah [Jaala] (jā'a-la [jā'a-la]; "elevation"). A servant of Solomon whose descendants returned from the Exile (Ezra 2:56; Neh. 7:58).

Jaalam (jā-a-lam "hidden"). A duke of Edom (Gen. 36:5, 14, 18; 1 Chron. 1:35).

Jaanai (jā'a-nī "answerer"). A descendant of Gad (1 Chron 5:12).

Jaare-oregim (jā'a-re-or'e-jim; "foresters"). Father of Elhanan, slayer of Goliath the Gittite (2 Sam. 21:19). Some suggest this is a copyist's error for Jair (cf. 1 Chron. 20:5), the "oregim" ("weavers") being a mistaken repetition of the last word in the verse.

Jaasau (jā'a-so; "maker"). One who married a foreign wife (Ezra 10:37).

Jaasiel [Jasiel] (ja-ā'si-el [jā'si-el]; "God is maker"). [1] One of David's mighty men (1 Chron. 11:47). [2] A cousin of Saul's (1 Chron. 27:21).

Jaazaniah (ja-az-a-nī'a; "Jehovah is hearing"). [1] A captain of the forces who joined Gedaliah (2 Kings 25:23). He is the Jezaniah ("Jehovah determines; Jehovah hears") of Jeremiah 40:8; 42:1, and possibly the Azariah of Jeremiah 43:2. [2] A chief of the tribe of Reuben, a son of a certain man named Jeremiah but not the prophet (Jer. 35:3). [3] One enticing the people to idolatry (Ezek. 8:11). [4] A wicked prince of Judah seen in Ezekiel's vision (Ezek. 11:1).

Jaazer [Jazer] (jā'a-zer [jā'zer]; "God helps"). A city east of the Jordan River, in or near the region of Gilead (Num. 21:32; 32:1).

Jaaziah (ja-a-zī-a; "Jehovah is determining"). A descendant of Merari living in Solomon's day (1 Chron. 24:26-27).

Jaaziel (ja-ā'zi-el; "God is determining"). A temple musician in David's time (1 Chron. 15:18). He is called Aziel in verse 20.

Jabal (jā'bal; "moving"). Son of Lamech, a nomad (Gen. 4:20).

Jabbok (jab'ok; "flowing"). An eastern tributary of the Jordan River, which served as the western border of Ammon (Gen. 32:22; Deut. 2:37).

Jabesh (jā'besh; "dry place"). Father of Shallum, who killed Zechariah and reigned in his place (2 Kings 15:10-14). *See also* Jabeshgilead.

Jabesh-gilead (jā'besh-gil'e-ad; "dry"). A city of Gilead (Judg. 21:8; 1 Sam. 11:1). It may have been located at a site now called Wadi Yabis, about 23 km. (20 mi.) south of the Sea of Galilee.

Jabez (jā'bez; "height"). Head of a family of Judah (1 Chron. 4:9-10).

Jabez (jā'bez; "sorrow"). A dwelling place of scribes, probably in Judah (1 Chron. 2:55).

Jabin (jā'bin; "intelligent; observed"). [1] A king of Hazor defeated by Joshua (Josh. 11:1). [2] Another king of Hazor who oppressed Israel and was defeated by Deborah (Judg. 4).

Jabneel [Jabneh] (jab'ne-el [jab'ne]; "building of God"). [1] A city marking the northern border of Judah (Josh. 15:11); modern Yebnah, about 6 km. (4 mi.) inland from the Mediterranean Sea and 14.5 km. (9 mi.) north-northeast of Ashdod (2 Chron. 26:6). [2] A border town of the tribe of Naphtali (Josh. 19:33); probably modern Khirbet Yemman, 11 km. (7 mi.) southwest of Tiberias.

Jabneh (jab'ne). *See* Jabneel.

Jachan (jā'kan; "afflicting"). A descendant of Gad (1 Chron. 5:13).

Jachin (jā'kin; "founding" or "he will establish"). [1] A son of Simeon (Gen. 46:10; Exod. 6:15; Num. 26:12). He is called Jarib in First Chronicles 4:24. [2] A priest in Jerusalem after the Babylonian Captivity (1 Chron. 9:10; Neh. 11:10). [3] Head of a family of Aaron (1 Chron. 24:17). *See* Jarib.

Jachin (jā'kin "God establishes"). The right hand pillar of Solomon's porch on the temple of Jerusalem (1 Kings 7:21).

Jacob (jā'kob; "supplanter; following after"). [1] Son of Isaac, twin of Esau, and an ancestor of Christ. He bought Esau's birthright and became the father of the Jewish nation (Gen. 25–50; Matt. 1:2). God changed his name from Jacob to Israel ("God strives"; Gen. 32:28; 35:10). **[2]** The father of Joseph, the husband of Mary (Matt. 1:15-16). *See also* Heli.

Jada (jā'da; "knowing"). A descendant of Judah (1 Chron. 2:28, 32).

Jadau (jā'do; "friend"). One who married a foreign wife (Ezra 10:43).

Jaddua (ja-dū'a; "very knowing; known"). **[1]** One who sealed the covenant (Neh. 10:21). **[2]** The last high priest mentioned in the Old Testament (Neh. 12:11, 22).

Jadon (jā'don; "judging"). One who helped repair the wall (Neh. 3:7).

Jael (jā'el; "a wild goat"). Wife of Heber who killed Sisera (Judg. 4:17-22; 5:6, 24).

Jagur (jā'ger "husbandman"). A town in extreme southern Judah (Josh. 15:21); probably modern Tell Ghurr.

Jahath (jā'hath; "comfort; revival"). **[1]** A descendant of Judah (1 Chron. 4:2). **[2]**, **[3]**, **[4]**, **[5]** Four descendants of Levi (1 Chron. 6:30, 43; 23:10-11; 24:22). **[5]** An overseer of temple repair (2 Chron. 34:12).

Jahaz [Jahaza, Jahazah] (jā'haz [jā'ha-za; ja-hā'za]; "a place trodden under foot"). A battlefield on the wastelands of Moab (Num. 21:23); its exact location is unknown.

Jahaziah (ja-ha-zī'a; "Jehovah reveals"). One who assisted in recording those who had foreign wives (Ezra 10:15).

Jahaziel (ja-hā'zi'el; "God reveals"). **[1]** One who joined David at Ziklag (1 Chron. 12:4). **[2]** A priest who helped bring the ark of the covenant into the temple (1 Chron. 16:6). **[3]** Son of Hebron (1 Chron. 23:19; 24:23). **[4]** A Levite who encouraged Jehoshaphat's army against the Moabites (2 Chron. 20:14). **[5]** A chief man whose son returned from Babylon (Ezra 8:5).

Jahdai (ja'da-ī; "Jehovah leads" or "leader; guide"). One of the family of Caleb the spy (1 Chron. 2:47).

Jahdiel (ja'di-el; "union of God; God gives joy"). Head of a family of Manasseh east of the Jordan (1 Chron. 5:24).

Jahdo (ja'do; "union"). Descendant of Gad (1 Chron. 5:14).

Jahleel (ja'le-el; "God waits; wait for God"). A son of Zebulun (Gen. 46:14; Num. 26:26).

Jahmai (ja'ma-ī; "Jehovah protects"). Head of a clan of Issachar (1 Chron. 7:2).

Jahzeel [Jahziel] (ja'ze-el; "God apportions"). A son of Naphtali listed three times (Gen. 46:24; Num 26:48; 1 Chron. 7:13).

Jahzerah (ja'ze-ra; "Jehovah protects"). A priest of the family of Immer whose descendants dwelt in Jerusalem (1 Chron. 9:12). Perhaps another name for Ahasai (q.v.).

Jahziel (ja'ze-el). *See* Jahzeel.

Jair (jā'ir; "Jehovah enlightens"). **[1]** A descendant of Judah through his father and of Manasseh through his mother (Num. 32:41; Deut. 3:14; 1 Kings 4:13; 1 Chron. 2:22). [2] Judge of Israel for twenty-three years (Judg. 10:3-5). [3] The father of Mordecai, Esther's cousin (Esther 2:5). [4] *See* Jaare-oregim.

Jairus (jā'i-rus; "enlightened"). A ruler of a synagogue near Capernaum whose daughter Jesus raised from the dead (Luke 8:41).

Jakan (jā'kan). *See* Jaakan.

Jakeh (jā'ke; "hearkening"). The father of Agur, the wise man (Prov. 30:1).

Jakim (jā'kim; "a setter up"). [1] Descendant of Benjamin (1 Chron. 8:19). [2] Head of a family descended from Aaron (1 Chron. 24:12).

Jalon (jā'lon; "Jehovah abides"). A descendant of Caleb the spy (1 Chron. 4:17).

Jambres (jam'brēz). One of the Egyptian magicians who opposed Moses (Exod. 7:9-13; 2 Tim. 3:8; cf. Exod. 7:9-13).

James (jāmz; Greek form of Jacob). [1] The son of Zebedee and brother of John called to be one of the twelve. He was slain by Herod Agrippa I (Matt. 4:21; Mark 5:37; Luke 9:54; Acts 12:2). [2] The son of Alpheus, another of the twelve apostles. He is probably the same as James "the less," the son of Mary. By "the less" is meant his age or height in relation to James the son of Zebedee (Matt. 10:3; Mark 15:40; Acts 1:13). [3] The brother of Jesus (Matt. 13:55). After Christ's resurrection, he became a believer (1 Cor. 15:7) and a leader of the church at Jerusalem (Acts 12:17; Gal. 1:19; 2:9). He wrote the Epistle of James (James 1:1). [4] Unknown person mentioned as "the brother of Judas." Most view this as an incorrect translation and would render ". . . Judas, the son of James" (Luke 6:16; Acts 1:13).

Jamin (jā'min; "right hand; favor"). [1] A son of Simeon (Gen. 46:10; Exod. 6:15; Num. 26:12; 1 Chron. 4:24). [2] A descendant of Ram (1 Chron. 2:27). [3] A priest who explained the Law (Neh. 8:7).

Jamlech (jam'lek; "Jehovah rules"). A prince of Simeon (1 Chron. 4:34).

Janna (jan'a). An ancestor of Christ (Luke 3:24).

Jannes (jan-ez; "he who seduces"). An Egyptian magician who opposed Moses (2 Tim. 3:8-9; cf. Exod. 7:9-13).

Janoah [Janohah] (ja-nō'a [ja-nō'ha]; "resting"). [1] A city of the tribe of Naphtali, north of Galilee (2 Kings 15:29); possibly modern Yanuh, 10.5 km. (6.5 mi.) southeast of Tyre. [2] A town on Ephraim's border (Josh. 16:6); possibly modern Yanun, 11 km. (7 mi.) southeast of Shechem.

Janum (jā'num; "sleeping"). A town in the mountains of Judah, west-southwest of Hebron (Josh. 15:53).

Japheth (jā'feth; "the extender; fair; enlarged"). Second son of Noah, considered the father of the Indo-European races (Gen. 5:32; 6:10; 7:13; 9:18, 23, 27; 1 Chron. 1:4-5).

Japhia (jā-fī'a; "high"). [1] Amorite king of Lachish defeated by

Joshua (Josh. 10:3). **[2]** A son of David (2 Sam. 5:15; 1 Chron. 3:7; 14:6).

Japhia (ja-fī'a; "enlarging"). A boundary town of Zebulun, 3 km. (2 mi.) southwest of Nazareth (Josh. 19:12).

Japhlet (jaf'let; "Jehovah causes to escape"). A descendant of Asher (1 Chron. 7:32-33).

Japhleti (jaf'le'-ti; "to shine"). A landmark on the southern boundary of Ephraim, near Beth-horon (Josh. 16:3).

Japho (ja'fo; "beauty"). A Palestinian city on the Mediterranean coast 56 km. (34 mi.) west of Jerusalem (Josh. 19:46). It was later called Joppa (q.v.).

Jarah (ja'ra; "unveiler; honey"). A son of Ahaz of the family of Saul (1 Chron. 9:42). He is called Jehoadah in First Chronicles 8:36.

Jareb (ja'reb; "contender; avenger"). A king of Assyria (Hos. 5:13; 10:6); surely a nickname.

Jared [Jered] (ja'red [je'red]; "descending"). A descendant of Seth and ancestor of Christ (Gen. 5:15-20; 1 Chron. 1:2; Luke 3:37).

Jaresiah (jar-e-sī'a; "Jehovah gives a couch"). A descendant of Benjamin (1 Chron. 8:27).

Jarha (jar'ha). An Egyptian servant who married his master's daughter (1 Chron. 2:34-35).

Jarib (ja'rib; "striving"). **[1]** A chief man under Ezra (Ezra 8:16). **[2]** A priest who took a foreign wife during the Exile (Ezra 10:18). **[3]** See Jachin [1].

Jarmuth (jar'muth; "height"). **[1]** A city in the lowlands of Judah (Josh. 10:3); modern Khirbet Yarmuk. **[2]** A city of the tribe of Issachar assigned to the Levites (Josh. 21:29); the same as Ramoth [3].

Jaroah (ja-rō'a; "new moon"). A descendant of Gad (1 Chron. 5:14).

Jashen (ja'shen "shining"). The father of some, or one, of David's mighty men (2 Sam. 23:32). But the text probably should read thus: ". . .Jashen, Jonathan the son of Shammah the Hararite." Thus, Jashen would be one of the mighty men, and Shage (1 Chron. 11:34) is the same as Shammah (2 Sam. 23:33). See also Hashem.

Jasher (ja'sher; "upright"). One who wrote a now lost book (Josh. 10:13; 2 Sam. 1:18).

Jashobeam (ja-shō-be-am; "the people return"). **[1]** One of David's mighty men (1 Chron. 11:11; 27:2). **[2]** One who joined David at Ziklag (1 Chron. 12:6). See Adino.

Jashub (ja'shub; "turning back"). **[1]** One who took a foreign wife (Ezra 10:29). See Jashubi-lehem. **[2]** See Job [2].

Jashubi-lehem (je-shū'bi-lē'hem; "turning back to Bethlehem"). A descendant of Judah (1 Chron. 4:22).

Jasiel (ja'si-el). See Jaasiel.

Jason (ja'sun; "healing"). **[1]** Paul's host during his stay at Thessalonica (Acts 17:5-9). **[2]** A Jewish Christian kinsman of Paul who sent salutations to Rome (Rom. 16:21). Both are possibly identical.

Jathniel (jath'ni-el; "God is giving"). A gatekeeper of the tabernacle (1 Chron. 26:2).

Jattir (jat'ir; "preeminence"). A town in the mountains of Judah, assigned to the Levites (Josh. 15:48; 21:14); possibly modern Khirbet 'Atti, 21 km. (13 mi.) south-southwest of Hebron.

Javan (jā'van). Fourth son of Japheth (Gen. 10:2, 4; 1 Chron. 1:5, 7). The name corresponds etymologically with Ionia and may denote the Greeks (cf. Isa. 66:19).

Javan (jā'van; "Ionians"). A trading post in southern Arabia (Ezek. 27:13).

Jaziz (jā'ziz; "shining"). David's chief shepherd (1 Chron. 27:31).

Jearim (jē'a-rim; "woods"). Mountains marking the boundary of Judah about 13 km. (8 mi.) northeast of Beth-shemesh (Josh. 15:10).

Jeaterai (je-at'e-rī; "steadfast"). A descendant of Gershon (1 Chron. 6:21).

Jeberechiah (je-ber-e-kī'a; "Jehovah is blessing"). The father of the Zechariah whom Isaiah took as a witness (Isa. 8:2).

Jebus (jē'bus; "manager"). Another name for Jerusalem (Judg. 19:10-11).

Jecamiah [Jekamiah] (jek-a-mī'a; "may Jehovah establish"). **[1]** A descendant of Judah (1 Chron. 2:41). **[2]** A son of King Jeconiah (Jehoiachin; 1 Chron. 3:18).

Jecholiah [Jecoliah] (jek-o-lī'a; "Jehovah is able"). Mother of Uzziah (or Azariah), king of Judah (2 Kings 15:2; 2 Chron. 26:3).

Jechonias (jek-o-nī'as). Greek form of Jeconiah. *See* Jehoiachin.

Jecoliah (jek-o-lī'a). *See* Jecholiah.

Jeconiah (jek-o-nī'a). *See* Jehoiachin.

Jedaiah (je-dā'ya; "Jehovah is praise"). **[1]** A descendant of Simeon (1 Chron. 4:37). **[2]** One who helped repair the wall (Neh. 3:10).

Jedaiah (je-dā'ya; "Jehovah is knowing"). **[1]** A priest of Jerusalem (1 Chron. 9:10; 24:7; Ezra 2:36; Neh. 7:39). **[2]** A priest who returned with Zerubbabel (Neh. 11:10; 12:6, 19). **[3]** Another priest who came up with Zerubbabel (Neh. 12:7, 21). **[4]** One who brought gifts to the temple (Zech. 6:10, 14).

Jediael (je-dī'a-el; "God knows"). **[1]** A son of Benjamin (1 Chron. 7:6, 10-11). Possibly the same as Ashbel (1 Chron. 8:1). **[2]** One of David's mighty men (1 Chron. 11:45). **[3]** One who joined David at Ziklag (1 Chron. 12:20). **[4]** A descendant of Korah, son of Meshelemiah (1 Chron. 26:2).

Jedidah (je-dī'da; "beloved"). Mother of King Josiah (2 Kings 22:1).

Jedidiah (je-di-dī-a; "beloved of Jehovah"). The name God gave Solomon through Nathan (2 Sam. 12:25).

Jeduthun (je-dū'thun; "a choir of praise"). **[1]** One of the three chief musicians of the service of song (1 Chron. 9:16; 25:1-6; Neh. 11:17).

He was also named Ethan (1 Chron. 6:44; 15:17, 19). **[2]** The father of Obed-edom (1 Chron. 16:38). Some believe him identical with [1].

Jeezer (je-ē'zer; contracted form of Abiezer, "father of help"). A descendant of Manasseh (Num. 26:30). Probably the same as the Abiezer of Joshua's time (Josh. 17:2; 1 Chron. 7:18).

Jegar-sahadutha [Galeed] (je'gar-sa-had-ū'tha [gal'e-ed]; "heap of witness"). A pile of stones erected by Laban to memorialize his pact with Jacob; near Mount Gilead north of the Jabbok River (Gen. 31:47). Galeed is Hebrew and Jegar-sahadutha is Aramaic; both mean the same thing.

Jehaleleel [Jehalelel] (je-hal-ē'le-el [je-hal'e-lel]; "God is praised"). **[1]** A descendant of Judah through Caleb the spy (1 Chron. 4:16). **[2]** A descendant of Merari in the time of Hezekiah (2 Chron. 29:12).

Jehdeiah (je-dē'ya; "union of Jehovah"). **[1]** A descendant of Levi in David's time (1 Chron. 24:20). **[2]** An overseer of David (1 Chron. 27:30).

Jehezekel (je-hez'e-kel; "God is strong"). A priest with sanctuary duty (1 Chron. 24:16).

Jehiah (je-hī'a; "Jehovah is living"). A Levite gatekeeper of the ark (1 Chron. 15:24). He was also called Jeiel (1 Chron. 15:18; 2 Chron. 20:14).

Jehiel (je-hī'el; "God is living"). **[1]** A singer in the tabernacle in David's time (1 Chron. 15:18; 16:5). **[2]** A descendant of Gershon (1 Chron. 23:8; 29:8). **[3]** A companion of the sons of David (1 Chron. 27:32). **[4]** A son of Jehoshaphat (2 Chron. 21:2). **[5]** A son of Heman the singer (2 Chron. 29:14). **[6]** A Levite in charge of the dedicated things in the temple (2 Chron. 31:13). **[7]** A chief priest in Josiah's day (2 Chron. 35:8). **[8]** Father of one who returned from the Exile (Ezra 8:9). **[9]** Father of the one who first admitted taking a foreign wife during the Exile (Ezra 10:2). **[10]**, **[11]** Two who had taken foreign wives (Ezra 10:21, 26).

Jehieli (je-hī'e-lī). A Levite set over the treasures of the sanctuary in David's time (1 Chron. 26:21-22). *See* Jehiel.

Jehizkiah (jē-hiz-kī'a; "Jehovah is strong" or "Jehovah strengthens"). An opponent of those who would have made fellow Jews slaves (2 Chron. 28:12). *See* Hezekiah.

Jehoadah (je-hō'a-da; "Jehovah unveils; Jehovah has numbered"). *See* Jarah.

Jehoaddan (je-ho-ad'an; "Jehovah gives delight"). Mother of King Amaziah and wife of King Joash (2 Kings 14:2; 2 Chron. 25:1).

Jehoahaz (je-hō'a-haz; "Jehovah upholds"). **[1]** Son and successor of Jehu on the throne of Israel. His reign was one of disaster (2 Kings 10:35; 13:2-25). **[2]** The son of Josiah and ruler of Judah for three months before he was deposed by Pharaoh Necho (2 Kings 23:30-34; 2 Chron. 36:1-4). He was also called Shallum before becoming king (1 Chron. 3:15; Jer. 22:11). **[3]** *See* Ahaziah [2].

Jehoash [Joash] (je'hō-ash [jō'ash); "Jehovah has given; Jehovah supports"). **[1]** The ninth king of Judah. Until the time of Jehoiada the priest's death Jehoash followed God; afterwards, he brought idolatry and disaster to his country (2 Kings 11:21-12:21). He is more frequently called by the shortened form of his name, Joash. **[2]** The twelfth king of Israel; he was successful in many military campaigns (2 Kings 13:9-14:16). He is most frequently called Joash, an abbreviated form of his name.

Jehohanan (je-hō-hā'nan; "Jehovah is gracious"). **[1]** A gatekeeper of the tabernacle in David's time (1 Chron. 26:3). **[2]** A chief captain of Judah (2 Chron. 17:15). **[3]** Father of one who aided Jehoiada (2 Chron. 23:1). **[4]]** One who married a foreign wife during the Exile (Ezra 10:28). **[5]** A priest who returned to Jerusalem with Zerubbabel (Neh. 12:13). **[6]** A singer at the purification of the wall of Jerusalem (Neh. 12:42). **[7]** Son of Tobiah the Ammonite (Neh. 6:17-18).

Jehoiachin (je-hoi'a-kin; "Jehovah establishes"). Ruler of Judah when it was captured by Nebuchadnezzar. He was an ancestor of Christ (2 Kings 24:8-15; 2 Chron. 36:9-10; Matt. 1:11-12). Jeconiah [Jechonias] ("Jehovah is able") is an altered form of his name (1 Chron. 3:16-17; Jer. 24:1) as is Coniah ("Jehovah is creating"; Jer. 22:24, 28; 37:1).

Jehoiada (je-hoi'a-da; "Jehovah knows"). **[1]** The father of one of David's officers (2 Sam. 8:18; 1 Kings 1:8, 26). **[2]** The chief priest of the temple for many years of the monarchy. He hid Joash from Athaliah for 6 years (2 Kings 11-12:9). **[3]** One who joined David at Ziklag (1 Chron. 12:27). **[4]** A counselor of David (1 Chron. 27:34). **[5]** One who helped to repair a gate of Jerusalem (Neh. 3:6). **[6]** A priest replaced by Zephaniah (Jer. 29:26). *See* Joiada.

Jehoiakim (je-hoi'a-kim; "Jehovah sets up" or "Jehovah has established"). The name given to Eliakim by Pharaoh Necho when he made him king of Judah. The name probably means that Necho claimed Jehovah had authorized him to put Eliakim on the throne (2 Kings 23:34–24:6). Not to be confused with Joiakim.

Jehoiarib (je-hoi'a-rib; "Jehovah contends"). **[1]** Head of a family of Aaron (1 Chron. 24:7). **[2]** *See* Joiarib [3].

Jehonadab [Jonadab] (je-hon'a-dab [jon'a-dab]; "Jehovah is liberal"). **[1]** Descendant of Rechab, who forbade his followers and descendants to drink wine and live in houses (Jer. 35:6-19; 2 Kings 10:15, 23). **[2]** The sly son of David's brother, Shimeah (2 Sam. 13:3, 5, 32, 35).

Jehonathan (je-hon'a-than; "Jehovah gives"). **[1]** An overseer of David's storehouses (1 Chron. 27:25). **[2]** One sent by Jehoshaphat to teach the Law (2 Chron. 17:8). **[3]** A priest (Neh. 12:18). He is called Jonathan in Nehemiah 12:35.

Jehoram [Joram] (je-hō'ram [jō'ram]; "Jehovah is high"). Joram is a shortened form of the name. **[1]** Son and successor of Jehoshaphat to the throne of Judah and an ancestor of Christ (2 Kings 8:16-24; Matt. 1:8). [2] The ninth king of Israel, slain by Jehu (2 Kings 1:17; 3:1-6; 9:24). [3] A priest commissioned to teach the people (2 Chron. 17:8).

Jehoshabeath [Jehosheba] (je-hō-shab'e-ath [je-hosh-e-ba]; "Jehovah makes oath"). A daughter of Jehoram, king of Judah, who helped conceal Joash (2 Chron. 22:11). In Second Kings 1:2, she is called Jehosheba.

Jehoshaphat [Josaphat] (je-hosh'a-fat [jos'a-fat]; "Jehovah is judge"). [1] The recorder of David (2 Sam. 8:16; 20:24; 1 Kings 4:3). [2] An officer of Solomon (1 Kings 4:17). [3] Father of Jehu, who conspired against Joram (2 Kings 9:2, 14). [4] A priest who helped to bring the ark of the covenant from Obed-edom (1 Chron. 15:24). [5] Faithful king of Judah and an ancestor of Christ (1 Kings 22:41-50; Matt. 1:8).

Jehoshaphat (je-hosh'a-fat; "judged of God"). The valley where the Last Judgment will take place (Joel 3:2); tradition identifies it as the Kidron Valley (q.v.).

Jehosheba (je-hosh'e-ba). See Jehoshabeath.

Jehoshua (je-hosh'u-a). See Joshua.

Jehovah-jireh (je-hō'va-jī're; "the Lord will provide"). The place where Abraham attempted to offer Isaac as a sacrifice (Gen. 22:14); its exact location is unknown.

Jehovah-nissi (je-hō'va-nis'ī; "the Lord my banner"). The altar that Moses built at Rephidim in honor of Israel's victory over Amalek (Exod. 17:15).

Jehovah-shalom (je-hō'va-sha'lom; "the Lord send peace"). An altar that Gideon built at Ophrah [2] (Judg. 6:24).

Jehozabad (je-hoz'a-bad; "Jehovah endows"). [1] A servant who killed Jehoash (2 Kings 12:21; 2 Chron. 24:26). [2] A gatekeeper descended from Korah (1 Chron. 26:4). [3] A chief captain of Jehoshaphat (2 Chron. 17:18). Not to be confused with Jozabad.

Jehozadak (je-hoz'a-dak). See Josedech.

Jehu (jē'hū; "Jehovah is he"). [1] The prophet who brought tidings of disaster to Baasha of Israel (1 Kings 16:1-12; 2 Chron. 19:2). [2] The tenth king of Israel (1 Kings 19:16-17; 2 Kings 9-10). His corrupt leadership weakened the nation. [3] A descendant of Hezron (1 Chron. 2:38). [4] A descendant of Simeon (1 Chron. 4:35). [5] One who joined David at Ziklag (1 Chron. 12:3).

Jehubbah (je-hūb'a; "hidden"). A descendant of Asher (1 Chron. 7:34).

Jehucal [Jucal] (je-hū'kal [joo'kal] "Jehovah is able"). A messenger of Zedekiah (Jer. 37:3; 38:1).

Jehud (jē'hud; "praising"). A town of the tribe of Dan located between Baalath and Bene-berak (Josh. 19:45); probably modern el-Yehudiyeh.

Jehudi (je-hū'dī; "a Jew"). A man who brought Baruch to the princes and read the king Jeremiah's prophecies (Jer. 36:14, 21, 23).

Jehudijah (je-hu-dī'ja; "the Jewess"). The wife of Ezra and descendant of Caleb (1 Chron. 4:18).

Jehush (jē'hush; "collector"). A man of the family of Saul (1 Chron. 8:39).

Jeiel [Jehiel] (je-ī'el [je-hī'el]; "God snatches away"). **[1]** A chief of the tribe of Reuben (1 Chron. 5:7). **[2]** An ancestor of Saul (1 Chron. 9:35). **[3]** One of David's mighty men (1 Chron. 11:44). **[4]** A singer and gatekeeper of the tabernacle (1 Chron. 15:18, 21; 16:5). **[5]** A descendant of Asaph (2 Chron. 20:14). **[6]** A scribe or recorder of Uzziah (2 Chron. 26:11). **[7]** A Levite in Hezekiah's time (2 Chron. 29:13). **[8]** A chief Levite in the days of Josiah (2 Chron. 35:9). **[9]** One who returned to Jerusalem with Ezra (Ezra 8:13). **[10]** One who married a foreign wife during the Exile (Ezra 10:43).

Jekabzeel (je-kab'ze-el; "congregation of God"). See Kabzeel.

Jekameam (jek-a-mē'am; "standing of the people"). A descendant of Levi (1 Chron. 23:19; 24:23).

Jekamiah (jek-a-mī'a). See Jecamiah.

Jekuthiel (je-kū'thi-el; "God is mighty"). A descendant of the spy Caleb (1 Chron. 4:18).

Jemima (je-mī'ma; "little dove"). First daughter of Job to be born after his restoration from affliction (Job 42:14).

Jemuel (jem'u-el; "God is light"). See Nemuel.

Jephthae (jef'the). Greek form of Jephthah (q.v.).

Jephthah [Jephthae] (jef'tha [jef'the]; "an opposer"). A judge of Israel who delivered his people from Ammon (Judg. 11–12:7).

Jephunneh (je-fun'e; "appearing"). **[1]** A man of Judah and father of Caleb the spy (Num. 13:6; 14:6; Deut. 1:36). **[2]** Head of a family of the tribe of Asher (1 Chron. 7:38).

Jerah (jē'ra; "moon"). A son of Joktan (Gen. 10:26; 1 Chron. 1:20). Possibly an Arabian tribe is intended.

Jerahmeel (je-ra'me-el; "God is merciful"). **[1]** A son of Hezron, grandson of Judah (1 Chron. 2:9, 25-27, 33, 42). **[2]** A son of Kish (1 Chron. 24:29). **[3]** An officer of Jehoiakim (Jer. 36:26).

Jered (je'red; "low; flowing"). **[1]** A son of Ezra, a descendant of Caleb (1 Chron. 4:18). **[2]** See Jared.

Jeremai (jer'e-mī; "Jehovah is high"). One who took a foreign wife during the Exile (Ezra 10:33).

Jeremiah [Jeremias; Jeremy] (jer-e-mī'a [jer-e-mī'as; jer'e-mī]; "Jehovah is high"). **[1]** A woman of Libnah whose daughter married King Josiah (2 Kings 23:31; Jer. 52:1). **[2]** Head of a family of the tribe of Manasseh (1 Chron. 5:24). **[3]** One who joined David at Ziklag (1 Chron. 12:4). **[4]** A man of Gad who joined David at Ziklag (1 Chron. 12:10). **[5]** Another who joined David at Ziklag (1 Chron. 12:13). **[6]** A priest who sealed the new covenant with God after the Exile (Neh. 10:2; 12:1, 12). **[7]** A descendant of Jonadab (Jer. 35:3). **[8]**

A prophet whose activity covered the reigns of the last five kings of Judah. He denounced the policies and idolatries of his nation (Jer. 1; 20; 26; 36).

Jeremias (jer-e-mī'as). Greek form of Jeremiah (q.v.).

Jeremoth (jer'e-mōth; "elevation"). [1] A son of Beriah (1 Chron. 8:14). [2], [3] Two who married foreign wives (Ezra 10:26-27). [4] A son of Mushi, descendant of Levi (1 Chron. 23:23). He is called Jerimoth in First Chronicles 24:30. [5] One appointed by David to the song service of the temple (1 Chron. 25:22). He is called Jerimoth in First Chronicles 25:4.

Jeriah [Jerijah] (jer-ī'a [jer-ī'ja]; "Jehovah is foundation"). A descendant of Hebron in the days of David (1 Chron. 23:19; 24:23; 26:31).

Jeribai (jer'i-bī; "Jehovah contends"). One of David's mighty men (1 Chron. 11:46).

Jericho (jer'i-kō "his sweet smell"). A fortified city of Canaan located about 8 km. (5 mi.) from the north end of the Dead Sea and 16 km. (10 mi.) northwest of the Jordan River (Num. 22:1; Deut. 32:49). Today it is the oldest continually inhabited city in the world.

Jeriel (jer'i-el; "foundation of God"). A descendant of Issachar (1 Chron. 7:2).

Jerijah (jer-ī'ja). *See* Jeriah.

Jerimoth (jer'i-moth; "elevation"). [1] A son of Bela (1 Chron. 7:7). [2] A son of Becher, son of Benjamin (1 Chron. 7:8). [3] One who joined David at Ziklag (1 Chron. 12:5). [4] A ruler of the tribe of Naphtali (1 Chron. 27:19). [5] A son of David (2 Chron. 11:18). [6] *See* Jeremoth [4], [5].

Terrain near Jericho.
This rugged mountain valley is typical of the area near Jericho, the city overwhelmed by Joshua. In this view, the monastery of St. George of Koziba overlooks the Wadi Qilt.

Jerioth (je'ri-oth; "tremulousness"). A wife or concubine of Caleb (1 Chron. 2:18).

Jeroboam (jer-o-bō'am; "enlarger; he pleads the people's cause"). [1] The first king of Israel after the division of the kingdom. He reigned for 22 years (1 Kings 11:26-40; 12:1-14:20). [2] The thirteenth king of Israel; his Israel was strong but overtly idolatrous (2 Kings 14:23-29).

Jeroham (je-rō'ham; "loved"). [1] A Levite, the grandfather of Samuel (1 Sam. 1:1; 1 Chron. 6:27). [2] A descendant of Benjamin (1 Chron. 9:8). [3] Head of a family of Benjamin (1 Chron. 8:27). [4] A priest whose son lived in Jerusalem after the Exile (1 Chron. 9:12; Neh. 11:12). [5] Father of two who joined David at Ziklag (1 Chron. 12:7). [6] Father of Azareel, prince of Dan (1 Chron. 27:22). [7] Father of one who helped Jehoiada to set Joash on the throne of Judah (2 Chron. 23:1).

Jerubbaal (jer-ub-bā'al; "let Baal contend" or possibly "let Baal show himself great"). The name given to Gideon by his father (Judg. 6:32; 7:1; 8:29).

Jerubbesheth (jer-ub-bē'sheth; "contender with the idol"). Name given to Jerubbaal (Gideon) by those who wanted to avoid pronouncing Baal (2 Sam. 11:21).

Jeruel (je-rū'el; "vision of God"). A wilderness area in Judah near the cliff of Ziz and En-gedi (2 Chron. 20:16).

Jerusalem (je-rū'sa-lem; "possession of peace"). Capital of the southern kingdom of Judah, located 48 km. (30 mi.) from the Mediterranean Sea and 27 km. (18 mi.) west of the Jordan River (Josh. 10:1; 2 Sam. 5:5).

Jerusha [Jerushah] (je-rū'sha [je-rū'sha]; "possession"). The wife of King Uzziah (2 Kings 15:33; 2 Chron. 27:1).

Jesaiah [Jeshaiah] (je-sā'ya [je-shā'ya]; "Jehovah is helper"). **[1]** A grandson of Zerubbabel (1 Chron. 3:21). **[2]** One appointed to the song service (1 Chron. 25:3, 15). **[3]** A grandson of Moses (1 Chron. 26:25). **[4]** One who returned from the Babylonian Captivity (Ezra 8:7). **[3]** A descendant of Merari who returned from Exile (Ezra 8:19). **[6]** One whose descendants dwelled in Jerusalem (Neh. 11:17).

Jeshanah (jesh'a-na; "old"). A city in the hill country of Ephraim (2 Chron. 13:19); variously identified as modern 'Ain Sinya, 6 km. (4 mi.) north of Bethel, or Burj el-Isanah, about 10 km. (6 mi.) north of Bethel.

Jesharelah (jesh-a-rē'la). *See* Asarelah.

Jeshebeab (je-sheb'e-ab; "seat of the father"). Head of the fourteenth course of priests (1 Chron. 24:13).

Jesher (je-sher; "rightness"). A son of Caleb (1 Chron. 2:18).

Jeshimon (jesh'i-mon; "solitude"). **[1]** A wilderness area lying west of the Dead Sea a few kilometers south of Hebron (1 Sam. 23:19; 26:1, 3). **[2]** A wilderness on the northeast end of the Dead Sea, near Pisgah and Peor (Num. 21:20).

Jerusalem and History

The most famous city in Bible lands is Jerusalem. From early times it was an important center. For example, Abram gave gifts to Melchizedek, who was the "king of Salem" (Gen. 14:18). This "Salem" was most likely the city of Jerusalem.

When the Israelites conquered the Promised Land, Benjamin's tribe was assigned the territory that included Jerusalem. But the invading armies were not strong enough to capture the city, and it was not until King David's time that Jerusalem finally became Hebrew territory (2 Sam. 5:6-7). David made the city his capital. He brought the ark of the covenant there, pitched a suitable tent for it, and began planning a temple to house the ark. His son Solomon completed the job (2 Sam. 7:12-16 and 1 Kings 5-6).

Later kings neglected both the temple and the city of Jerusalem. But at the height of its glory, Jerusalem was a showplace of the nation and the temple was world-famous. The greatest era in the history of the city and temple was under Solomon.

The city was protected by God when the national leaders worshiped Him and trusted Him. When Sennacherib attempted to destroy it, the Assyrian army was destroyed by a miracle from God (2 Kings 19:35-37).

In 587 B.C., Nebuchadnezzar of Babylon invaded Palestine, overran the city, and took the people away as slaves. The expensive treasures that were housed in the city and the many skilled craftsmen who maintained the valuable works of art and architectural design are described in 2 Kings 24:10-17.

For fifty years the city of Jerusalem lay in waste, but in 537 B.C. Zerubbabel and 50,000 followers were allowed to return and start rebuilding (Ezra 2:64-65; 3:8). Nehemiah rebuilt the walls of Jerusalem in about 444 B.C. (Neh. 6:15). Slowly, the Hebrews

Jeshishai (je-shi'sha-i; "Jehovah is ancient" or "aged"). A descendant of Gad (1 Chron. 5:14).

Jeshohaiah (je-sho-hā'ya; "humbled by Jehovah"). A descendant of Simeon (1 Chron. 4:36).

Jeshua [Jeshuah] (jesh'u-a [jesh'u-a]; "Jehovah is deliverance"). **[1]** A priest of the sanctuary (1 Chron. 24:11; Ezra 2:36; Neh. 7:39). **[2]** A Levite in charge of various offerings to the temple (2 Chron. 31:15). **[3]** A priest who returned to Jerusalem with Zerubbabel (Ezra 2:2; 3:2-9; 4:3; Neh. 7:7; 12:1-26). **[4]** Father of Jozabad the Levite (Ezra 8:33). **[5]** One whose descendants returned from the Exile (Ezra 2:6; Neh. 7:11). **[6]** Father of one who repaired the wall of Jerusalem (Neh. 3:19). **[7]** A Levite who explained the Law to the people (Neh. 8:7; 9:4-5). **[8]** One who sealed the new covenant with God after the Exile (Ezra 2:40; Neh. 7:43; 10:9). Some believe he is identical with **[6]**. **[9]** *See* Joshua.

Jeshua (jesh'u-a; "a savior"). A town in southern Judah that was repopulated by Jews returning from the Babylonian Captivity (Neh. 11:26); probably modern Tell es-Sa'roeh, about 18 km. (11 mi.) east-northeast of Beer-sheba.

Jeshurun [Jesurun] (jesh'u-run [jes'oo-run]; "blessed"). A symbolic name for Israel (Deut. 32:15; Isa. 44:2).

Jesiah (je-sī'a; "Jehovah exists"). **[1]** One who joined David at Ziklag (1 Chron. 12:6). **[2]** A descendant of Uzziel and a Levite (1 Chron. 23:20). He is called Isshiah in First Chronicles 24:25.

---

returned from their captivity and worked at rebuilding other sections of their city.

Other strong nations arose—the Greeks under Alexander the Great, the Egyptians, and the Persians. In 198 B.C., Jerusalem became a part of the Seleucid Empire. Judas Maccabee, one of Israel's greatest heros, retook the city in 165 B.C. and purified the temple.

In 63 B.C., Roman armies swept through Palestine and captured Jerusalem, ruining what was left of Zerubbabel's attempts to rebuild the temple. However, in 37 B.C., Herod the Great began rebuilding the temple on a grand scale; his work was so complex that the temple wasn't complete when Jesus was taken there as a baby (Luke 2:21-39). The end of Jerusalem's history in biblical times came when Titus, the Roman emperor, leveled the city and temple in A.D. 70.

Despite the troubled history of the "holy city," it still stands as a symbol of the Jewish people. "Zion" is one name given to it (although this really refers to one of the several hills around Jerusalem). The Bible calls the city by various names of honor: "city of David" (2 Sam. 5:7); "city of God" (Psa. 46:4); "city of truth" (Zec. 8:3); "holy city" (Neh. 11:1); "throne of the Lord" (Jer. 3:17) and many more.

The Egyptian pharaoh's daughter visited Solomon there (1 Kings 3:1), the Queen of Sheba also visited (1 Kings 10:1-2). Many events of Jesus' earthly ministry occurred there: Palm Sunday, the meal in an upper room, the trials and death of Christ, and His appearance after the Resurrection (Luke 24:33ff.).

In both Hebrews and Revelation, Jerusalem symbolizes the future hope of Christians who are faithful. The fact that heaven is called the "New Jerusalem" (Rev. 21:2) shows that eternal life will be beautiful and wonderful, even as a perfect Jerusalem would be (Heb. 12:22; Rev. 21:10; 22:19).

Even today, Jerusalem is a center for historical study and international struggle. Three world religions claim it as a holy city—Islam, Judaism, and Christianity.

Jezebel's Idolatry

Jezebel, daughter of King Ethbaal of Sidon, was raised in Sidon, a commercial city on the coast of the Mediterranean Sea. Sidon was considered to be a center of vice and ungodliness. When Jezebel married King Ahab of Israel, she moved to Jezreel, a city that served Jehovah. Jezebel soon decided to turn Jezreel into a city similar to her native town.

Jezebel tried to convince her husband to begin serving the golden calf, under the pretense that such worship would really be a service to Jehovah. Actually, the calf was a central idol in the worship of Baal, a sun-god who was important to ancient Phoenicians. Because Baal was believed to have power over crops, flocks, and the fertility of farm families, the golden calf was often linked with him. As the worship of Baal spread to countries bordering Phoenicia, more peoples adopted the religion's lascivious rites, which included human sacrifice, self-torture, and kissing the image. The practices of the Baal cult offended pious Jews, but because King Ahab was easily manipulated by Jezebel, beautiful temples honoring Baal were soon erected throughout Israel.

The priests of Jehovah opposed Jezebel; many of them were murdered. Even the great prophet Elijah fled from her wrath (1 Kings 18:4-19).

In her effort to erase the mark of Jehovah throughout Israel, Jezebel became the first female religious persecutor in Bible history. She so effectively injected the poison of idolatry into the veins of Israel that the nation suffered.

Elijah said, "The dogs shall eat Jezebel by the wall of Jezreel" (1 Kings 21:23). This prophesy came true; only Jezebel's skull, feet, and the palms of her hands were left to bury (2 Kings 9:36-37).

The hearts of the Israelites must have been ripe for idolatry, or Jezebel would not have been able to so pervert their religion. King Ahab committed a grave sin against God by marrying her, because Jezebel worshiped Baal (1 Kings 21:25-26).

Jesimiel (je-sim'i-el; "God sets"). A descendant of Simeon (1 Chron. 4:36).

Jesse (jes'e; "Jehovah exists; wealthy"). Father of David and an ancestor of Christ (Ruth 4:17, 22; 1 Sam. 17:17; Matt. 1:5-6).

Jesui (jes'u-ī). See Ishui.

Jesurun (jes'oo-run). See Jeshurun.

Jesus (jē'zus; Greek form of Joshua). [1] A Christian who, with Paul, sent greetings to the Colossians (Col. 4:11); he was also called Justus. [2] See Joshua.

Jesus Christ (jē'zus krīst; Jesus—"Jehovah is salvation," Christ— "the anointed one"). The son of the Virgin Mary who came to earth to fulfill the prophecies of the King who would die for the sins of His people. The account of His ministry is found in the Gospels of Matthew, Mark, Luke, and John.

Jether (jē'ther; "pre-eminent"). [1] The firstborn son of Gideon (Judg. 8:20). [2] A son of Jerahmeel (1 Chron. 2:32). [3] A descendant of Caleb the spy (1 Chron. 4:17). [4] A descendant of Asher (1 Chron. 7:38). [5] See Ithra.

Jetheth (jē'theth; "subjection"). A duke of Edom (Gen. 36:40; 1 Chron. 1:51).

Jethlah (jeth'la). A town of Dan (Josh. 19:42).

Jethro (jeth'ro; "pre-eminence"). The father-in-law of Moses. He advised Moses to delegate the time-consuming administration of justice (Exod. 3:1; 4: 8; 18:1-12). He is called Reuel in Exodus 2:18. In Numbers 10:29, the KJV calls him Raguel; but the Hebrew text reads Reuel.

Jetur (jē'tur). A son of Ishmael (Gen. 25:15; 1 Chron. 1:31).

Jeuel (je-ū'el; "snatching away"). A descendant of Judah (1 Chron. 9:6).

Jeush (jē'ush; "collector"). [1] A son of Esau (Gen. 36:5, 14, 18; 1 Chron. 1:35). [2] A descendant of Benjamin (1 Chron. 7:10). [3] A descendant of Gershon and the head of a clan (1 Chron. 23:10-11). [4] A son of Rehoboam (2 Chron. 11:19).

Jeuz (jē'uz; "counselor"). Son of Shaharaim, a descendant of Benjamin (1 Chron. 8:10).

Jezaniah (jez-a-nī'a). *See* Jaazaniah [1].

Jezebel (jez'e-bel; "unexalted; unhusbanded"). [1] The wicked, idolatrous queen of Israel (1 Kings 16:31; 18:4–21:25; 2 Kings 9:7-37). [2] A false prophetess at Thyatira (Rev. 2:20). Possibly the name is symbolic and not the prophetess's real name.

Jezer (jē'zer; "formation"). The third son of Naphtali (Gen. 46:24; Num. 26:49; 1 Chron. 7:13).

Jeziah (je-zī'a; "Jehovah unites"). One who took a foreign wife (Ezra 10:25).

Jeziel (jē'zi-el; "God unites"). Man of valor who joined David at Ziklag (1 Chron. 12:3).

Jezliah (jez-lī'a "Jehovah delivers"). A descendant of Benjamin (1 Chron. 8:18).

Jezoar (je-zō'er). A descendant of Caleb, the son of Hur (1 Chron. 4:7).

Jezrahiah (jez-ra-hī'a; "Jehovah is shining"). An overseer of the singers at the purification of the people (Neh. 12:42). *See* Izrahiah.

Jezreel (jez're-el; "God sows"). [1] A descendant of Etam (1 Chron. 4:3). [2] The symbolic name of a son of Hosea (Hos. 1:4).

Jezreel (jez're-el; "seed of God"). [1] A city on the Plain of Jezreel between Mount Gilboa and Mount Carmel (Josh. 19:18; 1 Kings 21:1). [2] A town in Judah's hill country (Josh. 15:56); probably modern Khirbet Terrama on the Plain of Dibleh.

Plain of Jezreel. King Ahab and his wife Jezebel conspired to murder a man named Naboth and seize his vineyard, which grew in this fertile region (1 Kings 21:1-15). The mountains of Gilboa rise in the background; their streams water the rich soil of the plain.

Jibsam (jib'sam; "lovely scent"). A son of Tola (1 Chron. 7:2).

Jidlaph (jid'laf; "melting away"). Son of Nahor and nephew of Abraham (Gen. 22:22).

Jimna (jim'na). *See* Imna.

Jiphtah (jif'ta; "breaking through"). A city in Judah near Ashnah and Nezib (Josh. 15:43).

Jiphthah-el (jif'tha-el; "God opens"). A valley that served as the boundary between the territories of Zebulun and Asher (Josh. 19:14, 27).

Joab (jō'ab; "Jehovah is father"). [1] A son of Zeruiah, David's sister. He was captain of David's army (2 Sam. 2:13-32; 3:23-31; 18; 1 Kings 2:22-23). [2] A descendant of Judah (1 Chron. 2:54). Some scholars believe a city of Judah is referred to here. The name would include the four words that follow in the KJV and be written: Atroth-beth-joab. [3] One of the tribe of Judah (1 Chron. 4:14). [4] An ancestor of returned captives (Ezra 2:6; 8:9; Neh. 7:11).

Joah (jō'a; "Jehovah is brother"). [1] A son of Asaph, the recorder in the time of Hezekiah (2 Kings 18:18, 26; Isa. 36:3, 11, 22). [2] A descendant of Gershom (1 Chron. 6:21; 2 Chron. 29:12). [3] A porter in the tabernacle (1 Chron. 26:4). [4] A Levite commissioned to repair the Lord's house (2 Chron. 34:8).

Joahaz (jō'a-haz; "Jehovah helps"). Father of Joah, Josiah's recorder (2 Chron. 34:8).

Joanna (jō-an'a; "God-given"). [1] An ancestor of Christ (Luke 3:27). [2] The wife of Chuza, Herod's steward, who ministered to Christ and the apostles (Luke 8:3; 24:10).

Joash (jō'ash; abbreviated form of Jehoash). [1] A man of Judah (1 Chron. 4:22). [2] Father of Gideon the judge (Judg. 6:11-32). [3] A son of Ahab (1 Kings 22:26; 2 Chron. 18:25). [4] One who joined David at Ziklag (1 Chron. 12:3). [5] *See* Jehoash [1]. [6] *See* Jehoash [2].

Joash (jō'ash; "Jehovah has aided"). [1] A son of Becher, a descendant of Benjamin (1 Chron. 7:8). [2] The keeper of David's stores of oil (1 Chron. 27:28).

Joatham (jō'a-tham). Greek form of Jotham (q.v.).

Job (jōb; "hated; persecuted"). [1] A pious man of Uz. His endurance in fierce trial resulted in marvelous blessing (Job 1-3; 42; Ezek. 14:14, 20). [2] The third son of Issachar (Gen. 46:13); he is also called Jashub (Num. 26:24; 1 Chron. 7:1).

Jobab (jō'bab). [1] A son of Joktan (Gen. 10:29; 1 Chron. 1:23). The name may possibly refer to an unknown Arabian tribe. [2] A king of Edom (Gen. 36:33-34; 1 Chron. 1:44-45). [3] A king of Canaan conquered by Joshua (Josh. 11:1). [4] A descendant of Benjamin (1 Chron. 8:9). [5] Another descendant of Benjamin (1 Chron. 8:18).

Jochebed (jok'e-bed; "Jehovah is honor or glory"). A descendant of Levi and mother of Moses (Exod. 6:20; Num. 26:59).

Joed (jō'ed; "Jehovah is witness"). A son of Pedaiah, a descendant of Benjamin (Neh. 11:7).

Joel (jō'el; "Jehovah is God"). [1] The firstborn son of Samuel the prophet (1 Sam. 8:2; 1 Chron. 6:33; 15:17). *See also* Vashni. [2] A descendant of Simeon (1 Chron. 4:35). [3] The father of Shemaiah, a descendant of Reuben (1 Chron. 5:4, 8). [4] A chief of the tribe of Gad (1 Chron. 5:12). [5] An ancestor of the prophet Samuel (1 Chron. 6:36). [6] A descendant of Tola (1 Chron. 7:3). [7] One of David's mighty men (1 Chron. 11:38). [8] A Levite in David's time (1 Chron. 15:7, 11; 23:8). [9] A keeper of the treasures of the Lord's house (1 Chron. 26:22). [10] A prince of Manasseh west of the Jordan (1 Chron. 27:20). [11] A Levite who aided in cleansing the temple (2 Chron. 29:12). [12] One who married a foreign wife during the Exile (Ezra 10:43). [13] An overseer of the descendants of Benjamin in Jerusalem (Neh. 11:9). [14] A prophet in the days of Uzziah (Joel 1:1; Acts 2:16).

Joelah (jo-ē'la; "God is snatching; may he avail!"). One who joined David at Ziklag (1 Chron. 12:7).

Joezer (jo-ē'zer; "Jehovah is help"). A warrior who joined David at Ziklag (1 Chron. 12:6).

Jogbehah (jog'be-ha; "high"). A city east of the Jordan River, inhabited by the tribe of Gad (Num. 32:35); present-day Jubeihat, located 10 km. (6 mi.) northwest of Rabbath-ammon.

Jogli (jog-li; "exiled"). A prince of Dan (Num. 34:22).

Joha (jō'ha; "Jehovah is living"). [1] A descendant of Benjamin (1 Chron. 8:16). [2] One of David's valiant men (1 Chron. 11:45).

Johanan (jō'hā'nan; "Jehovah is gracious"). [1] A captain who allied with Gedaliah after the fall of Jerusalem (2 Kings 25:23; Jer. 40:8, 13). [2] Eldest son of Josiah, king of Judah (1 Chron. 3:15). [3] A son of Elionai (1 Chron. 3:24). [4] Father of a priest in Solomon's time (1 Chron. 6:9-10). [5], [6] Two valiant men who joined David at Ziklag (1 Chron. 12:4, 12). [7] One who opposed making slaves of Judean captives in Ahaz's time (2 Chron. 28:12). [8] A returned exile (Ezra 8:12). [9] A priest who beckoned the exiles to Jerusalem (Ezra 10:6). [10] A son of Tobiah the Ammonite (Neh. 6:18). [11] A priest in the days of Joiakim (Neh. 12:22-23).

John (jon; a contraction of Jehohanan, "gift of God"). [1] The son of Zacharias and Elizabeth who came to prepare the way for the Messiah. He was called John the Baptist and was beheaded by Herod (Matt. 3; 11:7-18; 14:1-10; Luke 1:13-17). [2] A son of Zebedee and one of the twelve apostles. He is traditionally accorded the authorship of the Revelation, the Fourth Gospel, and the three epistles bearing his name (Matt. 4:21; 10:2; Acts 1:13; Gal. 2:9; Rev. 1:1). [3] A relative of the high priest Annas, who sat in judgment on Peter (Acts 4:6). [4] A missionary better known by his surname, Mark (q.v.). *See also* Jehohanan; Johanan.

Joiada (joi'a-da; "Jehovah knows"). An ancestor of the priest Jeshua (Neh. 12:10-11, 22; 13:28). *See* Jehoiada.

Joiakim (joi'a-kim; "Jehovah sets up"). The son of Jeshua who returned from the Babylonian Captivity (Neh. 12:10, 12, 26). Not to be confused with Jehoiakim.

Joiárib (joi'a-rib; "Jehovah knows"). [1] One whom Ezra sent to persuade ministers to return to the land of Israel (Ezra 8:16). [2] An ancestor of a family living in Jerusalem (Neh. 11:5). [3] A priest who returned from captivity (Neh. 11:10; 12:6, 19). He is called Jehoiarib in First Chronicles 9:10.

Jokdeam (jok'de-am; "anger of the people"). A city in the mountains of Judah south of Hebron (Josh. 15:56).

Jokim (jō'kim; "Jehovah sets up"). A descendant of Judah (1 Chron. 4:22).

Jokmeam (jok'mē-am; "revenge of the people"). A city of the tribe of Ephraim, given to the Levites. It stood nearly opposite the mouth of the Jabbok River (1 Chron. 6:68); probably the same as Kibzaim (q.v.).

Jokneam (jok'nē-am; "building up of the people"). [1] A city in Zebulun allotted to the Levites (Josh. 21:34). It stood on or near Mount Carmel, probably Tell Kaimun, about 11.3 km. (7 mi.) northwest of Megiddo. [2] A city in Ephraim (1 Kings 4:12). We should probably read Jokmeam (q.v.).

Jokshan (jok'shan; "fowler"). A son of Abraham by Keturah (Gen. 25:2-3; 1 Chron 1:32).

Joktan (jok'tan). A son of Eber of Shem's line (Gen. 10:25-26; 1 Chron. 1:19-20, 23). Perhaps the reference is to an Arabian tribe from whom many other Arabian groups sprang.

Joktheel (jok'the-el; "subdued by God"). [1] A city located in the lowlands of Judah (Josh. 15:38). [2] The name given to Sela [now Petra], capital of the Edomites (2 Kings 14:7).

Jona [Jonah; Jonas] (jō'na; [jō'na; jō'nas]; "a dove"). [1] The father of Simon Peter (John 1:42; 21:15-17). [2] A Hebrew prophet sent to preach to Nineveh in the days of Jeroboam II. He was the first Hebrew prophet sent to a heathen nation (2 Kings 14:25; Jon. 1:1, 3, 5, 17; 2:10; Matt. 12:39-41).

Jonadab (jon'a-dab). *See* Jehonadab.

Jonah (jō'na). *See* Jona.

Jonan (jō'nan; "grace"). An ancestor of Christ (Luke 3:30).

Jonathan (jon'a-than; "Jehovah is given"). [1] A priest of an idol shrine in the territory of Ephraim (Judg. 18:30). [2] A son of Abiathar the high priest (2 Sam. 15:27, 36; 17:17; 1 Kings 1:42). [3] A son of Shimea, David's brother (2 Sam. 21:21; 1 Chron. 20:7). [4] One of David's mighty men (2 Sam. 23:32; 1 Chron. 11:34). [5] A grandson of Onam (1 Chron. 2:32-33). [6] An uncle of David (1 Chron. 27:32). [7] Father of one who returned with Ezra (Ezra 8:6). [8] One involved with the foreign wife controversy (Ezra 10:15). [9] A descendant of

Jeshua the high priest (Neh. 12:11). **[10]** A priest (Neh. 12:14). **[11]** A scribe in whose house Jeremiah was kept prisoner (Jer. 37:15, 20; 38:26). **[12]** One who joined Gedaliah after the fall of Jerusalem (Jer. 40:8) **[13]**)A son of Saul and close friend of David (1 Sam. 14; 18:1-4; 31:2). **[14]** See Jehonathan [3].

Joppa (jop'pa; "beauty"). A town on the coast of Palestine (2 Chron. 2:16; Acts 9:36). See Japho.

Jorah (jō'ra; "harvest-born"). See Hariph [2].

Jorai (jō'ra-ī; "taught of God"). A chief of the tribe of Gad (1 Chron. 5:13).

Joram (jō'ram; shortened form of Jehoram). **[1]** A descendant of Moses (1 Chron. 26:25). **[2]** See Hadoram [2]. **[3]** See Jehoram [1], [2].

Jordan (jor'dan; meaning uncertain). The major river of Palestine. It rises in a valley between Mount Lebanon and Hermon. It follows a twisting route to enter the north end of the Dead Sea (Gen. 13:10; Josh. 2:7).

Jorim (jō'rim; a shortened form of Jehoram). An ancestor of Christ (Luke 3:29).

Jorkoam (jor'kō'am; "spreading the people"). A son of Raham, or a city he founded (1 Chron. 2:44).

Jorkoam (jor'kō'am; "paleness"). A place belonging to the tribe of Judah (1 Chron. 2:44). It may be identical with Jokdeam (q.v.).

Josabad (jos'a-bad). See Jozabad.

Josaphat (jos'a-fat). Greek form of Jehoshaphat (q.v.).

Jose (jō'se). An ancestor of Christ (Luke 3:29). Not to be confused with Joses.

Josedech (jos'e-dek; "Jehovah is righteous"). A priest and father of Jeshua the high priest (Hag. 1:1, 12, 14; Zech. 6:11). He is also called Jozadak (Ezra 3:2, 8; 5:2; 10:18; Neh. 12:26) and Jehozadak (1 Chron. 6:14-15).

Joseph (jō'zef; "increaser"). **[1]** The son of Jacob and Rachel. He was sold into slavery but became the prime minister of Egypt (Gen. 37; 39–50). **[2]** Father of one of the spies sent into Canaan (Num. 13:7). **[3]** A son of Asaph (1 Chron. 25:2, 9). **[4]** One who married a foreign wife during the Exile (Ezra 10:42). **[5]** A priest of the family of Shebaniah (Neh. 12:14). **[6]** The husband of Mary, mother of Jesus (Matt. 1:16-24; 2:13; Luke 1:27; 2:4). **[7]** A converted Jew of Arimathea in whose tomb Jesus was laid (Matt. 27:57. 59; Luke 15:43). **[8]** An ancestor of Christ (Luke 3:24). **[9]** Another ancestor of Christ (Luke 3:26). **[10]** Yet another ancestor of Christ (Luke 3:30). **[11]** A disciple considered to take the place of Judas Iscariot (Acts 1:23). He was also known as Barsabas and Justus.

Joses (jō'sez; "helped"). **[1]** One of the brothers of Christ (Matt. 13:55; Mark 6:3). **[2]** The son of Mary, the wife of Cleophas (Matt. 27:56; Mark 15:40, 47). Not to be confused with Jose.

Joshah (jō'sha; "Jehovah is a gift"). A descendant of Simeon (1 Chron. 4:34).

Joshaphat (josh'a-fat; "Jehovah judges"). One of David's valiant men (1 Chron. 11:43). Not to be confused with Jehoshaphat.

Joshaviah (josh-a-vī'a; "Jehovah is equality"). One of David's valiant men (1 Chron. 11:46).

Joshbekashah (josh-be-kā'sha; "seated in hardness"). A son of Heman, David's song leader (1 Chron. 25:4, 24).

Joshua [**Jehoshua; Jeshua**] (josh'u-a [je-hosh'u-a; jesh'u-a]; "Jehovah is salvation"). **[1]** The successor of Moses; the general who led the conquest of the Promised Land (Exod. 17:9-14; 24:13; Deut. 31:1-23; 34:9). Moses changed his name from Hoshea ("Jehovah is help") to Joshua. Oshea is another form of Hoshea (Num. 13:8, 16; Deut. 32:44). Joshua and Jehoshua are forms of the same name. He is also called Jeshua (Neh. 8:17). **[2]** A native of Beth-shem in the days of Eli (1 Sam. 6:14, 18). **[3]** The governor of Jerusalem under Josiah (2 Kings 23:8). **[4]** High priest at the rebuilding of the temple (Hag. 1:1, 12, 14; 2:2, 4; Zech. 3:1, 3, 6).

Josiah [**Josias**] (jō-sī'a [jō-sī'as]; "Jehovah supports"). **[1]** Godly king of Judah during whose reign the Book of the Law was found (1 Kings 13:2; 2 Kings 22:1–23:30). He was an ancestor of Christ (Matt. 1:10-11). **[2]** A son of Zephaniah living in Jerusalem (Zech. 6:10). *See also* Hen.

Josias (jō-sī'as). Greek form of Josiah (q.v.).

Josibiah (jo-si-bī'a; "Jehovah causes to dwell"). A descendant of Simeon (1 Chron. 4:35).

Josiphiah (jos-i-fī'a; "Jehovah abides"). Father of one who returned from the Exile (Ezra 8:10).

Jotbath [**Jotbathah**] (jot'ba [jot'ba-tha]; "goodness"). An encampment of the Israelites in the wilderness. Apparently it was near Ezion-geber (Num. 33:33; Deut. 10:7); it is possibly modern el-Taba.

Jotham [**Joatham**] (jō'tham [jō'a-tham]; "Jehovah is perfect"). **[1]** The son of Gideon who managed to escape from Abimelech (Judg. 9:5, 7, 21, 57). **[2]** A son of Jahdai (1 Chron. 2:47). **[3]** The twelfth king of Judah and an ancestor of Christ (2 Kings 15:5-38; Isa. 1:1; 7:1; Matt. 1:9).

Jozabad [**Josabad**] (joz'a-bad [jos'a-bad]; "Jehovah endows"). **[1]** One who joined David at Ziklag (1 Chron. 12:4). **[2]**, **[3]** Two descendants of Manasseh who joined David at Ziklag (1 Chron. 12:20). **[4]** An overseer of the dedicated things of the temple under Hezekiah (2 Chron. 31:13). **[5]** A chief of the Levites in Josiah's time (2 Chron. 35:9). **[6]** One who helped weigh the sanctuary vessels (Ezra 8:33). **[7]**, **[8]** Two who had married foreign wives (Ezra 10:22-23). **[9]** One who interpreted the Law (Neh. 8:7). **[10]** A chief Levite after the Exile (Neh. 11:16). Not to be confused with Jehozabad.

Jozachar (joz'a-kar; "Jehovah remembers"). The servant and murderer of King Joash of Judah (2 Kings 12:21). He is called Zabad in Second Chronicles 24:26.

Jozadak (joz'a-dak). *See* Josedech.

Jubal (joo'bal; "playing; nomad"). Son of Lamech; he was skilled with musical instruments (Gen. 4:21).

Jucal (joo'kal). *See* Jehucal.

Juda [Judah; Judas; Jude] (joo'da [joo'da; joo'das; jood]; "praise"). [1] A son of Jacob by Leah and an ancestor of Christ. He acquired the birthright Reuben lost. His descendants became one of the twelve tribes of Israel (Gen. 29:35; 37:26-28; 43:3-10; Matt. 1:2-3; Luke 3:33). [2] An ancestor of one who helped to rebuild the temple (Ezra 3:9). [3] One who married a foreign wife during the Exile (Ezra 10:23). [4] Second in authority over Jerusalem after the Exile (Neh. 11:9). [5] One who came up to Jerusalem with Zerubbabel (Neh. 12:8). [6] A prince of Judah (Neh. 12:34). [7] A priest and musician (Neh. 12:36). [8] One of the twelve apostles. He betrayed his Lord and hanged himself (Matt. 10:4; 26:14, 25, 47; 27:3; Luke 6:16; 22:3, 47-48). He was called Iscariot, apparently meaning "a man of Kerioth," a town 19 km. (12 mi.) from Hebron. [9] One of the brothers of Jesus (Matt. 13:55; Mark 6:3). He wrote the epistle bearing his name (Jude 1). [10] A Galilean who caused a rebellion against Rome (Acts 5:37). [11] One with whom Paul stayed at Damascus (Acts 9:11). [12] A prophet sent to Antioch with Silas (Acts 15:22, 27); he was surnamed Barsabas. [13] *See* Thaddeus. [14], [15] Two ancestors of Christ (Luke 3:26, 30).

Judah [Joda] (joo'da [jo'da]; "the praise of the Lord"). The territory of one of the original twelve tribes. Judah, along with Benjamin, formed the southern kingdom after Solomon's death. The uncertain border between Israel and Judah ran between Bethel in Israel and Ramah in Judah. Jerusalem was its capital (2 Chron. 13:18; 15:8).

Judea [Jewry] (joo-dē'a [joo'rī]; "the praise of the Lord"). First mentioned as a Persian province (Ezra 3:8). Later it became a Roman province (Matt. 2:1). Its northern boundary was Joppa on the west to a point 16.1 km. (10 mi.) north of the Dead Sea on the east. Its southern boundary was about 7 miles southwest of Gaza, through Beer-sheba, to the southern end of the Dead Sea.

Judith (joo'dith; "Jewess"). A wife of Esau (Gen. 26:34). *See* Esau's Wives.

Julia (joo'li-a; "soft-haired"). A woman Christian to whom Paul sent greetings (Rom. 16:15).

Julius (joo'li'us; "soft-haired"). A centurion who delivered Paul to Rome (Acts 27:1, 3).

Junia (joo'ni-a; "youth"). A man or woman (probably a man) to whom Paul sent greetings (Rom. 16:7).

Jushab-hesed (joo'shab-hē'sed; "kindness is returned"). A son of Zerubbabel (1 Chron. 3:20).

Justus (jus'tus; "just"). [1] A believer in Corinth with whom Paul lodged (Acts 18:7). [2] *See* Jesus [2]. [3] *See* Joseph [11].

Juttah (jut'a; "turning away"). A city in the mountains of Judah. It is near Maon, Carmel, and Ziph (now Yatta), 8.8 km. (5.5 mi.) southwest of Hebron (Josh. 15:55; 21:16).

K

Kabzeel (kab'ze-el; "the congregation of God"). A city in Judah (Josh. 15:21; 2 Sam. 23:20); probably modern Khirbet Hora. In Nehemiah 11:25 the city was also known as Jekabzeel (q.v.).

Kadesh (kā'desh). *See* Kadesh-barnea; also Meribah [2].

Kadesh-barnea (kā'desh-bar'ne-a; "holy"). A wilderness on Palestine's southern frontier. It was on the border between the wilderness of Paran on the south and the wilderness of Zin on the north of the Sinai Peninsula (Num. 32:8; 34:4). It is also called simply Kadesh (Num. 13:26; 20:1). In Genesis 14:7 the region is called Enmishpat.

Kadmiel (kad'mi-el; "God the primeval" or "before God"). [1] One whose descendants returned from Exile (Ezra 2:40; Neh. 7:43). [2] One who helped rebuild the temple (Ezra 3:9). [3] Levite who led the devotions of the people (Neh. 9:4-5; 10:9).

Kallai (kal'a-ī; "Jehovah is light" or "swift"). A priest who returned with Zerubbabel (Neh. 12:20).

Kanah (kā'na; "of reeds"). [1] A stream that divided the territories of Ephraim and Manasseh; perhaps Wadi Kanah which enters the Mediterranean 6.4 km. (4 mi.) north of Joppa (Josh. 16:8; 17:9). [2] A city in Asher not far from Sidon, presently known as Ain Kanah (Josh. 19:28).

Kareah [Careah] (ka-rē'a [ka-rē'a]; "bald head"). The father of Johanan and Jonathan (Jer. 40:8). The KJV spells the name Careah in Second Kings 25:23.

Karkaa (kar'ka-a; "floor; deep ground"). An unknown site on the southern boundary of the tribe of Judah (Josh. 15:3).

Karkor (kar'kor; "they rested; even or deep ground"). A city in Gad, east of the Jordan. The site of Gideon's victory over Zebah and Zalmunna (Judg. 8:10). It is present-day Karkar.

Kartah (kar'ta; "city"). A city in Zebulun given to the Merarite Levites (Josh. 21:34). The site has been identified with Ailit on the seacoast 14.5 km. (9 mi.) south of the point where Carmel reaches the sea.

Kartan (kar'tan; "town; city"). City of Naphtali given to the Gershonite Levites (Josh. 21:32); it is the same as Kirjathaim in First Chronicles 6:76 and is modern Khirbet el-Kureiyeh.

Kattath (kat'ath; "small"). A town in Zebulun (Josh. 19:15). It is probably identical with the Kitron in Judges 1:30.

Kedar (kē'der; "powerful" or "dark"). Second son of Ishmael (Gen. 25:13; 1 Chron. 1:29).

Kedemah (ked'e-ma; "eastward"). A son of Ishmael, head of a clan (Gen. 25:13; 1 Chron. 1:31).

Kedemoth (ked'e-moth; "antiquity; old age"). A Levitical town east of the Dead Sea (Josh. 13:18; 21:37; 1 Chron. 6:79).

Kedesh (ke'desh; "holy"). **[1]** A city of the Canaanites near the northern border, defeated by Joshua (Josh. 12:22; 19:37). **[2]** Levitical city of refuge in Naphtali. It was sometimes called Kedesh Naphtali (Josh. 20:7; Judg. 4:6, 9). It is probably modern Kades, about 7.2 km. (4.5 mi.) northwest of Lake Huleh. **[3]** A Levitical city in Issachar (1 Chron. 6:72). **[4]** A city of Judah near Hazor and Ithan (Josh. 15:23).

Kehelathah (ke-he-lā'tha; "a whole; a congregation"). A desert encampment of the Israelites (Num. 33:22-23). It is probably Krintilet Krayeh, also called Ajrud.

Keilah (ke-ī'la; "fortress"). A descendant of Caleb (1 Chron. 4:19).

Keilah (ke-ī'la; "fortress"). A town in the lowlands of Judah (1 Sam. 23:1, 13; Josh. 15:44). It is 8.5 mi. north of Hebron at Khirbet Kila.

Kelaiah (ke-lā'ya; "Jehovah is light; swift for Jehovah"). One of the priests who married a foreign wife during the Exile (Ezra 10:23). Possibly the same as Kelita (q.v.).

Kelita (kel'i-ta; "littleness"). **[1]** A priest who explained the Law when it was read by Ezra (Neh. 8:7). **[2]** One of those who sealed the covenant (Neh. 10:10); possibly the same as [1]. One or both of these may be identical with each other and/or Kelaiah (q.v.).

Kemuel (kem'u-el; "God stands" or "God's mound"). **[1]** A son of Nahor and a nephew of Abraham (Gen. 22:21). **[2]** A prince of Ephraim (Num. 34:24). **[3]** A Levite (1 Chron. 27:17).

Kenan (ke'nan). *See* Cainan.

Kenath (ke'nath; "possession"). A town on the extreme northeastern border of Israelite territory, the easternmost of the ten cities of the Decapolis (Num. 32:42). It is identified with Kanawat.

Kenaz [Kenez] (ke'naz [ke'nez]; "side" or "hunting"). **[1]** A duke of Edom (Gen. 36:42; 1 Chron. 1:53). **[2]** The fourth son of Eliphaz (Gen. 36:11, 15; 1 Chron. 1:36); perhaps the same as [1]. **[3]** Father of Othniel the judge (Josh. 15:17; Judg. 1:13). **[4]** A grandson of Caleb (1 Chron. 4:15).

Keren-Happuch (ker'en-hap'uk; "horn of antimony"). The third daughter of Job to be born after his restoration to health (Job 42:14).

Kerioth [Kirioth] (ke'ri-oth [ki'ri-oth]; "the cities"). **[1]** A town in extreme southern Judah (Josh. 15:25). **[2]** A city of Moab (Jer. 48:24, 41; Amos 2:2); possibly the same as Ar.

Keros (ke'ros; "fortress; crooked"). Ancestor of a clan who returned from Exile to the land of Israel (Ezra 2:44; Neh. 7:47).

Keturah (ke-tū'ra; "incense"). A wife of Abraham (Gen. 25:1, 4; 1 Chron. 1:32).

Keziah (ke-zī'a; "cassia"). The second daughter of Job to be born after his restoration from affliction (Job 42:14).

Keziz (ke'ziz; "the angle; border; cassia tree"). A valley and town of Benjamin (Josh. 18:21).

Kibroth-Hattaavah (kib'roth-ha-ta'a-va; "the graves of lust"). A campsite on the Sinai Peninsula where the Israelites grew tired of manna (Num. 11:34-35). This may be Rueis el-Ebeirig, northeast of Jebel Mesa.

Kibzaim (kib'zā'ım; "double gathering"). A city of Ephraim given to the Levites (Josh. 21:22). It may be the same as Jokmeam.

Kidron [Cedron] (kid'ron [kē'dron]; "obscure; making black or sad"). A valley in Jerusalem between the Mount of Ophel and the Mount of Olives (2 Sam. 15:23; John 18:1). Today it is called Wadi Sitti Maryan.

Kinah (kī'na; "buying; dirge; lamentation"). A city on the extreme southern boundary of Judah (Josh. 15:22).

Kir (kir; "a city; wall; meeting"). **[1]** An eastern country whose location has not been determined (2 Kings 16:9; Amos 9:7). The Arameans migrated from this place to Syria. It may have been the area between the Caspian and Black Seas, the modern Georgia. **[2]** See Kir-haraseth.

Kir-haraseth [Kir-hareseth, Kir-haresh, Kir-heres] (kir-har'a-seth [kir-har'e-seth, kir-har'esh, kir-her'es]; "city of the sun; wall of burnt brick"). A fortified city, probably the same as Kir (2 Kings 3:25; 16:9; Isa. 16:7, 11; Jer. 48:31). Its modern name is Kerak and it is located about 17.7 km. (11 mi.) east of the south bay of the Dead Sea.

Kir-heres (kir-her'es). See Kir-haraseth.

Kirioth (kir'i-oth). See Kerioth.

Kirjath (kir'jath; "city; vocation; meeting"). A city belonging to the tribe of Benjamin (Josh. 18:28). It is probably Kirjath-jearim (q.v.).

Kirjathaim [Kiriathaim] (kir-jath-thā'im; "double city"). **[1]** A Moabite city on the east of the Jordan (Num. 32:37); probably Khirbet-el-Kureiyat, north of the Arnon. **[2]** See Kartan.

Kirjath-arba (kir'jath-ar'ba; "fourth city"). An early name for the city of Hebron (Gen. 23:2; Josh. 14:15). See Hebron.

Kirjath-arim (kir'jath-a-rim'). See Kirjath-jearim.

Kirjath-baal (kir'jath-bā'al). See Kirjath-jearim.

Kirjath-huzoth (kir'jath-hū'zoth; "city of streets"). A town of Moab (Num. 22:39). Its location is unknown, but Kirjathaim and Kerioth are possibilities.

Kirjath-jearim (kir'jath-jē'a-rim; "city of woods"). Originally one of the cities of the Gibeonites located at the northwestern boundary of Judah (Josh. 9:17; Judg. 18:14). It is identical with Baalah (Josh. 15:9), Kirjath-arim (Ezra 2:25), Kirjath-baal (Josh. 18:14), and Baale-judah (2 Sam. 6:2). It is thought to be modern Deir el-Azhar, about 13.4 km. (8.3 mi.) northwest of Jerusalem.

Kirjath-sannah (kir'jath-sa'na; "city of instruction"). See Debir [1].

Kirjath-sepher (kir'jath-sēf'er; "city of books"). See Debir [1].

Kish [Cis] (kish [sis]; "bow; power"). **[1]** A son of Gibeon (1 Chron. 8:30; 9:36). **[2]** A Levite in David's time (1 Chron. 23:21; 24:29). **[3]** A descendant of Levi who assisted in the cleansing of the temple under Hezekiah (2 Chron. 29:12). **[4]** Great-grandfather of Mordecai (Esther

2:5). [5] The father of King Saul (1 Sam. 9:1, 3; 14:51; Acts 13:21).

Kishi (kish'ī; "snarer; fowler"). Father of Ethan, also known as Kushaiah (1 Chron. 6:44; 15:17).

Kishion [Kishon] (kish'i-on [kī'shon]; "hardness"). A city on the boundary of the tribe of Issachar (Josh. 19:20; 21:28). It is probably modern Tell el-Ajjul, 20.1 km. (12.5 mi.) northeast of Megiddo.

Kishon [Kison] (kī'shon [kī'son]; "bending; crooked"). A river in central Palestine which rises in Mount Tabor and, flowing westward, drains the valley of Esdraelon [Jezreel] (Judg. 4:7, 13; 1 Kings 18:40; Psa. 83:9). Next to the Jordan, it is the most important river in Palestine. *See* Kishion

Kithlish (kith'lish; "it is a wall"). A city located in the lowlands of Judah, perhaps the same as Dilean (Josh. 15:40); identified with Khirbet el-Mak-haz.

Kitron (kit'ron; "making sweet"). One of the towns of Zebulun (Judg. 1:30); perhaps the same as Kattath. It is identified with modern Tell el-Far, about 9.7 km. (6 mi.) southeast of Haifa.

Kittim (kit'im; "knotty"). A son of Javan (Gen. 10:4; 1 Chron. 1:7). Possibly the name refers to the inhabitants of Cyprus and the islands nearby.

Koa (kō'a; "male camel"). A prince or people dwelling between Egypt and Syria; named as enemy of Jerusalem (Ezek. 23:23).

Kohath (kō'hath; "assembly"). The second son of Levi and beginning of a priestly clan (Gen. 46:11; Exod. 6:16, 18).

Kolaiah (ko-lā'ya; "voice of Jehovah"). [1] A descendant of Benjamin (Neh. 11:7). [2] Father of the false prophet Ahab (Jer. 29:21).

Korah [Core] (kō'ra [ko're]; "baldness"). [1] A son of Esau by Aholibamah (Gen. 36:5, 14, 18; 1 Chron. 1:35). [2] A son of Eliphaz (Gen. 36:16). [3] A son of Hebron (1 Chron. 2:43). [4] Grandson of Kohath and ancestor of some sacred musicians (1 Chron. 6:22; Psa. 42; 45–46 titles). He was one of the leaders of the rebellion against Moses and Aaron; the earth swallowed them up (Num. 16:1-35).

Kore (kō're; "one who proclaims; quail"). [1] A Levite in charge of the freewill offerings in Hezekiah's time (2 Chron. 31:14). [2] A son of Asaph whose descendants were gatekeepers at the tabernacle (1 Chron. 9:19; 26:1, 19).

Koz (koz; "thorn"). [1] The ancestor of a priestly family returning from captivity (Ezra 2:61 Neh. 7:63). In the Hebrew text, the name appears as *Hakkoz*; the KJV considers the *Ha-* of the name to be the prefixed Hebrew definite article—here denoting a *certain* family. Others take all the word as a name (i.e., *Hakkoz*). If this be the case, the Hakkoz of First Chronicles 24:10 probably also refers to this person. [2] An ancestor of one who helped to repair the walls of Jerusalem (Neh. 3:4, 21).

Kushaiah (ku-shā'ya; "bow of Jehovah"). *See* Kishi.

L

Laadah (lā'a-da; "order; festival"). A descendant of Judah (1 Chron. 4:21).

Laadan (lā'a-dan; "festive-born; ordered"). [1] A descendant of Ephraim (1 Chron. 7:26). [2] A Levite from the family of Gershon (1 Chron. 23:7-9; 26:21). Also known as Libni (Exod. 6:17; Num. 3:18).

Laban (lā'ban; "white; glorious"). The brother of Rebekah and father of Rachel and Leah. Jacob served him for seven years in order to marry Rachel, but Laban tricked him by substituting Leah at the wedding festivals (Gen. 24–31).

Laban (lā'ban; "whiteness"). An obscure place in the Sinai Peninsula (Deut. 1:1); perhaps the same as Libnah [1].

Lachish (lā'kish; "who exists of himself"). A southern city of Judah midway between Jerusalem and Gaza (Josh. 10:3, 5; 2 Kings 18:17). The modern site of this Amorite city is Tell-ed-Duweir.

Lael (lā'el; "belonging to God"). A descendant of Gershon (Num. 3:24).

Lahad (lā'had; "oppression; dark colored"). A descendant of Judah (1 Chron. 4:2).

Lahai-roi (la-hī'roi). *See* Beer-lahai-roi.

Lahmam (la'mam; "their bread"). A city located in the lowlands of Judah (Josh. 15:40); probably Khirbet el-Lahm.

Lahmi (la'mī; "warrior"). Brother of Goliath, the giant (1 Chron. 20:5).

Laish (lā'ish; "lion"). Father of Phalti, who became the husband of Michal (1 Sam. 25:44; 2 Sam. 3:15).

Laish [Leshem] (lā'ish [lē'shem]; "a lion"). [1] The northern limit of the tribe of Dan (Judg. 18:7-29; Isa. 10:30; Josh. 19:47). The Danites changed its name to Dan (q.v.). [2] A place named in Isaiah 10:30 with Gallim and Anathoth.

Lakum (lāk'am; "fortress"). One of the landmarks on the boundary of Naphtali (Josh. 19:33); probably modern Mansura near the head of Wadi Pejjas.

Lamech (lā'mek; "strong youth; overthrower"). [1] Father of Noah and ancestor of Christ (Gen. 5:25-31; Luke 3:36). [2] Father of Jabal and Jubal; he is the first recorded polygamist (Gen. 4:18-26).

Laodicea (la-od-i-sē'a; "just people"). A chief city of Phrygia in Asia Minor (Col. 2:1; 4:15; Rev. 1:11). It is located on the Lycous River, a tributary of the Meander.

Lapidoth (lap'i-doth; "flames; torches"). The husband of Deborah, the prophetess (Judg. 4:4).

Lasea (la-sē'a; "wise"). A seaport of Crete (Acts 27:8). It is about 8 km. (5 mi.) east of Fair Havens.

Lebanon Mountains. The snow-capped Lebanon Mountains parallel the Palestinean coast for a distance of about 161 km. (100 mi.) from Kadesh to Sidon. At its highest point, the range reaches more than 3,300 m. (10,000 ft.) above sea level. These mountains formed the northwestern boundary of the Promised Land (Deut. 1:7).

Lasha (lā'sha; "to anoint"). A Canaanite boundary somewhere in the southeast of Palestine (Gen. 10:19). It has been identified with Callirhoe, a ravine east of the Dead Sea known for its hot springs. Now called Wadi Zerka Ma'in, it enters the Dead Sea about 17.7 km. (11 mi.) east of the mouth of the Jordan.

Lasharon (la-shā'ron; "of or to Sharon"). A town belonging to the Canaanites (Josh. 12:18) It may be the same as Aphek [3].

Lazarus (laz'a-rus; abridged form of Eleazar, "God has helped"). [1] The brother of Mary and Martha whom Jesus raised from the dead (John 11:1-12:17). [2] A believing beggar who was carried to Abraham's bosom (Luke 16:19-31).

Leah (lē'a; "weary"). Jacob's wife through the deception of her father, Laban (Gen. 29-31).

Lebana [Lebanah] (le-ba'na [leb'a-na]; "white"). Chief of a family of returning exiles (Ezra 2:45; Neh. 7:48).

Lebanah (leb'a-na). *See* Lebana.

Lebanon (leb'a-non; "white"). One of two ranges of mountains in northern Palestine (Deut. 1:7; Josh. 1:4). The second is called the Anti-Lebanons; Mount Hermon is its highest peak. Running for about 161 km. (100 mi.), the chain begins about 24.1 km. (15 mi.) southeast of Sidon and runs north to about 19.3 km. (12 mi.) north-northeast of Tripolis in Syria.

Lebaoth (le-bā'oth; "lioness"). One of the towns of southern Judah in Simeon (Josh. 15:32). It is the same as Beth-lebaoth and perhaps identical with Beth-birei (q.v.).

Lebbaeus (le-bē'us). *See* Thaddeus.

Lebonah (le-bō'na; "incense"). A place 12.9 km. (8 mi.) north of Bethel (Judg. 21:19).

Lecah (lē'ka; "walking; addition"). A descendant of Judah (1 Chron. 4:21).

Lehabim (le-hā'bim; "flame, red"). A descendant of Mizraim (Gen. 10:13; 1 Chron. 1:11). Possibly a reference to a tribe of Egyptians.

Lehi (lē'hī; "jawbone"). The location in Judah where Samson slew many Philistines (Judg. 15:9, 14, 19). The site is unknown. In verse 17 it is called Ramath-lehi ("elevation of the jawbone").

Lemuel (lem'u-el; "Godward; dedicated"). An unknown king often supposed to be Solomon or Hezekiah, whose words are recorded in Proverbs 31:1-9.

Leshem (lē'shem). *See* Laish.

Letushim (le-tū'shim; "hammered"). A son of Dedan (Gen. 25:3).

Leummim (le-um'im; "nations"). A son of Dedan (Gen. 25:3).

Levi (lē'vī; "joined"). [1] The third son of Jacob who avenged Dinah's wrong (Gen. 34:25-31), and went to Egypt with his father (Gen. 39:34; Exod. 6:16). His descendants became the priests of Israel. [2] An ancestor of Christ (Luke 3:24). [3] An ancestor of Christ (Luke 3:29). [4] Another name of Matthew (q.v.).

Libnah (lib'na; "white"). [1] An encampment of the Israelites during their journey in the wilderness (Num. 33:20-21). It may be identical with Laban. [2] A Levitical city of Jerusalem (Josh. 10:29-31; 2 Kings 19:8). It is now called Tel-el-safieh.

Libni (lib'nī; "whiteness; distinguished"). [1] A son of Merari (1 Chron. 6:29). [2] *See* Laadan.

Libya (lib'ya; "heart of the sea"). The Greek name for the continent of Africa, west of Egypt (Acts 2:10). The Hebrews called this region Phut [Put]. Even though the Hebrew text of Ezekiel 30:5 and 38:5 read Phut, the KJV rendered the word *Libya*. *See also* Lubim.

Likhi (lik'hī; "learned"). A descendant of Benjamin (1 Chron. 7:19).

Linus (lī'nus; "net"). A Roman friend of Paul (2 Tim. 4:21).

Lo-ammi (lō-am'ī; "not my people"). Symbolic name of Hosea's son (Hos. 1:9).

Lod (lod; "nativity"). A city of Benjamin in the Plain of Sharon (1 Chron. 8:12; Ezra 2:33). Today it is Ludd, about 17.7 km. (11 mi.) southeast of Joppa. In New Testament times it was called Lydda.

Lo-debar (lo-dē'bar; "barren"). A place east of the Jordan River (2 Sam. 9:4); probably the same as Debir [3].

Lois (lō'is; "pleasing; better"). The pious grandmother of Timothy (2 Tim. 1:5).

Lo-ruhamah (lō-roo-ha'ma; "receiving no compassion"). A figurative name of Hosea's daughter, indicating God's rejection of Israel (Hos. 1:6).

Lot (lot; "veiled"). Abraham's nephew that escaped from wicked Sodom (Gen. 13:1-14; Gen. 19).

Lotan (lō'tan; "hidden"). An Edomite duke (Gen. 36:20-29).

Lubim (lū'bim; "dwellers in a thirsty land"). The North African continent west of Egypt (Neh. 3:9). *See also* Libya.

Lucas (lū'kas). *See* Luke.

Lucifer (loo'si-fer; Latin, "light-bearer"). An epithet for the king of Babylon (Isa. 14:12). Lucifer translates a Hebrew word meaning "light-bearer." The title came to be applied to Satan.

Lucius (lū'shi-us; "morning born; of light"). **[1]** A prophet or teacher from Cyrene ministering at Antioch (Acts 13:1). **[2]** A Jewish Christian who saluted the community at Rome (Rom. 16:21). Perhaps the same as [1].

Lud (lud). A son of Shem (Gen. 10:22). Possibly the Lydians are intended.

Ludim (lū'dim). A son of Mizraim (Gen. 10:13). Possibly a reference to the inhabitants of an unknown country connected with the Egyptians.

Luhith (lu'hith; "made of boards"). A town in Moab, between Areopolis and Zoar (Isa. 15:5; Jer. 48:5).

Luke [Lucas] (lūk [lu'kas]; "light-giving"). Evangelist, physician, and author of the Third Gospel and Acts (Col. 4:14; 2 Tim. 4:11; Philem. 24).

Luz (luz; "separation"). **[1]** A city 17.7 km. (11 mi.) north of Jerusalem. In later times it was called Beth-el (Gen. 28:19; Josh. 16:2). **[2]** A town of the Hittites (Judg. 1:22-26). The ruin Luweiziyeh, about 4.5 miles northwest of Baniyas, has been proposed as the site.

Lycaonia (lik-a-ō'ni-a; "she-wolf"). An inland district of Asia Minor. Paul twice visited in the cities of Derbe and Lystra here (Acts 14:6-11). It was bordered on the north by Galatia and on the south by Cilicia.

Lycia (li'shi-a; "land of Lycus"). A region in southwestern Asia Minor (Acts 27:5); the place juts into the Mediterranean Sea.

Lydda (lid'a; "a standing pool"). A town located on the Plains of Sharon (Acts 9:32). It is identical with Lod (q.v.).

Lydia (lid'i-a "native of Lydia"). A woman convert of Thyatira (Acts 16:14-15).

Lydia (lid'i-a "Lydus land"). A country and people in Northern Africa, west of Egypt (Ezek. 30:5).

Lysanias (li-sā'ni-us "that drives away sorrow"). The tetrarch of Abilene (Luke 3:1).

Lysias (lis'i-as). *See* Claudius Lysias.

Lystra (lis'tra; "that dissolves"). A city of Lycaonia in central Asia Minor. Paul was stoned here (Acts 14:6-21).

M

Maachah [Maacah] (mā'a-ka [mā'a-ka]; "oppression"). **[1]** The son of Nahor, Abraham's brother (Gen. 22:24). **[2]** One of David's wives and mother of Absalom (2 Sam. 3:3; 1 Chron. 3:2). **[3]** A king of Maachah (2 Sam. 10:6). Some translate "the king of Maacah." **[4]** Father of Achish, king of Gath (1 Kings 2:39). He is called Maoch in First Samuel 27:2. **[5]** The mother of Asa, king of Judah (1 Kings 15:10, 13; 2 Chron. 15:16). She is called Michaiah (2 Chron. 13:2). **[6]** Concubine of Caleb (1 Chron. 2:48). **[7]** Wife of Machir, son of Manasseh (1 Chron. 7:15-16). **[8]** Wife of Jehiel (1 Chron. 8:29; 9:35). **[9]** Father of one of David's warriors (1 Chron. 11:43). **[10]** Father of Shephatiah, ruler of Simeon (1 Chron. 27:16).

Maachathi [properly Maacah] (ma-ak'a-thi [mā'a-ka]. A small kingdom that adjoined Geshur on the western border of Bashan (Deut. 3:14), the inhabitants of which were called Maachathites (Josh. 12:5; 13:13).

Maadai (ma-a-dā'ī; "Jehovah is ornament"). One who married a foreign wife (Ezra 10:34; Neh. 12:5).

Maadiah (ma-a-dī'a; "Jehovah is ornament"). A priest who returned from the Babylonian Captivity (Neh. 12:5). He is called Moadiah in Nehemiah 12:17.

Maai (ma-ā'ī; "Jehovah is compassionate"). A priest who helped to purify the people who returned from the Exile (Neh. 12:36).

Maaleh-acrabbim [Akrabbim] (ma-al'e-a-krab'im [a-krab'bim] "ascent of scorpions"). A high place which marks part of the boundary of Judah between Kedish and the Dead Sea (Josh. 15:3; Num. 34:4). Akrabbim is a shortened form of the name.

Maarath (mā'a-rath; "den"). A town located in the mountains of Judah (Josh. 15:59). It is near Beth-aron and is now called Umman.

Maaseiah (mā-a-sē'ya; "Jehovah is a refuge"). **[1]** A Levite of the praise service (1 Chron. 15:18, 20). **[2]** A captain who helped to make Joash king (2 Chron. 23:1). **[3]** Officer of King Uzziah (2 Chron. 26:11). **[4]** A son of Ahaz, king of Judah (2 Chron. 28:7). **[5]** Governor of Jerusalem under Josiah's reign (2 Chron. 34:8). **[6]**, **[7]**, **[8]**, **[9]** Four men who took foreign wives during the Exile (Ezra 10:18, 21-22, 30). **[10]** Father of Azariah, who repaired part of the wall of Jerusalem (Neh. 3:23). **[11]** A priest who stood with Ezra while he read the Law (Neh. 8:4). **[12]** A priest who explained the Law (Neh. 8:7); possibly the same as [11]. **[13]** One who sealed the new covenant with God after the Exile (Neh. 10:25). **[14]** A descendant of Pharez living in Jerusalem (Neh. 11:5). **[15]** One whose descendants lived in Jerusalem (Neh. 11:7). **[16]**, **[17]** Two priests who took part in the purification of the wall of Jerusalem (Neh. 12:41-42). **[18]** A priest whose son was sent by King Zedekiah to inquire of the Lord (Jer. 21:1; 29:25). [19] Father of a false prophet (Jer. 29:21). [20] An officer of the temple (Jer. 35:4). [21] Grandfather of Baruch, Jeremiah's scribe (Jer. 32:12).

Maasiai (ma-as'i-ī; "work of Jehovah"). A descendant of Aaron (1 Chron. 9:12).

Maath (mā'ath; "small"). An ancestor of Christ (Luke 3:26).

Maaz (mā'az; "counselor"). A son of Ram (1 Chron. 2:27).

Maaziah (ma-a-zī'a; "strength of Jehovah"). [1] Priest to whom certain sanctuary duties were charged (1 Chron. 24:18). [2] A priest who sealed the new covenant with God after the Exile (Neh. 10:8).

Macedonia (mas-e-dō ni-a; meaning unknown). A nation lying to the north of Greece proper (Acts 16:9; 18:5).

Machbanai (mak'ba-nī; "thick"). Warrior who joined David at Ziklag (1 Chron. 12:13).

Machbenah (mak-bē'ra; "knob, lump"). [1] A descendant of Caleb (1 Chron. 2:49). [2] Possibly a place identical with Cabbon (q.v.).

Machi (mā'kî; "decrease"). Father of one of the spies sent into Canaan (Num. 13:15).

Machir (mā'kir; "salesman; sold"). [1] A son of Manasseh (Gen. 50:23; Num. 26:29; Josh. 13:31). [2] A descendant of Manasseh living near Mahanaim (2 Sam. 9:4-5; 17:27).

Machnadebai (mach-na-dē'bī; "liberal; gift of the noble one"). One who had married a foreign wife (Ezra 10:40).

Machpelah (mak-pē'la; "double"). The place where the burial cave of Abraham is located, near Hebron (Gen. 23:17; 25:9).

Madai (ma-dā'ī). Son of Japheth (Gen. 10:2; 1 Chron. 1:5). The name possibly refers to the inhabitants of Media.

Madian (mā'di'an). See Midian.

Madmannah (mad-man'a; "measure of a gift"). A town near Gaza in southern Judah (Josh. 15:31). It is perhaps the same as Beth-marcaboth, which is Umm pemneh, about 19.3 km. (12 mi.) northeast of Beer-sheba.

Madmen (mad'men; "dunghill"). A location in Moab (Jer. 48:2). It may be modern Khirbet D mneh, 4 km. (2.5 mi.) northwest of Rabba.

Madmenah (mad-mē'na; "dung heap"). A village north of Jerusalem in the territory belonging to Benjamin (Isa. 10:31).

Madon (mā'don; "strife"). A city of northern Canaan (Josh. 11:1; 12:19). The name still exists in Khirbet Madin, 5 km. (3 mi.) south of Hattin.

Magbish (mag'bish; probably "sturdy; strong"). An unidentified town in Benjamin (Ezra 2:30).

Magdala (mag'da-la; "tower"). A village located on the western edge of the Sea of Galilee (Matt. 15:39). It is present-day el-Mejdel, 4.8 km. (3 mi.) north-northwest of Tiberias.

Magdiel (mag'di-el; "God is renowned"). A duke of Edom (Gen. 36:43; 1 Chron. 1:54).

Magog (mā'gog; "covering; roof"). The second son of Japheth (Gen.

10:2; 1 Chron. 1:5). Possibly a people inhabiting the north land. The name may denote the Scythians or be a comprehensive term for northern barbarians.

Magog (mā'gog; "region of Gog"). A country of undetermined location, generally described as being in a northerly direction from Palestine (Ezek. 38:2; 39:6). The first-century Jewish historian Josephus identified the land with the Scythians.

Magor-missabib (mā'gor-mis'a-bib; "terror is about"). Symbolic name given to Pashur by Jeremiah (Jer. 20:1-3).

Magpiash (mag'pi-ash; "collector of a cluster of stars; moth-killer"). One who sealed the new covenant with God after the Exile (Neh. 10:20).

Mahalah (ma-hā'la; "tenderness"). Descendant of Manasseh (1 Chron. 7:18). *See* Mahlah.

Mahalaleel [Maleleel] (ma-hā'la-lē'el [ma-lē'le-el]; "God is splendor"). [1] Son of Cainan and an ancestor of Christ (Gen. 5:12-13, 15; Luke 3:37). [2] One whose descendants lived at Jerusalem (Neh. 11:4).

Mahalath (mā'ha-lath; "mild"). [1] One of Esau's wives (Gen. 28:9). *See* Esau's Wives. [2] Wife of Rehoboam (2 Chron. 11:18).

Mahali (mā'ha-lī). *See* Mahli.

Mahanaim (ma-ha-nā'im; "tents"). A place on the boundary between Reuben and Gad (Gen. 32:2; Josh. 21:38). It is east of the Jordan and south of the Jabbok. The exact site is undetermined.

Mahaneh-dan (mā'ha-ne-dan; "tents of judgment"). A campsite between Zorah and Eshtaol (Judg. 18:12). It is west of Kirjath-jearim.

Maharai (ma-har'a-ī; "hasty"). One of David's warriors (2 Sam. 23:28; 1 Chron. 11:30; 27:13).

Mahath (mā'hath; "dissolution; snatching"). [1] A descendant of Kohath who helped to purify the sanctuary (1 Chron. 6:35; 2 Chron. 29:12). [2] A Levite overseer of dedicated things during Hezekiah's reign (2 Chron. 31:13).

Mahazioth (ma-hā'zi-oth; "visions"). One set over the song service of the temple (1 Chron. 25:4, 30).

Maher-Shalal-Hash-Baz (mā'her-shal'al-hash'baz; "the spoil hastens, the prey speeds"). Symbolic name of Isaiah's son (Isa. 8:1-4).

Mahlah (ma'la; "mildness; sick"). Eldest daughter of Zelophehad allowed a share of the land because her father had no sons (Num. 26:33; 27:1; Josh. 17:3). *See* Mahalah.

Mahli [Mahali] (ma'lī [mā'la-lī]; "mild; sickly"). [1] A son of Merari (Exod. 6:19; Num. 3:20; 1 Chron. 6:19, 29; Ezra 8:18). [2] A descendant of Levi (1 Chron. 6:47; 23:23; 24:30).

Mahlon (ma'lon; "mild; sickly"). The first husband of Ruth who died in Moab (Ruth 1:2-5).

Mahol (mā'hol; "dancer"). Father of renowned wise men (1 Kings 4:31).

Makaz (ma'kaz; "an end"). A place mentioned in First Kings 4:9; it is thought to be Khirbet el-Mukheigin, south of Ekron.

Makheloth (mak-ē'loth "congregations"). A desert encampment of the Israelites (Num. 33:25); probably modern Kuntilet Krayeh or Ajurd.

Makkedah (mak-ē'da; "worshipping"). A city of the Canaanites located on the Plain of Judah (Josh. 10:10; 12:16). It is 19.3 km. (12 mi.) southwest of Jerusalem in the plain country of Judah, and is now called Mughar.

Maktesh (mak'tesh; "mortar"). A section of Jerusalem where merchants gathered (Zeph. 1:11); probably the northern portion of the city.

Malachi (mal'a-kī; "messenger of Jehovah" or "my messenger"). The last of the prophets recorded in the Old Testament; he was contemporary with Nehemiah (Mal. 1:1).

Malcham (mal'kam; "their king"). A descendant of Benjamin (1 Chron. 8:9).

Malchiah [Malchijah; Melchiah] (mal-kī'a [mal-kī'ja; mel-kī'a]; "Jehovah is king"). [1] A leader of singing under David's reign (1 Chron. 6:40). [2] An Aaronite whose descendants dwelled in Jerusalem after the Captivity (1 Chron. 9:12; Neh. 11:12). [3] Head of a priestly family (1 Chron. 24:9). [4], [5], [6] Three who married foreign wives during the Exile (Ezra 10:25, 31). [7], [8], [9] Three who helped to rebuild the wall of Jerusalem (Neh. 3:11, 14, 31). [10] A prince or Levite who stood beside Ezra as he read the Law (Neh. 8:4). [11] A priest who helped to purify the wall of Jerusalem (Neh. 10:3; 12:42). [12] Father of Pashur (Jer. 21:1; 38:1).

Malchiel (mal'ki-el; "God is a King"). A descendant of Asher (Gen. 46:17; Num. 26:45; 1 Chron. 7:31).

Malchijah (mal'kī-ja). See Malchiah.

Malchiram (mal-kī'ram; "my king is exalted"). A descendant of King Jehoiakim (1 Chron. 3:18).

Malchi-shua (mal'kī-shoo'a). See Melchi-shua.

Malchus (mal'kus; "counselor; ruler"). A servant of the high priest whose ear Peter cut off (John 18:10).

Maleleel (ma-lē'le-el). Greek form of Mahalaleel (q.v.).

Mallothi (mal'lo-thi; "Jehovah is speaking"). One who was set over the song service of the temple (1 Chron. 25:4, 26).

Malluch (mal'uk; "counselor; ruling"). [1] A descendant of Levi (1 Chron. 6:44). [2], [3] Two who took foreign wives during the Exile (Ezra 10:29, 32). [4] A priest who sealed the covenant (Neh. 10:4). [5] A leader who sealed the new covenant with God after the Exile (Neh. 10:27). [6] One of the priests who returned with Zerubbabel (Neh. 12:2); he is called Melicu in verse 14.

Mamre (mam're; "firmness; vigor"). An Amorite chief who allied with Abraham (Gen. 14:13, 24).

Mamre (mam're; "firmness; vigor"). A place in the Hebron district, west of Machpelah (Gen. 23:17, 19; 49:30). The site has been identified at Râmet el-Khalil, 2 mi. north of Hebron.

Manaen (man'a-en; "comforter"). A teacher or prophet at Antioch (Acts 13:1).

Manahath (man'a-hath; "resting place; rest"). A descendant of Seir (Gen. 36:23; 1 Chron. 1:40).

Manahath (man'a-hath; "resting place; rest"). A city of Benjamin (1 Chron. 8:6).

Manasseh [Manasses] (ma-nas'e [ma-nas'ez]; "causing forgetfulness"). **[1]** The first son of Joseph (Gen. 41:51). His descendants became one of the twelve tribes of Israel and occupied both sides of the Jordan (Josh. 16:4-9; 17). **[2]** The idolatrous successor of Hezekiah to the throne of Judah. He was an ancestor of Christ (2 Kings 21:1-18; Matt. 1:10). **[3]** One whose descendants set up graven images at Laish (Judg. 18:30). Most scholars suggest that we should read Moses here instead. Perhaps a scribe felt an idolatrous descendant would cast reproach on the great lawgiver. A few manuscripts of the Septuagint, Old Latin, and the Vulgate read Moses here. **[4]**, **[5]** Two who had taken foreign wives (Ezra 10:30, 33).

Manasses (ma-nas'ez). Greek form of Manasseh (q.v.).

Manoah (ma-nō'a; "rest"). The father of Samson the judge (Judg. 13:1-23).

Maoch (mā'ok; "poor"). *See* Maachah [4].

Maon (mā'on; "abode"). A son of Shammai or a city he founded (1 Chron. 2:45).

Maon (mā'on; "place of sin"). A mountain city of Judah (Josh. 15:55; 1 Sam. 23:24). It is modern Tell Main, about 13.8 km. (8.5 mi.) south of Hebron.

Mara (ma'ra; "bitter"). Name assumed by Naomi after the death of her husband (Ruth 1:20).

Marah (ma'ra; "bitter"). The fountain of bitter water in the wilderness of Shur where the Israelites first halted after crossing the Red Sea (Exod. 15:23; Num. 33:8). The traditional site is 'Ain Hawarah, about 75.6 km. (47 mi.) from Suez.

Maralah (mar'a-la; "sleep"). A boundary village of Zebulun (Josh. 19:11). It is probably Tell Ghalta in the Plain of Kishon.

Marcus (mar'kus). *See* Mark.

Mareshah (ma-rē'sha; "possession"). **[1]** Father of Hebron (1 Chron. 2:42). **[2]** Son of Laadah (1 Chron. 4:21).

Mareshah (ma-rē'sha; "from the beginning"). A city in the lowlands of Judah (Josh. 15:44; 2 Chron. 11:8). Its ruins are placed at 1.6 km. (1 mi.) southeast of Beit Jibrin.

Mark [Marcus] (mark [mar'kus]; "polite; shining"). A Christian convert and missionary companion of Paul (Acts 12:12, 25; 15:37, 39; Col. 4:10). Mark is his Latin name, John his Hebrew name. He wrote the Gospel bearing his name.

Maroth (mā'roth; "bitterness"). A town in the lowlands of Judah (Mic. 1:12); possibly the same as Maarath (q.v.).

Marsena (mar'se-na; "worthy"). A prince of Persia (Esther 1:14).

Mars Hill. *See* Areopagus.

Martha (mar'tha; "lady"). Sister of Mary and Lazarus in Bethany (Luke 10:38, 40-41; John 11:1-39).

Mary (mā'ri; Greek form of Miriam, "strong"). [1] The mother of Jesus Christ; her song of faith (Luke 1:46-55) reveals her deep faith (Matt. 1:16-20; cf. John 2:1-11). [2] Mary the sister of Martha. She anointed the Lord with ointment and received His approval (Luke 10:39, 42; John 11:1-45). [3] A woman of Magdala in Galilee. She had been converted after having "seven devils" cast out of her (Matt. 27:56, 61; 28:1; Luke 8:2; John 19:25). [4] The mother of John Mark (Acts 12:12). [5] A Roman Christian to whom Paul sent greetings (Rom. 16:6). [6] Mary, the mother of Joses (Mark 15:47) and James (Luke 24:10), the "other Mary" (Matt. 28:1), and the Mary, wife of Cleophas (John 19:25), are possibly to be identified as the same person (Mark 15:40).

Mash (mash; "drawn out"). Son or grandson of Shem (Gen. 10:23). In First Chronicles 1:18 he is called Meshech. Possibly an Aramean people dwelling near Mount Masius in northern Mesopotamia is meant.

Mashal (ma'shal; "parable"). A city in Asher given to the Levites (1 Chron. 6:74). It is probably located on the plain south of Accho. It is identical with Mishal (q.v.).

Masrekah (mas're-ka; "whistling"). An ancient city in Edom (Gen. 36:36; 1 Chron. 1:47). It is Jebel el-Mushrat, about 35.4 km. (22 mi.) south-southwest of Maan.

Massa (mas'a; "burden; oracle"). A son of Ishmael (Gen. 25:14; 1 Chron. 1:30).

Massah (mas'a; "temptation"). The name of a spot in the vicinity of Horeb where the Israelites tempted God (Exod. 17:7; Deut. 6:16). *See also* Meribah [1].

Mathusala (ma-thū'sa-la). Greek form of Methuselah (q.v.).

Matred (mā'trid; "God is pursuer" or "expulsion"). Mother of Mehetabel, wife of Hadar (Gen. 36:39; 1 Chron. 1:50).

Matri (mā'trī; "Jehovah is watching" or "rainy"). Ancestor of a tribe of Benjamin to which Saul belonged (1 Sam. 10:21).

Mattan (mat'an; "gift"). [1] A priest of Baal slain by the Jews (2 Kings 11:18; 2 Chron. 23:17). [2] Father of a prince of Judah (Jer. 38:1).

Mattanah (mat'a-na; "gift of Jehovah"). An encampment during the latter part of Israel's wandering (Num. 21:18-19). It was north of the Arnon River and west of the wilderness of Kedemoth.

Mattaniah (mat-a-nī'a; "gift of Jehovah"). [1] The original name of King Zedekiah (2 Kings 24:17). [2] A descendant of Asaph whose family dwelt at Jerusalem (1 Chron. 9:15; 2 Chron. 20:14; Neh. 11:17, 22; 13:13). [3] A son of Heman the singer (1 Chron. 25:4, 16). [4] One who helped to cleanse the temple (2 Chron. 29:13). [5], [6], [7], [8]

Four who married foreign wives during the Exile (Ezra 10:26-27, 30, 37). **[9]** One of the gatekeepers (Neh. 12:25).

Mattatha (mat'a-tha; "gift"). Ancestor of Jesus (Luke 3:31). Not to be confused with Mattathah.

Mattathah (mat'a-tha; "gift"). One who married a foreign wife (Ezra 10:33). Not to be confused with Mattatha.

Mattathias (mat-a-thī'as; "God's gift"). **[1]** An ancestor of Jesus (Luke 3:25). **[2]** Another ancestor of Christ (Luke 3:26).

Mattenai (mat-te-nā'i; "gift of Jehovah"). **[1]**, **[2]** Two who married foreign wives during the Exile (Ezra 10:33, 37). **[3]** A priest who returned from the Exile (Neh. 12:19).

Matthan (mat'than; "gift"). An ancestor of Jesus (Matt. 1:15).

Matthat (mat'that; "gift"). **[1]** Grandfather of Joseph and ancestor of Jesus (Luke 3:24). **[2]** Another ancestor of Jesus (Luke 3:29).

Matthew (math'ū; "gift of God"). One of the twelve apostles; he was a tax collector before his call. He was also known as Levi (Matt. 9:9; 10:3; Mark 2:14). He wrote the Gospel bearing his name.

Matthias (ma-thī'as; "God's gift"). A Christian chosen to become an apostle to fill the place of Judas (Acts 1:23, 26). He was surnamed Justus.

Mattithiah (mat-i-thī'a; "gift of Jehovah"). **[1]** A Levite in charge of "things made in pans" (1 Chron. 9:31). **[2]** A Levite singer and gatekeeper (1 Chron. 15:18, 21; 16:5). **[3]** A son of Jeduthun (1 Chron. 25:3, 21). **[4]** One who took a foreign wife during the Exile (Ezra 10:43). **[5]** One who stood with Ezra when he read the Law (Neh. 8:4).

Meah (mē'a; "hundred"). A tower at Jerusalem not far from the Sheep Gate (Neh. 3:1; 12:39).

Mearah (me-ā'ra; "den"). A place, possibly a cavern, in Sidon in northern Canaan (Josh. 13:4).

Mebunnai (me-bun'ī; "built up"). *See* Sibbecai.

Medad (mē'dad; "love"). One of the elders of the Hebrews on whom the spirit fell (Num. 11:26-27).

Medan (mē'dan; "judgment"). A son of Abraham by Keturah (Gen. 25:2; 1 Chron. 1:32).

Medeba (med'e-ba; "waters of grief"). A Moabite town on the Jordan River in the territory of Reuben east of the Arnon (Num. 21:30; Josh. 13:9). It is now Madaba, 9.7 km. (6 mi.) south of Heshbon.

Media (mē'di-a "middle land"). A country of Asia located south of the Caspian Sea, west of Parthia, north of Elam, and east of the Yagros Mountains. During the 400's B.C. the Persians and Medes had a powerful empire here (Esther 1:3, 14, 18; Dan. 8:20).

Megiddo [Megiddon] (me-gid'ō [me-gid'on]; "declaring a message"). A city on the southern edge of the Plain of Esdraelon (Jezreel) at the northeast of Mount Carmel (Josh. 12:21; 17:11; Zech. 12:11).

Megiddon (me-gid'on). *See* Megiddo.

Mehetabel [Mehetabeel] (me-het'e-bel [me-het'a-bel]; "God is doing good"). **[1]** Wife of King Hadar of Edom (Gen. 36:39; 1 Chron. 1:50). **[2]** Father of Delaiah who defied Nehemiah (Neh. 6:10).

Mehida (me-hī'da; "famous"). An ancestor of returned captives (Ezra 2:52; Neh. 7:54).

Mehir (mē'her; "dexterity"). A descendant of Caleb of Hur (1 Chron. 4:11).

Mehujael (me-hū'ja-el; "God is combating"). A descendant of Cain (Gen. 4:18).

Mehuman (me-hū'man; "true"). One of the chamberlains of Ahasuerus (Esther 1:10).

Me-jarkon (me-jar'kon; "the waters of Jordan"). A city in the territory of Dan near Joppa (Josh. 19:46).

Mekonah (me-kō'na; "provision"). A town of Judah named in connection with Ziklag and other towns of the far south (Neh. 11:28).

Melatiah (mel-a-ti'a; "Jehovah delivers"). An assistant wall-builder (Neh. 3:7).

Melchi (mel'kī; "my King"). **[1]** An ancestor of Jesus (Luke 3:24). **[2]** Another ancestor of Jesus (Luke 3:28).

Melchiah (mel-kī'a). *See* Malchiah.

Melchisedec (mel-kis'e-dek). Greek form of Melchizedek (q.v.).

Melchi-shua [Malchi-shua] (mel-kī-shoo'a [mal-kī-shoo'a; "the king, i.e., [God] is salvation"]). The third son of King Saul (1 Sam. 14:49; 31:2; 1 Chron. 8:33).

Melchizedek [Melchisedec] (mel-kis'e-dek [mel-kis'e-dek] "king of righteousness"). King and high priest of Salem. He was a prophetic symbol or "type" of Christ (Gen. 14:18-20; Psa. 110:4; Heb. 5-7).

Melea (mel'e-a; "full"). Ancestor of Christ (Luke 3:31).

Melech (me'lek; "King"). Great-grandson of Saul (1 Chron. 8:35; 9:41).

Meggido. Joshua conquered the city which stood at this site in the Carmel Mountains during his conquest of Canaan (Josh. 12:21); it was then given to the tribe of Manasseh (Josh. 17:11). King Solomon fortified the city and established accommodations for his chariots and horses here (1 Kings 9:15-19). Many people believe that the end-time battle of Armageddon (Hebrew, "hill of Meggido") will take place in this area.

Melicu (mel'i-kū). *See* Malluch [4].

Melita (mel'i-ta; "affording honey"). The island of Malta, located in the Mediterranean Sea (Acts 28:1). It is 96.5 km. (60 mi.) south of Sicily.

Melzar (mel'zar; "the overseer"). One to whom Daniel and his companions were entrusted (Dan. 1:11, 16); this is possibly a title, rather than a proper name.

Memphis (mem'fis; "abode of the good"). An ancient Egyptian city located on the western bank of the Nile in the central portion of the country (Hos. 9:6). It was also called Noph (Jer. 2:16).

Memucan (me-mū'kan). A Persian prince (Esther 1:14-21).

Menahem (men'a-hem; "comforter"). The idolatrous and cruel usurper of the throne of Israel who killed Shallum (2 Kings 15:14-23).

Menan (mē'nan). An ancestor of Christ (Luke 3:31).

Meonenim (me-on'e-nim; "regardless of time"). A place near Shechem in Ephraim (Judg. 9:37).

Meonothai (me-on'o-thī; "Jehovah is dwelling" or "my dwelling"). A descendant of Judah (1 Chron. 4:14).

Mephaath (mef'a-ath; "force of waters"). A city allotted to Reuben and assigned to the Levites (Josh. 13:18). It was near Kedemoth or Kirjath-aim.

Mephibosheth (me-fib'o-sheth; "idol breaker"). [1] Son of Saul by his concubine Rizpah (2 Sam. 21:8). [2] A grandson of Saul. He was loyal to David, even though Ziba told David he was a traitor (2 Sam. 4:4; 9:6-13). He was also called Merib-baal ("Baal contends") (1 Chron. 8:34; 9:40).

Merab (mē'rab; "increase"). Daughter of Saul promised to David but given to Adriel (1 Sam. 14:49; 18:17, 19). Apparently she was a sister of Michal.

Meraiah (me-rā'ya; "revelation of Jehovah"). A priest of Jerusalem in the days of Joiakim (Neh. 12:12).

Meraioth (me-rā'yoth; "revelations"). [1] A descendant of Aaron and ancestor of Azariah (1 Chron. 6:6-7, 52; Ezra 7:3). [2] Another priest of the same line (1 Chron. 9:11; Neh. 11:11). [3] Another priest at the end of the Exile (Neh. 12:15); possibly the same as Meremoth [1] or [3].

Merari (me-rā'rī; "bitter; excited"). The third son of Levi and founder of a priestly clan (Gen. 46:11; Exod. 6:16, 19; Num. 3; 4:29-45).

Merathaim (mer-a-thā'im; "double rebellion"). The country of the Chaldeans, also known as Babylon (Jer. 50:21).

Mered (mē'red; "rebellious"). Son of Ezra, descendant of Judah (1 Chron. 4:17-18).

Meremoth (mer'e-moth; "strong; firm"). [1] A priest who weighed the gold and silver vessels of the temple (Ezra 8:33; Neh. 3:4, 21). [2] One who took a foreign wife during the Exile (Ezra 10:36). [3] One who sealed the New Covenant with God after the Exile (Neh. 10:5; 12:3).

Meres (mē'rez; "worthy"). One of the seven princes of Persia (Esther 1:14).

Meribah (mer'i-ba; "quarrel"). [1] The desert location where Moses smote the rock (Exod. 17:7). [2] Another name for Kadesh-barnea in the wilderness of Zin, where the Hebrew people rebelled against Moses (Num. 20:13). In Deuteronomy 32:51 the place is called Meribah-Kadesh.

Meribah-Kadesh (mer'i-ba-kā'desh). *See* Meribah [2].

Merib-baal (mer'ib-bā'al). *See* Mephibosheth.

Merodach-baladan (me-rō'dak-bal'a-dan; Babylonian, *Marduk-baladan*—"[the god] Marduk has given a son"). A king of Babylon in the days of Hezekiah (Jer. 50:2). Also called Berodach-baladan (2 Kings 20:12).

Merom (mē'rom; "elevations"). A lake 16.1 km. (10 mi.) north of the Sea of Galilee (Josh. 11:5, 7).

Meroz (mē'roz; "secret"). A place near Kishon (Judg. 5:23). Its exact location is unknown, but may be modern Khirbet Marus, about 12.1 km. (7.5 mi.) south of Kedesh of Naphtali.

Mesha (mē'sha; "freedom"). [1] A king of Moab who rebelled against Ahaziah (2 Kings 3:4). [2] Eldest son of Caleb (1 Chron. 2:42). [3] A descendant of Benjamin (1 Chron. 8:9).

Mesha (mē'sha; "salvation"). A boundary marker of the descendants of Joktan (Gen. 10:30). It seems to be west of Sephar.

Meshach (mē'shak; "the shadow of the prince; who is this?"). The name given to Mishael after he went into Babylonian captivity. He was delivered from the fiery furnace (Dan. 1:7; 3:12-30).

Meshech [Mesech] (mē'shek [mē'sek]; "long; tall"). [1] A son of Japheth (Gen. 10:2; 1 Chron. 1:5). Possibly a people inhabiting the land in the mountains north of Assyria; it was called Musku. [2] *See* Mash.

Meshelemiah (me-shel-e-mī'a; "Jehovah recompenses"). A descendant of Levi (1 Chron. 9:21; 26:1-2, 9). He is also called Shelemiah (1 Chron. 26:14).

Meshezabeel (me-shez'a-bēl; "God is deliverer"). [1] A priest who helped rebuild the wall (Neh. 3:4). [2] One who signed the covenant (Neh. 10:21). [3] A descendant of Judah (Neh. 11:24).

Meshillemith (me-shil'e-mith; "retribution"). A priest whose descendants lived in Jerusalem (1 Chron. 9:12). He is called Meshillemoth in Nehemiah 11:13.

Meshillemoth (me-shil'e-moth; "recompense"). [1] A descendant of Ephraim (2 Chron. 28:12). [2] *See* Meshillemith.

Meshobab (me-shō'bab). A prince of Simeon (1 Chron. 4 34).

Meshullam (me-shul'am; "associate; friend"). [1] Grandfather of Shaphan, a scribe (2 Kings 22:3). [2] A descendant of King Jehoiakim (1 Chron. 3:19). [3] Head of a family of Gad (1 Chron. 5:13). [4] A descendant of Benjamin (1 Chron. 8:17). **[5]** One whose son lived in Jerusalem (1 Chron. 9:7). **[6]** One who lived in Jerusalem (1 Chron. 9:8). **[7]** A descendant of Aaron and an ancestor of Ezra (1 Chron. 9:11; Neh. 11:11). He is also called Shallum (1 Chron. 6:12-13; Ezra 7:2). **[8]** A priest (1 Chron. 9:12). **[9]** An overseer of the temple work (2 Chron. 34:12). **[10]** A chief man who returned with Ezra to Jerusalem (Ezra 8:16). **[11]** One who assisted in taking account of those who had foreign wives after the Exile (Ezra 10:15). **[12]** One who took a foreign wife during the Exile (Ezra 10:29). **[13]**, **[14]** Two who rebuilt part of the wall of Jerusalem (Neh. 3:4, 6, 30; 6:18). **[15]** A prince or priest who stood with Ezra while he read the Law (Neh. 8:4). **[16]** A priest who sealed the New Covenant with God after the Exile (Neh. 10:7). **[17]** One who sealed the New Covenant with God after the Exile (Neh. 10:20). **[18]** One whose descendants lived in Jerusalem (Neh. 11:7). **[19]** A priest who assisted in the dedication of the wall of Jerusalem (Neh. 12:13, 33). **[20]** A descendant of Ginnethon (Neh. 12:16). **[21]** A Levite and gatekeeper after the Exile (Neh. 12:25).

Meshullemeth (me-shul′e-meth; "friend"). Wife of Manasseh and mother of Amon (2 Kings 21:19).

Mesopotamia (mes-o-po-tā′mi-a; "between two rivers"). A region located between the Tigris and Euphrates Rivers (Gen. 24:10; Deut. 23:4), excluding the mountain regions where the rivers take their rise and the low-lying plains of Babylon.

Metheg-ammah (mē′theg-am′a; "bridle of bondage"). A stronghold of the Philistines captured by David (2 Sam. 8:1). Many scholars believe that the name refers to Gath.

Methusael (me-thū′sa-el; "man of God"). The father of Lamech (Gen. 4:18).

Methuselah [Mathusala] (me-thū′ze′la [ma-thū′sa-la]; "man of the dart"). The longest living human recorded in the Bible, the grandfather of Noah and an ancestor of Christ (Gen. 5:21-27; Luke 3:37).

Mezahab (mez′a-hab; "offspring of the shining one"). Grandfather of Mehetabel, wife of Hadar, the eighth king of Edom (Gen. 36:39; 1 Chron. 1:50).

Miamin (mī′a-min; "fortunate"). **[1]** One who took a foreign wife during the Exile (Ezra 10:25). **[2]** A priest who returned from the Exile (Neh. 12:5).

Mibhar (mib′har; "choice; youth"). One of David's mighty men (1 Chron. 11:38).

Mibsam (mib-sam; "sweet odor"). **[1]** A son of Ishmael (Gen. 25:13; 1 Chron. 1:29). **[2]** A son of Simeon (1 Chron. 4:25).

Mibzar (mib′zar; "fortified"). Chief of Edom (Gen. 36:42; 1 Chron. 1:53).

Mica [Micah, Micha, Michah] (mī′ka; all probably contractions of Micaiah). **[1]** Owner of a small private sanctuary (Judg. 17:1-5). **[2]** A descendant of Reuben (1 Chron. 5:5). **[3]** A son of Merib-baal,

Mephibosheth in Second Samuel 4:4 (1 Chron. 8:34). **[4]** A descendant of Kohath, son of Levi (1 Chron. 23:20; 24:24). **[5]** The father of Abdon (2 Chron. 34:20). He is called Michaiah in Second Kings 22:12. **[6]** A prophet (Jer. 26:18; Mic. 1:1). **[7]** The son of Zichri (1 Chron. 9:15; Neh. 11:17). **[8]** One who signed the covenant (Neh. 10:11).

Michael (mī'ka-el; "who is like God?"). **[1]** One sent to spy out the land of Canaan (Num. 13:13). **[2]** A descendant of Gad (1 Chron. 5:13). **[3]** Another descendant of Gad (1 Chron. 5:14). **[4]** An ancestor of Asaph (1 Chron. 6:40). **[5]** A chief of the tribe of Issachar (1 Chron. 7:3). **[6]** One residing in Jerusalem (1 Chron. 8:16). **[7]** A warrior who joined David at Ziklag (1 Chron. 12:20). **[8]** Father of Omri, a prince of Issachar (1 Chron. 27:18). **[9]** A son of Jehoshaphat (2 Chron. 21:2). **[10]** An ancestor of one who returned from the Exile (Ezra 8:8).

Michah (mī'ka). *See* Mica.

Michaiah [Micaiah] (mī-kā'ya [mī'kā'ya]; "who is like Jehovah?"). **[1]** Wife of Rehoboam (2 Chron. 13:2). She is also called Maachah (1 Kings 15:2; 2 Chron. 11:20). *See* Maachah [5]. **[2]** *See* Mica [5]. **[3]** A prince of Judah (2 Chron. 17:7). **[4]** The son of Zaccur (Neh. 12:35). **[5]** One present at the dedication of the wall (Neh. 12:41). **[6]** A prophet who predicted Ahab's downfall (1 Kings 22:8-28; 2 Chron. 18:7-27).

Michal (mī'kel; "who is like God?"). A daughter of Saul whom David married (1 Sam. 14:49). Michal "had no child unto the day of her death" (2 Sam. 6:23). Yet Second Samuel 21:8 states she had five sons. The KJV rendering, "whom she brought up for Adriel," is not a permissible translation—the Hebrew text states she bore them. A few Hebrew, Greek, and Syriac manuscripts read: "the five sons of Merab" instead of Michal, which seems a plausible solution to the problem. See First Samuel 18:19.

Michmash [Michmas] (mik'mash [mik'mas]; "he that strikes"). A town of Benjamin (1 Sam. 13:5; Isa. 10:28; Ezra 2:27). The pass of Mukkmas retains the name. The town is 12.1 km. (7.5 mi.) northeast of Jerusalem and east of Bethaven.

Michmethah (mik'me-tha; "the gift of a striker"). A landmark boundary of Manasseh on the western side of the Jordan, east of Shechem (Josh. 17:7).

Michri (mik'rī; "Jehovah possesses"). An ancestor of a clan of Benjamin in Jerusalem (1 Chron. 9:8).

Middin (mid'in; "judgment"). A village in the wilderness of Judah (Josh. 15:61). It is probably modern Khirbet Abu Tabak in the Valley of Achor.

Midian (mid'i-an; "contention"). A son of Abraham by Keturah and founder of the Midianites (Gen. 25:2, 4; 36:35; 1 Chron. 1:32).

Midian [Madian] (mid'i-an [mā'di-an]; "contention"). The land of the descendants of Midian beyond the Jordan. It included Edom, the Sinai Peninsula, and Arabian Petra (Exod. 2:15-16; Judg. 6:1; Acts 7:29).

Migdalel (mig'dal-el; "tower of God"). A fortified city of Naphtali (Josh. 19:38). It may be modern Mujeidil 20.1 km. (12.5 mi.) northwest of Kedesh [Kades].

Migdalgad (mig'dal-gad; "tower compassed about"). A lowland city of Judah (Josh. 15:37); probably modern Khirbet el-Mejdeleh 8 km. (5 mi.) south of Beit Jibrin.

Migdol (mig'dol; "tower"). [1] A location in the extreme north of Egypt (Jer. 44:1; 46:14). [2] An encampment of the Israelites west of the Red Sea (Exod. 14:2; Num. 33:7).

Migron (mig'ron; "fear"). [1] A Benjamite village north of Michmash (Isa. 10:28). It may be modern Makrum. [2] If there were two Migrons, the second was located at the outermost part of Gibeah and considerably south of Michmash (1 Sam. 14:2). Tell Miryam has been suggested as the site.

Mijamin (mij'a-min; "fortunate"). [1] A priest in the time of David (1 Chron. 24:9). *See also* Miniamin [2]. [2] One who sealed the new covenant (Neh. 10:7). [3] One who married a foreign wife (Ezra. 10:25).

Mikloth (mik'loth; "twigs; sticks"). [1] A descendant of Benjamin living in Jerusalem (1 Chron. 8:32; 9:37-38). [2] A chief military officer under David (1 Chron. 27:4).

Mikneiah (mik-nē'ya; "Jehovah is jealous"). A Levite musician (1 Chron. 15:18, 21).

Milalai (mil-a-lā'i; "Jehovah is elevated"). A priest who aided in the purification of the wall (Neh. 12:36).

Milcah (mil'ka; "counsel"). [1] A daughter of Haran, Abraham's brother, and wife of Nahor (Gen. 11:29; 22:20, 23). [2] A daughter of Zelophehad (Num. 26:33; 27:1).

Miletus [Miletum] (mī-lē'tus [mī-lē'tum]; "scarlet"). A coastal city of Ionia (Acts 20:15; 2 Tim. 4:20). It was 57.9 km. (36 mi.) south of Ephesus.

Millo (mil'ō; "fulness"). [1] A bastion in Jerusalem built in anticipation of an Assyrian siege (2 Sam. 5:9; 1 Kings 9:15). [2] An acropolis of Shechem, a high platform of artificial fill (Judg. 9:6, 20).

Miniamin (min'ya-min; "fortunate"). [1] A Levite who apportioned the tithes (2 Chron. 31:15). [2] A priest in the days of Joiakim (Neh. 12:17). He is possibly the same as Mijamin in First Chronicles 24:9. *See* Mijamin [1]. [3] A priest who helped dedicate the wall (Neh. 12:41).

Minni (min'ī; "prepared"). A portion of the land of Armenia (Jer. 51:27). It was directly south of Lake Urmia and next to the Kingdom of Ararah of the Araxes River.

Minnith (min'ith; "prepared"). A location east of the Jordan where Jephthah slaughtered the Ammonites (Judg. 11:33; Ezek. 27:17). It may be modern Khirbet Hamzeh 6.4 km. (4 mi.) northeast of Hebron.

Miphkad (mif'kad, "appointment; census"). A gate in or near the northern end of the east wall of Jerusalem (Neh. 3:31).

Miriam (mir'i-am; "fat; thick; strong"). [1] The sister of Moses and Aaron. She rebelled against Moses with Aaron at Hazeroth (Exod. 2:4-10; Num. 12:1-15; 20:1). [2] A woman descendant of Judah (1 Chron. 4:17).

Mirma (mir'ma; "height"). Descendant of Benjamin (1 Chron. 8:10).

Misgab (mis'gab; "light"). An unidentified location in Moab (Jer. 48:1). It may not be a proper name.

Mishael (mish'a-el; "who is what God is?"). One who carried away the dead Nadab and Abihu (Exod. 6:22; Lev. 10:4). [2] One who stood with Ezra at the reading of the Law (Neh. 8:4). [3] One of the companions of Danie in Babylon (Dan. 1:6-7, 11, 19). *See* Meshach.

Mishal [Misheal] (mi'shal [mi'she-al]; "requiring"). A territorial town of Asher (Josh. 19:26; 21:30); not to be confused with Mashal.

Misham (mi'sham; "impetuous; fame"). A descendant of Benjamin (1 Chron. 8:12).

Mishma (mish'ma; "fame"). [1] A son of Ishmael (Gen. 25:14; 1 Chron. 1:30). [2] A descendant of Simeon (1 Chron. 4:25).

Mishmannah (mish-man'a; "strength; vigor"). One who joined David at Ziklag (1 Chron. 12:10).

Mispar (mis'par). *See* Mispereth.

Mispereth (mis'pe-reth; "writing"). One who returned from captivity (Neh. 7:7). He is called Mispar in Ezra 2:2.

Misrephoth-maim (mis're-foth-ma'im; "hot waters"). A location in northern Palestine (Josh. 11:8; 13:6). It was on the frontier of the country of the Sidonians. It is identified with modern Khirbet el-Musheir-efeh 17.7 km. (11 mi.) north of Accho and 8 km. (5 mi.) from the Mediterranean.

Mithcah (mith'ka; "sweetness"). An unidentified encampment of the Israelites in the wilderness (Num. 33:28).

Mithredath (mith're-dath; "given by [the god] Mithra"). [1] The treasurer of Cyrus through whom he restored the temple vessels (Ezra 1:8). [2] One who wrote to the king of Persia protesting the restoration of Jerusalem (Ezra 4:7).

Mitylene (mit-i-le'ne; "purity"). The principal city of the Island of Lesbos off the western coast of Asia Minor (Acts 20:14).

Mizar (mi'zar; "little"). A hill east of the Jordan, probably within sight of Mount Hermor on Lebanon's eastern slope (Psa. 42:6).

Mizpah [Mizpeh] (miz'pa [miz'pe]; "a watchtower"). [1] A mound of stones on Mount Gilead (Gen. 31:49). [2] A Hivite settlement in northern Palestine at the foot of Mount Hermon (Josh. 11:3). [3] A city in the lowlands of Judah (Josh. 15:38). It was just north of Eleutheropolis [Beit Jibrin] [4] A town in Gilead east of the Jordan (Judg. 11:34). It is possibly identical with Ramath-Mizpeh. [5] A town of

Benjamin just north of Jerusalem (Josh. 18:26; 1 Kings 15:22). The exact site is uncertain. [6] A place in Moab (1 Sam. 22:3); perhaps modern Rujm el-Meshrefeh west-southwest of Madaba.

Mizraim (miz′ra-im). The second son of Ham (Gen. 10:6, 13; 1 Chron. 1:8, 11). Possibly the Egyptian people are intended.

Mizzah (miz′a; "terror; joy"). A duke of Edom (Gen. 36:13, 17; 1 Chron. 1:37).

Mnason (nā′son; "remembering"). A Cyprian convert who accompanied Paul from Caesarea on Paul's last visit to Jerusalem (Acts 21:16).

Moab (mō′ab; "from my father"). The son of Lot by his daughter and an ancestor of the Moabites (Gen. 19:34-37).

Moab (mō′ab). A land that consisted of the plateau east of the Dead Sea between the wadis Arnon and Zered, though at certain periods extending to the north of the Arnon (Deut. 1:5; Num. 22–25).

Moadiah (mo-a-dī′a). *See* Maadiah.

Moladah (mol′a-da; "generation"). A southern city of Judah (Josh. 15:26; Neh. 11:26).

Molid (mō′lid; "begetter"). A descendant of Judah (1 Chron. 2:29).

Mordecai (mor′de′kī; "dedicated to Mars"). [1] A Jewish exile who became a vizier of Persia. He helped save the Jews from destruction (Esther 2-10). [2] A leader who returned from the Babylonian Captivity (Ezra 2:2; Neh. 7:7).

Moreh (mō′re; "stretching"). [1] The first stopping place of Abraham after he entered Canaan (Gen. 12:6). It was near Shechem. [2] A hill lying at the foot of the valley of Jezreel (Judg. 7:1). It is probably modern Jebel Dahy or Little Hermon about 12.9 km. (8 mi.) northwest of Mount Gilboa.

Moresheth-gath (mō′resh-eth-gath; "possession of Gath"). The hometown of Micah (Mic. 1:14). It may be modern Tell ej-Judeiyeh about 3.2 km. (2 mi.) north of Eleutheropolis.

Moriah (mo-rī′a; "bitterness of the Lord"). [1] An elevation in Jerusalem on which Solomon built the temple (2 Chron. 3:1). Probably the same hilltop was used as the threshing floor of Araunah. The name Moriah was possibly ascribed by the Chronicler because of its traditional meaning (2 Sam. 24:18; 2 Chron. 3:1). [2] The hill on which Abraham was prepared to sacrifice Isaac (Gen. 22:2). The site is uncertain, but Samaritans identify Moriah with Moreh [1]. This seems unlikely.

Mosera (mo-sē′ra; "bonds"). The location of an Israelite wilderness encampment near Mount Hor on the border of Edom (Deut. 10:6).

Moseroth (mō-sē′roth; "discipline"). A desert encampment of the Hebrews (Num. 33:30). Some identify it with Mosera (q.v.).

Moses (mō′zez; "drawer-out; child; one-born"). The great prophet and lawgiver of Israel. He led his people from Egyptian bondage. The Book of Exodus tells his story. He wrote the first five books of the Bible.

Moza (mō'za; "origin; offspring"). **[1]** A son of Caleb (1 Chron. 2:46). **[2]** A descendant of Saul (1 Chron. 8:36-37; 9:42-43).

Mozah (mō'za; "unleavened"). A city allotted to Benjamin (Josh. 18:26); probably Kalunya 7.6 km. (4.7 mi.) northwest of Jerusalem on the road to Jaffa.

Muppim (mup'im; "obscurities"). A son of Benjamin (Gen. 46:21). He is also called Shuppim (1 Chron. 7:12, 15; 26:16), Shupham (Num. 26:39), Shephuphan (1 Chron. 8:5). These last three names mean "serpent." While this individual may have borne many names, probably copyists' errors account for some of the diversity.

Mushi (mū'shī; "drawn out; deserted"). A son of Merari, son of Levi (Exod. 6:19; Num. 3:20; 1 Chron. 6:19, 47).

Myra (mī'ra; "weep"). A town of Lycia where Paul changed ships on his way to Rome (Acts 27:5). It is now called Dembre.

Mysia (mish'i-a "abominable"). A province in northwestern Asia Minor (Acts 16:7). Lydia is to the south and the Aegean Sea to the west of this province.

N

Naam (nā'am; "pleasantness"). A son of Caleb (1 Chron. 4:15).

Naamah (nā'a-ma; "pleasant"). **[1]** Daughter of Lamech and Zillah (Gen. 4:22). **[2]** A wife of Solomon and mother of Rehoboam (1 Kings 14:21; 2 Chron. 12:13).

Naamah (na'a-ma; "beautiful"). A town in the southwestern lowlands of Judah (Josh. 15:41). It is probably modern Khirbet Fered near Arak Ma'aman.

Naaman (nā'a-man; "pleasantness"). **[1]** A Syrian general who was healed of leprosy by bathing in the Jordan (2 Kings 5; Luke 4:27). **[2]** Grandson of Benjamin (Gen. 26:38, 40). **[3]** A son of Benjamin and founder of a tribal family (Gen. 46:21).

Naarah (nā'a-ra; "a girl" or "posterity"). A wife of Ashur (1 Chron. 4:5-6).

Naarai (nā'a-rī; "youthful"). One of David's valiant men (1 Chron. 11:37). Probably the same as Paarai (2 Sam. 23:35).

Naaran [Naarath] (nā'a-ran [nā'a-rath]; "youthful"). A border town of Ephraim (1 Chron. 7:28). It was east of Bethel and near Jericho, and was also called Naarath (Josh. 16:7).

Naarath (nā'a-rath). *See* Naaran.

Naashon (nā'a-shon). *See* Nahson.

Naasson (nā'a-son). Greek form of Nahshon (q.v.).

Nabal (nā'bal; "foolish; wicked"). A wealthy Carmelite who refused David and his men food (1 Sam. 25).

Naboth (nā'both; "a sprout"). The owner whom Jezebel had killed in order to obtain his vineyard (1 Kings 21:1-18).

Nachon (nā'kon; "stroke"). Scripture refers to the threshing floor of Nachon/Chidon (1 Sam. 6:6; 1 Chron. 13:9). This is either the combined name of two individuals, of two place names, or a combination of both. *Chidon* possibly means "destruction or a javelin."

Nachon (nā'kon). *See* Chidon.

Nachor (nā'kor). Greek form of Nahor (q.v.).

Nadab (nā'dab; "liberal"). **[1]** Firstborn son of Aaron, struck dead for offering "strange fire" to God (Exod. 6:23; Lev. 10:1-3). **[2]** A descendant of Jerahmeel (1 Chron. 2:28, 30). **[3]** A brother of Gibeon (1 Chron. 8:30). **[4]** Son of Jeroboam I; he ruled Israel for two years (1 Kings 15:25-31).

Nagge (na'gē; "splendor"). Ancestor of Jesus (Luke 3:25). *See also* Neariah.

Nahalal [**Nahallal; Nahalol**] (nā'ha-lal [nā'hal-al; nā'ha-lol]; "pasture"). A city of Zebulun assigned to the Levites (Josh. 19:15; 21:35; Judg. 1:30). It is probably modern Khirbet el-Teim, south of Accho.

Nahaliel (na-hā'li-el; "valley of God"). An Israelite encampment north of the Arnon River and east of Moab (Num. 21:19). It may be modern Wadi el-Waleh or Wadi Zerka Ma'in.

Nahallal (nā'hal-al). *See* Nahalal.

Nahalol (nā'ha-lol). *See* Nahalal.

Naham (nā'ham; "comfort"). A descendant of Judah, a chieftain (1 Chron. 4:19).

Nahamani (na-ha-mā'nī; "compassionate"). One who returned with Zerubbabel (Neh. 7:7).

Naharai [**Nahari**] (nā'ha-rī; "snorting one"). Joab's armor-bearer (1 Chron. 11:39; 2 Sam. 23:37).

Nahari (nā'ha-rī). *See* Naharai.

Nahash (nā-hash; "oracle" or "serpent"). **[1]** The father of Abigail and Zeruiah (2 Sam. 17:25). **[2]** An Ammonite king that was defeated by Saul (1 Sam. 11:1-2; 12:12). **[3]** Another king of Ammon (2 Sam. 10:2; 17:27; 1 Chron. 19:1-2). Not to be confused with Ir-nahash.

Nahath (nā'hath; "lowness"). **[1]** A descendant of Esau (Gen. 36:13; 1 Chron. 1:37). **[2]** An overseer of the offerings at the temple (2 Chron. 31:13). **[3]** *See* Toah.

Nahbi (nā'bī; "Jehovah is protection"). The spy of Naphtali whom Moses sent out to explore Canaan (Num. 13:14).

Nahor [**Nachor**] (nā'hor [nā'kor]; "piercer"). **[1]** Grandfather of Abraham and ancestor of Christ (Gen. 11:22-25; Luke 3:34). **[2]** A brother of Abraham (Gen. 11:26-27, 29; 22:20, 23; Josh. 24:2).

Nahor (nā'hor). A city mentioned in Genesis 24:10. This is possibly Haran so-called after Abraham's brother, Nahor.

Nahshon [**Naashon; Naasson**] (na'shon [nā'a-shon; nā'a-shon]; "oracle"). A descendant of Judah and ancestor of Christ. Perhaps Aaron's brother-in-law (Exod. 6:23; Num. 1:7; Matt. 1:4).

Nahum (nā'hum; "comforter"). One of the later prophets; he prophesied against Nineveh (Nah. 1:1). Not to be confused with Naum.

Nain (nā'in; "beauty"). A village in Galilee where Christ resurrected a widow's son (Luke 7:11). It is located 3.2 km. (2 mi.) south of Mount Tabor and a little southwest of the Sea of Galilee.

Naioth (nā'oth; "habitation"). The place in Ramah where a community of prophets gathered around Samuel (1 Sam. 19:18-23; 20:1). Its location is not clearly identified. *See also* Ramah [2].

Naomi (na-ō'mi; "pleasantness; my joy"). Mother-in-law to Ruth (Ruth 1:2–4:17).

Naphish (nā'fish; "numerous"). Son of Ishmael (Gen. 25:15; 1 Chron. 1:31).

Naphtali (naf'ta-lī; "wrestling"). The sixth son of Jacob (Gen. 30:7-8). His descendants became one of the twelve tribes.

Naphtali [Nephthalim] (naf'ta-lī [nef'tha-lim]; "that struggles"). A territory assigned to the tribe of Naphtali, located in mountainous northern Palestine (Josh. 19:32-39; Matt. 4:13). It was bounded on the east by the Upper Jordan River and the Sea of Galilee and on the west by the territories of Zebulun and Asher.

Naphtuhim (naf'tu-him). A son of Mizraim (Gen. 10:13; 1 Chron. 1:11). Many think this refers to a district in Egypt, possibly a designation for the people of the Egyptian Delta.

Narcissus (nar-sis'us; meaning unknown). A Roman Christian (Rom. 16:11).

Nathan (nā'than; "gift"). **[1]** Prophet and royal advisor to David (2 Sam. 7:2-17; 12:1-25). **[2]** A son of King David and ancestor of Christ (2 Sam. 5:14; 1 Chron. 3:5; Luke 3:31). **[3]** Father of Igal (2 Sam. 23:36). **[4]** A descendant of Jerahmeel (1 Chron. 2:36). **[5]** A companion of Ezra (Ezra 8:16). **[6]** One of those who had married a foreign wife (Ezra 10:39). **[7]** Brother of Joel, one of David's valiant men (1 Chron. 11:38). **[8]** Father of Solomon's chief officer (1 Kings 4:5). **[9]** A chief man of Israel (Zech. 10:10). *See* Nathan-melech.

Nathanael (na-than'a-el; "God has given"). A Galilean called by Christ to be a disciple. He is probably to be identified with Bartholomew (John 1:45-49; 21:2; Acts 1:13). *See also* Bartholomew.

Nathan-Melech (nā'than-mel'ek; "King's gift"). An official under Josiah (2 Kings 23:11).

Naum (nā'um; "comforter"). An ancestor of Christ (Luke 3:25). Not to be confused with Nahum.

Nazareth (naz'a-reth; "sanctified"). The hometown of Jesus in lower Galilee, north of the Plain of Esdraelon [Jezreel] (Matt. 4:13; Mark 1:9). It is 8 km. (5 mi.) west-southwest of Tiberias, 32.2 km. (20 mi.) southwest of modern Tell Hum [Capernaum] and 141.6 km. (88 mi.) north of Jerusalem.

Neah (nē'a; "moved"). A landmark boundary of Zebulun (Josh. 19:13). It is probably modern Tell el-wawiyat.

Neapolis (ne-ap'o-lis; "the new city"). A seaport of Philippi in

Macedonia (Acts 16:11; cf. 20:6). It is on the Strymonian Gulf 16.1 km. (10 mi.) east-southeast of Philippi.

Neariah (ne-a-rī'a; "Jehovah drives away"). [1] A descendant of David (1 Chron. 3:22). [2] A descendant of Simeon who smote the Amalekites in Mount Seir (1 Chron. 4:42).

Nebai (nē'bī; "projecting"). A co-covenanter with Ezra (Neh. 10:19).

Nebaioth [Nebajoth] (ne-ba'yoth [ne-bā'joth]; "husbandry"). Oldest son of Ishmael (Gen. 25:13; 28:9; 36:3; 1 Chron. 1:29).

Nebajoth (ne-bā'joth). *See* Nebaioth.

Neballat (ne-bal'at; "prophecy"). A town of Benjamin repopulated after the Babylonian Captivity (Neh. 11:34). It is now Beit Nabala 6.4 km. (4 mi.) northeast of Lydda.

Nebat (nē'bat; "cultivation"). Father of Jeroboam I (1 Kings 11:26).

Nebo (nē'bō; "height"). An ancestor of Jews who had taken foreign wives during the Exile (Ezra 10:43). This reference quite possibly refers to a city.

Nebo (nē'bō; "that prophesies"). [1] The mountain from which Moses saw the Promised Land (Deut. 32:49; 34:1). It is a peak in the Abarim Mountains east of the Jordan, opposite Jericho; probably modern Jebel en Neba, 12.9 km. (8 mi.) east of the mouth of the Jordan. On a clear day, all of Palestine can be seen from this peak. [2] A city of Reuben that fell again to the Moabites (Num. 32:3, 38; 33:47). It is probably modern Khirbet el-Mekhayyet, south of Mount Nebo. [3] A city in Judah (Ezra 2:29; Neh. 7:33), probably modern Beth-Nube, near Lydda.

Nebuchadnezzar [Nebuchadrezzar] (neb-u-kad-nez'er [neb-u-kad-rez'er]; Babylonian, *Nabur-kudurri-utsur*—"may [the god] Nabu guard my boundary stones"). Great king of the Babylonian Empire; he captured Jerusalem three times and carried Judah into captivity (2 Kings 24:1, 10-11; 25:1, 8, 22; Dan. 1–4).

Nebushasban (neb'ū-shaz'ban; "Nabu delivers me"). A Babylonian prince (Jer. 39:13).

Nebuzaradan (neb-u-zar-ā'dan; Babylonian, "[the god] Nabu has given seed"). A Babylonian captain of the guard at the siege of Jerusalem (2 Kings 25:8, 11, 20).

Necho (nē'ko). Pharaoh of Egypt who fought Josiah at Megiddo (2 Chron. 35:20).

Nedabiah (ned-a-bī'a; "Jehovah is willing"). A descendant of Jehoiakim king of Judah (1 Chron. 3:18).

Nehemiah (nē'he-mī'a; "Jehovah is consolation"). [1] Governor of Jerusalem; he helped rebuild the fallen city (Neh. 1:1; 8:9; 12:47). [2] A chief man who returned from the Exile (Ezra 2:2; Neh. 7:7). [3] One who repaired the wall of Jerusalem (Neh. 3:16).

Nehum (nē'hum). *See* Rehum.

Nehushta (ne-hush'ta; "basis; ground"). Wife of Jehoiakim; mother of Jehoiachin (2 Kings 24:8).

Neiel (ne-ī'el; "commotion of God"). A landmark boundary of Asher (Josh. 19:27). It is probably modern Khirbet Ya'hin on the edge of the Plain of Acre [Accho].

Nekeb (nē'keb; "cave"). A town on the boundary of the territory of Naphtali (Josh. 19:33) perhaps the same as Adami (q.v.).

Nekoda (ne-kō'da; "herdsman"). [1] Head of a family of Nethinim (Ezra 2:48; Neh. 7:50). [2] The head of a family without genealogy after the Exile (Ezra 2:60; Neh. 7:62).

Nemuel (nem'u-el; "God is speaking"). [1] A descendant of Reuben (Num. 26:9). [2] A son of Simeon (Num. 26:12; 1 Chron. 4:24). In Genesis 46:10; Exodus 6:15, he is called Jemuel.

Nepheg (nē'feg; "sprout; shoot"). [1] A brother of Korah (Exod. 6:21). [2] A son of David (2 Sam. 5:15; 1 Chron. 3:7; 14:6).

Nephishesim [Nephusim] (ne-fish'e-sim [ne'fu-zim]; "expansions"). Ancestor of returned captives (Neh. 7:52). He is called Nephusim in Ezra 2:50. This man is possibly identical with Naphish.

Nephthalim (nef'tha-lim). *See* Naphtali.

Nephtoah (nef-tō'a; "open"). A spring that marks the boundary between Judah and Benjamin (Josh. 15:9). It is identified with modern Lifta, 3.2 km. (2 mi.) northwest of Jerusalem.

Nephusim (ne-fū'sim). *See* Nephishesim.

Ner (nur; "light"). [1] An uncle (?) of Saul, father of Abner (1 Sam. 14:50). [2] Grandfather of Saul (1 Chron. 8:33; 9:39). These relationships are unclear. Abner may have been Saul's uncle. If so, Ner [1] and [2] are the same. He is also called Abiel (1 Sam. 9:1). It is also

Street Scene, Nazareth. Nazareth was a small city of low repute, yet Jesus' parents lived here and it became the boyhood home of the Savior (Luke 2:39-51). This narrow, winding alley of Nazareth looks much as the streets of Jesus' times would have appeared.

possible that Ner [2] (Abiel) had sons named Ner [1] and Kish, the father of Saul.

Nereus (nē're-us; "lamp"). A Roman Christian (Rom. 16:15).

Nergal-sharezer (nur'gal-sha-rē'zer; "May the god Nergal defend the prince"). A Babylonian officer who released Jeremiah (Jer. 39:3, 13-14).

Neri (nē'rī; "whose lamp is Jehovah"). Ancestor of Christ (Luke 3:27).

Neriah (ne-rī'a; "whose lamp is Jehovah"). Father of Baruch (Jer. 32:12, 16; 36:4, 8, 32).

Nethaneel (ne-than'e-el; "God gives"). [1] Chief of Issachar whom Moses sent to spy out the land of Canaan (Num. 1:8; 2:5; 7:18, 23; 10:15). [2] Fourth son of Jesse (1 Chron. 2:14). [3] One of the trumpet blowers when the ark of the covenant was brought up (1 Chron. 15:24). [4] A Levite (1 Chron. 24:6). [5] A son of Obed-edom and gatekeeper of the tabernacle (1 Chron. 26:4). [6] A prince commissioned by Jehoshaphat to teach the people (2 Chron. 17:7). [7] A Levite in the days of Josiah (2 Chron. 35:9). [8] A priest who married a foreign wife (Ezra 10:22). [9] A priest in the days of Joiakim (Neh. 12:21). [10] Levite musician at the purification ceremony (Neh. 12:36).

Nethaniah (neth-a-nī'a; "Jehovah gives"). [1] A musician in David's worship services (1 Chron. 25:2, 12). [2] A Levite whom Jehoshaphat sent to teach in Judah's cities (2 Chron. 17:8). [3] Father of Jehudi (Jer. 36:14). [4] Father of Ishmael, the murderer of Gedaliah (Jer. 40:8, 14-15; 41:11).

Netophah (ne-tō'fa). A city in Judah (Ezra 2:22). A Netophathite is one from this city (1 Chron. 2:54).

Neziah (ne-zī'a; "preeminent"). Head of a Nethinim family that returned to Jerusalem with Zerubbabel (Ezra 2:54; Neh. 7:56).

Nezib (nē'zib; "standing-place"). A city in the lowlands of Judah (Josh. 15:43). It is now Beit Nasib, near Ashna.

Nibshan (nib'shan; "prophecy"). A wilderness town of Judah (Josh. 15:62); possibly modern Khirbet el-Makari south of Jericho between Beth-araban and En-gev.

Nicanor (ni-kā'nor; "conqueror"). One of the seven chosen in the ministry to the poor (Acts 6:5).

Nicodemus (nik-o-dē'mus; "innocent blood"). A Pharisee and ruler of the Jews who assisted in Christ's burial (John 3:1-15; 7:50-52; 19:39-42).

Nicolaus (nik-o-lā'us; "conqueror of the people"). One of the seven chosen to aid in the ministration to the poor (Acts 6:5).

Nicopolis (ni-kop'o-lis; "the city of victory"). [1] A town in Epirus in western Greece about 6.4 km. (4 mi.) north of Actium. [2] A city on both sides of the Nestus River, the boundary between Thrace and Macedonia. Paul referred to one of the above in Titus 3:12; the first is preferred.

Niger (nī'jer). Surname of Simeon (q.v.).

Nile (nīl; "dark blue"). The greatest river of Egypt and the world's longest. It is simply referred to in Scripture as "the river" (Gen. 13:1; Exod. 2:3; 7:21). The Nile is about 6,669.3 km. (4,145 mi.) long.

Nimrah (nim'ra). *See* Beth-Nimrah.

Nimrim (nim'rim; "bitterness"). A brook in Moab (Isa. 15:6; Jer. 48:34). The name still exists in Wadi en-Nemeirah near the southeast end of the Dead Sea.

Nimrod (nim'rod; "valiant; strong"). A son of Cush (Gen. 10:8-9; 1 Chron. 1:10). His kingdom included Babel, Erech, Accad, and Calneh, cities in Shinar, but also included Assyria.

Nimshi (nim'shi; "Jehovah reveals"). An ancestor of Jehu (1 Kings 19:16; 2 Kings 9:2, 14).

Nineveh [Nineve] (nin'e-ve; meaning unknown). The capital of the Kingdom of Assyria (Nah. 1:1; cf. 3:1; Zeph. 2:13; Luke 11:32). It was located east of the Tigris River in the area north of the point the Tigris joins the Upper Zab. The ruins are now called Tell Kuyunjik and Tell Nebi Yunus.

No (nō; "stirring up"). An Egyptian city better known as Thebes (Ezek. 30:14-16; Jer. 46:25). It was the capital of Upper Egypt.

Noadiah (nō-a-dī'a; "Jehovah assembles"). [1] Son of Binnui to whom Ezra entrusted the sacred vessels of the temple (Ezra 8:33). [2] A prophetess opposed to Nehemiah (Neh. 6:14).

Noah [Noe] (nō'a [nō'e]; "rest"). Son of Lamech; the patriarch chosen to build the ark. Only his family survived the flood (Gen. 5:28-32; 6:8-22; 7–10). He was an ancestor of Christ (Luke 3:36).

Noah (nō'a; "flattery; movement"). A daughter of Zelophehad (Num. 26:33; Josh. 17:3).

Nob (nōb; "prophecy"). A city of the tribe of Benjamin located northeast of Jerusalem, within sight of the city (1 Sam. 21:1; 22:19).

Nobah (nō'ba; "prominent"). A descendant of Manasseh who conquered Kenath (Num. 32:42).

Nobah (nō'ba; "prominent"). A town of Gad east of the Jordan (Judg. 8:11). Its site is a tell near Safut.

Nod (nod; "vagabond"). An unidentified land east of Eden to which Cain fled after the murder of Abel (Gen. 4:16). Some suppose it to be China, but this is speculation.

Noe (nō'e). Greek form of Noah (q.v.).

Nogah (nō'ga; "splendor"). A son of David (1 Chron. 3:7; 14:6).

Nohah (nō'ha; "rest"). A son of Benjamin (1 Chron. 8:2).

Non (non). *See* Nun.

Noph (nōf). *See* Memphis.

Nophah (nō'fa; "fearful"). A city in Moab (Num. 21:30). It is not referred to elsewhere and may not be a place name. However, it may be another name for Nobah (q.v.).

Nun [Non] (nun [non]; "continuation; fish"). [1] A descendant of

Ephraim (1 Chron. 7:27); possibly the same as [2]. [2] The father of Joshua (Exod. 33:11; 1 Kings 16:34).

Nymphas (nim'fas; "bridegroom"). A Christian of Laodicea to whom Paul sends greetings (Col. 4:15). Some manuscripts read Nympha, which would make this individual a woman.

O

Obadiah (ō-ba-dī'a; "servant of Jehovah"). [1] The governor or prime minister of Ahab who tried to protect the prophets against Jezebel (1 Kings 18:3-16). [2] A descendant of David (1 Chron. 3:21). [3] A chief of the tribe of Issachar (1 Chron. 7:3). [4] A descendant of King Saul (1 Chron. 8:38; 9:44). [5] A man of the tribe of Zebulun (1 Chron. 27:19). [6] A chief of the Gadites who joined David at Ziklag (1 Chron. 12:9). [7] One of the princes whom Jehoshaphat commissioned to teach the Law (2 Chron. 17:7-9). [8] A Levite overseer in work done on the temple (2 Chron. 34:12). [9] The chief of a family that returned to Jerusalem (Ezra 8:9). [10] One who sealed the covenant with Nehemiah (Neh. 10:5). [11] A gatekeeper for the sanctuary of the temple (Neh. 12:25). [12] The fourth of the "minor prophets." His message was directed against Edom (Obad. 1). [13] See Abda [2].

Obal (ō'bal). See Ebal.

Obed (ō'bed; "servant"). [1] A son of Boaz and Ruth, father of Jesse, and ancestor of Christ (Ruth 4:17; Matt. 1:5; Luke 3:32). [2] A descendant of Judah (1 Chron. 2:37-38). [3] One of David's warriors (1 Chron. 11:47). [4] A Levite gatekeeper in David's time (1 Chron. 26:7). [5] Father of Azariah, who helped make Joash king of Judah (2 Chron. 23:1).

Obed-edom (ō'bed-ē'dom; "servant of [the god] Edom"). [1] A man who housed the ark for three months (2 Sam. 6:10-12; 1 Chron. 13:13-14). [2] One of the chief Levitical singers and doorkeepers (1 Chron. 15:18, 21, 24; 16:5, 38; 26:4, 8, 15). [3] A temple treasurer or official, or perhaps the tribe that sprang from [2] (2 Chron. 25:24).

Obil (ō'bil; "camel-keeper" or "lender"). A descendant of Ishmael who attended to David's camels (1 Chron. 27:30).

Oboth (ō'both; "desires"). An encampment of the Israelites east of Moab (Num. 21:10; 33:43). It is probably modern 'Ain el-Weiba.

Ocran (ok'ran; "troubler"). A descendant of Asher (Num. 1:13; 2:27).

Oded (ō'ded; "aiding" or "restorer"). [1] Father of Azariah the prophet (2 Chron. 15:1). [2] A prophet of Samaria who persuaded the northern army to free their Judean slaves (2 Chron. 28:9-15).

Og (og; "giant"). The giant king of Bashan, defeated at Edrei (Num. 21:33-35; Deut. 3:1-13).

Ohad (ō'had; "strength"). A son of Simeon (Gen. 46:10; Exod. 6:15).

Ohel (ō'hel; "tent"). A son of Zerubbabel (1 Chron. 3:20).

Olives, Mount of [**Mount of Corruption; Olivet**]. A ridge east of Jerusalem and separated from Jerusalem by the Kidron Valley (2 Sam. 15:30; Mark 11:1; Acts 1:12). It is called the Mount of Corruption in Second Kings 23:13.

Olympas (ō-lim'pas; meaning unknown). A Roman Christian (Rom. 16:15).

Omar (ō'mar; "speaker; mountaineer"). A grandson of Esau and a duke of Edom (Gen. 36 15).

Omri (om'ri "Jehovah apportions; pupil"). **[1]** The sixth king of Israel and founder of the third dynasty. He founded Samaria and made it Israel's capital (1 Kings 16:15-28). **[2]** A descendant of Benjamin, the son of Becher (1 Chron. 7:8). **[3]** A descendant of Perez living at Jerusalem (1 Chron. 9:4). **[4]** A prince of Issachar in the days of David (1 Chron. 27:18).

On (on; "sun" or "strength"). A Reubenite who rebelled against Moses and Aaron (Num. 16:1).

On (on; "strength"). An ancient city of Lower Egypt situated on the Nile Delta (Gen. 41:45, 50). It is identical with Beth-Shemesh [4], 30.6 km. (19 mi.) north of Memphis.

Onam (ō'nam; "vigorous"). **[1]** A grandson of Seir (Gen. 36:23; 1 Chron. 1:40). **[2]** A son of Jerahmeel of Judah (1 Chron. 2:26, 28).

Onan (ō'nan; "vigorous"). The second son of Judah. He was slain by God for disobedience (Gen. 38:4-10; Num. 26:19).

Onesimus (o-nes'i-mus; "useful"). A slave on whose behalf Paul wrote an epistle to his master, Philemon (Col. 4:9; Philem. 10, 15).

Onesiphorus (on-e-sif'o-rus; "profit-bringer"). A loyal friend of Paul's who often refreshed him in prison (2 Tim. 1:16; 4:19).

Ono (ō'no; "grief of him"). A city of Benjamin (1 Chron. 8:12; Ezra 2:33). It is probably modern Kafr 'Ana 11.3 km. (7 mi.) southeast of Joppa.

Ophel (ō'fel; "small wh te cloud"). A hill in southeastern Jerusalem (2 Chron. 27:3; Neh. 3:26; 11:21). It was near the Water Gate, Horse Gate, Pool of Siloam, the east court of the temple, and the Kidron Valley.

Ophir (ō'fer; "fruitful; rich"). A son of Joktan (Gen. 10:29; 1 Chron. 1:23). The name may possibly refer to a tribe who inhabited modern Somaliland.

Ophir (ō'fer; "fruitful region"). A region where Solomon mined gold (1 Kings 9:28; 1 Chron. 29:4). The location is highly uncertain. Josephus thought it was India, but the African coast in modern Somaliland is more probable.

Ophni (of'nī "wearisomeness"). A city of Benjamin (Josh. 18:24). It was 4.8 km. (3 mi.) north-northwest of Bethel.

Ophrah (of'ra; "fawn; hamlet"). A descendant of Judah (1 Chron. 4:14).

Ophrah (of'ra; "a fawn"). **[1]** A city of Benjamin (Josh. 18:23; 1 Sam. 13:17). It is probably modern el Taiyibeh, about 6.4 km. (4 mi.) east-northeast of Bethel. **[2]** A city in Manasseh (Judg. 6:11, 24; 9:5). It is now called Arrabeh.

Oreb (ō'reb; "raven"). A Midianite chieftain defeated by Gibeon and beheaded by the Ephraimites (Judg. 7:25).

Oreb (ō'reb; "a raven"). The rock east of Jordan near Beth-bareh where the Midianite chieftain Oreb died (Judg. 7:25; Isa. 10:26). It is now called Ash-el-Ghorab.

Oren (ō'ren; "pine; strength"). A son of Jerahmeel of Judah (1 Chron. 2:25).

Ornan (or'nan; "active"). A Jebusite from whom David bought a piece of land, on which Solomon's temple was erected (1 Chron. 21:15-25). He is called Araunah in Second Samuel 24:16.

Orpah (or'pa; "fawn; youthful freshness"). Daughter-in-law of Naomi (Ruth 1:4-14).

Osee (ō'ze). Greek form of Hosea (q.v.).

Oshea (o-shē'a). *See* Joshua.

Othni (oth'ni; "Jehovah is power"). A Levite, son of Shemaiah and tabernacle gatekeeper in David's time (1 Chron. 26:7).

Othniel (oth'ni-el; "God is power"). Caleb's younger brother who liberated Israel from foreign rule (Judg. 1:13; 3:8-11; 1 Chron. 27:15).

Ozem (ō'zem; "strength"). **[1]** A brother of David (1 Chron. 2:15). **[2]** A son of Jerahmeel of Judah (1 Chron. 2:25).

Ozias (o-zī'as). Greek form of Uzziah (q.v.).

Ozni (oz'ni). *See* Ezbon [1].

P

Paarai (pā'a-rī; "revelation of Jehovah" or "devotee of Peor"). One of David's mighty men (2 Sam. 23:35); probably the same as Naarai (1 Chron. 11:37).

Padan-aram [Padan] (pā'dan-ā'ram [pā'dan]; "plain [tableland] of Aram"). The plain region of Mesopotamia from the Lebanon Mountains to beyond the Euphrates, and from the Taurus Mountains on the north to beyond Damascus on the south (Gen. 25:20; 28:2; 31:18). It is called simply Padan in Genesis 48:7.

Padon (pā'don; "redemption"). One who returned with Zerubbabel (Ezra 2:44; Neh. 7:47).

Pagiel (pā'gi-el; "God's intervention"). A chief of Asher (Num. 1:13; 2:27).

Pahath-Moab (pā'hath-mō'ab; "ruler of Moab"). A Jewish family named after an ancestor of the above name or title (Ezra 2:6; Neh. 3:11). The one who sealed the covenant bearing this name is either another Jew or else the above family is intended (Neh. 10:1, 14).

Pai [Pau] (pā'ī [pā'u]; "howling"). The capital of Hadar, King of Edom (Gen. 36:39; 1 Chron. 1:50). Its location is unknown.

Palal (pā'lal; "judge"). One who helped rebuild the wall (Neh. 3:25).

Palestine [Palestina] (pal-es-tīn [pal-es-tin'a]; "which is covered"). An ill-defined region between the Jordan River and the Dead Sea on the east and the Mediterranean on the west (Gen. 15:18; Exod. 15:14; Joel 3:4). Its northern border is roughly the Lebanon Mountain range. It stretches in a southwesterly triangle to the Gulf of Aqaba on the Red Sea.

Pallu [Phallu] (pal'u [fal'u]; "distinguished"). A son of Reuben (Gen. 46:9; Exod. 6:14; 1 Chron. 5:3).

Palti (pal'tī; "Jehovah delivers"). [1] The man selected from Benjamin to spy out the land (Num. 13:9). [2] *See* Paltiel [2].

Paltiel [Phaltiel] (pal'ti-el [fal'ti-el]; "God delivers"). [1] A prince of the tribe of Issachar (Num. 34:26). [2] The man who married David's wife (2 Sam. 3:15). He is called Phalti in First Samuel 25:44.

Pamphylia (pam-fil'i-a; "a nation made up of every tribe"). A southern coastal area in Asia Minor; its main city is Perga (Acts 13:13; 14:24; 27:5).

Paphos (pa'fos; "that which boils"). A town on the southwest extremity of Cyprus; it was visited by Paul and Barnabas (Acts 13:6-13). It is modern Baffa.

Paradise (par'a-dīs; "pleasure ground; park"). Figurative name for the place where God dwells (2 Cor. 12:3) and the abode of the righteous (Luke 23:43; Rev. 2:7).

Parah (pa'ra; "increasing"). A town of Benjamin (Josh. 18:23). It is probably modern Wadi el-Farah 5.5 miles northeast of Jerusalem.

Paran (pā'ran; "beauty"). A wilderness seven days' march from Mount Sinai (Gen. 21:21; Num. 10:12; 1 Sam. 25:1). It is located east of the wilderness of Beer-sheba and Shurj, and it merges with the Wilderness of Sin with no clearly marked boundary. The area borders on Edom and Midian; it is sometimes called Mount Paran (Hab. 3:3) and El-Paran (Gen. 14:6).

Parbar (par'bar; "a suburb"). An area on the west side of the temple containing officials' chambers and cattle stalls (1 Chron. 26:18).

Parmashta (par-mash'ta; "stronger"). A son of Haman (Esther 9:9).

Parmenas (par'me-nas; "steadfast"). One of the seven deacons (Acts 6:5).

Parnach (par'nak; "gifted"). A descendant of Zebulun (Num. 34:25).

Parosh [Pharosh] (pā'rosh [fā'rosh]; "fleeing; fugitive"). [1] One whose descendants returned from the Exile (Ezra 2:3; Neh. 7:8). [2]

Another whose family returned from the Exile (Ezra 8:3). **[3]** One whose descendants had taken foreign wives during the Exile (Ezra 10:25). **[4]** One who sealed the covenant (Neh. 10:14). **[5]** The father of one who helped repair the wall of Jerusalem (Neh. 3:25). All of these are possibly the same.

Parshandatha (par-shan-dā'tha; "given by prayer"). A son of Haman slain by the Jews (Esther 9:7).

Paruah (pa-roo'a; "blooming"). Father of Jehoshaphat (1 Kings 4:17).

Parvaim (par-vā'im; "eastern"). A place where gold was obtained for the decoration of Solomon's temple (2 Chron. 3:6). It may be modern Sak el-Farwain in southern Arabia.

Pasach (pā'sak; "limping"). A descendant of Asher (1 Chron. 7:33).

Pas-dammim (pas-dam'im). *See* Ephes-dammim.

Paseah [Phaseah] (pa-sē'a [fa-sē'a]; "limping"). **[1]** A descendant of Judah through Caleb (1 Chron. 4:12). **[2]** One whose family returned (Ezra 2:49; Neh. 7:51). **[3]** Father of Jehoiada, who helped repair the wall (Neh. 3:6).

Pashur (pash'er; "splitter; cleaver"). **[1]** Head of a priestly family (Ezra 2:38; 10:22; Neh. 7:41). **[2]** A priest who sealed the covenant with God after the Exile (Neh. 10:1, 3). Possibly identical with [1]. **[3]** A priest, the "chief governor in the house of the Lord," who persecuted Jeremiah (Jer. 20:1-6). **[4]** Son of Melchiah, whose family returned to Jerusalem (1 Chron. 9:12; Neh. 11:12; Jer. 21:1; 38:1).

Patara (pat'a-ra; "trodden under foot"). A seacoast city of southwest Lycia in Asia Minor (Acts 21:1).

Pathros (path'ros; "persuasion of ruin"). The country of Upper Egypt inhabited by the Pathrusim (Isa. 11:11; Jer. 44:1-12), one of the seven peoples coming out of Egypt.

Pathrusim (path-roo'sim). A descendant of Mizraim (Gen. 10:14; 1 Chron. 1:12). Possibly the inhabitants of Pathros.

Patmos (pat'mos; "mortal"). A barren island to which John was banished (Rev. 1:9). It is in the Greek archipelagos and is now called Patino.

Patrobas (pat'ro-bas; "paternal"). A Roman Christian (Rom. 16:14).

Pau (pā'u). *See* Pai.

Paul (pol; Latin, *Paulus*—"little"). A Pharisee who studied Jewish law under Gamaliel (Acts 21:39). He was converted and made an apostle to the Gentiles (Acts 26:12-20). Perhaps he used his Roman name in humility. The Book of Acts tells of his missionary journeys.

Pedahel (ped'a-hel; "whom God redeems"). A prince of Naphtali (Num. 34:28).

Pedahzur (pe-da'zer; "the rock delivers"). Father of Gamaliel (Num. 1:10; 2:20).

Pedaiah (pe-dī'ya; "Jehovah delivers"). **[1]** Father of Joel (1 Chron. 27:20). **[2]** Grandfather of King Josiah (2 Kings 23:36). **[3]** Son or grandson of Jeconiah (1 Chron. 3:18-19). **[4]** One who helped to rebuild the wall of Jerusalem (Neh. 3:25). **[5]** One who stood with Ezra when he read the Law (Neh. 8:4; 13:13). **[6]** A descendant of Benjamin (Neh. 11:7).

Pekah (pē'ka; "opening"). A usurper of the throne cf Israel; he ruled for twenty years (2 Kings 15:25-31).

Pekahiah (pek-a-hī'a; "Jehovah watches"). Son and successor of Menahem on the throne of Israel. He was murdered by Pekah (2 Kings 15:22-26).

Pelaiah (pe-lā'ya; "Jehovah is distinguished"). **[1]** A son of Elioenai (1 Chron. 3:24). **[2]** A Levite who explained the Law when Ezra read it (Neh. 8:7). **[3]** A Levite who sealed the covenant (Neh. 10:10); he may be the same as [2].

Pelaliah (pel-a-lī'a; "Jehovah judges"). A priest whose grandson dwelled in Jerusalem after the Exile (Neh. 11:12).

Pelatiah (pel-a-tī'a; "Jehovah delivers"). **[1]** One who sealed the new covenant with Goc after the Exile (Neh. 10:22). **[2]** A descendant of David (1 Chron. 3:21). **[3]** A captain of Simeon (1 Chron. 4:42-43). **[4]** A wicked prince seen in Ezekiel's vision (Ezek. 11:1, 13).

Amphitheater in Pergamum. The citizens of Pergamum (KJV, Pergamos) were the first to establish the worship of the Roman emperor, Augustus Caesar; John referred to the city as the "seat of Satan" (Rev. 2:13). It is located 80 km. (50 mi.) north of Smyrna in present-day Turkey. In the heart of the city the Greeks built this magnificent amphitheater with 78 rows of seats. Behind the row of columns was the Asclepieum, where the people of Pergamum worshiped the god of healing, Asclepias.

Peleg [Phalec] (pē'leg [fā'lek]; "division"). Son of Eber and ancestor of Christ (Gen. 10:25; 11:16; Luke 3:35).

Pelet (pē'let; "deliverance"). **[1]** A son of Jahdai of the family of Caleb (1 Chron. 2:47). **[2]** One who joined David at Ziklag (1 Chron. 12:3).

Peleth (pē'leth "flight; haste"). **[1]** Father of On (Num. 16:1). **[2]** A son of Jonathan and a descendant of Pharez (1 Chron. 2:33).

Peniel (pe-nī'el). *See* Penvel.

Peninnah (pe-nin'na; "coral; pearl"). Second wife of Elkanah, father of Samuel (1 Sam. 1:2, 4).

Penuel (pe-nū'el; "face of God"). **[1]** A descendant of Benjamin (1 Chron. 8:25). **[2]** A chief or father of Gedar (1 Chron. 4:4).

Penuel [Peniel] (pe-nu'el [pe-nī'el]; "face of God"). An encampment of the Hebrews east of Jordan (Gen. 32:30-31; Judg. 8:8, 17). It derived its name from the fact that Jacob had seen God face-to-face there.

Peor (pē'or; "opening"). A mountain peak near Pisgah in Moab (Num. 23:28). It stood across the Jordan River from Jericho.

Perazim (pe-rā'zɪm). *See* Baal-perazim.

Peresh (per'esh; "separate"). Son of Machir, son of Manasseh (1 Chron. 7:16).

Perez [Phares; Pharez] (pē'rez [fā'rez]; "bursting through"). Eldest son of Judah and an ancestor of Christ (1 Chron. 27:3; Neh. 11:4). He is also called Pharez (Gen. 38:29; 46:12; Luke 3:33).

Perez-Uzzah (pē'rez-uz'a; "breech of Uzzah"). The name David gave to the place Uzzah was struck by God (2 Sam. 6:8).

Perga (pur'ga; "very earthy"). The capital of Pamphylia in Asia Minor during the Roman period (Acts 13:13).

Pergamos (pur'ga-mos; "elevation"). A city of Mysia in northwest Asia Minor and the site of one of the seven churches of Asia (Rev. 2:12-17).

Perida [Peruda] (pe-rī'da [pe-roo'da]; "separation"). One whose descendants returned from the Exile (Neh. 7:57; Ezra 2:55).

Persia (per'sha; "cuts or divides"). A great empire including all of western Asia and parts of Europe and Africa (Ezra 1:8; Ezek. 38:5). Persia proper corresponded to what is now the province of Fars in Iran.

Persis (pur'sis; "Persian"). A Christian woman at Rome (Rom. 16:12).

Peruda (pe'roo'da). *See* Perida.

Peter (pē'ter; "stone; rock"). A fisherman called to be an apostle of Christ. He became one of the leaders of the early church (Matt. 4:18-20; 16:15-19; Acts 2). Christ changed this man's name from Simon to a name meaning "rock" (*Cephas* in Aramaic, *Peter* in Greek).

Pethahiah (peth-a-hī'a; "Jehovah opens up"). **[1]** A chief Levite in the time of David (1 Chron. 24:16). **[2]** A Levite having a foreign wife

(Ezra 10:23). **[3]** A descendant of Judah (Neh. 11:24). **[4]** A Levite who regulated the devotions of the people after Ezra had finished reading the Law (Neh. 9:5).

Pethor (pē'thor; "soothsayer"). The residence of Balaam (Num. 22:5; Deut. 23:4). The town was near the Euphrates River and the mountains of Aram. It was a few kilometers south of Carchemish.

Pethuel (pe-thū'el; "God's opening"). Father of Joel the prophet (Joel 1:1).

Peullethai (pē-ūl'e-thī; "Jehovah's seed"). A son of Obed-edom and gatekeeper in the time of David (1 Chron. 26:5).

Phalec (fā'lek). Greek form of Peleg (q.v.).

Phallu (fal'oo). *See* Pallu.

Phalti (fal'tī). *See* Paltiel [2].

Phaltiel (fal'ti-el). *See* Paltiel.

Phanuel (fa-noo'el; "vision of God"). Father of Anna (Luke 2:36).

Pharaoh (far'ō; "inhabitant of the palace"). Royal title of Egyptian kings, equivalent to our word *king* (Gen. 12:15; 37:36; Exod. 2:15; 1 Kings 3:1; Isa. 19:11).

Phares (fā'rez). Greek form of Perez (q.v.).

Pharez (fā'rez). *See* Perez.

Pharosh (fā'rosh). *See* Parosh.

Pharpar (far'par; "that produces fruit"). One of the two rivers of Damascus (2 Kings 5:12). It is probably the modern Nahr el-'A'waj.

Phaseah (fa-sē'a). *See* Paseah.

Phebe (fē'be; "shining"). A servant of the church at Corinth or Cenchrea who helped Paul (Rom. 16:1).

Phenice (fē'nis; "land of palm trees"). **[1]** A harbor in southern Crete (Acts 27:12). **[2]** *See* Phoenicia.

Phichol (fī'kol; "dark water"). A captain or captains of the army of Abimelech, king of the Philistines (Gen. 21:22; 26:26). Some scholars think this is not a proper name (nor Abimelech), but a Philistine military title. Abraham and Isaac journeyed to Gerar many years apart but yet both encountered an Abimelech and Phichol residing there. If these names are titles, that would help explain this puzzling situation; *See* Abimelech.

Philadelphia (fil-a-del'fi-a; "love of a brother"). A town of Lydia in Asia Minor. It was the site of one of the seven churches of Asia (Rev. 1:11; 3:7-13). It was 45.5 km. (28.3 mi.) southeast of Sardis.

Philemon (fi-lē'mon; "friendship"). A convert at Colossae to whom Paul wrote an epistle on behalf of his runaway servant, Onesimus (Philem. 1, 5-7).

Philetus (fī-lē'tus; "amiable"). A convert who was condemned by Paul because of his stand on the Resurrection (2 Tim. 2:17).

Philip (fil'ip; "lover of horses"). **[1]** One of the twelve apostles of Christ (Matt. 10:3; John 1:44-48; 6:5-9). **[2]** An evangelist mentioned several times in Acts (Acts 6:5; 8:5-13). **[3]** *See* Herod [3], [4].

Philippi (fi-lip'ī; "the same"). A city of Macedonia founded by Philip the Great and named for him (Acts 16:12; 20:3-6). It lies inland about 16.1 km. (10 mi.) northwest of its seaport, Neapolis.

Philistia (fil-is'ti-a; "land of sojourners"). An area on the southwest coast of Palestine (Psa. 60:8; 87:4; 108:9). This land, which was the home of traditional enemies of Israel, was 80 km. (50 mi.) long and only 24 km. (15 mi.) wide.

Philistim (fil-is'tim). The reference to Philistim in Genesis 10:14 is to the Philistines.

Philologus (fi-lol'o-gus; "a lover of learning"). A Roman Christian to whom Paul sent greetings (Rom. 16:15).

Phinehas (fin'e-as; "mouth of brass"). [1] Grandson of Aaron and high priest (Exod. 6:25; Num. 25:6-18; 1 Chron. 6:4; 9:20). [2] Younger son of Eli; he was a priest who abused his office (1 Sam. 1:3; 2:22-24, 34). [3] Father of Eleazar (Ezra 8:33).

Phlegon (flē'gon; "burning"). A Roman Christian (Rom. 16:14).

Phoenicia [Phenice] (fe-nish'i-a [fē'nis]; "land of palm trees"). A thin strip of territory between the Mediterranean Sea on the west and on the east the mountains of Lebanon (Acts 21:2; 11:19; 15:3). It included the hills running south from those mountains.

Phrygia (frij'i-a; "barren"). A large and important inland province of Asia Minor (Acts 2:10; 16:6).

Phurah (fū'ra; "beauty"). A servant of Gideon (Judg. 7:10-11).

Phut [Put] (fut [put]; "bow"). The third son of Ham (Gen. 10:6; 1 Chron. 1:8). Possibly a reference to a people related to the Egyptians. Many consider the reference to be to a people related to the Libyans.

Phut (fut). *See* Libya.

Phuvah [Pua; Puah] (fū'va [pū'a]; "utterance"). [1] Second son of Issachar (Gen. 46:13; Num. 26:23; 1 Chron. 7:1). [2] Father of Tola the judge (Judg. 10:1).

Phygellus (fi-gel'us; "fugitive"). One who deserted Paul in Asia (2 Tim. 1:15).

Pibeseth (pi-bē'seth; "house of Bast"). An Egyptian town located on the west bank of the Pelusiac branch of the Nile (Ezek. 30:17). It is now called Tell Basta, about 72.4 km. (45 mi.) east-northeast of Cairo.

Pi-hahiroth (pī-ha-hī'roth; "the mouth"). The location of the final Israelite encampment prior to crossing the Red Sea (Exod. 14:2, 9; Num. 33:7-8). The site is uncertain, but it may be the swamps of Jeneffel at the edge of the pass between Baal-zephon and the Great Bitter Lake.

Pilate (pī'lat). *See* Pontius Pilate.

Pildash (pil'dash; "flame of fire"). A son of Nahor, Abraham's brother (Gen. 22:22).

Pileha (pil'e-ha; "worship"). One who sealed the covenant (Neh. 10:24).

Piltai (pil'tī; "Jehovah causes to escape"). A priest in Jerusalem in the days of Joiakim (Neh. 12:17).

Pinon (pī'non; "darkness"). A chief of Edom (Gen. 36:41; 1 Chron. 1:52).

Piram (pī'ram; "indomitable" or "wild"). An Amorite king slain by Joshua (Josh. 10:3).

Pirathon (pir'a-thon; "princely"). The town where Abdon the judge was buried (Judg. 12:15). It is now called Ferata and is 12 km. (7.5 mi.) southwest of Shechem.

Pisgah (pis'ga; "fortress"). The mountain ranges from which Moses viewed the Promised Land (Num. 21:20; Deut. 3:27). This part of the Abarim Range is near the northeast end of the Dead Sea.

Pisidia (pi-sid'i-a; "pitch"). An island district of Asia Minor with Antioch as its capital (Acts 13:14).

Pison (pī'son; "changing"). A river of Eden (Gen. 2:11). It has traditionally been identified with the Phasis (modern Rion) or the Kur, a tributary of the Araxes. The Palla Copas canal has been suggested also.

Pispah (pis-pa; "expansion"). A descendant of Asher (1 Chron. 7:38).

Pithom (pī'thom; "their mouthful"). An Egyptian store-city built by the Israelites (Exod. 1:11). It was located in the valley connecting the Nile and Lake Timsah. The ruins are at Tell el-Maskhutah.

Pithon (pī'thon; "harmless"). A son of Micah and great-grandson of Saul (1 Chron. 8:35).

Pochereth (pok'e-reth; "binding"). One whose children returned (Ezra 2:57; Neh. 7:59).

Pontius Pilate (pon'shus pī'lat; Latin, *Pontius Pilatus*—"marine dart-carrier"). A Roman procurator of Judea. When Christ was brought before him for judgment, Pilate, fearing the Jews, turned Him over to the people even though he found Him not guilty (Matt. 27:2-24; John 18:28-40).

Pontus (pon'tus; "the sea"). A district in northeastern Asia Minor on the Pontus Euxinus (Acts 2:9; 1 Pet. 1:1).

Poratha (pōr'a-tha; "favored"). A son of Haman slain by the Jews (Esther 9:8).

Porcius Festus (por'shi-us fes'tus). *See* Festus.

Potiphar (pot'i-fer; "belonging to the sun-god"). Egyptian captain of the guard who became the master of Joseph (Gen. 37:36; 39).

Potipherah (po-tif'er-a; "given of the sun-god"). A priest of On; father-in-law of Joseph (Gen. 41:45, 50).

Potter's Field. *See* Aceldama.

Praetorium (pre-tō'ri-um). The Praetorium was originally the head-quarters of a Roman camp, but in the provinces the name was used to designate the official residence. Jesus was brought to Pilate's Praetorium in Jerusalem (Mark 15:16).

Prisca (pris'ka). Shortened form of Priscilla (q.v.).

Priscilla [Prisca] (pri-sil'a [pris'ka]; "ancient one"). The wife of Aquila; a Jewish Christian deeply loyal to her faith (Acts 18:2, 18, 26; Rom. 16:3).

Prochorus (prok'o-rus; "choir leader"). One of the seven deacons (Acts 6:5).

Ptolemais (tol-e-mā'is). *See* Accho.

Pua (pū'a). *See* Phuvah.

Puah (pū'a). *See* Phuvah.

Publius (pub'li-us; "common; first"). Governor of Malta who courteously received Paul and his company when they were ship-wrecked (Acts 28:1-10).

Pudens (pū'denz; "shame faced"). A Roman Christian (2 Tim. 4:21).

Pul (pul). *See* Tiglath-pileser.

Pul (pul; "Lord"). A country of undetermined location (Isa. 66:19), sometimes considered to be Libya.

Punon (pū'non; "precious stone"). An Israelite encampment during the last portion of the wilderness wandering (Num. 33:42). It is probably modern Feeinan on the east side of the Aravah.

Put (put). *See* Phut.

Put (put). *See* Libya.

Puteoli (pu-tē'o-lī; "sulphurous wells"). A seaport on the northern shore of the Bay of Naples (Acts 28:13). The modern city of Pozzuoli stands there.

Putiel (pū'ti-el; "God enlightens"). Father-in-law of Eleazer, son of Aaron (Exod. 6:25).

Q

Quartus (kwor'tus; "fourth"). A Corinthian Christian who sent greetings to the church in Rome (Rom. 16:23).

Quicksands, the. *See* Syrtis.

R

Raamah (rā'a-ma; "trembling"). A son of Cush (Gen. 10:7; 1 Chron. 1:9). Possibly a reference to the inhabitants of a place in southwest Arabia.

Raamah (rā'a-ma; "to constrain, humiliate"). A place near Ma'in in southwest Arabia (Ezek. 27:22). It is called Regma in inscriptions from that area.

Raamiah (rā-a-mī'a; "Jehovah causes trembling"). A chief who returned to the land (Neh. 7:7). In Ezra 2:2, he is called Reelaiah ("Jehovah causes trembling").

Raamses (ram'sēz; "child of the sun"). One of the cities the Israelites built for the Egyptians (Exod. 1:11). It is thought to be San el-Hazar or modern Kantir.

Rabbah [Rabbath] (rab'a [rab'ath]; "great"). [1] The chief city of the Ammonites (Deut. 3:11; Josh. 13:25). It was located 37 km. (23 mi.) east of the Jordan River at the headwaters of the Jabbok. [2] A city in Judah near Kirjath-jearim (Josh. 15:60).

Rabbith (rab'ith; "great"). A boundary town of Issachar (Josh. 19:20). It is perhaps the present village of Raba 12.9 km. (8 mi.) south of Mount Gilboa.

Rabmag (rab'mag; "chief magician" or "priest"). This is not a proper name, but an official position of some sort. It is unclear whether it is a high religious or governmental position (Jer. 39:3, 13). Nergal-sharezer of Babylonia bore this title.

Rabsaris (rab'sa-ris). Not a proper name, but an official position in the Babylonian and Assyrian governments. Its precise nature is unknown (Jer. 39:3, 13; 1 Kings 18:17).

Rabshakeh (rab'sha-ke). The title of an office in the Assyrian government. Its precise function is unknown. but suggestions include that of a field marshal or governor of the Assyrian provinces east of Haran (2 Kings 18:17-28; 19:4, 8).

Rachab (rā'kab). Greek form of Rahab (q.v.).

Rachal (rā'kal; "to whisper"). A town in Judah (1 Sam. 30:29). Some believe the text should read Carmel and would be identical with Carmel [2].

Rachel [Rahel] (rā'chel [rā'hel]; "ewe"). Daughter of Laban, wife of Jacob, and mother of Joseph and Benjamin (Gen. 29–35).

Raddai (rad'ā'ī; "Jehovah subdues" or "beating down"). Brother of David (1 Chron. 2:14).

Ragau (rā'go). Greek form of Reu (q.v.).

Raguel (ra'gū'el). *See* Jethro.

Rahab [Rachab] (rā'hab [rā'kab]; "broad"). The harlot of Jericho who helped the Hebrew spies and who became an ancestor of Christ (Josh. 2:1-21; 6:17-25; Matt. 1:5).

Raham (rā'ham; "pity; love"). A descendant of Caleb (1 Chron. 2:44).

Rahel (rā'hel). *See* Rachel.

Rakem (rā'kem; "friendship"). A descendant of Manasseh (1 Chron. 7:16).

Rakkath (rak'ath; "empty"). A fortress city in Naphtali on the western shore of the Sea of Galilee (Josh. 19:35); probably Tell el-latiyeh.

Rakkon (rak'on; "void"). A place near Joppa in the territory of Dan (Josh. 19:46).

Ram [Aram] (ram [a'ram]; "exalted"). [1] An ancestor of David and of Christ (Ruth 4:19; Matt. 1:3-4; Luke 3:33). [2] Son of Jerahmeel of Judah (1 Chron. 2:27). [3] Head of the family of Elihu (Job 32:2).

Ramah [Rama] (rā'ma [rā'ma]; "elevated"). [1] A town in Benjamin near Gibeah, Geba, and Bethel (Josh. 18:25; Judg. 4:5; Isa. 10:29; Matt. 2:18). It has been identified as modern Er-Ram 8 km. (5 mi.) north of Jerusalem. [2] The town where Samuel was born (1 Sam. 1:1). It is also called Ramathaim-Zophim (1 Sam. 1:11). Its location is uncertain but has been identified with Ramah [1] and modern-day Rentis, about 14.5 km. (9 mi.) northeast of Lydda. It may be Arimathea. [3] A frontier town of Asher (Josh. 19:29). If not the same as Ramah [4] it may be Rameh, about 20.9 km. (13 mi.) south-southeast of Tyre. [4] A fortified city of Naphtali (Josh. 19:36). The site may be modern Rameh, 27.4 km. (17 mi.) east-northeast of Accho. [5] *See* Ramoth-gilead. [6] *See* Ramath.

Ramath [Ramoth] (rā'math [rā'moth]; "height, elevation"). A city of Simeon called "Ramath of the South" (Josh. 19:8). It is now Kurnab. It is also called "Ramoth" in First Samuel 30:27.

Ramathaim-Zophim (rā'ma-thā'im-zō'fim). *See* Ramah [2].

Ramath-Lehi (rā'math-lē'hī; "elevation of the jawbone"). *See* Lehi.

Ramath-Mizpeh (rā'math-miz'pe; "place of the watchtower"). A city of Gad in Gilead (Josh. 13:26). It was 24 km. (15 mi.) northwest of Rabbath of Ammon, at the Jabbok. It may be identical with Mizpeh [4].

Rameses (ram'e-sēz; "child of the sun"). A fertile district of Egypt where the Israelites settled (Gen. 47:11; Exod. 12:37). It was possibly the Land of Goshen.

Ramiah (ra-mī'a; "Jehovah is high"). One who married a foreign wife during the Exile (Ezra 10:25).

Ramoth (rā'moth; "heights"). One who had taken a foreign wife (Ezra 10:29).

Ramoth (rā'moth; "high places" or "heights"). [1] A Levitical city of Gilead in Gad (Deut. 4:43; Josh. 20:8). It is identical with Ramoth-gilead. [2] A city of Levi in Issachar (1 Chron. 6:37). It is identical with Jarmuth [2] and Remeth (q.v.). [3] *See* Ramath.

Ramoth-gilead [Ramoth] (rā'moth-gil'e-ad [rā'moth]; "heights of Gilead"). The chief city of Gad. It was a city of refuge ascribed to the Levites (1 Kings 4:13; 22:4). Sometimes it is called simply Ramoth (Deut. 4:43; Josh. 20:8). It has been identified with both Tell Ramith and Tell el-Hush.

Rapha (ra'fa; "fearful"). [1] The fifth son of Benjamin (1 Chron. 8:2). He is called Rephaiah in First Chronicles 9:43. [2] A descendant of King Saul (1 Chron. 8:37).

Raphu (ra'fū; "feared; one healed"). Father of a spy sent into Canaan (Num. 13:9).

Reaia [Reaiah] (re-ā'ya [re-ā'ya]; "Jehovah sees"). [1] A descendant of Reuben (1 Chron. 5:5). [2] One whose descendants returned from the Exile (Ezra 2:47; Neh. 7:50). [3] A descendant of Judah (1 Chron. 4:2); perhaps the same as Haroeh (1 Chron. 2:52).

Reba (rē'ba; "fourth part"; "sprout"; or "off-spring"). One of the Midianite chieftains slain by the Israelites under Moses (Num. 31:8; Josh. 13:21).

Rebecca (re-bek'a). Greek form of Rebekah (q.v.).

Rebekah [Rebecca] (re-bek'a [re-bek'a]; "flattering"). Wife of Isaac and mother of Jacob and Esau (Gen. 22:23; 24–28).

Rechab (rē'kab; "companionship"). [1] A descendant of Benjamin who murdered Ish-bosheth (2 Sam. 4:2, 5-9). [2] Founder of a tribe called Rechabites (2 Kings 10:15; Jer. 35). [3] A descendant of Hemath (1 Chron. 2:55). [4] One who helped to build the wall of Jerusalem (Neh. 3:14).

Rechah (rē'ka; "uttermost part"). A village in Judah (1 Chron. 4:12). Its location is not known.

Red Sea. A sea that divides Egypt and Arabia. It was across this body of water that the Israelites escaped from Egypt (Exod. 10:19). The Hebrews called it the Sea of Deliverance; others called it the "Sea of Reeds."

Reelaiah (re-el-ā'ya). *See* Raamiah.

Refuge, Cities of. *See* Cities of Refuge.

Regem (rē'gem; "friendship"). A descendant of Caleb (2 Chron. 2:47). *See* Regem-melech.

Regem-melech (rē'gem-mē'lek; "royal friend"). A messenger sent out by some Jews. Some authorities do not take this as a proper name but read: ". . .Sherezer, the friend of the king" (Zech. 7:2).

Rehabiah (re-ha-bī'a; "Jehovah is a widener"). Eldest son of Eliezer, son of Moses (1 Chron. 23:17; 24:21).

Rehob (rē'hob; "breadth; width"). [1] Father of Hadadezer, king of Zobah (2 Sam. 8:3, 12). [2] A Levite who sealed the covenant (Neh. 10:11).

Rehob (rē'hob; "breadth; width"). [1] *See* Beth-rehob. [2], [3] Two towns of Asher (Josh. 19:28, 30). One of them was given to the Levites and one remained in the hands of the Canaanites (Judg. 1:31; Josh. 21:31).

Rehoboam [Roboam] (re'ho-bō'am [ro'bō'am]; "freer of the people"). The son of Solomon; when he was king, ten tribes revolted from him and he set up the southern kingdom of Judah (1 Kings 11:43; 12; 14). He was an ancestor of Christ (Matt. 1:7).

Rehoboth (re-hō'both; "spaces"). [1] A well dug by Isaac in the Valley of Gerar (Gen. 26:22). It is probably modern Wadi Ruheibeh, 30.6 km. (19 mi.) southwest of Beer-sheba. [2] A suburb of Nineveh (Gen. 10:11). [3] A city somewhere in northern Edom (Gen. 36:37; 1 Chron. 1:48). Its location is unidentified.

Rehum (rē'hum; "pity"). [1] A chief man that returned from Exile with Zerubbabel (Ezra 2:2). He is called Nehum ("comfort") in Nehemiah 7:7. [2] A chancellor of Artaxerxes (Ezra 4:8, 17). [3] A Levite who helped to repair the wall of Jerusalem (Neh. 3:17). [4] One who sealed the covenant (Neh. 10:25). **[5]** One who went up with Zerubbabel (Neh. 12:3).

Rei (rē'i; "friendly"). A friend of David (1 Kings 1:8).

Rekem (rē'kem; "friendship"). **[1]** A Midianite king slain by the Israelites (Num. 31:8; Josh. 13:21). **[2]** A son of Hebron (1 Chron. 2:43-44).

Rekem (re'kem; "mercy"). A city of Benjamin (Josh. 18:27). It is probably modern Ar Kalandujeh.

Remaliah (rem-a-lī'a; "Jehovah increases" or "whom Jehovah has adorned"). Father of Pekah (2 Kings 15:25-37). This is perhaps not a proper name, but a slur on Pekah's impoverished background.

Remeth (rē'meth; "height"). A city of the tribe of Issachar (Josh. 19:21); not to be confused with Ramath.

Remmon (rem'on). *See* Rimmon.

Remmon-methoar (rem'on-meth'o-ar). *See* Rimmon [3].

Rephael (rē'fa-el; "God has healed"). Firstborn son of Obed-edom and tabernacle gatekeeper (1 Chron. 26:7).

Rephah (rē'fa; "healing; support"). A descendant of Ephraim (1 Chron. 7:25).

Rephaiah (re-fā'ya; "Jehovah is healing"). **[1]** Head of a family of the house of David (1 Chron. 3:21). **[2]** A captain of Simeon (1 Chron. 4:42). **[3]** A son of Tola (1 Chron. 7:2). **[4]** One who helped to rebuild the wall of Jerusalem (Neh. 3:9). **[5]** *See* Rapha [1].

Rephaim, Valley of (ref'a-im; "valley of giants"). The site in Judah where David defeated the Philistines (Isa. 17:5; 2 Sam. 5:18). It lies between Jerusalem and Bethlehem, southwest of Jerusalem and the Valley of Hinnom. It is probably the present-day Valley el-Bukaa.

Rephidim (ref'i-dim; "beds"). An Israelite encampment between the Wilderness of Sin and Mount Sinai (Exod. 17:1, 8). It may be the Wadi Refayid, northwest of Jebel Musa.

Resen (rē'sen; "bride"). A city between Nineveh and Calah in Assyria (Gen. 10:12).

Resheph (rē'shef; the name of a Canaanite deity; meaning unknown). A descendant of Ephraim (1 Chron. 7:25).

Reu [Ragau] (rē'ū [rā'go]; "friendship"). Son of Peleg and ancestor of Christ (Gen. 11:18-21; Luke 3:35).

Reuben (roo'ben; "behold, a son"). Eldest son of Jacob and Leah; he lost his birthright through sin against his father (Gen. 29:32; 35:22; 37:29). His descendants became one of the twelve tribes of Israel.

Reuel (roo'el; "God is his friend"). **[1]** A son of Esau by Bashemath (Gen. 36:4; 1 Chron. 1:35, 37). **[2]** Descendant of Benjamin (1 Chron. 9:8). **[3]** *See* Jethro. **[4]** *See* Deuel.

Reumah (roo'ma; "pearl; coral"). Nahor's concubine (Gen. 22:24).

Rezeph (rē'zef; "pavement"). A city of Syria taken by Sennacherib (2 Kings 19:12; Isa. 37:12). It is perhaps the modern Rusafah several kilometers west of the Euphrates toward Palmyra.

Rezia (re-zī'a; "Jehovah is pleasing"). A descendant of Asher (1 Chron. 7:39).

Rezin (rēz'in; "dominion"). [1] The last king of Syria who, along with Pekah, fought Judah (2 Kings 15:37; 16:5-10). [2] One whose descendants returned from the Babylonian Captivity (Ezra 2:48; Neh. 7:50).

Rezon (rē'zon; "prince; noble"). A Syrian rebel who set up his own government in Damascus (1 Kings 11:23). Many scholars think Rezon simply is a title denoting a prince and identify him with Hezion (q.v.).

Rhegium (rē'ji-um; "fracture"). A town located in southern Italy (Acts 28:13). It was opposite Messina in Sicily and is now called Reggio.

Rhesa (rē'sa; "head"). An ancestor of Christ (Luke 3:27).

Rhoda (rō'da; "rose"). A maid in the house of Mary (Acts 12:12-15).

Rhodes (rōdz; "rose"). An island located off the coast of Caria in southwest Asia Minor (Acts 21:1).

Ribai (rī'bī; "Jehovah contends"). Father of Ittai, one of David's valiant men (2 Sam. 23:29; 1 Chron. 11:31).

Riblah (rib'la; "quarrel"). [1] A city on the Orontes where the sons of Zedekiah were slain (Jer. 39:5-7; 2 Kings 23:33). It was 30 km. (50 mi.) south of Hamath. It may be modern Ribleh in the Plain of Coelesyria. [2] A border city of the Promised Land (Num. 34:11). It is perhaps modern Harmel northeast of the source of the Orontes.

Rimmon (rim'on; "pomegranate"). Father of Ishbosheth's murderers (2 Sam. 4:2-9).

Rimmon [Remmon] (rim'on [rem'on]; "pomegranate"). [1] A town in southern Judah (Josh. 15:32; 1 Chron. 4:32; Zech. 14:10). It is identified with Khirbet Umm er-Ramānīn, about 9 mi. from Beersheba. [2] A rock near Gibeah (Judg. 20:45-47; 21:13). It is possibly a limestone projection 3.5 mi. east of Bethel. [3] A border town of Zebulun (1 Chron. 6:77). The town is called Dimnah in Joshua 21:35, a reading many scholars consider a corruption of Rimmon. The site is referred to in Joshua 19:13 as Remmon-methoar. Many translate verse 13: . . . [the border] goes out to Ittah-Kazin and goes to Kemmon and bends [methoar] to Neah.

Rimmon-parez (rim'on-pē'rez; "pomegranates of the wrath"). The fifteenth encampment of the Israelites (Num. 33:19). It is somewhere between Rithmah and Libnah and is possibly Nakt el-Biyar.

Rinnah (rin'a; "praise to God; strength"). A descendant of Judah (1 Chron. 4:20).

Riphath (ri'fath; "spoken"). A son of Gomer (Gen. 10:3). A copyist's mistake makes him Diphath in First Chronicles 1:6. Possibly a reference to the Paphlagonians on the Black Sea.

Rissah (ris'a; "dew"). An encampment in the wilderness (Num. 33:21-22). It is probably modern Kuntilet el-Jerafi.

Rithmah (rith'ma; "noise"). The fourteenth encampment of Israel in the wilderness (Num. 33:18). It is perhaps the same as Kadesh.

Rizpah (riz'pa; "variegated" or "hot stone"). A concubine of Saul (2 Sam. 3:7; 21:8-11).

Roboam (ro-bō'am). Greek form of Rehoboam.

Rodanim (rō'da-nim). *See* Dodanim.

Rogelim (rō'ge-lim; "footmen"). The dwelling place of Barzillai (2 Sam. 17:27). It was located in Gilead and is probably Bersiniya 8.8 km. (5.5 mi.) southwest of Irbid.

Rohgah (rō'ga; "outcry; alarm"). A chief of Asher (1 Chron. 7:34).

Romamti-ezer (ro-mam'ti-ē'zer; "highest help"). Son of Heman appointed over the service of song (1 Chron. 25:4, 31).

Rome (rōm; "city of Romulus"). The capital of the great Roman Empire (Acts 23:11). It is located in Italy on the Tiber River.

Rosh (rosh; "head"). A descendant of Benjamin (Gen. 46:21).

Rufus (roo'fus; "red"). [1] A son of Simon of Cyrene (Mark 15:21). He was probably well-known to those to whom Mark wrote his gospel. [2] A Roman Christian (Rom. 16:13); some identify him with [1].

Rumah (rū'ma; "exalted"). A town whose locality is uncertain (2 Kings 23:36). Perhaps it is Arumah near Shechem or Rumah [Khirbet Rumeh] in Galilee, 9.7 km. (6 mi.) north of Nazareth.

Ruth (rooth; "friendship; companion"). Moabite wife of Mahlon and Boaz; she was the great-grandmother of David and an ancestor of Christ (Ruth 1:4-5, 14-16; 4:10; Matt. 1:5).

S

Sabta [Sabtah] (sab'ta; "striking"). The third son of Cush (Gen. 10:7; 1 Chron. 1:9). Possibly a people of southern Arabia is intended.

Sabtecha [Sabtechah] (sab'te-ka; "striking"). The fifth son of Cush (Gen. 10:7; 1 Chron. 1:9). Possibly a reference to a people of south Arabia.

Sacar (sā'kar; "hired"). [1] The father of one of David's mighty men (1 Chron. 11:35). He is called Sharar ("strong") in Second Samuel 23:33. [2] A Levite tabernacle gatekeeper in the days of David (1 Chron. 26:4).

Sadoc (sā'dok; Greek form of Zadok—"righteous"). An ancestor of Christ (Matt. 1:14).

Sala [Salah] (sā'la; "petition; sprout"). A son of Arphaxad and ancestor of Christ (Gen. 10:24; 11:12; Luke 3:35). He is called Shelah in First Chronicles 1:18, 24.

Salamis (sal'a-mis; "shaken"). A town located on the east end of Cyprus (Acts 13:5). It is 4.8 km. (3 mi.) northwest of modern Famagusta.

Salathiel (sa-lā'thi-el). Greek form of Shealtiel (q.v.).

Salcah [Salchah] (sal'ka; "thy lifting up"). A city located at the extreme limits of Bashan (Deut. 3:10; Josh. 12:5). It is now Salkhad 106.2 km. (66 mi.) east of the Jordan, opposite Beth-shean in Samaria.

Salem (sā'lem; "perfect peace"). The city of Melchizedek (Gen. 14:18; Psa. 76:2). It is possibly modern Salim; however, many believe it to be Jerusalem.

Salim (sa'lim; "path"). The place where John baptized (John 3:23). It is near the waters of Aenon which were probably north of Shechem, although the site is uncertain.

Sallai (sal'a-ī; "rejecter"). [1] A chief man of the tribe of Benjamin (Neh. 11:8). [2] A priest who returned with Zerubbabel from the Exile (Neh. 12:20). He is called Sallu in Nehemiah 12:7.

Sallu (sal'u; "weighed; dear"). [1] A descendant of Benjamin dwelling in Jerusalem (1 Chron. 9:7; Neh. 11:7). [2] *See* Sallai [2].

Salma [Salmon] (sal ma [sal'mon]; "strength; clothing"). [1] A son of Caleb, son of Hur (1 Chron. 2:51, 54). [2] Father of Boaz and ancestor of Christ (Ruth 4:20-21; Matt. 1:4-5; Luke 3:32). Not to be confused with Zalmon.

Salmon (sal'mon). *See* Zalmon.

Salmone (sal-mō'ne; "peace"). The easternmost point of the island of Crete (Acts 27:7). It is now known as Cape Sidero.

Salome (sa-lō'me; "clothing; strength"). [1] One of the women who saw the Crucifixion (Mark 15:40; 16:1). Matthew 27:56 mentions that the mother of the sons of Zebedee was present; she is probably to be identified with Salome. John 19:25 lists the sister of Jesus' mother among those near the cross; some scholars identify her with Salome, but others deny this. [2] The daughter of Herodias who danced before Herod (Matt. 14:6; Mark 6:22).

Salt, City of. *See* City of Salt.

Salt Sea [Dead Sea; East Sea]. The body of water at the southern end of the Jordan Valley, which contains no marine life because of its heavy mineral contents (Gen. 14:3; Num. 34:12). Its modern name is the Dead Sea.

Salt, Valley of. A plain traditionally located at the lower end of the Dead Sea (2 Sam. 8:13). Another such valley, the Wadi el-Milh (salt), is east of Beer-sheba, and may be the site of the defeat of the Edomites.

Salu (sā'lu; "miserable; unfortunate"). Father of Zimri, who was slain (Num. 25:14).

Samaria (sa-mā'ri-a; "watch mountain"). [1] The capital of the northern kingdom of Israel (1 Kings 20:1; 2 Chron. 18:2; Jer. 41:5). It was 67.6 km. (42 mi.) north of Jerusalem. [2] Another name for the kingdom of Israel (1 Kings 13:32; 2 Kings 17:24). [3] A district of Palestine in Christ's time (Luke 17:11-19). Galilee was on its north and Judea on the south.

Samgar-nebo (sam'gar-nē'bo). A Babylonian officer who sat with other officials in the middle gate of Jerusalem (Jer. 39:3). Some take

Ruins of Samaria. A city with a long history, Samaria was capital of the northern kingdom of Israel from the reign of Omri in the ninth century B.C. This basilica near the forum at Samaria was built by Herod the Great, who named the town Sebaste in honor of his Roman patron, Augustus (*Sebaste* is the Greek equivalent of the Latin *Augustus*). The evangelist Philip preached here, as did Peter and John (Acts 8:5-25).

this as a proper name (perhaps meaning "be gracious, Nebo"). Others view it as a title of Nergal-sharezer.

Samlah (sam'la; "garment"). King of Edom (Gen. 36:36; 1 Chron. 1:47-48).

Samos (sā'mos; "full of gravel"). An island of Greece (Acts 20:15). It is off the eastern coast of Asia Minor southwest of Ephesus.

Samothracia (sam-o-thrās'ē-a; "of the Samians and Thracians"). A small island in the Aegean Sea off the southern coast of Thrace (Acts 16:11).

Samson (sam'son; "distinguished; strong"). Judge of Israel for 20 years. His great strength and moral weakness have made him famous (Judg. 13:24; 14-16).

Samuel [Shemuel] (sam'ū-el [she-mū'el]; "asked of God; heard of God"). Prophet and last judge of Israel. He anointed Saul and later David as king (1 Sam. 1:20; 3-13; 15-16; 19; 25:1; Heb. 11:32).

Sanballat (san-bal'at; "strong"). A leading opponent of the Jews at the time they were rebuilding the walls of Jerusalem (Neh. 2:10; 4:1, 7; 6:1-14).

Sansannah (san-san'a; "branch"). A village in extreme southern Judah (Josh. 15:31). It is probably modern Khirbet esh-Shamsaniyat about 16.1 km. (10 mi.) north-northeast of Beer-sheba.

Saph (saf; "preserver"). A descendant of Rapha the giant (2 Sam. 21:18). He is called Sippai ("Jehovah is preserver") in First Chronicles 20:4.

Saphir (sā'fer; "delightful"). A town in Judah (Mic. 1:11). It was west of Hebron and may be Khirbet el-Kom.

Sapphira (sa'fī'ra; "beautiful; sapphire"). The dishonest wife of Ananias, who was struck dead by God (Acts 5:1-10).

Sara (sā'ra). Greek form of Sarah (q.v.).

Sarah [Sara; Sarai] (sā'ra [sā'ra; sā'rī]; "princess"). The wife of Abraham and mother of Isaac (Gen. 17–18; 20–21; Heb. 11:11; 1 Pet. 3:6). Her name was changed from Sarai ("Jehovah is prince") to Sarah ("princess") because she would be the progenitor of a great nation (Gen. 17:15). See Serah.

Sarai (sā'rī). See Sarah.

Saraph (sā'raf; "burning"). A descendant of Judah (1 Chron. 4:22).

Sardis (sar'dis; "prince of joy"). The capital city of Lydia where a church was located (Rev. 1:11; 3:1, 4). It was on the east bank of the Pactolus River about 80.5 km. (50 mi.) east of Smyrna.

Sargon (sar'gon; "the [the god] has established the king [ship]"). An important king of Assyria who finished the siege of Samaria and carried away Israel. He is called by name only once in Scripture (Isa. 20:1).

Sarid (sā'rid; "survivor"). A landmark in the territory of Zebulun (Josh. 19:10, 12). It is modern Tell Shadud in the northern portion of the Plain of Esdraelon [Jezreel] about 8 km. (5 mi.) southwest of Nazareth.

Saron (sā'ron). The Greek form of Sharon (q.v.).

Sarsechim (sar'se-kim; "chief of the eunuchs"). A prince of Babylon who sat at the gate (Jer 39:3).

Saruch (sā'ruk). Greek form of Serug (q.v.).

Saul [Shaul] (sol [shol]; "asked"). [1] The first king of Israel; God eventually gave him up. He tried several times to slay David, but was killed himself at Gilboa (1 Sam. 9–31). [2] The original name of Paul (q.v.). [3] See Shaul [1].

Sceva (sē'va; "fitted"). A Jewish priest at Ephesus whose sons attempted to cast out a demon, but were wounded by it instead (Acts 19:14-16).

Seba (sē'ba; "drunkard"). Eldest son of Cush (Gen. 10:7; 1 Chron. 1:9). Not to be confused with Sheba. Possibly the name refers to a people of southern Arabia.

Seba (sē'ba; meaning unknown). An African nation bordering the land of Cush (Psa. 72:10; Isa. 43:3). There is some confusion between Sheba and Seba, but they are probably two distinct locations.

Secacah (se-kā'ka; "thicket"). A city of Judah near the Dead Sea (Josh. 15:61). It was situated in the Valley of Achor.

Sechu (sē'kū; "defense"). A location with a well on the route from Gibeah to Ramah (1 Sam. 19:22).

Secundus (se-kun'dus; "second"). A Thessalonian Christian and friend of Paul (Acts 20:4).

Segub (sē'gub; "might; protection"). **[1]** Younger son of Hiel who rebuilt Jericho in the days of Ahab (1 Kings 16:34). **[2]** A grandson of Judah (1 Chron. 2:21-22).

Seir (sē'ir; "tempest"). **[1]** The valley and mountains of Aravah from the Dead Sea south to the Elanitic Gulf (Gen. 14:6; 32:3). Seir was the name of the mountain range in Edom and the name came to include the entire territory. **[2]** A ridge on Judah's border west of Kirjath-jearim (Josh. 15:10).

Seirath (se-ī'rath; "tempest"). A place in Mount Ephraim to which Ehud fled after he murdered Eglon (Judg. 3:26).

Sela [Selah] (sē'la; "a rock"). **[1]** The capital of Edom, located between the Dead Sea and the Gulf of Aqaba (2 Kings 14:7; Isa. 16:1). It is also called Petra. **[2]** A rock formation about 1,160 m. (3,800 ft.) above sea level, which dominates the city of Petra (cf. Judg. 1:36). It is now called Ummel-Bizarah.

Sela-hammahlekoth (sē'la-ha-ma'le-koth; "rock of divisions"). A cliff in the wilderness near Moan where David escaped from Saul (1 Sam. 23:28).

Seled (sē'led; "exultation"). A descendant of Judah (1 Chron. 2:30).

Seleucia (sē-lū'shi-a; "beaten by the waves"). A Syrian seaport from which Paul and Barnabas began their first missionary journey (Acts 13:4). It is located 8 km. (5 mi.) north of the mouth of the Orontes River.

Sem (sem). Greek form of Shem (q.v.).

Semachiah (sem-a-kī'a; "Jehovah supports"). A gatekeeper of the tabernacle in David's day (1 Chron. 26:7).

Semei (sem'e-i; Greek form of Shimei). An ancestor of Christ (Luke 3:26).

Senaah (se-nā'a). *See* Hassenaah.

Seneh (sē'ne; "enemy"). The more southerly of two rocks in the passage between Michmash and Geba (1 Sam. 14:4-5). It is 10.5 km. (6.5 mi.) northeast of Jerusalem.

Senir (sē'nir). *See* Shenir.

Sennacherib (se-nak'er-ib; Babylonian, *Sin-ahi-eriba*—"[the god] Sin has substituted for my brother"). An Assyrian king who killed his brother to usurp the throne. He unsuccessfully invaded Judah. The amazing story of the destruction of his army is told in Second Kings 19 (2 Kings 18:13; Isa. 36:1; 37:17, 21, 37).

Senuah (se-nū'a; "the violated"). A descendant of Benjamin (Neh. 11:9). Possibly the same as Hasenuah (q.v.).

Seorim (sē-ōr'im; "fear; distress"). A priest in the days of David (1 Chron. 24:8).

Sephar (se'far; "scribe"). An area in the southeastern portion of Arabia (Gen. 10:30).

Sepharad (se-fa'rad; "a book descending"). A place where the Jerusalem exiles lived (Obad. 20). It is probably Sardis in Asia Minor (q.v.).

Sepharvaim (se-far-va'yim; "the two scribes"). A city formerly identified with Sippar on the east bank of the Euphrates; it is now believed to be the Syrian city Shabara (Isa. 37:13).

Serah (se'ra; "extension"). A daughter of Asher (Gen. 46:17; 1 Chron. 7:30). Numbers 26:46 should read Serah, not Sarah.

Seraiah (se-ra'ya; "Jehovah is prince; Jehovah has prevailed"). [1] A scribe of David (2 Sam. 8:17). In Second Samuel 20:25, he is called Sheva and Shavsha in First Chronicles 18:16. He is also called Shisha in First Kings 4:3. [2] Chief priest of Jerusalem (2 Kings 25:18; 1 Chron. 6:14; Ezra 7:1). [3] One whom Gedaliah advised to submit to Chaldea (2 Kings 25:23; Jer. 40:8). [4] The brother of Othniel (1 Chron. 4:13-14). [5] A descendant of Simeon (1 Chron. 4:35). [6] A priest that returned to Jerusalem with Zerubbabel (Ezra 2:2). [7] A leader sent to capture Jeremiah (Jer. 36:26). [8] A prince of Judah who went to Babylon (Jer. 51:59, 61). [9] A son of Hilkiah dwelling in Jerusalem after the Exile (Neh. 11:11). [10] A chief of the priests who returned from Babylon (Neh. 12:1, 7).

Sered (se'red; "escape; deliverance"). Eldest son of Zebulun (Gen. 46:14; Num. 26:26).

Sergius Paulus (sur'ji-us po'lus). The Roman deputy of Cyprus who was converted because Elymas was struck blind (Acts 13:7).

Serug [Saruch] (se'rug [sa'ruk]; "strength; firmness"). Father of Nahor and ancestor of Christ (Gen. 11:20-21; Luke 3:35).

Seth [Sheth] (seth [sheth]; "compensation; sprout"). Son of Adam and Eve, and an ancestor of Christ (Gen. 4:25-26; 1 Chron. 1:1; Luke 3:38).

Sethur (se'thur; "secreted; hidden"). One sent to spy out the land (Num. 13:13).

Shaalabbin [Shaalbim] (sha-a-lab'in [sha-al'bim]). A city of the tribe of Dan (Josh. 19:42; Judg. 1:35). It may be modern Silbit 4.8 km. (3 mi.) northwest of Aijalon.

Shaaph (sha'af; "union; friendship"). [1] A descendant of Judah (1 Chron. 2:47). [2] A son of Caleb (1 Chron. 2:49).

Shaaraim [Sharaim] (sha-a-ra'im [sha-ra'im]; "gates"). [1] A town in lowland Judah west of Socoh (1 Sam. 17:52; Josh. 15:36). [2] A town of Simeon (1 Chron. 4:31). It is identified with Tell el-Far'ah about 24.9 km. (15.5 mi.) south-southeast of Gaza.

Shaashgaz (sha-ash'gaz; "lover of beauty; one anxious to learn"). A chamberlain of Ahasuerus (Esther 2:14).

Shabbethai ("shab'e-thi; "sabbath-born"). [1] An assistant to Ezra (Ezra 10:15). [2] One who explained the Law to the people (Neh. 8:7).

[3] A chief Levite in Jerusalem (Neh. 11:16). All three may be identical.

Shachia (sha-kī'a; "fame of Jehovah"). A descendant of Benjamin (1 Chron. 8:10).

Shadrach (shā'drak; "servant of [the god] Sin"). The name given to Hananiah at Babylon. He was cast into a fiery furnace and rescued (Dan. 1:7; 3).

Shage (sha'ge; "erring; wandering"). Father of one of David's mighty men (1 Chron. 11:34). Possibly another name of Shammah (q.v.).

Shaharaim (shā-ha-rā'im; "double dawn"). A descendant of Benjamin who went to Moab (1 Chron. 8:8).

Shahazimah (sha-ha-zē'ma; "heights"). A city of Issachar (Josh. 19:22). It is between Mount Tabor and the Jordan, and is probably modern Tell el-Mekarkash [Mukarkash].

Shalem (shā'lem; "peaceful; secure"). A town near Shechem (Gen. 33:18). Most scholars translate: "And Jacob came in peace [Shalem] to the city of Shechem."

Shalim (shā'lim; "foxes"). A district in Ephraim through which Saul passed when searching for his father's livestock (1 Sam. 9:4).

Shalisha (sha-lī'sha; "the third"). An area near Mount Ephraim through which Saul passed when searching for his father's livestock (1 Sam. 9:4). It was probably northeast of Lydda.

Shallum [Shallun] (shal'um [shal'un]; "recompenser"). **[1]** The youngest son of Naphtali (1 Chron. 7:13). He is also called Shillem (Gen. 46:24; Num. 26:49). **[2]** A descendant of Simeon (1 Chron. 4:25). **[3]** A descendant of Judah (1 Chron. 2:40-41). **[4]** One who usurped the throne of Israel and reigned for one month (2 Kings 15:10-15). **[5]** Husband of Huldah the prophetess (2 Kings 22:14; 2 Chron. 34:22). **[6]** See Jehoahaz [2]. **[7]** See Meshullam [7]. **[8]** A gatekeeper of the tabernacle (1 Chron. 9:17-19, 31; Ezra 2:42; Neh. 7:45). **[9]** Father of Jehizkiah (2 Chron. 28:12). **[10]**, **[11]** Two who married foreign wives during the Exile (Ezra 10:24, 42). **[12]** One who helped to repair the wall of Jerusalem (Neh. 3:12). **[13]** One who helped to repair the gate of Jerusalem (Neh. 3:15). **[14]** An uncle of Jeremiah (Jer. 32:7). **[15]** Father of one who was a temple officer in the days of Jehoiakim (Jer. 35:4).

Shalmai (shal'mī; "Jehovah is recompenser"). Ancestor of returned exiles (Ezra 2:46; Neh. 7:48).

Shalman (shal'man). The king who sacked Beth-arbel (Hos. 10:14). Perhaps he was either Shalmaneser V of Assyria or Shalman king of Moab.

Shalmaneser (shal-man-ē'zer; Babylonian, *Shulmaner-asharidu*— "[the god] Shulman is chief"). The king of Assyria to whom Hoshea became subject was Shalmaneser V (2 Kings 17:3). Either Shalmaneser or Sargon, his successor, was the king to whom Samaria fell after a long siege (2 Kings 17:6; 18:9).

Shama (shā'ma; "hearer"). One of David's heroes (1 Chron. 11:44).

Shamariah (sham-a-rī'a). *See* Shemariah.

Shamed (sha'med; "destroyer"). A son of Elpaal (1 Chron. 8:12).

Shamer (sha'mer; "preserver"). [1] A descendant of Merari (1 Chron. 6:46). [2] A descendant of Asher (1 Chron. 7:34). He is called Shomer in First Chronicles 7:32.

Shamgar (sham'gar; "cupbearer; fleer"). Judge of Israel who rescued his people from the Philistines (Judg. 3:31; 5:6).

Shamhuth (sham'huth; "fame; renown"). A captain of David's army (1 Chron. 27:8).

Shamir (shā'mir; "thorn hedge; approved"). A son of Micah, a Levite (1 Chron. 24:24).

Shamir (shā'mir; "thorn"). [1] A city in the mountainous district of Judah (Josh. 15:48). It is probably modern el-Bireh. [2] A town in Mount Ephraim (Judg. 10:1-2). Sanur between Samaria and Engannim have been suggested as sites.

Shamma (sham'a; "fame; renown"). A descendant of Asher (1 Chron. 7:37). *See* Shammah.

Shammah (sham'a; "fame; renown"). [1] A grandson of Esau (Gen. 36:13, 17; 1 Chron. 1:37). [2] A son of Jesse (1 Sam. 16:9; 17:13). He is also called Shimeah or Shimea (2 Sam. 13:3; 21:21; 1 Chron. 20:7), and Shimma (1 Chron. 2:13). [3] One of David's mighty men or the father of one of David's mighty men (2 Sam. 23:11). [4] Another of David's mighty men (2 Sam. 23:33), called Shammoth in First Chronicles 11:27. [5] Yet another of David's mighty men (2 Sam. 23:25).

Shammai (sham'a-ī; "celebrated"). [1] A descendant of Judah (1 Chron. 2:28, 32). [2] A descendant of Caleb, son of Hezron (1 Chron. 2:44-45). [3] A son or grandson of Ezra (1 Chron. 4:17).

Shammoth (sham'oth). *See* Shammah [4].

Shammua [Shammuah] (sha-mū'a; "famous"). [1] One sent to spy out the land of Canaan (Num. 13:4). [2] One of David's sons (2 Sam. 5:14; 1 Chron. 14:4). In First Chronicles 3:5, he is called Shimea. [3] A Levite who led the temple worship after the Exile (Neh. 11:17). He is also called Shemaiah (1 Chron. 9:16). [4] The head of a priestly family in Nehemiah's day (Neh. 12:18).

Shamsherai (sham'she-rī; "heroic"). A descendant of Benjamin (1 Chron. 8:26).

Shapham (shā'fam; "youthful; vigorous"). A chief of Gad (1 Chron. 5:12).

Shaphan (shā'fan; "prudent; sly"). [1] A scribe of Josiah who read him the Law (2 Kings 22:3; 2 Chron. 34:8-21). [2] Father of a chief officer under Josiah (2 Kings 22:12; 2 Chron. 34:20). [3] Father of Elasah (Jer. 29:3). [4] Father of Jaazaniah whom Ezekiel saw in a vision (Ezek. 8:11). Many scholars consider all of the above to be identical.

Shaphat (shā'fat; "judge"). [1] One sent to spy out the land of Canaan (Num. 13:5). [2] Father of Elisha the prophet (1 Kings 19:16,

19; 2 Kings 3:11; 6:31). [3] One of the family of David (1 Chron. 3:22). [4] A chief of Gad (1 Chron. 5:12). [5] One over David's herds in the valley (1 Chron. 27:29).

Shapher (shā'fer; "bright"). A mountain encampment during the Hebrews' wanderings in the wilderness (Num. 33:23). Jebel 'Araif en-Nakah, south of Kadesh, has been suggested as the site.

Sharai (shā'ra-i; "Jehovah is deliverer"). One who took a foreign wife (Ezra 10:40).

Sharaim (sha-rā'im). *See* Shaaraim [1].

Sharar (shā'rar). *See* Sacar [1].

Sharezer [Sherezer] (sha-rē'zer [she-rē'zer]; Babylonian, *Sharutsur*—"he has protected the king"). [1] A son of the Assyrian king Sennacherib who, with his brother, killed their father (2 Kings 19:37; Isa. 37:38). [2] One sent to consult the priests and prophets (Zech. 7:2).

Sharon [Saron] (shar-un [sar'un]; "his song"). [1] A region that lies between the Mediterranean Sea from Joppa to Carmel and the central portion of Palestine (1 Chron. 27:29; Acts 9:35). [2] A district east of the Jordan occupied by the tribe of Gad (1 Chron. 5:16).

Sharuhen (sha-roo'hen; "gracious house"). A city in Simeon near Beth-lebaoth (Josh. 19:6). It is perhaps identical with Shaaraim [2].

Shashai (shā'shī; "noble; free"). One who married a foreign wife during the Exile (Ezra 10:40).

Shashak (shā'shak; "assaulter; runner"). A descendant of Benjamin (1 Chron. 8:14, 25).

Shaul [Saul] (shā'ul [sol]; variant form of Saul). [1] The sixth king of Edom (Gen. 36:37-38; 1 Chron. 1:48-49). [2] A descendant of Levi (1 Chron. 6:24). [3] A son of Simeon found in several lists (Gen. 46:10; Exod. 6:15; 1 Chron. 4:24).

Shaveh (shā've; "the plain"). A place near Salem mentioned as the King's Valley (Gen. 14:17; 2 Sam. 18:18). It may be the same as the Kidron Valley.

Shaveh-kiriathaim (shā've-kir-ya-thā'im; "plains of Kiriathaim"). A plain near Kirjathaim [1], the dwelling place of the Emim (Gen. 14:5).

Shavsha (shav'sha). *See* Seraiah [1].

Sheal (shē'al; "request"). One who took a foreign wife (Ezra 10:29).

Shealtiel [Salathiel] (she-al'ti-el [sa-la'thi-el]; "lent by God"). Father of Zerubbabel and an ancestor of Christ (Ezra 3:2, 8; 5:2; Hag. 1:1, 12; Matt. 1:12).

Sheariah (she-a-rī'a; "Jehovah is decider"). A descendant of Saul (1 Chron. 8:38; 9:44).

Shearing House. The location where the royal family of King Ahaziah of Judah was slaughtered (2 Kings 10:12-14). The Hebrew name is *Beth 'eked;* the site is probably Beit Kad, about 25.7 km. (16 mi.) north-northeast of Samaria.

Shear-jashub (shē'ar-ja'shub; "a remnant returns"). Symbolic name given a son of Isaiah (Isa. 7:3).

Sheba (shē'ba; "oath; covenant"). [1] A chief of Gad (1 Chron. 5:13). [2] One who rebelled against David and was beheaded for it (2 Sam. 20). [3] A grandson of Abraham (Gen. 25:3; 1 Chron. 1:32). [4] A descendant of Shem (Gen. 10:28; 1 Chron. 1:22). Some scholars identify [5] with [4]. They believe Sheba is a tribe or people and stress that close genealogical ties account for the occurrence of the name in both Ham's and Shem's genealogy. [5] A descendant of Ham (Gen. 10:7; 1 Chron. 1:9).

Sheba (shē'ba; "oath"). [1] A country in southwest Arabia (1 Kings 10:1-13; 2 Chron. 9:1-12). Its capital was Ma'rib, which was about 60 miles east-northeast of San'a, the present capital of Yemen. [2] A town of Simeon mentioned after Beer-sheba (Josh. 19:2). Its location is uncertain.

Shebah (shē'ba; "seven"). The well at Beer-sheba where Isaac made a covenant with Abimelech (Gen. 26:33).

Shebam (shē'bam; "fragrance"). A city east of the Jordan given to the tribes of Reuben and Gad (Num. 32:3). It is located 8 km. (5 mi.) from Heshbon. It is identical with Sibmah (q.v.).

Shebaniah (sheb-a-nī'a; "Jehovah is powerful"). [1] A priest who aided in bringing the ark of the covenant to the temple (1 Chron. 15:24). [2] A Levite who guided the devotions of the people (Neh. 9:4-5; 10:10). [3], [4] Two priests who sealed the covenant (Neh. 10:4, 12, 14).

Shebarim (she'ba-rim; "hopes"). A place to which the Israelites ran on their flight from Ai (Josh. 7:5). The location of the site is unknown.

Sheber (shē'ber; "breach"). A descendant of Jephunneh (1 Chron. 2:48).

Shebna (sheb'na; "youthfulness"). The scribe or secretary of Hezekiah replaced by Eliakim (2 Kings 18:18; Isa. 22:15-25; 36:3-22).

Shebuel (she-bū'el; "God is renown"). [1] A son of Gershom (1 Chron. 23:16; 26:24). [2] A son of Haman, chief singer in the sanctuary (1 Chron. 24:4). He is called Shubael in verse 20.

Shechaniah [Shecaniah] (shek-a-nī'a; "Jehovah is a neighbor"). [1] Head of a family of the house of David (1 Chron. 3:21-22). [2], [3] Two whose descendants returned from the Babylonian Captivity (Ezra 8:3, 5). [4] One who took a foreign wife during the Exile (Ezra 10:2). [5] Father of one who repaired the wall of Jerusalem (Neh. 3:29). [6] Father-in-law to one who opposed Nehemiah (Neh. 6:18). [7] A priest who returned from the Exile (Neh. 12:3). [8] A priest in the time of David (1 Chron. 24:11). [9] A priest in Hezekiah's day (2 Chron. 31:15).

Shechem [Sychem] (shē'kem [sī'kem]; "shoulder"). [1] Son of Hamor who defiled Dinah; he and his family were soon destroyed for that act (Gen. 33:19; 34). [2] A descendant of Manasseh (Num. 26:31; Josh. 17:2). [3] Another descendant of Manasseh (1 Chron. 7:19).

Shechem [Sichem; Sychem] (shē'kem [sī'kem; sī'kem]; "portion"). An ancient city in central Palestine (Gen. 12:6; 33:18; Josh. 24:32;

Acts 7:16) in the hill country of Ephraim. It is present-day Nablus, located about 66 km. (41 mi.) north of Jerusalem between Mount Ebal and Mount Gerizim.

Shedeur (shed′e-er; "shedder of light"). One who helped number the people (Num. 1:5; 2:10; 7:30, 35).

Shehariah (she-ha-rī′ah; "Jehovah is the dawn"). A descendant of Benjamin (1 Chron. 8:26).

Shelah (shē′la; "peace"). **[1]** The youngest son of Judah (Gen. 38:5-26; 1 Chron. 2:3; 4:21). **[2]** *See* Sala.

Shelemiah (shel-e-mī′a; "Jehovah is recompense"). **[1]** *See* Meshelemiah. **[2]**, **[3]** Two who married foreign wives during the Exile (Ezra 10:39, 41). **[4]** Father of Hananiah (Neh. 3:30). **[5]** A priest over the treasury (Neh. 13:13). **[6]** An ancestor of one who was sent by the princes to get Baruch (Jer. 36:14). **[7]** One ordered to capture Baruch and Jeremiah (Jer. 36:26). **[8]** Father of one sent to Jeremiah to ask for prayers (Jer. 37:3; 38:1). **[9]** Father of the guard who apprehended Jeremiah (Jer. 37:13).

Sheleph (shē′lef; "drawn out"). A son of Joktan (Gen. 10:26; 1 Chron. 1:20). A Semitic people dwelling in Arabia is possibly intended.

Shelesh (shē′lesh; "might"). A descendant of Asher (1 Chron. 7:35).

Shelomi (she-lō′mi; "Jehovah is peace"). Father of a prince of Asher (Num. 34:27).

Shelomith (shel′o-mith; "peacefulness"). **[1]** Mother of one stoned for blasphemy in the wilderness (Lev. 24:11). **[2]** Daughter of Zerubbabel (1 Chron. 3:19). **[3]** A descendant of Gershon (1 Chron. 23:9). **[4]** A descendant of Levi and Kohath (1 Chron. 23:18). **[5]** One over the treasures in the days of David (1 Chron. 26:25-28). **[6]** Child of Rehoboam (2 Chron. 11:20). **[7]** An ancestor of a family that returned from the Exile (Ezra 8:10). Not to be confused with Shelomoth.

Shelomoth (shel′o-moth; "peacefulness"). A descendant of Izhar (1 Chron. 24:22). Many identify him with Shelomith **[4]**.

Shelumiel (she-lū′mi-el; "God is peace"). A chief of Simeon appointed to assist Moses (Num. 1:6; 2:12; 7:36).

Shem [Sem] (shem [sem]; "name; renown"). Son of Noah and ancestor of Christ (Gen. 5:32; 6:10; 10:1; Luke 3:36).

Shema (shē′ma; "fame; repute"). **[1]** A son of Hebron (1 Chron. 2:43-44). **[2]** A descendant of Reuben (1 Chron. 5:8). **[3]** A chief of the tribe of Benjamin (1 Chron. 8:13). **[4]** One who stood with Ezra when he read the Law (Neh. 8:4).

Shema (shē′ma; "report; rumor; fame"). A city of Judah in the Negeb (Josh. 15:26).

Shemaah (she-mā′a; "the fame"). Father of two valiant men who joined David (1 Chron. 12:3).

Shemaiah (she-mā′ya; "Jehovah is fame" or "Jehovah hears"). **[1]** A prophet who warned Rehoboam against war (1 Kings 12:22;

2 Chron. 11:2). **[2]** A descendant of David (1 Chron. 3:22). **[3]** Head of a family of Simeon (1 Chron. 4:37). **[4]** Son of Joel (1 Chron. 5:4). **[5]** A descendant of Merari (1 Chron. 9:14; Neh. 11:15). **[6]** One who helped to bring the ark of the covenant to the temple (1 Chron. 15:8, 11). **[7]** A Levite who recorded the allotment in David's day (1 Chron. 24:6). **[8]** A gatekeeper for the tabernacle (1 Chron. 26:4, 6-7). **[9]** A Levite whom Jehoshaphat sent to teach the people (2 Chron. 17:8). **[10]** One who helped to cleanse the temple (2 Chron. 29:14). **[11]** A Levite in Hezekiah's day (2 Chron. 31:15). **[12]** A chief Levite in Josiah's day (2 Chron. 35:9). **[13]** One who returned with Ezra (Ezra 8:13). **[14]** A person sent to Iddo to enlist ministers (Ezra 8:16). **[15]**, **[16]** Two who married foreign wives during the Exile (Ezra 10:21, 31). **[17]** One who helped to repair the wall of Jerusalem (Neh. 3:29). **[18]** One who tried to intimidate Nehemiah (Neh. 6:10). **[19]** One who sealed the new covenant with God after the Exile (Neh. 10:8). **[20]** One who helped to purify the wall of Jerusalem (Neh. 12:36). **[21]** One at the dedication of the wall of Jerusalem (Neh. 12:42). **[22]** Father of the prophet Urijah (Jer. 26:20). **[23]** One who wanted the priests to reprimand Jeremiah (Jer. 29:24, 31). **[24]** Father of a prince of the Jews (Jer. 36:12). **[25]** *See* Shammua **[3]**. **[26]** A prince of Judah who took part in the dedication of the wall (Neh. 12:34). **[27]** A Levite of the line of Asaph (Neh. 12:35). **[28]** A chief of the priests who returned with Zerubbabel (Neh. 12:6-7).

Shemariah [Shamariah] (shem-a-rī′a [sham-a-rī′a]; "whom Jehovah guards"). **[1]** One who joined David at Ziklag (1 Chron. 12:5). **[2]** A son of King Rehoboam (2 Chron. 11:19). **[3]**, **[4]** Two who married foreign wives during the Exile (Ezra 10:32, 41).

Shemeber (shem-ē′ber; "splendor of heroism"). The king of Zeboim in the days of Abraham (Gen. 14:2).

Shemer (shē′mer; "watch"). Owner of the hill which Omri bought and on which he built Samaria (1 Kings 16:24).

Shemida [Shemidah] (she-mī′da; "fame of knowing"). A grandson of Manasseh (Num. 26:32; Josh. 17:2; 1 Chron. 7:19).

Shemidah (she-mī′da). *See* Shemida.

Shemiramoth (she-mīr′a-moth; "fame of the highest"). **[1]** A Levite in the choral service (1 Chron. 15:18, 20; 16:5). **[2]** One sent by Jehoshaphat to teach the Law (2 Chron. 17:8).

Shemuel (she-mū′el; variant form of Samuel—"asked of God") **[1]** One appointed to divide the land of Canaan (Num. 34:20). **[2]** Head of a family of Issachar (1 Chron. 7:2). **[3]** *See* Samuel.

Shen (shen; "tooth"). A place near which Samuel erected a stone memorial to the victory over the Philistines (1 Sam. 7:12).

Shenazar (she-naz′ar; "ivory keeper; Sin [the god] protect"). Son or grandson of Jeconiah (1 Chron. 3:18).

Shenir [Senir] (shē′ner [sē′nir]; "light that sleeps"). The Amorite name for Hermon (Deut. 3:9; Ezek. 27:5).

Shepham (she'fam; "wild"). A location on the northeastern boundary of the Promised Land near Riblah (Num. 34:10).

Shephathiah [**Shephatiah**] (shef-a-thī'a [shef-a-tī'a]; "Jehovah is judge"). [1] A son of David by Abital (2 Sam. 3:4; 1 Chron. 3:3). [2] Father of Meshullam who dwelled in Jerusalem (1 Chron. 9:8). [3] A valiant man who joined David at Ziklag (1 Chron. 12:5). [4] A prince of Simeon (1 Chron. 27:16). [5] A son of Jehoshaphat (2 Chron. 21:2). [6] An ancestor of returned captives (Ezra 2:4; Neh. 7:9). [7] One of Solomon's servants whose descendants returned from the Babylonian Captivity (Ezra 2:57; Neh. 7:59). [8] An ancestor of returned captives (Ezra 8:8). He is possibly identical with [6]. [9] A descendant of Pharez whose descendants dwelled in Jerusalem (Neh. 11:4). [10] A prince of Judah in Zedekiah's time (Jer. 38:1).

Shephi [**Shepho**] (shē'fī [shē'fo]; "unconcern"). A descendant of Seir the Horite (1 Chron. 1:40). He is called Shepho in Genesis 36:23.

Shepho (shē'fo). *See* Shephi.

Shephuphan (she-fū'fan). *See* Muppim.

Sherah (shē'ra; "blood-relationship"). A woman descendant of Ephraim (1 Chron. 7:24). She was either his daughter or granddaughter; the text is unclear.

Sherebiah (sher-e-bī'a; "Jehovah is originator"). [1] A priest who returned from the Exile (Ezra 8:18, 24; Neh. 8:7; 9:4-5). [2] A Levite who sealed the new covenant with God after the Exile (Neh. 10:12; 12:8, 24).

Sheresh (shē'resh; "union"). A descendant of Manasseh (1 Chron. 7:16).

Sherezer (she-ē'zer). *See* Sharezer.

Sheshach (shē'shak; "humiliation"). Possibly a cipher form of Babel (Babylon) (Jer. 25:26). Other scholars view this as a part of Babylon or a Babylonian district.

Sheshai (shē'shī; "free; noble"). A son of Anak slain by Caleb (Num. 13:22; Josh. 15:14).

Sheshan (shē'shan; "free; noble"). A descendant of Judah through Jerahmeel (1 Chron. 2:31, 34-35).

Sheshbazzar (shesh-baz'er; "O Shamash [the god], protect the father"). The prince of Judah into whose hands Cyrus placed the temple vessels. Many believe he is the same as Zerubbabel, but others deny this. They claim Sheshbazzar was governor under Cyrus and Zerubbabel under Darius (Ezra 1:8, 11; 5:14-16).

Sheth (sheth; "compassion"). A chief of the Moabites (Num. 24:17). Not to be confused with Seth.

Sheth (sheth; "tumult"). A descriptive name given to Moabites (Num. 24:17). Possibly an ancient tribal name of the Moabites.

Shethar (shē'thar; "star; commander"). One of the seven princes of Persia and Media (Esther 1:14). Not to be confused with Shethar-boznai.

Shethar-boznai (shē'thar-boz'nī; "starry splendor"). An official of the king of Persia (Ezra 5:3, 6; 6:6, 13).

Sheva (shē'va; "self-satisfying"). **[1]** A son of Caleb (1 Chron. 2:49). **[2]** *See* Seraiah [1].

Shibmah (shib'ma). *See* Sibmah.

Shicron (shik'ron; "his wages"). A town on the northern boundary of Judah (Josh. 15:11).

Shihon (shī'hon; "wall of strength"). A town near Mount Tabor (Josh. 19:19). It is perhaps at Modern 'Ayun esh-Sha'in.

Shihor [Sihor] (shī'hor [sī'hor]; "blackness"). The east branch of the Nile River (1 Chron. 13:5; Jer. 2:18). Ideally, this was to be Israel's southern boundary.

Shihor-libnath (shī'hor-lib'nath; "black of whiteness"). A boundary stream of Asher (Josh. 19:26). It is probably the Nahr ez-Zirka 9.7 km. (6 mi.) south of Dor.

Shilhi (shil'hī; "a warrior; one with darts"). Grandfather of King Jehoshaphat (1 Kings 22:42; 2 Chron. 20:31).

Shilhim (shil'him; "armed"). A city in southern Judah near Lebaoth (Josh. 15:32). It is identified with Shaaraim [2].

Shillem (shil'em; "retribution"). *See* Shallum [1].

Shiloah [Siloah] (shi-lō'a [si'lōa]; "sent"). A waterway of Jerusalem (Isa. 8:6; Neh. 3:15). It carried water from the spring of Gihon to the Pool of Shelah to irrigate the Kidron Valley outside the city. It is identical with Siloam [1].

Shiloh (shī'lō; "peace"). A town in Ephraim (Josh. 18:1-10; Judg. 21:19). It is halfway between Shechem and Bethel.

Shiloni (shī-lō'nī; "weapon; armor"). Father of Zechariah (Neh. 11:5).

Shilshah (shil'sha; "might; heroism"). A son of Zophath (1 Chron. 7:37).

Shimea [Shimeah] (shim'e-a [shim'e-a]; "[God] has heard [a prayer]"). **[1]** A descendant of Merari (1 Chron. 6:30). **[2]** Father of Berachiah (1 Chron. 6:39). **[3]** *See* Shammah [2]. **[4]** *See* Shammua [2]. **[5]** One of the family of King Saul whose descendants dwelled in Jerusalem (1 Chron. 8:32; 9:38). In the latter passage he is called Shimeam.

Shimeam (shim'e-am; "fame; rumor"). *See* Shimeah [2].

Shimeath (shim'e-ath; "fame"). Mother of one who aided in killing King Jehoash (2 Kings 12:21; 2 Chron. 24:26).

Shimei [Shimhi; Shimi] (shim'e-ī [shim'hī; shim'ī]; "Jehovah is fame; Jehovah hear me"). **[1]** A son of Gershon and a grandson of Gershon (Exod. 6:17; Num. 3:18, 21; Zech. 12:13). **[2]** A descendant of Benjamin who cursed David when he was fleeing from Absalom (2 Sam. 16:5-13; 19:16-23). **[3]** A loyal officer of David (1 Kings 1:8). **[4]** An officer of Solomon (1 Kings 4:18). **[5]** Grandson of King Jeconiah (1 Chron. 3:19). **[6]** A man who had sixteen sons and six daughters

(1 Chron. 4:26-27). **[7]** A descendant of Reuben (1 Chron. 5:4. **[8]** A son of Libni (1 Chron. 6:29). **[9]** Father of a chief of Judah (1 Chron. 8:21). **[10]** A Levite (1 Chron. 23:9). **[11]** A Levite in the temple song service in the days of David (1 Chron. 25:17). **[12]** One in charge of many vineyards (1 Chron. 27:27). **[13]** One who helped to cleanse the temple (2 Chron. 29:14). **[14]** A Levite in charge of the temple offerings under Hezekiah (2 Chron. 31:12-13). **[15]**, **[16]**, **[17]** Three men who took foreign wives during the Exile (Ezra 10:23, 33, 38). **[18]** Grandfather of Mordecai (Esther 2:5).

Shimeon (shim′e-on; "hearing"). One who married a foreign wife (Ezra 10:31). Not to be confused with Simeon.

Shimhi (shim′hī). *See* Shimei.

Shimi (shim′ī). *See* Shimei.

Shimma (shim′a). *See* Shammah [2].

Shimon (shī′mon; "trier; valuer"). A descendant of Caleb (1 Chron. 4:20).

Shimrath (shim′rath; "watch"). A descendant of Benjamin (1 Chron. 8:21).

Shimri [Simri] (shim′rī [sim′rī]; "Jehovah is watching"). **[1]** Head of a family of Simeon (1 Chron. 4:37). **[2]** Father of one of David's mighty men (1 Chron. 11:45). **[3]** Gatekeeper of the tabernacle in David's day (1 Chron. 26:10). **[4]** One who helped to cleanse the temple (2 Chron. 29:13).

Shimrith (shim′rith; "watch"). A woman of Moab, mother of Jehozabad who killed Joash (2 Chron. 24:26). She is called Shomer in Second Kings 12:21.

Shimrom [Shimron] (shim′rom [shim′ron]; "watch"). The fourth son of Issachar (Gen. 46:13; Num. 26:24; 1 Chron. 7:1). *See also* Shimron.

Shimron (shim′ron; "watch-height"). An ancient city belonging to Zebulun (Josh. 11:1; 19:15). It is possibly Semuniyeh 10.1 km. (6.3 mi.) west of Nazareth.

Shimron-meron (shim′ron-mē′ron). A royal city of the Canaanites, whose king was slain by Joshua (Josh. 12:20). Probably the full name of Shimron (q.v.).

Shimshai (shim′shī; "Jehovah is splendor"). A scribe who, with Rehum, wrote to the king of Persia opposing the rebuilding of the wall of Jerusalem (Ezra 4:8-9, 17, 23).

Shinab (shī′nab). The king of Admah attacked by Chedorlaomer and his allies (Gen. 14:2).

Shinar (shī′nar; "watch of him that sleeps"). The plains later known as Babylonia or Chaldea, through which the Tigris and Euphrates Rivers flow (Gen. 10:10; Isa. 11:11).

Shiphi (shī′fī; "Jehovah is fulness"). Father of a chief of Simeon (1 Chron. 4:37).

Shiphrah (shif′ra; "beauty"). One of the Hebrew midwives at the time of the birth of Moses (Exod. 1:15).

Shiphtan (shif'tan; ' judge"). Father of Kemuel, a chief of Ephraim (Num. 34:24).

Shisha (shī'sha; "distinction; nobility"). Father of two of Solomon's scribes (1 Kings 4:3). Possibly the same as Seraiah [1].

Shishak (shī'shak). Another name for Shishak I, king of Egypt. He sheltered Jeroboam against Solomon and in later years invaded Judah (1 Kings 11:40; 14:25; 2 Chron. 12).

Shitrai (shit'rī; "Jehovah is deciding"). A man in charge of David's herds in Sharon (1 Chron. 27:29).

Shittim (shit'im; "thorns"). [1] The final Israelite encampment before crossing the Jordan. Here Moses bade farewell and the Law was completed (Num. 25:1; Josh. 2:1). It was in Moab, east of Jordan, opposite Jericho. [2] A dry and unfruitful valley (Joel 3:18). The name may not denote any particular valley, but it may refer to the Kidron Wadi which starts northwest of Jerusalem, moves toward the east and runs toward the Dead Sea. It may also be a portion of the Arabah around the Dead Sea.

Shiza (shī'za; "splendor"). Father of one of David's valiant men (1 Chron. 11:42).

Shoa (shō'a; "kings". A location mentioned along with Babylon, Chaldea, and Assyria (Ezek. 23:23); it probably refers to a settlement of the Sutu nomads of the Syrian Desert.

Shobab (shō'bab; "returning"). [1] A son of David (2 Sam. 5:14; 1 Chron. 3:5). [2] A son of Caleb (1 Chron. 2:18).

Shobach (shō'bak; "expansion"). Captain of the army of Hadarezer of Zobah (2 Sam. 10:16, 18); he is also called Shophach (1 Chron. 19:16).

Shobai (shō'bī; "Jehovah is glorious"). A tabernacle gatekeeper whose descendants returned from the Babylonian Captivity (Ezra 2:42; Neh. 7:45).

Shobal (shō'bal; "wandering"). [1] A son of Seir (Gen. 36:20, 23; 1 Chron. 1:38, 40). [2] A son of Caleb, son of Hur (1 Chron. 2:50, 52). [3] A son of Judah (1 Chron. 4:1-2).

Shobek (shō'bek; "free"). One who sealed the covenant with Nehemiah (Neh. 10:24).

Shobi (shō'bī; "Jehovah is glorious"). A man who helped David when he fled from Absalom (2 Sam. 17:27).

Shocho [Shochoh; Shoco; Socoh; Socho; Sochoh] (shō'ko [shō'ko; shō'ko; sō'ko; sō'ko; sō'ko]; "defense"). [1] A town in lowland Judah or the hilly border of the Valley of Elah (Josh. 15:35; 2 Chron. 11:7; 28:18; 1 Sam. 17:1). [2] A town in Judah's hill country (Josh. 15:48). It is modern Khirbet Shuweikeh 16.1 km. (10 mi.) south-southwest of Hebron. [3] A place in one of Solomon's administrative districts (1 Kings 4:10). It is modern Tell-er-Ras about 16.1 km. (10 mi.) northwest of Samaria.

Shochoh. (sho'ko). See Shocho.

Shoco (sho'ko). See Shocho.

Shoham (shō'ham; "leek-green beryl"). A descendant of Merari (1 Chron. 24:27).

Shomer (shō'mer; "keeper"). [1] *See* Shamer [2]. [2] *See* Shimrith.

Shophach (shō'fak). *See* Shobach.

Shophan (shō'fan; "burrow"). A fortress city east of the Jordan River that was captured and rebuilt by the tribe of Gad (Num. 32:35).

Shua [Shuah] (shoo'a [shoo'a]; "prosperity"). [1] A daughter of Heber (1 Chron. 7:32). [2] A Canaanite whose daughter Judah married (Gen. 38:2, 12; 1 Chron. 2:3).

Shuah (shoo'a; "depression"). [1] A son of Abraham by Keturah (Gen. 25:2; 1 Chron. 1:32). [2] A brother of Chelub; descendant of Caleb (1 Chron. 4:11).

Shual (shoo'al; "jackal"). The third son of Zophah (1 Chron. 7:36).

Shual (shoo'al; "fox"). A district north of Michmash (1 Sam. 13:17).

Shubael (shoo'ba-el; "God's captive"). [1] A son or descendant of Amram, a descendant of Levi (1 Chron. 24:20). [2] *See* Shebuel [2].

Shuham (shoo'ham; "depression"). *See* Hushim [1].

Shunem (shoo'nem; "their sleep"). A town near Jezreel that was allotted to the tribe of Issachar (Josh. 19:18; 1 Sam. 28:4). It was opposite Mount Gilboa. The site is present-day Solem or Sulam.

Shuni (shoo'nī; "fortunate"). A son of Gad (Gen. 46:16; Num. 26:15).

Shupham (shoo'fam). *See* Muppim.

Shuppim (shup'im; "serpent") [1] A gatekeeper in the days of David (1 Chron. 26:16). [2] *See* Muppim.

Shur (shoor; "wall"). A desert in the northwest part of the Sinai Peninsula (Gen. 16:7; 25:18). It was outside the eastern border of Egypt and was probably a caravan route between Egypt and Beersheba.

Shushan [Susa] (shoo'shan [soo'sa]; "a lily"). The capital of Elam inhabited by the Babylonians; later a royal residence and capital of the Persian Empire (Neh. 1:1; Dan. 8:2). The city was also known as Susa. The site is modern Shush on the Ulai River.

Shuthelah (shoo'the-la; "setting of Telah"). [1] A son of Ephraim (Num. 26:35-36; 1 Chron. 7:20). [2] Another descendant of Ephraim (1 Chron. 7:21).

Siaha [Sia] (sī'a-ha [sī'a]; "congregation"). Ancestor of returned captives (Ezra 2:44; Neh. 7:47).

Sibbechai (sib'e-kī; "Jehovah is intervening"). A mighty man who killed a Philistine giant (2 Sam. 21:18; 1 Chron. 11:29; 20:4). He is called Mebunnai in Second Samuel 23:27.

Sibmah [Shibmah] (sib'ma [shib'ma]; "to be cold"). A town of Reuben and Gad (Num. 32:38; Josh. 13:19). It is identical with Shebam (q.v.).

Sibraim (sib-rā'im; "twofold hope"). A northern boundary marker of Canaan (Ezek. 47:16). It is probably Sepharvaim.

Sichem (sī'kem). *See* Shechem.

Siddim (sid'im; "the tilled field"). A valley near the Dead Sea (Gen. 14:3, 8, 10), full of bitumen pits.

Sidon [Zidon] (sī'don [zī'don]; "fortress"). Eldest son of Canaan, son of Ham (Gen. 10:15). He is called Zidon in First Chronicles 1:13. Possibly a reference to the inhabitants of the ancient city of Sidon.

Sidon [Zidon] (sī'don [zī'don]; "hunting"). An ancient city of Canaan (Gen. 10:15, 19; Josh. 11:8; Luke 4:26).

Sihon (sī'hon; "great; bold"). An Amorite king that was defeated by Israel (Num. 21:21-31; Deut. 1:4; 2:24-32; Josh. 13:15-28).

Sihor (sī'hor). *See* Shihor.

Silas [Silvanus] (sī'las [sil-vā'nus]; "forest; woody; third; asked"). An eminent member of the early church who traveled with Paul through Asia Minor and Greece and was imprisoned with him at Philippi (Acts 15:22, 32-34; 2 Cor. 1:19; 1 Thess. 1:1).

Silla (sil'a; "exalting"). A place near Millo where King Joash was murdered (2 Kings 12:20).

Siloah (sī-lō'a). *See* Shiloah.

Siloam (sī-lō'am); "sent"). [1] A famous pool of Jerusalem at the south end of Hezekiah's tunnel (John 9:7). It is identical with Shiloah (q.v.). [2] A tower on the Ophel ridge near Siloam (Luke 13:4).

Silvanus (sil-vā'nus]. *See* Silas.

Simeon [Simon] (sim'e-un [sī'mon]; "hearing"). [1] The second son of Jacob by Leah (Gen. 29:33; 34:25; 48:5; 49:5). His descendants became one of the twelve tribes of Israel. [2] A devout Jew who blessed the Christ child in the temple (Luke 2:25-34). [3] An ancestor of Jesus (Luke 3:30). [4] A disciple and prophet at Antioch (Acts 13:1); he was surnamed Niger ("black"). [5] Original name of Peter (q.v.). Simon is but another form of Simeon. Not to be confused with Shimeon.

Simon (sī'mon; "hearing"). [1] Original name of the apostle Peter (Matt. 4:18; 16:16-17; Luke 4:38; Acts 10:18). [2] Another of the twelve apostles, called Simon the Canaanite, indicating his fierce loyalty either to Israel or to his faith (Matt. 10:4; Mark 3:18; Luke 6:15; Acts 1:13). [3] One of Christ's brothers (Matt. 13:55; Mark 6:3). [4] A leper of Bethany in whose house Christ was anointed (Matt. 26:6; Mark 14:3). [5] A Cyrenian who was forced to bear the cross of Christ (Matt. 27:32; Mark 15:21). [6] A Pharisee in whose house the feet of Christ were anointed (Luke 7:40, 43-44). [7] The father of Judas Iscariot (John 6:71; 12:4; 13:2). [8] A sorcerer who tried to buy the gifts of the Holy Spirit (Acts 8:9, 13, 18, 24). [9] A tanner of Joppa with whom Peter lodged (Acts 9:43; 10:6, 17, 32).

Simri (sim'rī). *See* Shimri.

Sin (sin; "bush"). [1] A city on the eastern side of the Nile (Ezek. 30:15-16). It is possibly Pelusium; but is also identified with Syene, which is present-day Aswan at the first cataract of the Nile. [2] A wilderness area located between the Gulf of Suez and Sinai (Exod. 16:1; Num. 33:11-12).

Sinai [Sina] (sī'nī [sī'na]; "a bush"). [1] An area in the center of the peninsula that lies between the horns of the Red Sea, the Gulf of Suez, and the Gulf of Aqaba (Exod. 16:1; Acts 7:30-38). [2] A mountain, also called Horeb, where the Israelites received the Ten Commandments (Exod. 19:18). The location of the site is uncertain, although it is generally agreed to be in central Sinai. The traditional site is Jebel Musa, but other possibilities are Mount Serbal and Ras es-Safsafeh.

Sinim (si'nim; "south country"). A land from which the scattered Israelites were again to be gathered (Isa. 49:12). It probably refers to Syene on the southern Egyptian frontier where there was a Jewish garrison. Earlier scholars believed that China was indicated, but that view has been abandoned.

Sion (sī'un; "breastplate"). [1] Another name for Mount Hermon (Deut. 4:48). [2] *See* Zion.

Siphmoth (sif'moth; "fruitful"). A place in southern Judah frequented by David (1 Sam. 30:28).

Sippai (sīp'ī). *See* Saph.

Sirah (sī'ra; "turning"). A well near Hebron where Abner was recalled by Joab (2 Sam. 3:26). It is probably modern 'Ain Sarah.

Sirion (sir'i-on; "breastplate"). The name given to Mount Hermon by the Sidonians (Deut. 3:9; Psa. 29:6).

Sisamai (sis'a-mī; "Jehovah is distinguished"). A descendant of Jerahmeel, son of Pharez (1 Chron. 2:40).

Sisera (sis'er-a; "mediation; array"). [1] Captain of the army of Jabin who was murdered by Jael (Judg. 4:1-22; 5:26, 28). [2] One whose descendants returned (Ezra 2:53; Neh. 7:55).

Sitnah (sit'na; "hatred"). The second well dug by Isaac, located in the Valley of Gerar (Gen. 26:21).

Smyrna (smur'na; "myrrh"). A city on the western coast of Asia Minor (Rev. 2:8-11). It is 64.4 km. (40 mi.) north of Ephesus.

So (sō; "vizier"). A king of Egypt, either Osorkon IV or Tefnakht. Others believe this name is a reference to a city (2 Kings 17:3-7).

Socho (sō'ko; "brambly"). A son of Heber (1 Chron. 4:18).

Socho (sō'ko). *See* Shocho.

Sochoh (sō'ko). *See* Shocho.

Socoh (sō'ko). *See* Shocho.

Sodi (sō'dī; "Jehovah determines"). Father of one of the spies sent into Canaan (Num. 13:10).

Sodom [Sodoma] (so'dom [sod'o-ma]; "their secret"). One of the five Cities of the Plain (Gen. 10:19; Rom. 9:29), destroyed because of its wickedness. The exact location of the site is unknown, but it is in the Dead Sea area.

Solomon (sol'o-mon; "peace"). Son of David by Bathsheba and king of a united, strong Israel for forty years. His wisdom and carnal sin stand out in his multi-faceted character (1 Kings 1:11; 2:11). He was an ancestor of Christ (Matt. 1:6-7).

Solomon's Pools. A repository of water built by Solomon near Bethlehem (Eccles. 2:6).

Solomon's Porch. A colonnade built by Solomon on the east side of the temple (John 10:23; Acts 3:11).

Sopater (sō'pa-ter; "one who defends the father"). A man of Berea who accompanied Paul to Asia (Acts 20:4). Perhaps the same as Sosipater (q.v.).

Sophereth (so-fē'reth; "learning"). Servant of Solomon whose ancestors returned from exile (Ezra 2:55; Neh. 7:57).

Sosipater (so-sip'a-ter; "one who defends the father"). One who sent greetings to the Roman Christians (Rom. 16:21). He was Jewish (a "kinsman" of Paul) and is possibly the same as Sopater (q.v.).

Sorek (sō'rek; "vine"). A valley in Gaza where Delilah lived (Judg. 16:4). It is modern Wadi es-Saran, which begins 20.9 km. (13 mi.) southwest of Jerusalem and twists northwest toward the Mediterranean.

Sosthenes (sos'the-nēz; "strong; powerful"). [1] Chief ruler of the synagogue at Corinth, beaten by the Greeks (Acts 18:17). [2] A believer who united with Paul in addressing the Corinthian church (1 Cor. 1:1). Some believe he was [1] after conversion.

Sotai (sō'tī). Head of a family of servants (Ezra 2:55; Neh. 7:57).

South Ramoth. See Ramath.

Spain (spān; "rain"). A peninsula in southwestern Europe (Rom. 15:24). The nation was known as Hispania to the Romans.

Stachys (stā'kis; "ear of corn"). A believer of Rome to whom Paul sent greetings (Rom. 16:9).

Stephanas (stef'a-nas; "crown"). One of the first believers of Achaia (1 Cor. 1:16; 16:15-17).

Stephen (stē'fen; "crown"). One of the seven deacons. He became the first martyr of the church after Christ (Acts 6:5-9; 7:59; 8:2).

Suah (sū'a; "riches; distinction"). A son of Zophah, a descendant of Asher (1 Chron. 7:36).

Succoth (suk'oth; "tents"). [1] A town where Jacob built himself a house (Gen. 33:17; Josh. 13:27). It was east of the Jordan between Peniel and Shechem. Its probable location is Deir 'Alla, about 1.6 km. (1 mi.) west of where the Jabbok bulges and turns south. [2] The first camping ground of the Israelites after leaving Egypt (Exod. 12:37; 13:20).

Sukkiim (suk'i-im; "booth-dweller"). A nation that assisted Shishak of Egypt when he invaded Judah (2 Chron. 12:3). Its population was probably of Libyan origin.

Sur (sur; "rebellion"). A gate in Jerusalem, possibly leading from the king's palace to the temple (2 Kings 11:6). The parallel passage calls it the Gate of the Foundation (2 Chron. 23:5).

Susa (soo'sa). *See* Shushan.

Susanna (su-zan'na; "lily"). One of the women who ministered to Christ and was His follower (Luke 8:3).

Susi (sū'sī; "Jehovah is swift or rejoicing"). Father of one of the spies (Num. 13:11).

Sychar (sī'kar; "end"). A town of Samaria near Jacob's well (John 4:5).

Sychem (sī-kem). *See* Shechem.

Syene (sī'ē'ne; "a bush"). A town on the southern frontier of Egypt (Ezek. 29:10; 30:6).

Syntyche (sin'ti-che; "fortunate"). A woman of the church at Philippi (Phil. 4:2).

Syracuse (sir'a-kus; "that draws violently"). A city on the east coast of Sicily (Acts 28:12).

Syria (sir'i-a; a form of the word *Assyria*). The country lying north and east of Palestine (Judg. 10:6; 1 Kings 10:29; Acts 15:23). It stretched far inland from the Mediterranean and was bounded by the Taurus Mountains to the north.

Syrtis Quicksands (sur'tis; "shallows"). Two shoals off the coast of Africa between Carthage and Cyrene (Acts 27:17). The greater Syrtis is now called the Gulf of Sidra, the lesser Syrtis the Gulf of Gabes.

T

Taanach [Tanach] (tā'a-nak [tā'nak]; "who humbles thee"). An ancient city in Canaan whose king was conquered by Joshua (Josh. 12:21; 21:25; Judg. 1:27). Its ruins, Tell Ta'annak, are on the southern edge of the Valley of Jezreel about 8 km. (5 mi.) southeast of Megiddo.

Taanath-shiloh (tā'a-nath-shī'lo; "breaking down a fig tree"). A border town between Manasseh and Ephraim (Josh. 16:6). It is now Khirbet Ta'na 11.3 km. (7 mi.) east-southeast of Shechem.

Tabbaoth (tab'a-oth; "spots; rings"). One whose descendants returned with Zerubbabel (Ezra 2:43; Neh. 7:46).

Tabbath (tab'ath; "celebrated"). A place where the Midianites stayed after Gideon's attack (Judg. 7:22). It is located in the Jordan Valley at Ras Abu Tabat.

Tabeal [Tabeel] (tā-bē-al [tā'be-el]; "God is good"). [1] Father of a man the kings of Israel and Damascus planned to make king of Judah (Isa. 7:6). [2] A Persian official who tried to hinder the rebuilding of the wall of Jerusalem (Ezra 4:7).

Tabeel (tā'be-el). *See* Tabeal.

Taberah (tab'e-ra; "burning"). A place three days north of Mount Sinai where Israel was punished for murmuring against God (Num. 11:3; Deut. 9:22).

Tabitha (tab'i-tha; "gazelle"). The Christian woman of Joppa whom Peter raised from the dead (Acts 9:36-42). Dorcas is the Greek form of the name.

Tabor (tā'ber; "purity"). [1] A mountain located in the northern part of the Valley of Jezreel (Judg. 4:6, 12, 14; Psa. 89:12). It is now called Jebel el-Tur and is 8.8 km. (5.5 mi.) southeast of Nazareth. [2] A town of Zebulun given to the Levites (1 Chron. 6:77). Its location is uncertain. It may be the Chisloth-tabor of Joshua 19:12 or Khirbet Dabural, which is on a hill between Tabor and Nazareth. [3] An oak (not a plain as in KJV) in Benjamin (1 Sam. 10:3).

Tabrimon (tab'rim-on; "[the god] Rimmon is good"). Father of Ben-hadad I, king of Syria (1 Kings 15:18).

Tadmor (tad'mor; "bitterness"). A city known to the Greeks and Romans as Palmyra; it facilitated trade with the East (1 Kings 9:18; 2 Chron. 8:4). Its ruin is Tadmar in an oasis east-northeast of Damascus about midway between the city and the Euphrates. Some believe the reading in First Kings should be *Tamar;* the Masoretic Hebrew scholars read *Tadmor* in the margin but *Tamar* in the text. If we read Tamar then the reference is to a city probably in southern Judah.

Tahan (tā'han; "graciousness"). [1] A descendant of Ephraim (Num. 26:35). [2] Another descendant of Ephraim (1 Chron. 7:25).

Tahath (tā'hath; "depression; humility"). [1] A descendant of Kohath (1 Chron. 6:24, 37). [2] A descendant of Ephraim (1 Chron. 7:20). [3] A grandson of the above (1 Chron. 7:20).

Tahath (tā'hath; "fear"). A desert encampment of the Israelites (Num. 33:26-27).

Tahapanes [Tahpanhes; Tehaphnehes] (ta-hap'a-nēz; [ta'pan-hēz; tē-haf'ne-hēz]; "secret temptation"). An Egyptian city on the Pelusiac channel of the Nile (Jer. 2:16; 43:7-9; 44:1; Ezek. 30:18). It is identified with modern Tell Defneh.

Tahpenes (ta'pan-hēz). An Egyptian queen, wife of the Pharaoh, who received the fleeing Hadad, an enemy of Solomon (1 Kings 11:18-20).

Tahrea [Tarea] (ta're-a [tā're-a]; "flight"). Son of Micah, descendant of Saul (1 Chron. 8:35; 9:41).

Tahtim-hodshi (ta'tim-hod'shī; "lowlands of Hodshi"). A location between Gilead and Dan-jaan visited by Joab during the census of Israel (2 Sam. 24:6). The location of the site is unknown.

Talmai (tal-mi; "bold; spirited"). [1] A man or clan defeated by Caleb (Num. 13:22; Josh. 15:14; Judg. 1:10). [2] King of Geshur and father-in-law of David (2 Sam. 3:3; 13:27).

Talmon (tal'mon; "oppressor; violent"). A Levite in Ezra's day; a temple porter (1 Chron. 9:17; Ezra 2:42; Neh. 7:45).

Tamah [Thamah] (tā'ma [thā'ma]; "combat"). One whose descendants returned from the Babylonian Captivity (Ezra 2:53; Neh. 7:55).

Tamar [Thamar] (tā'mer [thā'mar]; "palm"). **[1]** The wife of Er, mother of Perez, and an ancestor of Christ (Gen. 38:6, 11, 13; Ruth 4:12; Matt. 1:3). **[2]** The daughter of David violated by Amnon (2 Sam. 13:1-32). **[3]** A daughter of Absalom (2 Sam. 14:27).

Tamar (tā'mer; "palm tree"). A place somewhere to the southwest of the Dead Sea; some identify the site with the village of Thamara, near Kurnub and Ain el-Arūs. Others deny this (Ezek. 47:18-19; 48:28).

Tanach (tā'nak). *See* Taanach.

Tanhumeth (tan-hū'meth; "comfort"). Father of one of Gedaliah's captains (2 Kings 25:23; Jer. 40:8).

Taphath (tā'fath; "ornament"). A daughter of Solomon (1 Kings 4:11).

Tappuah (tap-pū'a; "apple; hill place"). A descendant of Judah (1 Chron. 2:43).

Tappuah (tap-pū'a; "swelling"). **[1]** A city in the lowlands of Judah (Josh. 15:34). It is probably modern Beit Nettif 6.4 km. (4 mi.) north of Hebron. **[2]** A border town of Ephraim west of Shechem (Josh. 16:8; 17:7-8). It is probably Sheikh Abu Zarad, about 12.9 km. (8 mi.) south of Shechem.

Tarah (tā'ra; "wretch"). The twelfth Israelite encampment in the wilderness (Num. 33:27). It was between Tahath and Mithcah.

Taralah (tar'a-la; "strength"). A city allotted to the tribe of Benjamin (Josh. 18:27). It was near Irpeel.

Tarea [Tharshish] (tā're-a [thar'shish]). *See* Tahrea.

Tarshish (tar'shish; "hard"). **[1]** A son of Javan and grandson of Noah (Gen. 10:4; 1 Chron. 1:7). Possibly a people who inhabited a region in Spain (Tartessus), near Gibraltar. **[2]** One of the seven princes of Persia (Esther 1:14). **[3]** A descendant of Benjamin (1 Chron. 7:10).

Tarshish [Tharshish] (tar'shish [thar'shish]; "contemplation"). A city in southern Spain with which the Phoenicians traded (Jer. 10:9; Ezek. 27:12; 1 Kings 10:22). It is believed to be modern Tartessus near Gibraltar.

Tarsus (tar'sus; "winged"). The most prominent city of Cilicia located on the river Cydnus in Asia Minor; it was the birthplace of Paul (Acts 9:11).

Tartan (tar'tan; meaning unknown). The title of a high Assyrian officer. There is evidence that the office was second only to the king. There are two tartans mentioned in Scripture (2 Kings 18:17; Isa. 20:1).

Tatnai (tat-nī; "gift"). A Persian governor of Samaria in the days of Zerubbabel (Ezra 5:3; 6:6, 13).

Tebah (tē'ba; "thick; strong"). A son of Nahor, the brother of Abraham (Gen. 22:24).

Tebaliah (teb-a-lī'a; "Jehovah is protector; Jehovah has purified").

A Levite gatekeeper in the days of David (1 Chron. 26:11).

Tehaphnehes (te-ha⁻'ne-hez). See Tahapanes.

Tehinnah (te-hin'na; "entreaty; supplication"). A descendant of Judah (1 Chron. 4:12).

Tekoa [Tekoah] (te-<ō'a; "that is confirmed"). A town of Judah on the hills near Hebron (2 Sam. 14:2; Jer. 6:1). It is modern Taku 'ais, a ruined village 9.7 km (6 mi.) south of Bethlehem.

Tel-abib (tel-ā'bib; "heap of new grain"). A town of Babylonia near the river Chebar where Jewish exiles were placed (Ezek. 3:15).

Telah (tē'la; "vigor"). A descendant of Ephraim (1 Chron. 7:25).

Telaim (tē-lā'im; "lambs"). The place where Saul gathered and numbered his forces before the attack on Amalek (1 Sam. 15:4). It was probably in extreme southern Judah.

Telassar [Thelasar] (te-las'er [the-lā'ser]; "taking away"). A city near Harran and Orfa in western Mesopotamia (2 Kings 19:12; Isa. 37:12).

Telem (tē'lem; "a lamb"). One who married a foreign wife during the Exile (Ezra 10:24).

Telem (tē'lem; "their shadow"). A town in extreme southern Judah (Josh. 15:24).

Tel-harsa [Tel-haresha] (tel-har'sa [tel-har'e-sha]; "suspension of the plow"). A Babylonian village used as a grouping point for Jews returning to Palestine (Ezra 2:59; Neh. 7:61).

Tel-melah (tel-mē'la. "hill of salt"). A Babylonian town mentioned in Ezra 2:59; Nehemiah 7:61. It possibly was situated on the low salt tract near the Persian Gulf.

Tema (tē'ma; "south" or "sun burnt"). A son of Ishmael (Gen. 25:15; 1 Chron. 1:30).

Tema (tē'ma; "south; south country; sun burnt"). A son of Ishmael (Gen. 25:15). The place his descendants dwelt was also called Tema (Job 6:19). It was located in Arabia midway between Damascus and Mecca.

Teman (tē'man; "south" or "sun burnt"). [1] A grandson of Esau (Gen. 36:11, 15; 1 Chron. 1:36). [2] A duke of Edom (Gen. 36:42; Chron. 1:53).

Temeni (tem'e-nī; "fortunate"). A son of Ashur (1 Chron. 4:5-6).

Temple. The structure in which the Israelites worshiped and offered sacrifices to God. There were three temples: Solomon's, Zerubbabel's, and Herod's.

Terah [Thara] (tē'ra [thā'ra]; "turning; duration"). The father of Abraham and ancestor of Christ (Gen. 11:27-32; Luke 3:34).

Teresh (tē'resh; "strictness; reverence"). A chamberlain of the Persian court that plotted against the crown (Esther 2:21; 6:2).

Tertius (tur'shi-us; "third"). The scribe to whom the Epistle to the Romans was dictated (Rom. 16:22). Some conjecture that he is Silas (q.v.).

Tertullus (ter-tul'us; "third"). An orator hired by the Jews to state skillfully their case against Paul before Felix (Acts 24:1-8).

Thaddeus (tha-dē'us; a name derived from an Aramaic word for the female breast). One of the twelve apostles (Matt. 10:3; Mark 3:18). He is the same as Judas, the brother of James (Luke 6:16; John 14:22; Acts 1:13). He was also named Lebbeus ("heart").

Thahash (thā'hash; "reddish"). A son of Nahor, Abraham's brother (Gen. 22:24).

Thamah (thā'ma). See Tamah.

Thamar (thā'mar). Greek form of Tamar (q.v.).

Thara (thā'ra). Greek form of Terah (q.v.).

Tharshish (thar'shish). See Tarshish.

Thebez (thē'bez; "muddy"). A place in the district of Neapolis (Judg. 9:50). It was 20.9 km. (13 mi.) southwest of Scythopolis [Beth-shean].

Thelasar (the-lā'ser). See Telassar.

Theophilus (the-of'i-lus; "loved by God"). An unknown person, possibly a Roman official, to whom Luke addressed his Gospel and Acts (Luke 1:3; Acts 1:1).

Thessalonica (thes-a-lo-nī'ka; "victory at sea"). A city situated on the Macedonian coast at the head of the Thermaic Gulf (Acts 17:1, 11, 13; 27:2). It is known as Salonika today.

Theudas (thū'das; "the gift of God"). Instigator of a rebellion against the Romans, which was crushed by them (Acts 5:36).

Thimnathah (thim'na-tha; "a portion"). A city in the allotment of Dan (Josh. 19:43). It was located between Elon and Ekron. Many identify it with Timnath [2]. See also Timnah.

Thomas (tom'as; "twin"). One of the twelve apostles of Jesus. When Christ rose from the dead, he was most skeptical (Matt. 10:3; Mark 3:18; John 20:24-29). His Aramaic name is Didymus in Greek.

Three Taverns. A station on the Appian Way near the modern city of Cisterna (Acts 28:15).

Thyatira (thī-a-tī'ra; "sacrifice of labor"). A city between Pergamos and Sardis (Acts 16:14; Rev. 2:18-29). It was in Lydia in Asia Minor.

Tiberias (ti-bē'ri-as; "good vision"). A city on the west coast of the Sea of Galilee (Josh. 6:1; 21:1).

Tiberius (ti-bē'ri-us; "son of [the river] Tiber"). Third emperor of the Roman Empire (Luke 3:1).

Tibhath (tib'hath; "extension"). A city of Amam-Zobah (1 Chron. 18:8). It is identical with Betah (q.v.).

Tibni (tib'nī; "intelligent"). One who rivaled Omri for the throne of Israel (1 Kings 16:21-22).

Tidal (tī'dal; "splendor; renown"). King of Goyim who, with his allies, invaded the Cities of the Plain (Gen. 14:1, 9).

Tiglath-pileser (tig'lath-pi-lē'zer; Babylonian, *Tukulti-apil-Esharra*—"my trust is in the son of Asharra"). A king of Assyria who invaded Naphtali during the time of Pekah of Israel. He conquered northern Palestine and deported many from Naphtali (2 Kings 15:29; 16:7, 10; 1 Chron. 5:6, 26). His native name was Pul (2 Kings 15:19). Realizing he bore two names, we should translate First Chronicles 5:26, ". . . God . . . stirred . . . Pul king of Assyria *even* [not *and*] Tilgath-pilneser king of Assyria."

Tikvah [Tikvath] (tik'va [tik'vath]; "hope"). **[1]** The father-in-law of Huldah the prophetess (2 Kings 22:14; 2 Chron. 34:22). **[2]** The father of Jahaziah (Ezra 10:15).

Tilon (tī'lon; "mockery; scorn"). A descendant of Judah (1 Chron. 4:20).

Timaeus (ti-mē'us; "honorable"). Father of the blind Bartimaeus (Mark 10:46).

Timna [Timnah] (tim'na; "allotted portion; restraining"). **[1]** A concubine of a son of Esau (Gen. 36:12). **[2]** A daughter of Seir the Horite (Gen. 36:22; 1 Chron. 1:39). **[3]** A chief of Edom (Gen. 36:40; 1 Chron. 1:51). **[4]** A son of Eliphaz (1 Chron. 1:36).

Timnah (tim'na; "allotted portion"). **[1]** A town on the northern border of Judah (Josh. 15:10). It was allotted to Dan and is called Thimnathah in Joshua 19:43. It was also known as Timnath (Gen. 38:12-14). Its site is Khirbet Tibnah, 15 mi. from Jerusalem. **[2]** A town in the hill country of Judah (Josh. 15:57). Possibly identical with [1]. *See also* Timna.

Timnath (tim'nath; "image"). **[1]** A border town in Judah (Gen. 38:12-14). It is probably identical with Timnah. **[2]** A city in the territory of Dan near Philistia (Judg. 14:1-2, 5).

Timnath-heres (tim'nath-hē'rez; "extra portion"). A village in Ephraim (Judg. 2:9). It is identical with Timnath-serah.

Timnath-serah (tim'nath-sē'ra; "image of the sun"). The home and burial place of Joshua (Josh. 19:50; 24:30). It is probably modern Tibnah, 19.3 km. (12 mi.) northeast of Lydda. It is identical with Timnath-heres.

Timon (tī'mon; "honorable"). One of the seven deacons (Acts 6:1-6).

Timotheus [Timothy] (ti-mō'the-us [tim'o-thi]; "honored of God"). A young friend and convert of Paul; he traveled extensively with the apostle. He was from Lystra and was the son of Eunice, a Jewess, and a Greek father (Acts 16:1; 17:14-15; 1 Tim. 1:2, 18; 6:20).

Timothy (tim'o-thi). *See* Timotheus.

Tiphsah (tif'sa; "passage"). **[1]** A crossing located on the Euphrates River (1 Kings 4:24). It is probably modern Thapsacus. **[2]** A place mentioned in connection with Tirzah (2 Kings 15:16). It may be the ruined village of Tafsah 10.5 km. (6.5 mi.) southwest of Shechem. Others identify it with Tappuah (q.v.).

Tiras (tī'ras; "longing"). Youngest son of Japheth (Gen. 10:2; 1 Chron. 1:5). Possibly the inhabitants of Thrace. Other scholars consider reference to be to the Tyrsenoi, a people who inhabited the islands and coastlands of the Aegean.

Tirhakah (tir'ha-ka). A king of Ethiopia and Egypt who aided Hezekiah in his fight against Sennacherib (2 Kings 19:9; Isa. 37:9).

Tirhanah (tir'ha-na; "kindness"). A descendant of Hezron (1 Chron. 2:48).

Tiria (tir'i-a; "foundation"). A descendant of Judah (1 Chron. 4:16).

Tirshatha (tur-shā'tha; "reverend—i.e., his excellency"). A title of the governor of Judea under Persian rule (Ezra 2:63; Neh. 7:65, 70; 8:9; 10:1).

Tirzah (tur'za; "delight"). Youngest daughter of Zelophehad (Num. 26:33; 27:1; Josh. 17:3).

Tirzah (tur'za; "benevolent"). A Canaanite city located north of Jerusalem (Josh. 12:24; 1 Kings 14:17). It was 48.3 km. (30 mi.) from Jerusalem.

Titus (tī'tus; "pleasant"). A converted Grecian entrusted with a mission to Crete (2 Cor. 2:13; Gal. 2:1; Titus 1:4).

Toah (tō'a; "depression; humility"). An ancestor of Samuel the prophet (1 Chron. 6:34). He is called Nahath in verse 26 and Tohu in First Samuel 1:1.

Tob (tob; "good"). An area east of the Jordan between Gilead and the eastern deserts (Judg. 11:3, 5).

Tob-adonijah (tob-ad-o-nī'ja; "the Lord Jehovah is good"). One sent by Jehoshaphat to teach the Law (1 Chron. 17:8).

Tobiah [Tobijah] (to-bī'a [to-bī'ja]; "Jehovah is good"). [1] A Levite sent by Jehoshaphat to teach the Law (2 Chron. 17:8). [2] An ancestor of returning captives who had lost their genealogy (Ezra 2:60; Neh. 7:62). [3] An Ammonite servant of Sanballat who opposed Nehemiah (Neh. 2:10-20). [4] A leader who returned from the Babylonian Captivity (Zech. 6:10, 14).

Tobijah (to-bī'ja). *See* Tobiah.

Tochen (tō'ken; "middle"). A town of Simeon (1 Chron. 4:32), near Rimmon. It is identical with Ether [2].

Togarmah (to-gar'ma). A son of Gomer (Gen. 10:3; 1 Chron. 1:6). Possibly a people of the far north who inhabited the mountains northwest of Mesopotamia, between the Anti-Taurus and the Euphrates, or possibly the area on the upper Euphrates between Samosata and Melita.

Togarmah (to-gar'ma; "all bone"). A country that supplied horses and mules to the Tyrians and soldiers to the army of Gog (Ezek. 27:14; 38:6). Many identify this land with Armenia.

Tohu (tō'hu). *See* Toah.

Toi [Tou] (tō'e [tō'oo]; "error; wandering"). A king of Hamath who sent his son to congratulate David on his victory over Hadadezer (2 Sam. 8:9-10; 1 Chron. 18:9-10).

Tola (tō'la; "warm; crimson"). [1] A son of Issachar (Gen. 46:13; 1 Chron. 7:1-2). [2] A judge of Israel (Judg. 10:1).

Tolad (tō'lad). *See* Eltolad.

Tophel (tō'fel; "ruin"). An area north of Bozra, toward the southeast corner of the Dead Sea (Deut. 1:1). It is perhaps Tafileh.

Tophet [Topheth] (tō'fet [tō'feth]; "a drum"). Once a part of a king's garden in Hinnom; it became a place where people in Jerusalem sacrificed their children (Isa. 30:33; Jer. 19:6, 11-14; 2 Kings 23:10).

Tou (tō'oo). *See* Toi.

Trachonitis (trak-o-nī'tis; "strong"). A Roman province south of Damascus and north of Jordan (Luke 3:1). It is now called al-Seja.

Treasure Cities [Treasure House; Store Cities]. Designated cities at which the kings of the ancient world kept their treasures and tithes (Exod. 1:11; Ezra 5:17).

Troas (trō'az; "penetrated"). An important city on the coast of Mysia (Acts 16:8; 2 Tim. 4:13). It was in northern Asia Minor and is also called Alexandria.

Trogyllium (tro-jil'i-um; "fruit port"). A rocky projection of the ridge of Mycale and a town (Acts 20:5). They were both located on the western coast of Asia Minor opposite the island of Samos.

Trophimus (trof'i-mus; "a foster child"). A Christian convert and afterward a companion-in-travel with Paul (Acts 20:4; 21:29; 2 Tim. 4:20).

Tryphena (trī-fē'na; "dainty; shining"). A Christian woman of Rome to whom Paul sent greetings (Rom. 16:12).

Tryphosa (trī'fō'sa: "delicate; shining"). A Christian woman at Rome sent greetings by Paul (Rom. 16:12).

Tubal (tū'bal). A son of Japheth (Gen. 10:2; 1 Chron. 1:5). Possibly a reference to a people in eastern Asia Minor; they are called Tabal in Assyrian inscriptions.

Tubal-cain (tū'bal-kān). One of the sons of Lamech and an expert metal-smith (Gen. 4:22).

Tychicus (tik'i-kus; "fortunate"). A disciple and messenger of Paul (Acts 20:4; Eph. 6:21; 2 Tim. 4:12).

Tyrannus (tī-ran'us; "tyrant"). A Greek rhetorician or Jewish rabbi in whose school Paul taught at Ephesus (Acts 19:9).

Tyre [Tyrus] (tīr [tīr'us]; "rock"). A city on the central coast of Phoenicia noted for its commercial activity (Josh. 19:29; 2 Sam. 5:11; Jer. 25:22). It is located halfway between Accho and Sidon.

Tyrus (tīr'us). *See* Tyre.

U

Ucal (ū'kal; "I can"; or a verb meaning "to be consumed"). *See* Ithiel.

Uel (ū'el; "will of God"). A son of Bani who had taken a foreign wife (Ezra 10:34).

Ur. This is all that remains of the city in which Abraham lived before migrating into Palestine. The mound in the rear was the ziggurat, or temple tower. The ruins of the city lie in the foreground.

Ulai (ū'lī; "pure water"). A river surrounding Shushan in Persia (Dan. 8:2, 16). It is now called Kerah or Kerkhah.

Ulam (ū'lam; "solitary" or "preceding"). [1] A descendant of Manasseh, the son of Peresh (1 Chron. 7:16-17). [2] A descendant of Benjamin whose sons were "mighty men of valor" (1 Chron. 8:39-40).

Ulla (ul'a; "elevation; burden"). A descendant of Asher (1 Chron. 7:39).

Ummah (ūm'a; "darkened"). A city of Asher on the Mediterranean coast (Josh. 19:30). It was near Aphek or Rehob; now it is called Alma.

Unni (ū'nī; "answering is with Jehovah"). [1] One of the Levites chosen as singers (1 Chron. 15:10, 18, 20). [2] A Levite that returned to the land with Zerubbabel (Neh. 12:9).

Uphaz (ū'faz; "pure gold"). A city generally regarded as being identical with Ophir (Jer. 10:9; Dan. 10:5).

Ur (ur; "flame; light"). Father of one of David's mighty men (1 Chron. 11:35).

Ur (ur; "light"). The city which Abram left to go to Haran (Gen. 11:28, 31). Ur is generally identified as ancient Ur (Uri), modern Tell el-Muqayyar located on the Euphrates in south Iraq.

Urbane [Urbanus] (ur'bān [ur-ba'nus]; "pleasant; witty"). A faithful Roman Christian whom Paul greeted (Rom. 16:9).

Uri (ū'rī; "enlightened; my light"). A contracted form of Uriah. [1] The son of Hur, and father of Bezaleel (Exod. 31:1-2; 1 Chron. 2:20). [2] The father of Geber (1 Kings 4:19). [3] A porter of Levi who had married a foreign wife (Ezra 10:24).

Uriah [Urias; Urijah] (u-rī'a [u-rī'as; u-rī'ja]; "Jehovah is my light"). **[1]** A Hittite soldier in David's army. He was killed in a fierce battle, for David, desiring to marry his wife, Bath-sheba, had placed him on the front battle line (2 Sam. 11). **[2]** A priest under Ahaz who built a pagan altar on the king's command; then placed it in the temple (2 Kings 16:10-16). **[3]** A prophet whose message of judgment so offended Jehoiakim that he murdered him (Jer. 26:20-23). **[4]** A priest, the father of Meremoth (Ezra 8:33; Neh. 3:4, 21). **[5]** A man who stood by Ezra when he read the Law (Neh. 8:4). Possibly the same as **[4]**. **[6]** A priest whom Isaiah took as a witness (Isa. 8:2).

Urias (u-rī'as). Greek form of Uriah (q.v.).

Uriel (ū'ri-el; "God is my light"). **[1]** A chief of the sons of Kohath (1 Chron. 6:24; 15:5, 11). Possibly the same as Zephaniah **[2]**. **[2]** Father of Michaiah, one of Rehoboam's sons (2 Chron. 13:2).

Urijah (u-rī'ja). See Uriah.

Uthai (ū'thī; "my iniquity; Jehovah is help"). **[1]** A son of Bigvai who returned to the land of Israel with Ezra (Ezra 8:14). **[2]** A descendant of Judah (1 Chron. 9:4).

Uz [Huz] (uz [huz]; "counsel; firmness"). **[1]** Eldest son of Aram (Gen. 10:23). Possibly the name refers to an Aramean tribe or people. **[2]** A son of Shem (1 Chron. 1:17). The Septuagint makes this Uz identical with **[1]** naming Aram as his father. It is also possible the Hebrew text was abbreviated here. **[3]** A son of Dishan, son of Seir (Gen. 36:28). **[4]** The son of Nahor by Milcah (Gen. 22:21).

Uz (uz; "counsel; firmness"). **[1]** The country where Job lived (Job 1:1). The two most likely locations are Hauran, south of Damascus, and the area between Edom and north Arabia. **[2]** A kingdom not far from Edom (Jer. 25:20; Lam. 4:21). Perhaps identical with **[1]**.

Uzai (ū'zī; "hoped for"). The father of Palal (Neh. 3:25).

Uzal (ū'zal; "wandering"). A son of Joktan (Gen. 10:27; 1 Chron. 1:21). Possibly the name refers to an Arabian tribe.

Uzza [Uzzah] (ūz'a [uz'a]; "strength"). **[1]** A man who was struck dead by God when he touched the ark of the covenant (2 Sam. 6:2-7; 1 Chron. 13:6-10). **[2]** A descendant of Merari (1 Chron. 6:29). **[3]** A descendant of Ehud (1 Chron. 8:7). **[4]** An ancestor of a Nethinim family that returned from Babylon (Ezra 2:49; Neh. 7:51).

Uzza, Garden of (ūz'a; "strength"). The place where Manasseh, king of Judah, and Amon, his son, were buried (2 Kings 21:18, 26).

Uzzah (ūz'a). See Uzza.

Uzzen-sherah (uz'en-shē'ra; "ear of the flesh"). A town established by Sherah, a daughter of Ephraim (1 Chron. 7:24). It was near the two Beth-horons and is now called Beit Sira.

Uzzi (uz'ī; "Jehovah is strong" or "my strength"). **[1]** A descendant of Issachar (1 Chron. 7:1-3). **[2]** Chief of a priestly family of Jedaiah (Neh. 12:19, 42). **[3]** Descendant of Benjamin (1 Chron. 7:7). **[4]** The overseer of the Levites at Jerusalem (Neh. 11:22). **[5]** The father of Elah, a descendant of Benjamin (1 Chron. 9:8). **[6]** A son of Bukki;

even though in the line of high priests, he does not seem to have held this office (1 Chron. 6:5-6, 51; Ezra 7:4).

Uzzia (u-zī'a; "Yahweh is strong"). One of David's valiant men (1 Chron. 11:44).

Uzziah [Ozias] (u-zī'a [o-zī'as]; "Jehovah is strong" or "my strength is Jehovah"). **[1]** The eleventh king of Judah. When he attempted to offer incense unlawfully, God struck him with leprosy. He was also called Azariah (2 Kings 15:1-8; 2 Chron. 26). He was an ancestor of Christ (Matt. 1:8-9). **[2]** A Levite descended from Kohath and ancestor of Samuel (1 Chron. 6:24). **[3]** Father of Jehonathan (1 Chron. 27:25). **[4]** A priest who had married a foreign wife (Ezra 10:21). **[5]** A descendant of Judah (Neh. 11:4).

Uzziel (u-zī'el; "God is my strength" or "God is strong"). **[1]** The ancestor of the Uzzielites; the son of Kohath (Exod. 6:18). **[2]** Captain of the sons of Simeon (1 Chron. 4:42). **[3]** A son of Bela and grandson to Benjamin (1 Chron. 7:7). **[4]** An assistant wall-builder (Neh. 3:8). **[5]** A Levite, son of Jeduthun, who helped to cleanse the temple (2 Chron. 29:14). **[6]** A musician set by David over the service of song in the temple (1 Chron. 25:4). Uzziel is the same as Azareel in verse 18.

V

Vajezatha (va-jez'a-tha; "born of Ized" or "given-of-the-Best-One"). One of the sons of Haman slain by the Jews (Esther 9:9).

Valley Gate. A gate in the southwest wall of Jerusalem leading to the Hinnom Valley (Neh. 2:13).

Vaniah (va-nī'a; "praise, or nourishment, of Jehovah"). A son of Bani who had sinned by marrying a foreign wife (Ezra 10:36).

Vashni (vash'nī; "the second"). According to First Chronicles 6:28, the firstborn son of Samuel, but First Samuel 8:2 states Joel was his firstborn. Because of this, some scholars follow the Septuagint and Syriac versions, where verse 28 reads thus: "And the sons of Samuel: the first-born, Joel, and *the second* Abiah."

Vashti (vash'tī; "beautiful woman; best"). The queen of Persia who was divorced by King Ahasuerus because she refused to come to his great feast (Esther 1:10-22).

Vineyards, Plain of the. A place east of the Jordan River, site of the battle in which Jephthah defeated the forces led by Ammon (Judg. 11:33). Many translations take this as a proper name and render it *Abel-cheramin.*

Vophsi (vof'sī; "fragrant; rich"). A descendant of Naphtali, the father of Nahbi the spy (Num. 13:14).

W

Water Gate. A gate on the east side of Jerusalem, above the spring of Gihon (Neh. 8:1, 3).

Wilderness. The area in which the Israelites wandered for 40 years before entering Canaan (Deut. 1:1; Josh. 5:6). Several places are encompassed in the designation Wilderness; these are listed under their individual names (e.g., Paran, Zin, etc.).

Willows, Brook of the. A small stream that marks the boundary between Moab and Ecom (Isa. 15:7). It is possibly the lower course of Wadi el-Hesa where i: meets the upper course of Seil el-Kerahi.

Z

Zaanaim (za-a-nā'im). *See* Zaanannim.

Zaanan (zā'a-nan; "pointed"). A town in Judah (Mic. 1:11). It is probably identical with Zenan (q.v.). The site is probably modern Arak el-Kharba.

Zaanannim [Zaanaim] (zā-a-nan'im [zā-a-nā-im]). A place on the southern border of Naphtali (Josh. 19:33; Judg. 4:11).

Zaavan [Zavan] (zā'van [zā'van]; "causing fear"). A descendant of Seir (Gen. 36:27). Also called Zavan (1 Chron. 1:42).

Zabad (zā'bad; "endower"). [1] A descendant of Jerahmeel of Judah (1 Chron. 2:36-37). [2] A man of Ephraim and son of Tahath (1 Chron. 7:21). [3] Son of Ahlai and one of David's mighty men (1 Chron. 11:41). [4], [5], [6] Three who married foreign wives during the Exile (Ezra 10:27, 33, 43). [7] *See* Jozachar.

Zabbai (zab'a-ī; "roving about; pure"). [1] One who took a foreign wife during the Exile (Ezra 10:28). [2] Father of Baruch (Neh. 3:20).

Zabbud (zab'ud; "endowed"). One who returned from the Exile with Ezra (Ezra 8:14).

Zabdi (zab'dī; "Jehovah is endower"). [1] Father of Carmi (Josh. 7:1, 17-18); called Zimri in First Chronicles 2:6. [2] A descendant of Benjamin (1 Chron. 8:19). [3] One of David's storekeepers (1 Chron. 27:27). [4] An ancestor of Mattaniah (Neh. 11:17); also called Zichri (1 Chron. 9:15) and Zaccur (1 Chron. 25:2, 10; Neh. 12:35).

Zabdiel (zab'di-el; "my gift is God"). [1] Father of Jashobeam, David's captain (1 Chron. 27:2). [2] An overseer of the priests (Neh. 11:14).

Zabud (zā'bud; "bestowed"). Officer and friend of Solomon (1 Kings 4:5).

Zabulon (zab'u-lon). Greek form of Zebulun (q.v.).

Zaccai (zak'a-ī; "pure"). One whose descendants returned (Ezra 2:9; Neh. 7:14). Possibly the same as Zabbai [2].

Zaccheus (za-kē'us; "pure"). A publican with whom Jesus lodged during His stay at Jericho (Luke 19:1-10).

Zaccur [Zacchur] (zak'ur; "well remembered"). [1] A descendant of Simeon (1 Chron. 4:26). [2] Father of Shammua, one of the spies (Num. 13:4). [3] Descendant of Merari (1 Chron. 24:27). [4] *See* Zabdi [4]. [5] A Levite who sealed the covenant (Neh. 10:12). [6] Father of Hanan (Neh. 13:13); possibly the same as [5]. [7] One who rebuilt part of the wall of Jerusalem (Neh. 3:2).

Zachariah [Zechariah] (zak-a-rī'a [zek-a-rī'a]; "memory of the Lord"). [1] Son and successor of Jeroboam II. He reigned only six months (2 Kings 14:29; 15:8-11). [2] Father of Abi or Abijah, mother of Hezekiah (2 Kings 18:2); written *Zechariah* in Second Chronicles 29:1.

Zacharias (zak-a-rī'as; Greek form of Zechariah—"memory of the Lord"). [1] The prophet whom the Jews stoned (Matt. 23:35; Luke 11:51). Some believe this prophet to be identical with Zechariah [11] or [16], though it is possible the reference is to an unknown prophet. [2] A priest, father of John the Baptist (Luke 1).

Zacher (zā'ker; "fame"). Son of Jeiel (1 Chron. 8:31); called Zechariah in First Chronicles 9:37.

Zadok (zā'dok; "righteous"). [1] A high priest in the time of David (2 Sam. 8:17; 15:24-36; 1 Kings 1:8-45). [2] Father of Jerusha, wife of Uzziah and mother of Jotham, both kings of Israel (2 Kings 15:33; 2 Chron. 27:1). [3] Son of Ahitub and father of Shallum or Meshullam (1 Chron. 6:12-13; Ezra 7:2). [4] A young man of valor (1 Chron. 12:28). [5], [6] Two who repaired the wall of Jerusalem (Neh. 3:4, 29). [7] One who sealed the covenant with Nehemiah (Neh. 10:21). [8] A scribe under Nehemiah (Neh. 13:13).

Zaham (zā'ham; "fatness"). A son of Rehoboam (2 Chron. 11:19).

Zair (zā-ir; "small"). The place in or near Edom where Joram defeated the Edomites (2 Kings 8:21). It is possibly Sa'ir, about 8 km. (5 mi.) north-northeast of Hebron. Some identify the city with Zior (q.v.).

Zalaph (zā'laf; "purification"). The father of one who repaired the wall of Jerusalem (Neh. 3:30).

Zalmon (zal'mon; "terrace; accent"). The Ahohite who was one of David's guards (2 Sam. 23:28). He is called Ilai ("exalted") in First Chronicles 11:29. Not to be confused with Salmon.

Zalmon [Salmon] (zal'mon [sal'mon]; "shady"). A wooded area in Shechem (Judg. 9:48-49; Psa. 68:14).

Zalmonah (zal-mo'nah; "shade"). An Israelite encampment in the desert (Num. 33:41-42). It was probably east of Jebel Harien.

Zalmunna (zal-mun'a; "withdrawn from protection"). A Midianite king slain by Gideon (Judg. 8:5-21).

Zanoah (za-nō′a; "broken district"). One of the family of Caleb (1 Chron. 4:18).

Zanoah (za-nō′a; "marsh"). [1] A town in lowland Judah (Josh. 15:34; Neh. 3:13). It is Khirbet Zanu' or Zanuh about 4.8 km. (3 mi.) south-southeast of Beth-shemesh. [2] A town in Judah's hill country about 2.1 km. (1.3 mi.) northwest of Yatta (Josh. 15:56; 1 Chron. 4:18).

Zaphnath-paaneah (zaf′e-nath-pa-nē′a; "savior of the world; revealer of secrets"). Name given to Joseph by Pharaoh (Gen. 41:45).

Zaphon (zā′fon; "north"). A place allotted to the tribe of Gad in the Jordan Valley east of the river (Josh. 13:27).

Zara (zā′ra). Greek form of Zara or Zerah (q.v.).

Zarah (zā′ra). See Zerah.

Zareah (zā′re-a; "wasp; hornet"). See also Zorah.

Zared [Zered] (zā′red [zē′red]; "brook"). A brook and valley that marks the greatest limit of the Hebrews' wandering in the wilderness (Num. 21:12; Deut. 2:13-14). It was south of the Arnon, probably Wadi el-Hesa.

Zarephath (zar′e-fath; "smelting place"). A town located near Zidon (Sidon) that was the residence of Elijah (2 Kings 17:9). It is probably modern Sarafand, 12.9 km. (8 mi.) south of Zidon.

Zaretan [Zartanah; Zarthan] (zar′e-tan [zar′ta-na; zar′than]; "cooling"). A village near Beth-shean in the territory of Manasseh (Josh. 3:16; 1 Kings 4:12). It is probably Tell es-Sa'idiyeh. The city is probably identical with Zereda (q.v.).

Zareth-shahar (zā′reth-shā′har; "beauty of the dawn"). A town allotted to the tribe of Reuben (Josh. 13:19). It is probably at Zarat on the eastern shore of the Dead Sea.

Zartanah (zar′ta-na) See Zaretan.

Zarthan(zar′than). See Zaretan.

Zattu [Zatthu] (zat′ū [zat-thu]; "lovely; pleasant"). [1] One whose descendants returned from the Exile (Ezra 2:8; 10:27; Neh. 7:13). [2] A cosealer of the new covenant (Neh. 10:14).

Zavan (zā′van). See Zaavan.

Zaza (zā′za; "projection"). A son of Jonathan (1 Chron. 2:33).

Zealotes (zē-lō′tēz). See Simon [2].

Zebadiah (zeb-a-dī′a. "Jehovah is endower"). [1] A descendant of Benjamin (1 Chron. 8:15). [2] A son of Elpaal (1 Chron. 8:17). [3] One who joined David (1 Chron. 12:7). [4] A descendant of Levi through Kohath (1 Chron. 26:2). [5] A son of Asahel (1 Chron. 27:7). [6] A Levite sent by Jehoshaphat to teach the Law (2 Chron. 17:8). [7] A son of Ishmael (2 Chron. 19:11). [8] Head of a family who returned from exile (Ezra 8:8). [9] A priest who had taken a foreign wife (Ezra 10:20).

Zebah (zē′ba; "victim"). Midianite king slain by Gideon (Judg. 8:5-21).

Zebaim (ze-bā'im; "gazelles"). The home of one whose descendants returned from the Babylonian Captivity (Ezra 2:57; Neh. 7:59). It is perhaps identical with Zeboim (q.v.).

Zebedee (zeb'e-dē; "the gift of Jehovah"). A fisherman of Galilee, husband of Salome, and father of the apostles James and John (Matt. 4:21; 27:56; Mark 1:19-20).

Zebina (ze-bī'na; "bought"). One who married a foreign wife during the Exile (Ezra 10:43).

Zeboim [Zeboiim] (ze-bo'im [ze-boi'im]; "gazelles"). [1] One of the five Cities of the Plain (Gen. 10:19; 14:2, 9). [2] A valley between Michmash and the wilderness to the east (1 Sam. 13:16-18). [3] A Benjamite town (Neh. 11:34). It is probably north of Lydda, perhaps at Khirbet Sabeyah.

Zebudah (ze-bū'da; "endowed"). Wife of Josiah, king of Judah (2 Kings 23:36).

Zebul (zē'bul; "dwelling"). Ruler of Shechem (Judg. 9:28-41).

Zebulun [Zabulon] (zeb'u-lun [zab'u-lon]; "dwelling"). Tenth son of Jacob and ancestor of one of the twelve tribes (Gen. 30:20; 49:13; 1 Chron. 2:1).

Zebulun (zeb'u-lun; "dwelling"). The territory given to the tribe of Zebulun (Josh. 19:27, 34). It was north of Issachar, east of Asher, and southwest of Naphtali.

Zechariah (zek-a-rī'a; "Jehovah my righteousness"). [1] A chief of the tribe of Reuben (1 Chron. 5:7). [2] A Levite gatekeeper in the days of David (1 Chron. 9:21; 26:2, 14). [3] A Levite set over the service of song in the days of David (1 Chron. 15:18, 20; 16:5). [4] A priest in the days of David (1 Chron. 15:24). [5] A descendant of Levi through Kohath (1 Chron. 24:25). [6] A descendant of Levi through Merari (1 Chron. 26:11). [7] Father of Iddo (1 Chron. 27:21). [8] A prince of Jehoshaphat sent to teach the people (2 Chron. 17:7). [9] A Levite who encouraged Jehoshaphat against Moab (2 Chron. 20:14). [10] A son of Jehoshaphat (2 Chron. 21:2). [11] A son of Jehoiada who was stoned (2 Chron. 24:20). *See* Zacharias [1]. [12] Prophet in the days of Uzziah (2 Chron. 26:5). [13] A Levite who helped to cleanse the temple (2 Chron. 29:13). [14] A descendant of Levi (2 Chron. 34:12). [15] A prince of Judah in the days of Josiah (2 Chron. 35:8). [16] A prophet in the days of Ezra. His book still exists (Ezra 5:1; 6:14; Zech. 1:1, 7; 7:1, 8). [17] A chief man of Israel (Ezra 8:3). [18] One who returned from the Exile (Ezra 8:11). The chief man in Ezra 8:16 was probably [17] or [18]. [19] One who took a foreign wife during the Exile (Ezra 10:26). [20] A prince with Ezra (Neh. 8:4). [21] A descendant of Perez (Neh. 11:4). [22] One whose descendants dwelled in Jerusalem (Neh. 11:5). [23] A priest (Neh. 11:12). [24] A Levite trumpeter (Neh. 12:35-36). [25] A priest who took part in the dedication ceremony (Neh. 12:41). [26] One whom Isaiah took as a witness (Isa. 8:2). [27] *See* Zachariah [2]. [28] *See* Zacher.

Zedad (zē'dad; "mountainside"). A northern boundary mark of Canaan (Num. 34:8; Ezek. 47:15). It is probably a tower and has been identified with Sadad, southwest of Homs.

Zedekiah (zed-e-kī'a; "Jehovah my righteousness; Jehovah is might"). [1] A false prophet who encouraged Ahab to attack the Syrians at Ramoth-gilead (1 Kings 22:11, 24; 2 Chron. 18: 10, 23). [2] A false prophet (Jer. 29:21-23). [3] A prince of Judah in the days of Jehoiakim (Jer. 36:12). [4] The last king of Judah; his rebellion spelled the doom of Judah (2 Kings 24:18–25:7; 2 Chron. 36:11-21). He is probably referred to in First Chronicles 3:16 as a "son" or successor of Jeconiah. *See* Mattaniah [1].

Zeeb (zē'eb; "wolf"). A prince of Midian slain by Gideon (Judg. 7:25; 8:3).

Zelah (zē'la; "rib"). A town of Benjamin containing Kish's tomb (2 Sam. 21:14). It is probably Khirbet Salah northwest of Jerusalem.

Zelek (zē'lek; "split"). An Ammonite, a valiant man of David (2 Sam. 23:37; 1 Chron. 11:39).

Zelophehad (ze-lō'fe-had; "firstborn"). Grandson of Gilead (Num. 26:33; 27:1, 7; Josh. 17:3).

Zelzah (zel'za; "noontide"). A town near Rachel's tomb (1 Sam. 10:2). It was 8 km. (5 mi.) southeast of Jerusalem.

Zemaraim (zem-a-rā'im; "wool"). [1] A city north of Jericho (Josh. 18:22); we now know that it was 6.4 km. (4 mi.) away from Jericho. [2] A mountain in Ephraim's hill country (2 Chron. 13:4). Possible locations are Burkah and Kafr Nata.

Zemira (ze-mī'ra; "song"). A son of Becher, a descendant of Benjamin (1 Chron. 7:8).

Zenan (zē'nan; "coldness"). A village in the allotment of Judah (Josh. 15:37). It is probably identical with Zaanan (q.v.).

Zenas (zē'nas; "living"). A Christian who had been a teacher of the Law (Titus 3:13).

Zephaniah (zef-a-ni'a; "Jehovah is darkness; Jehovah has treasured"). [1] A prophet in the days of Josiah (Zeph. 1:1). [2] A Levite or priest, ancestor of Samuel (1 Chron. 6:36). Possibly the same as Uriel [1]. [3] Son of Josiah the priest (Zech. 6:10, 14). [4] A priest who opposed Babylonian rule (2 Kings 25:18; Jer. 21:1; 37:3).

Zephath (zē'fath; "which beholds"). A city of Canaan in the mountains of Kadesh near the Edomite border (Judg. 1:17). It was later called Hormah (q.v.).

Zephathah (zef'a-tha; "watchtower"). The valley in Judah's territory near Mareshah in which Asa and Zerah battled (2 Chron. 14:9-10). It is possibly modern Wadi Safiyeh.

Zephi [Zepho] (zē'fī [zē'fō]; "watch"). A son of Eliphaz (Gen. 36:11, 15; 1 Chron. 1:36).

Zepho (zē'fō). *See* Zephi.

Zephon (zē'fon; "dark; wintry"). A son of Gad (Num. 26:15). Also called Ziphion in Genesis 46:16.

Zer (zur; "perplexity"). A fortress city of Naphtali (Josh. 19:35). It was located near the southwest bank of the Sea of Galilee. It may be Madon (q.v.).

Zerah [Zara; Zarah] (zē'ra [zā'ra; zā'ra]; "sprout"). **[1]** A son of Reuel (Gen. 36:13, 17; 1 Chron. 1:37). **[2]** Father of Jobab (Gen. 36:33; 1 Chron. 1:44). **[3]** A son of Judah (Gen. 38:30; 1 Chron. 2:4, 6). **[4]** A descendant of Gershon (1 Chron. 6:21). **[5]** A Levite (1 Chron. 6:41). **[6]** A king of Ethiopia who warred with Asa (2 Chron. 14:9). **[7]** *See* Zohar [2].

Zerahiah (zer-a-hī'a; "Jehovah has come forth"). **[1]** A priest of the line of Eleazar (1 Chron. 6:6, 51; Ezra 7:4). **[2]** Head of a family who returned from the Exile with Ezra (Ezra 8:4).

Zered (zē'red). *See* Zared.

Zereda (zer'e-da; "ambush"). A village in Manasseh (1 Kings 11:26). It was located to the north of Mount Ephraim about 24.1 km. (15 mi.) southwest of Shechem. It is identical with Zaretan (q.v.).

Zeredathah (zer-e-dā'tha; "cool"). A village near Bethshean (2 Chron. 4:17). Many suppose this place is identical with Zaretan (q.v.).

Zeresh (zē'resh; "gold"). Wife of Haman (Esther 5:10, 14; 6:13).

Zereth (zē'reth; "brightness"). A descendant of Judah (1 Chron. 4:7).

Zeri (zë'rī; "balm"). A musician in the days of David (1 Chron. 25:3); perhaps the same as Izri (v. 11).

Zeror (zē'ror; "bundle"). An ancestor of Kish (1 Sam. 9:1).

Zeruah (ze-roo'a; "full-breasted"). The mother of Jeroboam I (1 Kings 11:26).

Zerubbabel [Zorobabel] (ze-rub'a-bel [zo-rob'a-bel]; "seed of Babylon"). **[1]** The leader of a group who returned from exile; he began the rebuilding of the temple (Ezra 3–5; Neh. 7:7; 12:1, 47). He was an ancestor of Christ (Matt. 1:12-13). **[2]** An ancestor of Christ (Luke 3:27); perhaps the same as [1].

Zeruiah (zer-u-ī'a; "balm"). A daughter of Jesse and David's sister (1 Sam. 26:6; 2 Sam. 2:13, 18).

Zetham (zē'tham; "shining"). Son or grandson of Laadan (1 Chron. 23:8; 26:22).

Zethan (zē'than; "olive tree"). A descendant of Benjamin (1 Chron. 7:10).

Zethar (zē'thar; "conqueror"). A eunuch of Ahasuerus (Esther 1:10).

Zia (zī'a; "terrified"). A descendant of Gad (1 Chron. 5:13).

Ziba (zī'ba; "plantation"). A steward of Saul (2 Sam. 9:2-13; 16:1-4; 19:17-29).

Zibeon (zib'e-un; "wild robber"). **[1]** A Hivite man (Gen. 36:2, 14). **[2]** A son of Seir (Gen. 36:20, 24; 1 Chron. 38, 40).

Zibia (zib'i-a; "gazelle"). A descendant of Benjamin (1 Chron. 8:9).

Zibiah (zib'i-a; "gazelle"). Mother of King Joash of Judah (2 Kings 12:1; 2 Chron. 24:1).

Zichri (zik'rī; "renowned"). [1] A son of Izhar (Exod. 6:21). [2] A descendant of Benjamin (1 Chron. 8:19). [3] A descendant of Benjamin of Shishak (1 Chron. 8:23). [4] A descendant of Benjamin of Jeroham (1 Chron. 8:27). [5] A descendant of Eliezer in the days of Moses (1 Chron. 26 25). [6] Father of Eliezer, a descendant of Reuben (1 Chron. 27:16). [7] Father of Amaziah (2 Chron. 17:16). [8] Father of Elishaphat (2 Chror. 23:1). [9] A man of valor who slew the son of King Ahaz (2 Chron. 28:7). [10] Father of Joel (Neh. 11:9). [11] A priest of the sons of Abijah (Neh. 12:17). [12] *See* Zabdi [4].

Ziddim (zid'im; "huntings"). A fortress city of Naphtali (Josh. 19:35). It is possibly Hattim, 8.8 km. (5.5 mi.) northwest of Tiberias.

Zidkijah (zid-kī'ja; "Jehovah my righteousness"). A chief prince of the Jews (Neh. 10:1).

Zidon (zī'don). *See* Sidon.

Ziha (zī'ha; "dried"). [1] One whose children returned from the Babylonian Captivity (Ezra 2:43; Neh. 7:46). [2] A ruler of the Nethinim (Ezra 2:43; Neh. 11:21).

Ziklag (zik'lag; "measure pressed down"). A city in the south of Judah (1 Sam. 30:1; 2 Sam. 1:1; 4:10). It is probably Tell el-Khutweilfel about 16.1 km. (10 mi.) north of Beer-sheba.

Zillah (zil'a; "protection; screen"). One of the wives of Lamech (Gen. 4:19, 22-23).

Zilpah (zil'pa; "myrrh dropping"). Mother of Gad and Asher (Gen. 29:24; 30:9-13; 35:26).

Zilthai (zil'thī; "shadow"). [1] A descendant of Benjamin (1 Chron. 8:20). [2] A captain who joined David at Ziklag (1 Chron. 12:20).

Zimmah (zim'a; "counsel"). [1] A Levite of the family of Gershon (1 Chron. 6:20). [2] A Levite in the fourth or fifth degree of temple service (1 Chron. 6:42). [3] A Levite who assisted in cleansing the temple (2 Chron. 29:12).

Zimran (zim'ran; "celebrated"). A son of Abraham by Keturah (Gen. 25:2; 1 Chron. 1:32).

Zimri (zim'rī; "celebrated"). [1] A disobedient Israelite slain by Phinehas (Num. 25:14). [2] A captain who slew Elah (1 Kings 16:9-20). [3] A son of Zerah of Judah (1 Chron. 2:6). [4] A descendant of Benjamin (1 Chron. 8 36; 9:42).

Zin (zin; "swelling"). A wilderness on the southern border of Canaan, not to be confused with the Wilderness of Sin. It was either a part of the Wilderness of Paran or bordered on the wilderness which contained Kadesh-barnea (Num. 20:1; 27:14; Josh. 15:1-3).

Zina (zī'na; "fruitful"). Second son of Shimei (1 Chron. 23:10). He is called Zizah in verse 11.

Zion [Sion] (zī'on [sī'on]; "monument; fortress; set up"). One of the hills on which Jerusalem stood. It came to be applied to the temple and the whole of Jerusalem and its people as a community whose destiny depends on God (2 Sam. 5:7; Psa. 48:11; Isa. 8:18; Joel 2:23). Zion also was a symbol of heaven (Rev. 14:1).

Zior (zī'or; "smallness"). A city in Judah near Hebron (Josh. 15:54). Some identify the city with Zair (q.v.).

Ziph (zif; "refining place"). **[1]** Grandson of Caleb (1 Chron. 2:42). **[2]** A son of Jehaleleel (1 Chron. 4:16).

Ziph (zif; "falsehood"). **[1]** A city in southern Judah (Josh. 15:24). It was located between Ithnan and Telem and is probably modern ez-Teifah. **[2]** A town in Judah's hill country (Josh. 15:55; 2 Chron. 11:8). It is Tell Zif, 4 mi. southeast of Hebron.

Ziphah (zī'fa; "lent"). A son of Jehaleleel (1 Chron. 4:16).

Ziphion (zif'i-on; "looking out; serpent; dark"). See Zephon.

Ziphron (zif'ron; "rejoicing"). A place specified by Moses as the northern boundary of the Promised Land (Num. 34:9). It is probably Za'feranh southeast of Restan.

Zippor (zip'or; "bird"). Father of Balak, king of Moab (Num. 22:2, 4, 10, 16).

Zipporah (zi-pō'ra; "little bird"). The wife of Moses and daughter of Reuel (Exod. 2:21; 4:25; 18:2).

Zithri (zith-rī; "Jehovah is protection"). A descendant of Levi through Kohath (Exod. 6:22).

Ziz (ziz; "flower"). The pass that runs from the western shore of the Dead Sea north of En-gedi to the wilderness of Judah (2 Chron. 20:16). It is probably Wadi Hasasah.

Ziza [Zizah] (zī'za [zī'za]; "shining; brightness"). **[1]** A chief of Simeon (1 Chron. 4:37). **[2]** A son of King Rehoboam (2 Chron. 11:20). **[3]** See Zina.

Zoan (zō'an; "motion"). A city on the eastern bank of the Nile Delta on the Tanitic branch of the river (Ezek. 30:14). It was known to the Greeks as Tanis and is now San el-Hagar.

Zoar (zō'er; "small"). One of the five Cities of the Plain of the Jordan (Gen. 14:2; 19:22). It probably was located at the southeast end of the Dead Sea near es-Safi. The original site is believed to be under the Dead Sea's waters.

Zobah [Zoba] (zō'ba [zō'ba]; "station"). A portion of Syria east of Coelesyria that was a separate empire during the days of Saul, David, and Solomon (1 Sam. 14:47; 2 Sam. 8:3; 10:6).

Zobebah (zō-bē'ba; "the affable"). A descendant of Judah (1 Chron. 4:8).

Zohar (zō'har; "nobility; distinction"). **[1]** Father of Ephron, from whom Abraham bought a field (Gen. 23:8; 25:9). **[2]** A son of Simeon of Judah (Gen. 46:10; Exod. 6:15). He is also called Zerah (1 Chron. 4:24).

Zoheleth (zō'he-leth; "that creeps; serpent"). A stone beside En-rogel near the Well of the Virgin. It was here that Adonijah sacrificed animals (1 Kings 1:9).

Zoheth (zō'heth; "strong"). A descendant of Judah (1 Chron. 4:20).

Zophah (zō'fa; "watch"). A descendant of Asher (1 Chron. 7:35-36).

Zophai (zō'fī; "watcher"). A brother of Samuel (1 Chron. 6:26). He is called Zuph in verse 35.

Zophar (zō'fer; "hairy; rough"). A Naamathite and "friend" of Job (Job 2:11; 11:1; 20:1).

Zophim (zō'fim; "place for a watchman"). A place or top of Pisgah where Balaam viewed the Israelite camp (Num. 23:14). It is possibly Tal'al es-Safa.

Zorah (zō'ra; "leprosy"). A city in the lowlands of Judah allotted to the tribe of Dan (Josh. 19:41; 2 Chron. 11:10). The site is Sar'ah about 22.5 km. (14 mi.) west of Jerusalem. It is identical with Zorean (q.v.). It is called Zoreah [Zareah] in Joshua 15:33 and Nehemiah 11:29.

Zoreah (zō're-a; "wasp; hornet"). *See also* Zorah.

Zorobabel (zo-rob'a-bel). Greek form of Zerubbabel (q.v.).

Zuar (zū'er; "little"). Father of Nethaneel and a chief of Issachar (Num. 1:8; 2:5).

Zuph (zuf). *See* Zophai.

Zuph (zuf; "covering"). A district of unknown location (1 Sam. 9:5). The usual location given is about 40.2 km. (25 mi.) southwest of Shechem.

Zur (zur; "rock"). [1] A prince of Midian slain by Phinehas (Num. 25:15; 31:8). [2] A son of Jehiel (1 Chron. 8:30; 9:36).

Zuriel (zū'ri-el; "God is my rock"). A chief of the Levites, descendant from Merari (Num. 3:35).

Zurishaddai (zū-ri-shad'ī; "the Almighty is a rock"). Father of Shelumiel (Num. 1:6; 2:12).

ACKNOWLEDGMENTS

The Publisher gratefully acknowledges the cooperation of these sources, whose illustrations appear in the present work:

British Museum, 29; L. H. Grollenberg, 16, 68, 76, 123, 133, 145; Levant Photo Service, 89; Thomas Nelson Inc., 59, 67, 153; Matson Photo Service, 82; M. J. Van der Ploeg, 71, 106; University Museum, 192; Willem Van De Poll, 35, 70, 111, 166; William White, 64.

The Publisher has attempted to observe the legal requirements with respect to the rights of suppliers of photographic materials. Nevertheless, persons who have claims are invited to apply to the Publisher.

THE ANCIENT WORLD
GENESIS

MILES
KILOMETERS

JEROME S. KATES, *Cartographer*
HERBERT G. MAY, PH.D., *Research Editor*
COPYRIGHT 1948. THOMAS NELSON AND SONS

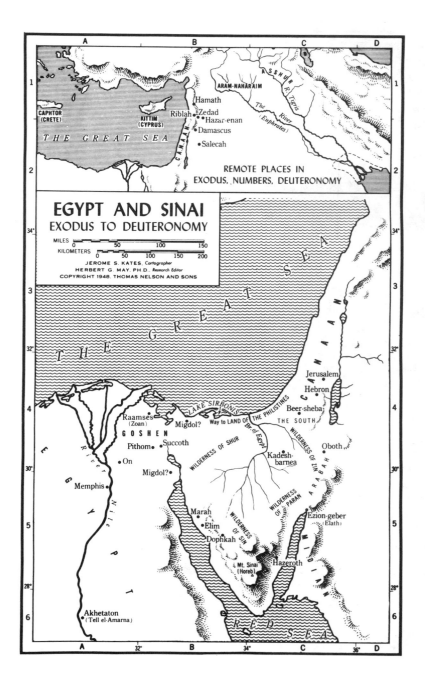

REMOTE PLACES IN EXODUS, NUMBERS, DEUTERONOMY

EGYPT AND SINAI
EXODUS TO DEUTERONOMY

MILES
0   50   100   150
KILOMETERS
0   50   100   150   200

JEROME S. KATES, Cartographer
HERBERT G. MAY, PH.D., Research Editor
COPYRIGHT 1948, THOMAS NELSON AND SONS

ARAM-NAHARAIM
Hamath
Zedad
Hazar-enan
Riblah
Damascus
Salecah

CAPHTOR (CRETE)

KITTIM (CYPRESS)

THE GREAT SEA

ASSHUR
R. Tigris
The Euphrates River

CANAAN

THE GREAT SEA

Jerusalem
Hebron
Beer-sheba

Raamses (Zoan)
Migdol?
GOSHEN
Pithom
Succoth
On
Migdol?
Memphis

LAKE SIRBONIS
Way to LAND OF THE PHILISTINES
Br. of EGYPT
THE SOUTH
WILDERNESS OF SHUR
Kadesh-barnea
Oboth
WILDERNESS OF ZIN
ARABAH

EGYPT

River Nile

Marah
Elim
Dophkah
WILDERNESS OF SIN
WILDERNESS OF PARAN
Ezion-geber (Elath)
Hazeroth
MIDIAN

Mt. Sinai (Horeb)

Akhetaton (Tell el-Amarna)

RED SEA

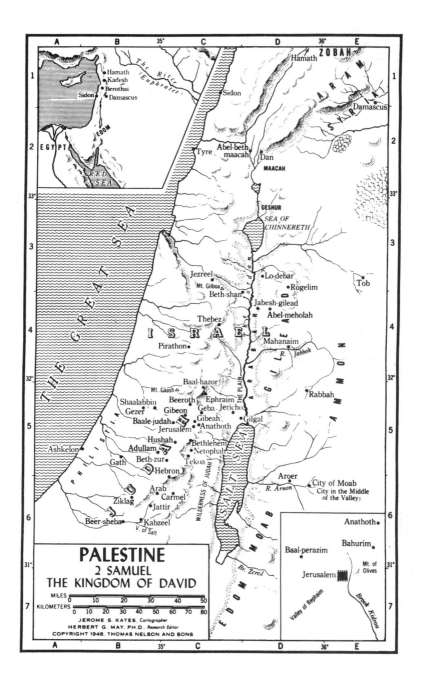

PALESTINE
2 SAMUEL
THE KINGDOM OF DAVID

MILES
0 10 20 30 40 50
KILOMETERS
0 10 20 30 40 50 60 70 80

JEROME S. KATES, *Cartographer*
HERBERT G. MAY, PH.D., *Research Editor*
COPYRIGHT 1948. THOMAS NELSON AND SONS

THE KINGDOMS OF THE
ANCIENT WORLD
DANIEL

JEROME S. KATES, Cartographer
HERBERT G. MAY, PH.D., Research Editor
COPYRIGHT 1948, THOMAS NELSON AND SONS

MILES
0 100 200 300 400 500 600 700 800
KILOMETERS
0 100 500 1000

PALESTINE
MATTHEW, MARK *and* LUKE

MILES 0 10 20 30 40 50
KILOMETERS 0 10 20 30 40 50 60 70 80

JEROME S. KATES, *Cartographer*
CHESTER C. McCOWN, PH.D., *Research Editor*
COPYRIGHT 1949, THOMAS NELSON AND SONS

JERUSALEM
IN NEW TESTAMENT TIMES

JEROME S. KATES, *Cartographer*

CHESTER C. McCOWN, PH.D., *Research Editor*

COPYRIGHT 1949, THOMAS NELSON AND SONS

KEY

ANCIENT WALLS (N. T. TIMES?) DISCOVERED ————

ANCIENT WALLS REASONABLY CONJECTURED = = = = =

WALLS DISCOVERED — DATE UNCERTAIN ....

SCARPS FOR WALLS — DATE UNCERTAIN ....

POSSIBLE COURSE OF WALLS ....

DRAIN OR UNDERGROUND STRUCTURE — — — — —

LATE AND MODERN BUILDINGS

MODERN ROADS AND STREETS ════

FEET

0   100   500   1000

THE TRAVELS
OF PAUL
in the
BOOK OF ACTS
CHAPTERS 13-28

JEROME S. KATES, Cartographer
CHESTER C. McCOWN, PH. D. Research Editor
COPYRIGHT 1949 THOMAS NELSON AND SONS